JUDGES AND UNJUST LAWS

Judges and Unjust Laws

Common Law Constitutionalism and
the Foundations of Judicial Review

Douglas E. Edlin

THE UNIVERSITY OF MICHIGAN PRESS

Ann Arbor

First paperback edition 2010
Copyright © by the University of Michigan 2008
All rights reserved
Published in the United States of America by
The University of Michigan Press
Manufactured in the United States of America
⊚ Printed on acid-free paper

2013   2012   2011   2010   4   3   2   1

A CIP catalog record for this book is available from the British Library.

Library of Congress Cataloging-in-Publication Data

Edlin, Douglas E.
    Judges and unjust laws : common law constitutionalism and the
foundations of judicial review / Douglas E. Edlin.
        p.   cm.
    Includes bibliographical references and index.
    ISBN-13: 978-0-472-11662-1 (cloth : alk. paper)
    ISBN-10: 0-472-11662-2 (cloth : alk. paper)
    1. Judge-made law—Great Britain.   2. Judge-made law—United
States.   3. Judicial review—Great Britain.   4. Judicial review—
United States.   I. Title.

K3367.E35   2008
347'.012—dc22   2008017464

ISBN 978-0-472-03415-4 (pbk. : alk. paper)
ISBN 978-0-472-02295-3 (e-book)

To Nancy
For Matthew

The law has "its epochs of ebb and flow." One of the flood seasons is upon us. Men are insisting, as perhaps never before, that law shall be made true to its ideal of justice. Let us gather up the driftwood, and leave the waters pure.

—BENJAMIN N. CARDOZO

Contents

Acknowledgments

I have been working on this book, in various ways, for some time. I am grateful to the journals that have afforded me the opportunity to present some of this work in print prior to the publication of this book. Sections of chapter 6 appeared as "Judicial Review without a Constitution" in 38 *Polity* 345 (2006), and sections of chapter 9 appeared as "From Ambiguity to Legality: The Future of English Judicial Review" in 52 *American Journal of Comparative Law* 383 (2004). I thank the editors of those journals for permission to reproduce and develop that work here.

Many people have read and commented on all or part of this book. For their very helpful suggestions and corrections, I thank Nicholas Barber, David Dyzenhaus, John Gardner, Mark Graber, Jeffrey Hackney, Ken Kersch, Bronwen Morgan, Richard Morgan, James Murphy, Amanda Perreau-Saussine, Harry Pohlman, Sylvia Snowiss, John Stanton-Ife, Nicos Stavropoulos, Lucas Swaine, and Brian Tamanaha.

I have been the student of many extraordinary scholars and teachers of public law, constitutional theory, legal philosophy, and legal history. Most of them are cited in the pages that follow, and that is probably the best evidence of their importance to me and of their influence on my understanding of these subjects. I hope that this is enough, although it does not seem adequate.

I am thankful for many people and places in my life. I am grateful to my parents and to my brother for their unwavering love and support. I had the good fortune to attend a fine liberal arts college that nurtured me in every conceivable way. I should like to thank the entire faculty of Hobart and William Smith Colleges, along with every building and blade of grass and vista on the campus. But for reasons of space, I must restrict myself to a much shorter list. Scott Brophy introduced me to many questions of legal theory and constitutional thought that have preoccupied me since. Scott and his colleagues—Steven Lee, Eugen Baer, Benjamin Daise, and many other remarkable individuals—saw me as someone I had not yet known and helped me to recognize myself in him. My relationships with them stand as the model of those I hope to have with my own students. In fact, they are the primary reason that I now have students of my own. From the first (or second) day we met, Beau Breslin has tirelessly, patiently, and enthusiastically encouraged, counseled, challenged, and sustained me. John Donato continues to demonstrate to me the meaning of being, here, now. In addition, when I think back on my time at Hobart, I find it impossible to separate time from place. So I thank Seneca Lake and the starlit walk to Houghton House for all that they did, and continue to do.

Most of the research and writing of this book was completed at Oxford University. I simply cannot imagine a more ideal environment in which to think, and talk, and write, about questions of Anglo-American constitutionalism, legal and political theory, and constitutional history (or any other area of human endeavor and experience, for that matter). Many more people there than I can acknowledge here have helped to improve the ideas and words in this book. I have thanked some of them by name in a previous paragraph. Of all these individuals, the one who must be singled out again for mention (but not for blame) is Nicos Stavropoulos. From our first meeting in the Mansfield College garden until our last meeting over dinner in Jericho, Nicos generously offered his guidance, judgment, good humor, and incisive analysis. All I can do is thank him. I doubt I will ever be able to repay him.

In addition to my good fortune in attending a fine college, I am even more privileged to teach at one now. It is entirely fitting that this book was completed at Dickinson College. Its exceptional faculty, its long tradition of excellence in teaching law and politics in broad social context, and its handsome buildings—financed (at the beginning) by, among others, John Marshall, James Madison, and William Paterson—leave me confident that Dickinson is a place where foundational questions of government and law have been and will be discussed for a very long time. More specifically, I thank Andy Rudalevige for his help and encouragement at a crucial stage in this book's development.

This book, like most things of value in my life, would not exist without my wife, Nancy. She has read much of this, debated most of it, and heard all of it. And as she put it late one evening in the midst of a frustrating (for her) discussion, she "reminded me what my argument was supposed to be." For all of this and so much more, words cannot express my feelings.

The most valuable part of my life, our son Matthew, also would not exist without Nancy. Matthew was born during the researching and writing of this book. As a result, what he gained in a mother, I lost in a commentator and editor. Perhaps someday he will read this and help his mom finish what she started.

1. Introduction: "The Justice of the Common Law"

A. Unjust Laws

Unjust laws have troubled lawyers, political scientists, and philosophers since they first reflected on the legal standards by which people govern themselves. Unjust laws raise difficult questions about our understanding of law, our aspirations for our laws, our obligations to one another, and our government's responsibilities to each of us. From Aristotle and Aquinas to Hart and Fuller, the debate about these questions has continued for millennia, and it will endure for as long as people need law to order their societies and to guide their lives.

There are several ways that a law might be unjust. It might prohibit or curtail conduct that should be permitted.[1] It might permit conduct that should be prohibited.[2] It might apply or enforce unfairly an otherwise unobjectionable law.[3] People can and will disagree about whether and in what way a particular law is unjust. I do not, however, wish to enter into that debate. For the purposes of this study, I want to posit a particular law as unjust and then ask by what legal basis, if any, a judge can resist and attempt to correct that injustice. It seemed to me that it might help clarify discussion to have a specific example of an unjust law in mind. The example of an unjust law that I will use in chapter 7 is one permitting government-sanctioned racial discrimination.[4] I will not attempt to defend the claim, if a defense is needed, that racially discriminatory laws are unjust.[5] I assume it for the purposes of my argument. Of course, someone might imagine a polity in which racially discriminatory laws are not necessarily unjust by definition. I am, however, interested in existing common law systems. My selection of racially discriminatory laws as paradigmatically unjust refers to the related experiences of common law nations regarding, for example, treatment of indigenous populations and the political and constitutional history of the United States with respect to slavery and legalized racial segregation and subjugation.

In addition to overtly or substantively unjust laws, certain laws also attempt, in various ways, to undermine the institutional position or constitutional obligations of common law courts. In chapters 8 and 9, I examine some specific examples of this type of law as well.[6] I analyze cases in which judges responded to these laws and refused to allow the integrity and authority of their courts to be enervated in this manner. In these discussions, I highlight specific fundamental common law principles that operate through judicial decisions to maintain the constitutional relationship of government organs and to enforce legal limitations on government action.

Despite the long history of interest in problems presented by unjust laws, relatively little has been written about the particular difficulties these laws raise for judges called on to enforce them. What little has been written tends to oversimplify or misconceive the genuine nature of the conflict unjust laws pose for judges.[7] My goal is to offer another way of looking at the conflict created by unjust laws and at judicial responses to it.

B. The "Moral-Formal Dilemma"

People generally assume that unjust laws create a conflict between a judge's moral obligations as a person and her legal obligations as a judge.[8] More specifically, these laws, it is said, force a judge to choose between her human obligation to resist iniquity and her legal obligation to enforce the law as it is. In his book *Justice Accused*, Robert Cover described the cognitive dissonance experienced by some abolitionist judges when faced with unjust laws as the "moral-formal dilemma."[9] Cover used laws permitting slavery, in particular the Fugitive Slave Act of 1850, as his example of unjust laws that gave rise to the moral-formal dilemma for judges who were, at least while they were off the bench, abolitionists, such as Joseph Story.

> In one sense there was a general, pervasive disparity between the individual's image of himself as a moral human being, opposed to human slavery as part of his moral code, and his image of himself as a faithful

judge, applying legal rules impersonally—which rules required in many instances recognition, facilitation, or legitimation of slavery.[10]

As Cover documents in his book, most of these judges resolved this conflict by taking the formal route, enforcing the act, and relying on platitudes about "fidelity to law"[11] or judicial deference and restraint required by the separation of powers.[12]

In his review of *Justice Accused,* Ronald Dworkin claims that Story and other abolitionist judges enforced laws they believed to be unjust because they rejected notions of natural law that might have provided a basis in fundamental legal principle for refusing to uphold the Fugitive Slave Act.[13] As others have noted, the judicial rejection of natural law asserted by Dworkin is historically baseless.[14] Nonetheless, as Anthony Sebok explains, "Cover's conclusion is that the leading legal theory of the age—legal positivism—so dominated these judges that they could see but not act upon the appeals made from natural law in their courtrooms."[15] As I will discuss later, Gustav Radbruch leveled a similar charge against positivism for fostering an environment in which the Nazi government could subvert the legal principles and constitutional values of Weimar.[16] Dworkin argues that judges who felt trapped by the moral-formal dilemma, such as Story, were in this predicament because they "had abandoned a theory of law . . . [according to which] the law of a community consists not simply in the discrete statutes and rules that its officials enact but in the general principles of justice and fairness that these statutes and rules, taken together, presuppose by way of implicit justification."[17]

Undoubtedly, Dworkin has his own theory of law in mind as the alternative that would have permitted abolitionist judges to invalidate the Fugitive Slave Act without resort to natural law theory. Dworkin argued that the Fugitive Slave Act violated the U.S. Constitution because of the Constitution's conceptions of individual freedom, procedural due process, and federalism.[18] Sebok argues convincingly, however, that Dworkin's claims are fundamentally inconsistent with the relevant constitutional language and history, state laws then existing, and important state and federal precedent.[19] Sebok also offers a reconstruction of Dworkin's argument that might support his conclusion about the unconstitutionality of the Fugitive Slave Act.[20] Moreover, in a later essay, Sebok further develops his argument about the unconstitutionality of the Fugitive Slave Act by demonstrating that Lord Mansfield's famous decision in *Somerset v. Stewart,*[21] which effectively ended slavery in England,[22] was incorporated into American law by precedent and statute.[23] Significantly for the argument I will develop, Sebok emphasizes in this later piece the importance that influential early American judges placed on authoritative sources for judicial reasoning and decision making in accordance with the common law.[24]

I will return to aspects of Dworkin's theory in later chapters. For now, I just want to mention that I agree with his statement (although not with the underlying argument in his review of *Justice Accused*) concerning the importance of "general principles of justice" to judicial decision making in cases involving unjust laws. For reasons I explain later, I believe a defense of the use of these principles by judges in these cases demands a more exacting theoretical and doctrinal explanation than Dworkin provides of their source and use in accordance with the method and history of the common law.

The moral-formal dilemma is not just a means of describing the quandary in which certain nineteenth-century American judges found themselves. The moral-formal dilemma has been so well and thoroughly osmosed by modern lawyers, judges, and scholars that we do not even question it anymore. But this is a mistake, and it has led contemporary legal and political theorists to further errors.

C. Unsatisfying Answers

Theorists conditioned to think only along the moral-formal axis assume that a judge faced with an unjust law has only three unpalatable options: "he would have to consider whether he should actually enforce it [the unjust law] . . . or whether he should lie and say that this was not the law after all, or whether he should resign."[25] To me and to others,[26] this Hobson's choice is deeply troubling. Looking through moral-formal eyes, though, no other options are available to a judge in this situation.

These theorists agree that, morally speaking, judges should refuse to enforce the law. But these theorists also agree that judges do so only at the expense of their countervailing legal duty to apply the law as they find it.[27] Some are willing to accept this form of civil disobedience practiced from the bench. In fact, some theorists claim that a judge's moral duty to resist injustice justifies his subverting the judicial process by telling legal lies about the actual bases for his decision.[28]

The problem is that, with moral-formal eyes, there seems nothing else a judge can do, legally speaking, to refuse to enforce unjust laws. There is another possibility, however. There are legal arguments that support a common law judge's ability and obligation, as a judge, to refuse to enforce unjust laws. *How do you refuse unjust laws?*

D. An Alternative

The moral-formal dilemma is, to my mind, a false dichotomy. It proceeds from an incomplete understanding of the judicial function to an impoverished account of judicial obligation. As the term indicates, the legal side of the dilemma provides judges with only a formalistic account of their legal authority and responsibilities. This limited, formal view sees the judge's legal authority as limited solely to the enforcement of the law as it is. But this is not a complete picture of the common law judicial function. Once the full extent of a judge's legal authority is considered, the dilemma's formulation can be corrected, and the problem can be reconsidered.

I argue that unjust laws do not create a moral-formal or moral-legal dilemma; they create a legal-legal dilemma. Unjust laws create a conflict between two of a common law judge's most fundamental legal obligations: to apply the law and to develop the law. The crucial point for my purposes here is that I intend to provide a legal, rather than a moral, justification for judges to refuse to enforce unjust laws without resigning or resorting to prevarication. *A legal argument for denying unjust laws*

I begin my argument in chapter 2 with a general discussion of the common law as a legal system, a judicial method, and a body of doctrine and principle. In that chapter, I explain the understanding of legal sources that I use throughout my argument. I then consider the judicial process and its central importance to the common law legal system and tradition. In doing so, I refer to the doctrines of precedent and to what Roscoe Pound and others refer to as the "supremacy of law." These doctrines function as descriptive indicators of common law systems, both in terms of the sources used in legal argumentation and in terms of the function of courts and law in defining and restraining the breadth of government power. Pound traced the doctrine of supremacy of law to Edward Coke's opinion in *Dr. Bonham's Case.*[29] Pound's reference to *Bonham* in relation to the supremacy of law connects directly to my discussion in chapters 5 and 6 of *Bonham* as a seminal legal source in the common law tradition for the establishment of judicial review and to my discussion in chapters 8 and 9 of the Anglo-American constitutional commitment to rule-of-law values. I also explain in chapter 2 that the doctrines of precedent and supremacy of law apply to the internal and external processes of adjudication and that the common law judicial process applies to all categories of adjudication, including cases involving statutory construction or constitutional interpretation. Chapter 2 concludes with an examination of various jurisprudential approaches to the identification of the law's content and the relationship of that content to its moral worth. More specifically, I address the perspectives of inclusive and exclusive positivism concerning this issue, along with the views of Ronald Dworkin. In reviewing these different theoretical perspectives, I hope to highlight the ways that they intersect with my argument in this book and the ways that they do not.

I then turn, in chapters 3 and 4, to the arguments for the judicial obligation to apply the law. In this discussion and in the later one for the judicial obligation to develop the law, I pursue two distinct but complementary lines or types of argument. The first line of argument relies on "legal sources" as I define that term in chapter 2. The second line of argument is conceptual—that is, based on the concept of the common law itself. These arguments are presented, as lawyers sometimes say, "in the alternative," meaning that the arguments are independent of one another[30] and that the reader is free to accept either one or both of them.

My analysis of the judicial obligation to apply the law starts, in chapter 3, with the source-based argument. It seems to me that the doctrine of stare decisis[31] grounds part of the judge's fundamental legal obligation to apply the law, when the law is found in judicial decisions. I explore the bedrock importance of stare decisis to the common law tradition and explain that, to have any meaningful effect on judicial decision making, stare decisis must sometimes (or often) require a judge to abide by precedent even where the judge would prefer to reach a different result. I examine the attempts by several theorists to avoid the repercussions of stare decisis when the doctrine demands that judges produce unjust rulings. I argue that each of these attempts fails because it attempts to avoid the strictures of stare decisis by denying its genuine force and prevalence. I argue that the only way to claim that stare decisis can yield in a given case is to locate an equally important and equally fundamental common law principle that will permit judges to avoid injustice. This principle is to be found in the judicial obligation to develop the law.

The second prong of the source-based argument for the judicial obligation to apply the law concerns legislative supremacy. Just as stare decisis requires judges to apply case law, legislative supremacy requires judges to enforce statutes. To some extent, this might seem more a matter of institutional interaction or political ideology. As I discuss in the second half of chapter 3, however, the judicial recognition of legislative authority to enact binding law results in the force of legislative supremacy as a legal constraint and not just as a political fact. I then examine, as I did with stare decisis, some attempts by scholars to avoid the constraints of legislative supremacy when it compels judges to enforce unjust statutes. As with stare decisis, I argue that these attempts to avoid legislative supremacy are merely attempts to reconstitute legislative supremacy, usually through the pretext of statutory interpretation, rather than efforts to meet the doctrine head-on. And as with stare decisis, I argue that legislative supremacy can be superseded only by a similarly foundational judicial obligation to develop the law.

After examining the source-based legal support for the judicial obligation to apply the law, I offer a short argument in chapter 4 to establish a judicial obligation to do so that is based on the systemic role occupied by common law judges. In that chapter, I observe that the common law method requires judges to engage in certain modes of reasoning that involve reference to and reliance on recognized, authoritative legal sources. When judges depart from the rules found in these sources, they are required to provide a justificatory explanation for this departure. This definition of the judicial role and this method of legal reasoning ordinarily result in judges applying the law as it is, because there is no legitimate legal basis for deviation or alteration. w/ no precedent, may apply law as is

Next, I begin my argument for the judicial obligation to develop the law by refusing to enforce unjust laws. As with the discussion of the judicial obligation to apply the law, I present a source-based argument and a conceptual argument. The source-based argument begins in chapter 5, with an extended examination of Coke's decision in *Bonham*. Academics debate the proper understanding of this case. Some claim that Coke intended his opinion to serve as a legal justification for judicial review of primary legislation as that doctrine would later develop in the United States. Others assert that Coke meant to offer nothing more than a statement of statutory construction, which posed no threat to the orthodoxy of English parliamentary sovereignty. Relying on the political climate of Coke's day, watershed events in Coke's life, analysis of case law, and the subsequent influence of the decision, I defend the first reading of *Bonham*. In particular, I defend a reading of *Bonham* as the historical and theoretical basis for judicial review of legislation according to common law principles rather than a canonical constitutional text. Allowed to repair law

After considering *Bonham*, I analyze statements by Lord Mansfield in

Omychund v. Barker.[32] *Omychund* is important to me for several reasons. First, it was in this case that Lord Mansfield articulated the idea that the common law "works itself pure." The case provides an excellent example of this aspect of the common law judicial process. In addition, the case relates to the applicability of the common law judicial process to all types of case: constitutional, statutory, and decisional. Finally, I connect Lord Mansfield's statements in *Omychund* to Lord Coke's decision in *Bonham* as a means of locating important affinities in their thought about the common law, specifically about the relation between reason and justice and the correlation between developing the law and correcting injustice through the application of reason in the adjudication of legal disputes.

I then shift my focus, in chapter 6, from England to the United States. Looking at American state and federal cases from the late eighteenth and early nineteenth centuries, I argue that the doctrine of judicial review as it developed during the formative years of the American Republic was not limited to evaluation of legislation in light of a written constitution. Instead, American courts used the common law and the Constitution as alternative bases for judicial review. Moreover, some state courts relied explicitly and implicitly on Coke's *Bonham* decision as the legal foundation for this judicial authority. I explain further that the U.S. Supreme Court and Chief Justice John Marshall himself continued to refer to constitutional and common law justifications for judicial review even after the *Marbury* decision.[33] I also explain that prominent American lawyers and judges of this period recognized a doctrinal and theoretical distinction between common law and natural law as bodies of principle and bases for judicial decision. I argue that the line of cases beginning with *Bonham* and traced through these early American decisions represents a coherent doctrine of judicial review based on common law principles rather than constitutional provisions. I refer to judicial review grounded on common law principles as "common law review" and to judicial review reliant on a constitutional document as "constitutional review." I also argue that this doctrine of common law review engenders a judicial obligation to develop the law by refusing to enforce laws determined to violate these principles, in much the same way that constitutional review requires judges to refuse to enforce laws determined to violate a constitutional provision.

After concluding the source-based argument in favor of a judicial obligation to develop the law, I begin the conceptual argument in chapter 7. This argument attempts to show that a judicial obligation to develop the law is inherent in the common law judicial role. In other words, I argue that a legal system cannot accurately be called a common law system unless its judges' function is understood to include a responsibility to develop the law through the adjudicative process. This argument has four parts: (1) the common law is designed to develop over time; (2) this development involves the effort to achieve substantive justice; (3) according to the common law tradition and method, judges are the institutional actors charged with ensuring that this development takes place; and (4) when judges fail to achieve this objective, drastic negative consequences sometimes result. In advancing this argument, I employ the change in American law involving racial segregation as an example of the developmental design of the common law and of the judicial role and responsibility in that process of development. No common law unless improvement is possible

After presenting these two complementary arguments in favor of the judicial obligation to develop the law, I try, in chapter 8, to explain some analytic features of that doctrine as it might operate in practice. In doing so, my goal is to demonstrate that common law review is a workable legal doctrine that can be used by real judges when deciding cases involving unjust laws. I outline the different forms that this judicial authority might take and different judicial attitudes toward its exercise. I then explore the interaction of common law review with the institutional and constitutional doctrines of stare decisis and legislative supremacy. Next, I connect the exercise of common law review to the existence of common law constitutionalism. An important aspect of this discussion is its demonstration of the importance of common law review in contemporary English and American constitutional law and theory. By examining cases in which judges apprehend a significant threat to the institutional autonomy of their courts, I describe specific situations and broader circumstances where common law review remains a viable and vital doctrine on which judges can and do rely in maintaining the integrity of the judiciary in the face of jurisdictional incursions by legislation, precedent, and executive action. These cases are especially important because a possible reaction to my argument is that the historical and doctrinal relevance of common law review has been obviated by the incorporation of the principles and practice of common law review, at least in U.S. law, through more recent interpretations of the due process and equal protection provisions of the Fourteenth Amendment. To the extent that this may be true for the more apparent instances of substantively unjust laws, the cases I analyze in chapters 8 and 9 demonstrate the contemporary salience of common law review in the United States and in the United Kingdom. Chapter 8 concludes with a response to the so-called Radbruch formula and highlights important distinctions between my argument and Radbruch's.

In chapter 9, I examine the possibility of introducing common law review in two common law regimes, England and the United States, the common law world's least and most hospitable habitats, respectively, for the doctrine. I consider the obstacles to the incorporation of common law review posed by, in particular, the English doctrines of stare decisis and parliamentary sovereignty. I argue that, properly understood, the English legal tradition and some recent English case law support the application of common law review in English courts—at the very least, in the House of Lords. Focusing principally on a recent House of Lords decision, I demonstrate the existence and operation of a fundamental common law principle that operates in English law to maintain fundamental commitments to constitutionalism and judicial protection of individual liberties through the review of government action.

Where the United States is concerned, I note in chapter 9 that the absence of some English hurdles eases the potential acceptance of common law review, although I recognize that there would be objections in America as well. I argue in chapter 9 that the Anglo-American constitutional commitments to the rule of law are more fundamental and meaningful than the apparent distinctions drawn from the presence or absence of a written constitution or from references to legislative supremacy. My emphasis here is on the shared constitutional values entrenched in the common law principles enforced by English and American courts when reviewing the legality of government action. And I emphasize the common law foundations of the constitutional protections articulated in the U.S. Constitution. The proper understanding of the Constitution at the time of ratification and today depends on an appreciation of the document as a reaffirmation of a commitment to fundamental common law rights and principles rather than a reconstruction or restriction of the nature and meaning of these principles. This shared common law tradition is what truly harmonizes and best informs Anglo-American constitutional thought and meaning.

Now that I have outlined this book's argument, it might be useful to address a couple of potential concerns about my project before revisiting the moral-formal dilemma and explaining some advantages of my method of analysis. My argument is limited to the common law's tradition, method, and sources. This is because the distinction between the common law and civil law traditions may be relevant when analyzing the ability and obligation of judges to refuse to enforce unjust laws. This distinction has been ignored by those theorists who have addressed the topic, and it seems to me that it might be worthwhile to consider whether common law judges and civil law judges operate under different constraints when asked to enforce unjust laws in their courtrooms. Let me stress that I am not asserting in any way that common law systems and the common law tradition are inherently more just than civil law systems and the civil law tradition. I mean only to suggest that the distinction is worth considering when thinking about how the different systems and traditions address, from an institutional perspective, the problems posed by unjust laws. My argument is an effort to address the common law portion of that broader inquiry.

Another issue of concern relates to the jurisprudential commitments that underlie my arguments. Legal theorists often like to determine what you are before deciding what they think about your position. Theorists frequently want to know whether a person is a legal positivist, a natural lawyer, or whatever, as a means of understanding that person's more specific arguments. I dislike this tendency and will resist it here. Nevertheless, I will not be coy about my arguments. I have explained that I present a source-based and a conceptual argument to support the judicial obligation to develop (or to apply) the law. Where the source-based argument is concerned, I concede that those individuals, if there are any, who do not believe that authoritative legal sources play a pivotal role in legal reasoning may conclude that my source-based argument is deficient as a result of its reliance on these sources. Where my conceptual argument is concerned, some people might think that I am arguing for a norm or rule of common law systems, one according to which judges are legally authorized to refuse to enforce egregiously unjust laws. I have no particular objection to conceiving of the argument in this way. I just wish to point out that this is not the only way to conceive of the argument. The argument is also amenable to those who do not perceive law as reducible to norms or rules. And for people of this inclination, there is no need to view the conceptual argument in terms of a norm or a rule.

Once the judicial obligation to develop the law by refusing to enforce unjust laws is established, the moral-formal dilemma can be reevaluated. The "formal" side of the dilemma can be viewed, less pejoratively and more appropriately, as the legal obligation to apply the law. Even more important, though, we can see that the other side of the dilemma is occupied not by a sweeping, human, moral obligation to oppose injustice but, instead, by a specific, judicial, legal obligation to develop the law. We can begin to see the dilemma posed by unjust laws as a legal-legal dilemma. Viewing the dilemma from this antinomic perspective has several advantages. First, judges and theorists may no longer be hidebound by the narrow view of judicial responsibility and authority presupposed by the formal side of the dilemma. Instead, this richer, more balanced account of common law judicial obligation allows us to appreciate that a judge's legal obligations are not encompassed and exhausted by the singular obligation to apply the law. There is more that a judge can do, from a legal standpoint, to correct injustice and to improve the law. Construing the dilemma as a conflict of legal obligations and fully apprehending the character and extent of these legal obligations allow us to see that a judge is not stepping outside the law by refusing to enforce unjust laws. By refusing to enforce an unjust law, the judge is changing the law in accordance with the common law's sources, methods, and traditions.[34]

Avoiding the moral-formal conception of the unjust laws dilemma will not eliminate disagreements about the law or about proper judicial decision making. But it will refocus the disagreement and our attention more precisely. Even those who accept that unjust laws create a legal conflict of judicial obligations may still disagree about whether a judge should properly have deferred to precedent or overridden a statute in a particular circumstance. But we must be careful to distinguish arguments about the morality of an action and the legality of a decision. In this regard, legal obligations are conceptually distinct from moral obligations.[35] When judges are confronted with unjust laws, moral convictions trigger or inform legal obligations. This is not to say, however, that moral obligations and legal obligations merge. They remain distinct, but related, in determining what a judge's legal responsibilities are.

E. Types of Injustice

Finally, I should say something about the types of injustice to which my argument applies and those to which it does not. The discussion of unjust laws in this book is not an abstract analysis of the nature of justice (distributive, corrective, or otherwise), nor is it a search for the definitive algorithm that will allow all judges in all jurisdictions at all times to know when to exercise common law review. Instead, it is an examination of "legal justice" as that term is understood and applied by courts of common law jurisdictions to address legal wrongs by legal means through the award of legal remedies through legal judgments. In chapter 8, I discuss the epistemic evaluation necessary for judges to determine if a particular case is appropriate for the exercise of common law review. At this point, I want to explain more generally the types of injustice to which common law review can properly be applied and the types of injustice that would be inappropriate for its application.

Judges operate in a legal, political, social, and historical context. Each common law nation has a differently configured constitutional and legal order that has defined and responded to its own unique political, social, and historical circumstances. And yet these nations also share, as common law nations, a mode of legal reasoning from legal sources, a form of judicial process, and a structure and relationship of legal institutions.[36] Only in accordance with this process, these institutions, and these sources can legal injustices be addressed by legal means. There are, needless to say, various forms of injustice in any human society and various ways that human beings attempt to correct these injustices. In what remains of this chapter, I will explain the distinctive nature of legal injustice to which common law judges might attempt to respond through judicial means. This is what might be called the "situated perspective" of the common-law tradition.[37] I also hope to explain, principally by implication and correlation, other sorts of extralegal social injustice to which common law judges cannot properly respond in a manner consistent with their institutional role as judicial officials.

The common law tradition has long recognized a relationship between the moral evaluations of judges and the legal rulings of courts. But the common law has also always maintained a conceptual distance between "background morality"[38] and the articulation of legal rights in legal sources. The fact that legal rights often bear a relationship to moral conventions does not mean that all widely or strongly held moral beliefs will generate legal rights. For the argument I develop here, there must be some common law norm through which the judge's moral conviction can honestly be expressed. Dworkin claims that a judge is "more likely" to recognize concrete legal rights where some preexisting legislative right exists.[39] But such a tendency does not seem sufficient to ground concrete legal rights in the sources of law and modes of reasoning that define the common law tradition. By saying that it is "more likely" that judges will rely on preexisting legal norms to articulate legal rights consistent with their moral evaluations, Dworkin intends to leave open the possibility that the moral evaluation alone, in certain instances, might be sufficient to construct "the best justification of legal practice" and, concomitantly, to determine "what rights people have to win law suits."[40] Pushed to its limits, this view would erode entirely the conceptual distinction between law and morality (or, at least, the separation of recognized legal sources from extralegal moral considerations). This may be Dworkin's view, although some of his other writings indicate that he would not permit judges simply to write morality into law with no mediating influence of historical and social context, institutional limitations, authoritative sources, and legal principles.[41] In any event, the argument made here does not permit judges simply to write their moral beliefs into law without any supporting legal principle or norm. But the common law tradition does, nevertheless, permit a more expansive role than is ordinarily assumed for the moral evaluations of judges in the correction of·injustice, because the common law offers a remarkably rich vein of legal concepts and principles on which judges may draw when they confront unjust laws in their courtrooms.

For judges to exercise any form of judicial review (including common law review), there must first be an identified party who has suffered an injury susceptible of articulation as a legal wrong with a legal remedy available in a judicial forum. This is one important aspect of the discussion of recognized, authoritative legal sources for judicial reasoning. To exercise common law review, judges must determine that there is some legal source on which to draw in fashioning a legal remedy. Many, if not most, perceived social inequities do not fall into this category. This is ultimately a moral evaluation, but it is not solely a moral evaluation. For common law review to be exercised appropriately, this considered moral evaluation must be capable of expression in terms of a recognized legal source.[42]

Judges will undoubtedly disagree about whether an injustice exists, whether that injustice is a genuinely legal injustice, and whether that injustice is amenable to judicial rectification. In republican democracies, major policy initiatives are left primarily and properly to the legislatures for their legal expression. In chapters 3 and 8, I refer to this phenomenon as "legislative primacy." Moreover, in republican democracies, judges usually and properly defer to legislative pronouncements when rendering judgments. In chapter 8, I call this "deference as respect," following David Dyzenhaus. Legislative primacy and deference as respect, along with the institutional limitations of the judiciary (requiring a lawsuit, proper parties, recognized claims, available remedies, etc.), limit the scope and availability of common law review. In this discussion of justice, I can only offer a sense, rather than a definition, of the types of injustice that common law courts can properly attempt to correct. Although concrete definitions are often helpful analytic tools and have their place in the study of the common law, they seem especially ill-suited to a discussion of the injustices to which common law judges may attempt to respond.

In describing the types of injustice to which common law judges may respond with legal means, the best place to start is with a somewhat self-evident but still crucial principle that unifies Anglo-American law (and the law of all common law jurisdictions): "The maxim that there is no wrong without a remedy does not mean, as it is sometimes supposed, that there is a legal remedy for every moral or political wrong. If this were its meaning, it would be manifestly untrue."[43] For the purposes of my argument, this raises three related points: (1) not all social, moral, or political injustices are legal injustices; (2) according to the common law tradition, unless and until a form of injustice is expressed in a form of law, the judiciary cannot properly attempt to correct it; and (3) we need to discern very carefully which types of injustice have been incorporated into the laws of a given common law system. If (and only if) a type of injustice can be found in a legal source, then it becomes a proper subject for judicial evaluation, although it still may not be an appropriate occasion for judicial repudiation via common law review. As a result, judges must accept that they cannot do anything, as judges, to correct certain deeply felt social injustices that cannot fairly and honestly be said to have been expressed in legal form.[44]

An example from U.S. constitutional law may help to illustrate this point. One might ask whether a judge who believes capital punishment is morally wrong must still enforce the death penalty in her courtroom. The answer will depend on the judge's ability to express the wrongness of capital punishment in terms of a concrete legal violation. A judge may not, on this account, refuse to enforce a penalty of death out of a deeply held religious conviction that capital punishment contravenes a biblical text.[45] However, in an appropriate legal framework, a judge could possibly refuse to enforce the death penalty because of a carefully reasoned legal conviction that capital punishment violates a constitutional text.[46] The point here is that, in both instances, there is a relationship between the judge's legal conclusion and her moral conviction. But the crucial difference, which requires real introspection, intellectual honesty, and institutional caution on the part of judges, is the recognition that in the first case, the judge's moral conviction rests ultimately on a religious text or tradition that is not recognized as an authoritative legal source.[47] To be sure, there could be (and are) legal systems in which a religious text is incorporated explicitly or by reference into a constitutional charter. In a system such as this, there might be no meaningful distinction between religious convic-

→ Morality ≠ Legality

tions that are not expressed in legal terms and moral convictions that are. But in every existing common law system, this is not the case.[48] Tolerance for the free exercise of religion (and the prohibition against establishment of a state religion in the United States), constitutional protections for minorities, and the expression of legal concepts and rules in discrete terms prevent the conclusion that religious beliefs can catalyze judicial review. Reliance on a religiously based moral conviction exemplifies a category of perceived injustice to which my argument would not apply and underscores the relevance, at every stage, of reliance on, on the one hand, expressions of moral principle within legal sources, which can form a basis for common law review, and, on the other, expressions of moral principle external to legal sources, which cannot.

In the context of U.S. law, however, the moral convictions of a judge who finds capital punishment unconscionable can fairly be articulated as a legal violation of a specific constitutional provision. Justice William Brennan, a notable example of a judge who refused to enforce the death penalty, accentuated an interpretation of the constitutional text informed, without question, by a deeply felt moral conviction: "I view the Eighth Amendment's prohibition of cruel and unusual punishments as embodying to a unique degree moral principles that substantively restrain the punishments our civilized society may impose on those persons who transgress its laws."[49] Brennan consistently (or persistently) relied on this conviction and this interpretation of the Eighth Amendment in his repeated dissents from decisions of the Supreme Court that upheld capital sentences.[50] Some people (including some judges) will view this as an intransigent and perhaps irresponsible refusal to abide by the settled precedent of the Supreme Court. Brennan recognized this.[51] His response, like his reasoning, was consistent with the purpose and exercise of common law review: "[W]hen a Justice perceives an interpretation *of the text* to have departed so far from its essential meaning, that Justice is bound, by a larger constitutional duty to the community, to expose the departure and point toward a different path."[52] Brennan's reference to the text stresses the basis in a legal source for the expression of his moral conviction. Brennan limits his statement to the correction of a legal error in the course of issuing a legal judgment. Judges are not permitted to engage in freewheeling pronouncements of policy or principle in the absence of a live dispute *sub judice*. Common law review, like constitutional review, is available only where judges are engaged in the attempt to correct a legal injustice, and *only* a legal injustice.

Brennan's explicit invocation of the moral conviction that undergirded his legal conclusion about the meaning of the Eighth Amendment is also entirely consistent with the method of common law review (although this example, of course, involves a constitutional provision rather than a common law principle). Again, the key here is the relationship between an individual judge's moral evaluation and the expression of that evaluation in an authoritative source. This would be a categorically different situation—and I would agree as to its inappropriateness—if Brennan had said, "I believe capital punishment is immoral, and so I will not enforce it in my courtroom." Judges must, at all times, engage in a form of legal reasoning and argumentation, which may incorporate or reference moral views, but always only in a manner consistent with the common law legal tradition and its method of reasoning.

The differentiation of religious convictions not grounded in legal texts from other moral convictions that are expressed in legal sources is, in many ways, a complex example. There are many other, more straightforward instances of social, political, economic, and other injustices that may likewise be perceived by certain judges as powerfully immoral but that are not expressed (and cannot in good faith be expressed) in terms of authoritative legal sources on which a judge can rely when exercising common law review (or constitutional review). Allan Hutchinson provides an example in his discussion of the problem of homelessness. Hutchinson says that attempts to engage with the common law at a theoretical level must seek to explain actual practice in particular instances rather than construct a grand theory that can explain the common law's proper response to injustice in whatever form. Hutchinson asserts that "available legal resources are sufficient to support a plausible argument that the common law could respond constructively, if not conclusively, to the plight of the homeless."[53] The problem is that Hutchinson does not tell us what those available legal resources are. In fact, Hutchinson concedes that established legal doctrine, "historical momentum," and the "deep moral integrity" of the common law may not support his argument and that such a response might never happen.[54] Hutchinson claims that an argument for correcting homelessness through the common law process of adjudication "is less about its legal validity and more about its political usefulness."[55]

I agree and disagree with Hutchinson. I agree that attempts to theorize about the common law must account for history, practice, and doctrine. I do not believe, however, that arguments about correcting homelessness (or any other injustice) through the common law process are more about political usefulness than legal validity. In fact, this impulse is at the root of the problem when considering types of injustice to which common law judges may properly respond while respecting their institutional position and constraints. The recognition that there is not a legal remedy for every moral and political wrong means that certain social injustices must be addressed through other means, no matter how much we might sometimes wish we could frame them in legal terms that would permit judicial intervention.[56] When thinking about institutional and other public responses to social problems, treating political usefulness as more central than legal validity is not an attempt to understand the common law process and practice as it is. There may very well be a way to combat homelessness through the common law process, but that will involve respecting the common law courts as legal institutions and the common law method, which requires some basis in legal sources on which courts and lawyers can frame legal arguments.

In distinguishing the types of injustice that common law judges can attempt to correct through the exercise of common law review from other types of injustice that must be addressed in other ways, an example of a specific fundamental common law principle from English law is helpful. This chapter takes its title from a famous line in the *Cooper* decision: "although there are no positive words in a statute requiring that a party shall be heard, yet the justice of the common law will supply the omission."[57] This principle has been applied broadly by English courts as a "vehicle of change" and "the engine of modern public law."[58] In other words, English courts have applied the notion of the justice of the common law not just to implement and supplement parliamentary intentions but also to review government action and to impose substantive constraints on public power in accordance with the common law and English constitutional principles.[59]

The justice of the common law is a broad principle, but its application is necessarily case-specific and constrained by the institutional limitations of the common law courts. For example, a specific common law principle derived from the broader notion of common law justice is the right of access to the courts, which I mention in chapter 8. The right of access to the courts is a fundamental common law right, long recognized by English courts as possessing a constitutional dimension.[60] It is no accident that Justice Byles's famous reference to "the justice of the common law" in *Cooper* arose in reference to the common law courts' intrinsic institutional obligation to allow parties to be heard in court. In virtue of its expression as a pre-existing common law right recognized in authoritative legal sources, the right of access to the courts, when infringed, is the type of injustice that could justify the exercise of common law review. Needless to say, the circumstances in which an asserted violation of the right of access to the courts will implicate the review authority of the courts inevitably depends on the particular characteristics of each case. All I want to explain now is that this is the sort of legal injustice to which common law courts may properly attempt to respond through common law review. And this sort of legal injustice is unlike other sorts of injustice, which are not historically and institutionally the purview of judges in the common law tradition.

With this in mind, we can return to Hutchinson's example of the problem of homelessness. Common law judges may not be well placed institutionally to address homelessness as a pervasive social ill, a dysfunction of policy implementation, or a failure for theories of distributive justice. However, the issue of homelessness helps us to consider other ways that common law judges can address issues related to poverty where they impede participation in the judicial process, which is the province of common law judges. Again, the goal here is not to formulate a litmus test for determining whether an issue related to poverty can be addressed judicially. Instead, I want to describe the sorts of problem courts can seek to correct through legal remedies in the judicial process.) *how legality can address morality*

English and U.S. courts have consistently held that people cannot be prevented from participating in the judicial process and asserting their individual rights. The historical and constitutional contexts are, of course, somewhat different in each nation, but the fundamental principle is the same. Accordingly, English and U.S. courts have refused to enforce statutory provisions that would require certain payments of court fees for poor litigants, because these statutes would violate the right to participate in the judicial process.[61] And U.S. courts and English law require counsel to be appointed for indigent defendants in criminal proceedings.[62] Of course, none of this is meant to suggest that the quality of participation in the judicial process does not vary according to the participants' respective financial means. Indeed, that is precisely the point. The courts cannot ensure that each litigant enjoys the same qualitative experience in court as every other litigant any more than the courts can ensure that wealth will not substantially impact people's lives outside the courthouse. Not all social, economic, and political injustices are legal injustices that permit judicial solutions. However, the Anglo-American legal tradition and substantive law do empower courts to ensure that everyone is entitled to a basic right of participation in the judicial process, so that those injustices that are fairly categorized as legal can be addressed through processes of legal argumentation and adjudication. Common law courts must preserve values and interests amenable to the judicial process and leave other areas of life to other institutions and processes of government.

Lon Fuller described the incongruity of attempting to correct certain nonlegal injustices through the judicial process as attempting "to accomplish through adjudicative forms what are essentially tasks of economic allocation."[63] As Fuller points out, statutory rights may be created for the provision of a minimum wage, job security, or procedures for dispute resolution. And alleged violations of these statutory rights may be heard in court. But as Fuller also explains, the creation of certain legal rights to limited economic protections "do[es] not change the essential nature of that calculation [as economic rather than judicial]."[64]

Distinguishing between types of injustice that can be addressed through the common law judicial process and those that cannot also touches on the infelicity of thinking of unjust laws through the moral-formal rubric. Whatever the merits of his more general theory, Fuller's recognition of the internal domain of law helps him (and us) to see that the circumscription of this domain "affects and limits the substantive aims that can be achieved through law."[65] In other words, seeing that unjust laws create a conflict internal to law for judges also helps us to see that there is more that judges can do within the legal domain to correct legal injustice, while at the same time reminding us that not all injustices are legal injustices that can be corrected by judges within the legal domain.

For an injustice to be the sort of injustice to which judges might respond via common law review, at least three elements must be met. First, the injustice must be expressed in the form of some legal source or government act that can give rise to a litigated dispute over legal claims with an available legal remedy recognized at common law. Second, the moral convictions of the judge confronting the unjust law must also be traceable to a legal source. By this I mean that the judge must be able to express her moral disapprobation in terms of an existing common law principle, right, or norm violated by the unjust law. Third, the moral convictions of the judge offended by the unjust law must be capable of expression in a legal source. By this I mean that the judge must be able to express her moral disapprobation in the form of a legal ruling supported by a reasoned judicial opinion. More simply put, each of the three components of this analysis—the unjust law, the judge's moral convictions, and the judge's legal response—must be expressed in and as a form of law. Accordingly, despite likely objections, the proper exercise of common law review does not permit unconstrained attempts by judges to write their personal moral beliefs into the law. The proper exercise of common law review only permits judges to respond to legal injustices through legal means by reference to legal sources. Common law review cannot, therefore, be invoked by a judge in response to perceived affronts to abstract or extralegal visions of social justice, religious doctrine, natural rights, or economic theory.

It is unsurprising that theorists steeped in the moral-formal dilemma, who assume that a judge's moral duty trumps his legal duty in cases involving unjust laws, conclude that a judge's only options in these cases are such unjudicial things as deliberate misrepresentation or the enforcement of injustice. Under the assumptions of the moral-formal dilemma, his legal obligations toward litigants, the integrity of the judicial process, and the health of the legal system have evaporated. But once the dilemma is instead viewed as a conflict of legal obligations, we suddenly find that his work as a judge is not done; he still has legal responsibilities to the parties, the public, the process, and the system, all of which have invested him with more expansive and solemn obligations.

2. The Common Law

The term *common law* is used to describe many things: a rule, a principle, a group of rules, a body of principles of justice and fairness, a type of legal system, a method, a process, and a tradition. However the term is used, courts constitute a focal point in the common law method, process, and tradition.[1] Some people therefore conclude that *common law* refers simply to "rules made by courts" or "judge-made law." But this understanding of the term is too narrow. As Roscoe Pound explained, the common law is better understood as "a mode of judicial and juristic thinking, a mode of treating legal problems rather than a fixed body of definite rules."[2] Pound realized that the term *common law* not only describes the legal rules made by courts but also encompasses the processes and principles by which courts make legal rules. In Pound's words, the common law consists of:

> the body of authoritative materials of judicial determination—the body of received materials in which those who decide cases are held and hold themselves bound to find the grounds of decision . . . [and] the process of determining controversies in accordance, so far as may be, with the authoritative materials for decision.[3]

According to Pound, when speaking of the common law as a legal system, we must have a grasp of the authoritative materials of judicial determination, which I will here call "legal sources," and of the judicial process of determining controversies in accordance with legal sources.[4]

These two central aspects of the common law—legal sources and judicial process—underlie the structure of my common law arguments. I argue that common law judges have two cardinal obligations: to apply the law and to develop the law. When discussing each of these obligations, I advance two parallel but independent arguments resting on legal sources and the judicial function within the common law adjudicative process. In other words, I argue that the judicial obligation to apply the law and the judicial obligation to develop the law can be derived from Anglo-American legal sources and from the common law judicial function.

A. Sources

Pound's view of legal sources is familiar to any lawyer in a common law regime. Sources are distinctively legal because they are recognized as authoritative within the profession. These are the materials to which lawyers turn in researching questions for clients and presenting arguments to judges and on which judges rely in drafting the opinions that support their rulings. Pound shares his notion of legal sources with, among others, John Chipman Gray.[5] This traditional view of legal sources is closely related to the "sources thesis" advanced by Joseph Raz. Sources, as viewed by Gray and Raz, are, as Raz says, "clearly related."[6] Gray and Raz disagree, however, about the status of moral norms as legal sources. Gray believed that moral principles are or can be legal sources.[7] It is not clear, however, whether Gray should be seen as a traditional natural lawyer[8] or an inclusive legal positivist.[9] In other words, it is unclear whether Gray viewed the association of moral principles and legal sources as necessary or contingent. Whichever Gray would have preferred, Raz disagrees.[10] For Raz's exclusive positivism, moral principles are never legal sources, although they may sometimes inform judicial reasoning.[11]

Pound does not align himself with Gray or Raz concerning the identification or connection of law and morality as necessary, contingent, or nonexistent. I will follow Pound's lead. Pound, Gray, and Raz, together with John Finnis,[12] all agree that there are certain materials recognized as authoritative legal sources. As I will use the term in the next few pages (and throughout this book), this is all I, too, mean by "legal sources."[13] I am interested in a fact about legal reasoning. According to the traditional view, to which I subscribe, legal reasoning proceeds from and relies on a "limited domain" of recognized, authoritative legal sources according to which lawyers and judges formulate and evaluate legal claims and arguments.[14]

Before discussing precisely which materials constitute legal sources, I should clarify some terminology. I conceive of a judicial system as consisting of three standard tiers: courts of first instance, intermediate appellate courts, and courts of last resort. I refer to courts of first instance as "trial courts," to intermediate appellate courts simply as "appellate courts," and to courts of last resort as "high courts." When discussing the American legal system, I use the denomination "high courts" to refer, where appropriate, to the court of last resort in a state judicial system and to the U.S. Supreme Court; in the English context, "high court" refers to the House of Lords.

Legal sources include official (or primary) sources, such as a constitution, statutes, regulations, and case law.[15] Official sources are not, however, the only legal sources in common law systems. Melvin Eisenberg supplements official sources by providing a comprehensive definition of common law legal sources:

> [C]ourts reason from doctrines found in texts that are not formally binding on the deciding court but are nevertheless generally recognized by the profession as authoritative legal sources. These texts include official sources, such as cases decided by courts outside the jurisdiction or by lower or parallel courts, and secondary sources authored by members or students of the profession, such as *Restatements*, treatises, and law review articles.[16]

By differentiating between official sources and secondary sources, Eisenberg's definition heeds a traditional distinction of the common law. Secondary sources are recognized as legitimate resources to which judges and lawyers may turn in making legal arguments, but they are not law *in se*, unless and until asseverated in a recognized official legal source.[17] In fact, there are two distinctions here. The first distinction is between official legal sources and secondary legal sources. The second distinction is between legal sources (official and secondary) and other, extralegal materials. At the risk of oversimplification, official sources constitute the law. Secondary legal sources contain legitimate bases for legal argument and reasoning. Extralegal sources may sometimes be relevant and referenced in a legal argument or decision, but they are not recognized as bases for legal argument.

Eisenberg includes as legal sources "texts that are not formally binding on the deciding court." One category of nonbinding official sources mentioned by Eisenberg is decisions of lower or parallel courts. From the appellate court perspective,[18] decisions of "lower courts" are decisions of trial courts. Eisenberg therefore includes trial court decisions as legal sources. This seems sensible and accurate. Trial courts have perhaps the greatest influence over what the law will become, because trial courts usually have the first say, even if not the last, about what the law is.[19] Of course, trial courts are sometimes overruled by appellate courts, but trial court rulings are far more frequently affirmed.[20] Furthermore, even where a trial court is initially overruled, high courts frequently overrule intermediate appellate decisions by adopting the rationale originally expressed by the lower court.[21]

In addition to the specific examples Eisenberg offers of nonbinding official sources, I would add dicta and dissenting opinions. I include dicta as legal sources because very often what begin as dicta later become the source of important judicial decisions.[22] The considered language of the U.S. Supreme Court should generally be treated as an authoritative legal source, whether contained in the holding or in dicta.[23] To take a famous example from American law, Chief Justice Harlan Fiske Stone's footnote 4 in the *Carolene Products* case became a wellspring for later awareness of the constitutional import of the distinction between economic and personal rights.[24] Stone's statement also guided courts in appreciating the distinct importance of personal rights and the courts' role in preserving and protecting these rights for American citizens.

I include dissenting opinions as a source of law for similar reasons. Yesterday's dissenting opinions have often become today's law. In fact, some of the most famous opinions of some of the most venerated figures in American law were written as dissenting opinions that ultimately shaped what the law would later become:

> [S]ome of the most significant decisions from which they [Justices Brandeis and Holmes] dissented had been reached by a bare majority of the Court, and increasingly their dissents came to be shared by one or two other Justices . . . [S]urely the dissenting opinions of two such powerful intellects as Holmes and Brandeis may be assumed to embody their most deeply felt precepts about the American constitutional system. What Felix Frankfurter wrote about Holmes in 1927 is equally true of Brandeis, "some of his weightiest utterances are dissenting opinions— but they are dissents that record prophecy and shape history."[25]

As with dicta, it is not necessary for dissenting opinions to become accepted and incorporated into majority opinions before they transmute into legal sources. They are recognized as legal sources when they are written.[26]

Eisenberg's definition of legal sources is responsive to certain facts about common law systems, common law reasoning, and the common law process. Legal sources must be discerned from the perspective of the court reviewing information that it can rely on or refer to in resolving a legal dispute.[27] Eisenberg labels this court the "deciding court." A suitably expansive definition of common law legal sources must include the entire universe of legal authority on which a deciding court can rely in resolving a pending case. Deciding courts can and do refer to and rely on trial court decisions, dicta, and dissenting opinions. Indeed, one important reason that trial court opinions, dicta, and dissenting opinions are published in common law systems is precisely so that they may be used later by judges and lawyers in reasoning about a legal problem to resolve a legal dispute. The definition of legal sources that I use includes official sources (understood to include trial court decisions, dissenting opinions, and dicta) and secondary sources.

B. Process

Pound thought that to comprehend the common law system, one must understand legal sources and the judicial process. I have just discussed legal sources. Now I will turn to the judicial process. As a judicial process, the common law refers to litigants raising claims in lawsuits, providing a court with different arguments in support of or defense against these claims, and having their claims resolved by a judgment, which is typically supported by stated reasons for the judge's decision. As a type of legal system, the common law focuses on the courts' role in fashioning rules as a result of the process of raising, reasoning about, and resolving legal claims. For Pound, two determinate concepts connect all common law systems:

> Along with the doctrine of judicial precedent . . . this doctrine of the supremacy of law is one of the . . . distinctively characteristic institutions of the Anglo-American legal system.[28]

In fact, Pound considered the doctrines of precedent and supremacy of law to be "the two fundamental doctrines of the common law."[29]

By "supremacy of law," Pound refers to a doctrine according to which courts are positioned and empowered to review executive and legislative acts and, if necessary, to invalidate them as inconsistent with the fundamental principles of the common law.[30] The legal source to which Pound traces the doctrine of supremacy of law is the famous statement of Edward Coke in *Dr. Bonham's Case*.[31] I will examine Lord Coke's opinion in *Bonham* in detail later. For now, it is sufficient simply to note that in Anglo-American legal history, *Bonham* was the first judicial pronouncement of the authority of common law courts to review legislative and executive acts to ensure compliance with common law principles. As Pound uses the phrase, supremacy of law refers to this power of judicial review.

Pound's belief that the doctrines of precedent and supremacy of law are distinctive signifiers of common law systems should not be regarded as a crude essentialist position. Pound does not suggest that a legal system must possess the dual doctrines of precedent and supremacy of law to be a common law system. Nor could he. As a legal system, the common law predates the development of both doctrines.[32] Pound is better understood as making a broad, descriptive claim that any vibrant, full-blooded common law system will possess these two doctrines. Pound noticed the historical fact that all modern common law systems possess some version of both doctrines. Pound also perceived that these doctrines best allow common law systems to balance the sometimes competing aims of stability, flexibility, and equity.

Pound maintained that we must understand the common law judicial process to understand the common law legal system. Understanding the doctrines of precedent and supremacy of law is fundamental to understanding the internal process of common law adjudication—that is, the institutional principles and methods according to which judges decide particular cases. But a full appreciation of the common law judicial process also requires an understanding of the external process of common law adjudication; that is, it requires abstracting the process of formulating, following, reviewing, and revising legal rules in the context of resolving lawsuits and viewing this process across the vista of different courts, times, and sources of a common law system.

The external process of common law adjudication overlays the entire legal system. Frequently, we conceive of the common law as the legal rules articulated by courts in the course of deciding cases,[33] and this is one meaning of the expression *common law*. But *common law* also describes a process of adjudication that applies not just to cases involving judge-made rules but to all cases that arise for resolution by courts within common law systems. The common law adjudicative process applies to constitutional[34] and statutory[35] cases as well as in the areas of law more typically categorized today as common law.

The dialectic method of common law reasoning through the adjudicative process contributes to the articulation, evaluation, and refinement of all areas of the law. We frequently differentiate bodies of law—constitutional, statutory, and common law—as distinct categories of official legal sources. But here we must be careful to distinguish between the common law as describing a body of legal principles and the common law as a method of reasoning and a process of adjudication. Considered in the latter sense, the common law method and process developmentally administer the realms of constitutional and statutory law just as they do in, say, tort or contract law.[36] Understood in the former sense, certain common law principles operate at a constitutional level, subjecting governmental action to the rule of law and curtailing abuses of legislative and executive power. Functionally and historically, the common law courts apply common law principles through the common law process to ensure that the rule of law governs the government and the individual, in public and private spheres of law.[37] The purported contrasts between constitutional and common law and between public and private law are neither sharp nor perspicuous in the common law. This is true, as I have said, as a matter of process and substance. The same method regulates the articulation and development of these areas of law, and the same principles and doctrines arise in each type of case.[38]

Retaining these somewhat artificial distinctions for the moment, constitutional law, as a body of law deemed to be subject to common law process and principle, is most relevant to the argument I will here pursue. As I explain more completely later, there was no historical splintering of constitutional law and common law.[39] Even though we are accustomed today to differentiate between common law cases and constitutional cases, this is a mistake that impedes a proper evaluation of contemporary constitutional adjudication in common law jurisdictions. The common law tradition and process best describe and explain constitutional adjudication in modern common law systems,[40] and common law principles of constitutional dimension operate in contemporary constitutional adjudication and decision making of high courts in common law jurisdictions.[41]

C. Content

The previous discussion of common law reasoning with authoritative sources through the judicial process requires that I address a debate in legal theory about the relationship between the identification of the law and the moral evaluation of the law. The notion that the content of the law can be identified through a rule of recognition without recourse to moral evaluation is most often associated with (exclusive) legal positivism. Among modern theorists, Joseph Raz articulates and defends this view most prominently.[42] Some contemporary (inclusive) positivists hold that the rule of recognition itself can, in particular jurisdictions, incorporate substantive moral criteria into the process of identifying what the law is. In other words, these positivists claim that what is identified as law, in certain jurisdictions, depends in part on its compliance with or expression of certain moral values.[43]

Ronald Dworkin rejects the rule of recognition entirely. Initially, Dworkin seemed motivated to reject the rule of recognition because he believed no rule of this type could identify the principles immanent in the law, which are sometimes cited and used by judges to resolve difficult cases.[44] In later work, Dworkin argued that the law's content can never be fully determined in isolation from its moral evaluation. According to Dworkin, the law's meaning is constructed by judges during an interpretive process that involves, at every stage, the evaluation of legal sources in terms of political morality (with due consideration of social norms, constitutional values, historical facts, and institutional obligations). Dworkin sometimes writes about these stages and dimensions of interpretation as though they are discrete and autonomous moments and modes of analysis.[45] He makes it clear, however, that even at the "preinterpretive" stage, when the "tentative content" of the materials to be interpreted is established, a form of interpretation takes place (about which different interpreters will disagree) concerning which materials are properly necessary for purposes of interpretation.[46] Another way Dworkin describes this interpretive dynamic is that the content of law is determined at the doctrinal stage in accordance with the aspirational values of law and justifications of legal practice formulated at the jurisprudential stage and expressed through the decisions of judges at the adjudicative stage, which are based on claims made at the semantic stage.[47] For Dworkin, morality is principally relevant to determining the content of the law at the doctrinal and adjudicative stages, when judges "decide both what the law is and how to honor their responsibilities as judges."[48] However he expresses it, Dworkin's idea here is that morality enters into the construction of the law's content through judicial interpretation of the moral values that underlie the law, the legal system, and legal practice in a given jurisdiction.

According to Dworkin's account, the rule of recognition cannot help us identify the content of the law, because of pervasive social disagreement about the meaning of language, history, morality, politics, justice, doctrine, and institutional responsibility. This is the core claim of Dworkin's "semantic sting" challenge to positivism.[49] As deployed in judicial reasoning, these concepts are interpretive rather than criterial or natural kind concepts, because their meaning is determined not by a conventional understanding we all share or by a true essence they possess but, rather, through the process of interpretation in light of the point or purpose of the practice being interpreted.[50] Some scholars conclude that Dworkin must therefore deny either that there are identifiable legal sources or the importance of legal sources for legal reasoning. This is incorrect. Dworkin offers an alternative account of legal sources and legal reasoning.[51]

I must briefly clarify a common misconception about Dworkin's position. The fact that morality is used to determine the content of the law does not mean that the content of the law is whatever would be morally desirable for the content of the law to be.[52] This point is crucial, because no one (Dworkin included) could responsibly claim that existing legal materials, concepts, and doctrines do not at all constrain the reasoning and decision making of judges in actual cases.[53] Dworkin explicitly acknowledges the importance of institutional and doctrinal constraints on the invocation of moral principles through judicial interpretation.[54] The fact that Dworkin rejects the sources thesis does not mean that he rejects the notion of legal sources or their relevance to legal reasoning. He believes instead that the content of these sources is determined through the process of interpretation, rather than through a rule of recognition, and that this interpretive process will ordinarily involve an assessment—at each interpretive stage—of the relevant legal data according to their substantive moral worth in light of the normative values and institutional constraints operative in that legal system and culture. For Dworkin, the substantive content of the law is not identified prior to adjudication (and possibly changed as a result of the adjudicative process); the content of the law is determined through the interpretive process of adjudication.

I am not here going to engage debates concerning whether positivism is or is not committed to or undermined by criterial semantics[55] or whether inclusive positivists are no longer truly positivists as a result of their acceptance of moral conditions for legal validity in certain jurisdictions.[56] For the purposes of my argument, legal positivists of whatever stripe will view the expression of a judge's moral convictions in terms of a common law norm through the analytic framework of the sources thesis. My argument can be understood in this fashion, though Dworkin would view my argument somewhat differently. In Dworkinian terms, my argument would mean that judges determine the content of the law in terms of moral principles that are imbedded in the common law and articulated through the process of judicial interpretation and decision making. Dworkin would argue that certain apparent forms of legal injustice are actually not part of Anglo-American legal doctrine, when properly interpreted by judges in accordance with fundamental commitments to justice intrinsic to this legal tradition. My argument can be read this way as well.

For purposes of applying Dworkin's theoretical approach to the argument of this book, the principle of legality, which I discuss in chapter 9, probably offers the best example of a fundamental common law principle whose content is determined through the interpretive process of adjudication. As I explain in detail in chapter 9, the content of the principle of legality as a constraint on government action can be understood to be determined through its interpretation and application by judges in accordance with their perception of the point of the "unwritten" English constitution. English judges disagree about the relationship between common law constitutionalism and parliamentary sovereignty, and these disagreements filter into their respective views of the constraints the principle of legality poses for government action. In other words, the substantive content of the principle of legality as it relates to the recognition and enforcement of specific legal rights against the government is determined by the rationales offered by judges reviewing alleged infringements of fundamental rights by the government.

For Dworkin, what the principle of legality means—what the content of the law is—can only be determined by carefully considering the arguments offered by judges to explain the rights that English citizens may possess in a particular case, not by attempting to fix at a moment in time what existing legal sources say about the principle's meaning.[57] Some (possibly most) English judges would not apply the principle of legality as vigorously as others in safeguarding individual rights, because of an expansive conception of parliamentary sovereignty that they believe is most fundamental to English constitutional values. Other judges believe that the principle of legality serves as a presumption of general application operative at a constitutional level to protect fundamental rights and to maintain fundamental constitutional commitments to the rule of law, at times by constraining government action. According to Dworkin, if the latter judicial interpretation of the principle of legality (regardless of whether it is the majority view) is the interpretation that coheres with English legal doctrine and constitutional commitments and also provides the best expression of English law in terms of substantive justice, then this *is* the meaning of the principle of legality. Considerations of justice cannot be dissociated from the articulation of the doctrinal content of the principle.

D. Structure

In this chapter, I have focused on two facets of the common law's structure: the recognition of certain distinctive legal sources and the centrality of the judicial process for any adequate appreciation of a common law legal system. As I discussed earlier, I will develop, in this book, two interrelated but independent lines of argument tied to each of these facets. The first derives from and depends on Anglo-American legal sources and is therefore tailored to particular common law systems. The second stems from the judicial process and common law judges' defined role within that process and applies generally to any properly designated common law system.

The two most fundamental common law principles, according to Pound, are the doctrines of precedent and supremacy of law. Grounded in their legal sources, these two fundamental principles are the bases for my arguments about the basic judicial obligations in common law systems. The doctrines of stare decisis and legislative supremacy inform the judicial obligation to apply the law. The doctrine of supremacy of law, which I will call "common law review" later in this study, is the principle that engenders the judicial obligation to develop the law. Analyzing legal sources and judicial function, I will examine each of these obligations in depth so that we can better apprehend the judicial process and the ways that this process forms the indispensable cynosure of the legal systems we describe with the term *common law*.

3. The Source-Based Argument for the Judicial Obligation to Apply the Law

A. Stare Decisis

Almost everyone agrees that judges have a fundamental obligation to apply the law.[1] We accept this judicial obligation as so basic to our legal system and to our conception of the judicial function that we rarely consider the obligation's origin.[2] This chapter and the one that follows it explore the legal foundation for the judicial obligation to apply the law.

Stare decisis is one of the most fundamental doctrines of common law systems.[3] The doctrine is sometimes referred to as the doctrine of precedent or the directive to "treat like cases alike." Some writers differentiate between the doctrine of precedent and the doctrine of stare decisis.[4] These writers claim that the doctrine of precedent reflects structural facts about hierarchical judicial systems that require lower courts to obey the decisions of higher courts; they claim that stare decisis is the doctrine that binds a court to its own prior rulings. Rather than this distinction, I prefer to refer to "vertical" and "horizontal" stare decisis to express the former and the latter idea, respectively.[5]

This is more than mere semantics. An artificial differentiation between doctrines of precedent and stare decisis misapprehends the generic nature of the binding force of precedent. Precedent influences all common law judges, to varying degrees. Distinguishing between a doctrine of precedent and a doctrine of stare decisis muddles the fundamental nature and importance of stare decisis in common law systems. Moreover, the putative distinction between doctrines of precedent and stare decisis conflicts with the reasoning and language of courts that invoke these principles when deciding cases.[6]

Having explained the terminology I will employ, I should examine briefly some central issues relating to the doctrine of stare decisis in theory and practice. Stare decisis is a doctrine created, respected, and applied by common law courts.[7] As Rupert Cross and J. W. Harris explain, the courts' acceptance and observance of the doctrine are its source and the basis of its legal validity:

> Precedent rules confer authority on the *rationes decidendi* of various courts; but they derive their authority, not from such *rationes,* but from a more widely diffused judicial practice which transcends the outcome of particular cases. To the extent that this practice is settled, they are conceived of as imposing obligations which are as peremptory as any other legal obligations, and in that sense they constitute rules of law. However, they dwell at a higher level than ordinary rules of substantive case-law whose authenticity they control.[8]

In the United States, stare decisis binds courts most stringently in cases involving prior judicial statutory interpretation[9] and least onerously in constitutional cases.[10] In common law cases, courts apply an intermediate stare decisis standard.[11] The traditional rationale for this sliding scale is that Congress may legislatively correct a judicial error in statutory interpretation. On this account, if Congress fails to act in the face of judicial interpretation, that may be taken as the legislature's tacit assent to the judicial construal of the statute, and the courts should be very reluctant to alter this implicitly accepted interpretation.[12] In constitutional cases, in comparison, Congress cannot easily manifest its disapproval of a judicial interpretation; the only corrective recourse available to Congress if it disagrees with the court is a constitutional amendment, which often is a practical impossibility.

Many judges and commentators have questioned the application of varying stare decisis standards to different types of case.[13] While I share their concerns, I am interested in examining the doctrine as it is actually applied by courts. Therefore, I will simply accept, for the purposes of the present discussion, this sliding scale of stare decisis in the United States.[14]

It is easiest to capture the relative weight of precedent according to the sliding scale by imagining a prism whose sides reflect three independent yet interrelated factors (1) the nature of the case involved (constitutional, common law, statutory), (2) the level of the court that issued the precedent (trial, appellate, high),[15] and (3) the level of the court reviewing the precedent (trial, appellate, high). For the first two factors, the precedential force of the previous case and its attendant binding weight on the deciding court increases as one moves up the scale (i.e., from left to right across the labels in parentheses). For the third factor, the converse is true; the precedential weight of the previous case decreases as one moves up the judicial hierarchy. *Precedent changes when courts change*

Viewed through this prism, the bindingness of precedent is directly proportional to the strength of the justification a court must proffer to deviate from the previous decision. On one end of the spectrum, the strength of the necessary justification may be rather weak. An example of this situation, as we have already seen, occurs when the U.S. Supreme Court concludes that one of its own prior constitutional decisions was erroneous. Even here, however, the Supreme Court must explain its departure from precedent; a weak justification is not the same as no justification. At the other end of the spectrum would be a federal trial court faced with a Supreme Court precedent involving interpretation of a federal statute. Only in extremely rare circumstances could the trial court refuse to follow the Supreme Court's prior decision.[16]

Some scholars debate whether stare decisis is more properly conceived as a presumption or a rule.[17] While efforts to sharpen our understanding of stare decisis are valuable, this debate threatens to obscure the more important point for my argument here. Stare decisis must be understood within common law methodology, according to which judges reason from and rely on legal sources in grounding their decisions. Where stare decisis is concerned, the legal source at issue is precedent. A case is "precedent" for stare decisis analysis[18] if—and only if—the case previously addressed the dispositive issue in the pending matter.[19] Precedent can be either persuasive or binding.[20] According to Eisenberg's previously cited discussion of the official sources on which courts sometimes rely,[21] persuasive precedent, which lawyers and judges sometimes call "persuasive authority,"[22] consists of cases from outside the deciding court's jurisdiction or cases decided within the deciding court's jurisdiction by courts parallel to or lower than the deciding court in the judicial hierarchy.[23] "Binding" precedent consists of the cases that resolve the dispositive issue before the deciding court, which were handed down by courts from within the deciding court's jurisdiction that are above the deciding court in the judicial hierarchy. A court may refer to or rely on persuasive precedent, but it is not obligated to do so. A court must refer to—and perhaps must defer to—binding precedent, and its failure to do so is a defect in common law reasoning and method that undermines the court's contribution to the judicial process, impairs the authority of its decision, and may even invalidate its decision as *per incuriam.*

Whether conceived as a presumption that may sometimes be rebutted or as a rule that may occasionally yield to another rule, the point remains the same: any time a court is presented with binding precedent, it is required, by common law method and reasoning, either to follow the precedent or to justify its deviation.[24] This is why stare decisis is the foundation of the judicial obligation to apply decisional law. The injunction to treat like cases alike, or "not to unsettle things which are established,"[25] requires courts to follow precedent. As this injunction has evolved within common law method, "any departure from the doctrine of stare decisis demands special justification."[26] So stare decisis requires judges to follow precedent and apply the law as they find it or to justify their deviation from the established rule. In the majority of cases, of course, there will be no justification for divergence; the judge will be obligated to apply the law as it is.

I should digress briefly to address a possible objection to my approach. I have here defined the term *binding precedent* somewhat expansively. I understand it to refer to those cases that bind a judge either to follow them or to explain his reasons for not following them. Some readers may claim that I am distorting the meaning of the word *binding.* After all, if a case is binding, it stands to reason that a judge must be bound to follow it. Although this might seem reasonable, it is only one, somewhat rigid understanding of what the word *binding* means. One may be bound to do one thing and one thing only, or one may be bound to act within a set or series of permissible options. This objection implicitly adopts the former definition of the word *binding,* while I choose the latter. In my view, the more inflexible definition inaccurately describes the way judges and lawyers often use the term *binding precedent.* A personal example will help to explain what I mean.

Once, when arguing before the U.S. District Court for the Southern District of New York, my adversary and I agreed that certain cases of the U.S. Court of Appeals for the Second Circuit were binding precedent,[27] but I argued nevertheless that the district court should adopt an alternative legal analysis dependent on a different line of Second Circuit precedent. My adversary argued that the district court was bound to follow Second Circuit cases holding that in disputes arising from textile contracts between experienced textile merchants (as this case involved), the existence of an arbitration clause in the agreement could be assumed. I argued that the district court should follow a line of Second Circuit decisions holding that parties seeking to enforce an arbitration agreement must always demonstrate the existence of an agreement to arbitrate between the parties involved (which I claimed the defendant could not do in the circumstances of our case). Despite the cases on which my adversary relied, I managed to convince the Southern District judge that the defendant was obligated to prove that my clients had agreed to arbitrate and that the defendant was unable to establish the existence of this agreement.[28]   Precedent follows from following rule

Although it might seem paradoxical for judges and lawyers to discuss binding precedent that a court sometimes does not follow, judges and attorneys frequently talk this way; my experience is shared by many lawyers—at least by many American lawyers. My definition of binding precedent accommodates the situation where judges choose not to follow binding precedent, provided that they explain their reasons,[29] as the Southern District judge did in my example. Therefore, although my definition might seem counterintuitive on the surface, it allows for situations where judges do not follow binding precedent. It best captures the way stare decisis constrains judges while remaining faithful to the way lawyers and judges actually think and talk.[30] Needless to say, judges and attorneys sometimes disagree about whether a precedent is truly binding. In such cases, if the judge becomes convinced that he is bound by precedent, he will simply follow it.[31] But at other times, as in my anecdotal example, judges and lawyers agree that certain precedent is binding, even though a judge sometimes chooses not to follow it.[32]

In my discussions of precedent in this book, I do not consider questions about how to define or locate the holding of a particular case to evaluate whether a decision is binding precedent for a lower court or for the issuing court at a later date.[33] For the purposes of my discussion, I assume that the precedent being reviewed by the deciding court is perfectly clear, directly applicable, admits of no linguistic or legal ambiguities, cannot properly be distinguished on any basis, and is therefore binding under principles of vertical and, in England, horizontal[34] stare decisis. As I have just explained, this does not automatically mean that a judge must follow this precedent, but it does mean that she must explain her reasons for departing from it and that her basis for departing from it cannot be fitted under the rubrics of distinguishment or interpretation.

Having explained that I will not discuss stare decisis as a presumption or a rule, I should clarify how I will discuss the doctrine. I think stare decisis is best conceived as an "institutional principle."[35] I prefer this conception for three reasons. First, the word *institutional* captures the role of the judiciary in developing and legitimating the doctrine as a legal standard. Second, the word *principle* best denotes the breadth and generality of stare decisis's operation within common law systems.[36] Third, the term *institutional principle* best underscores the analytic position of stare decisis within the common law landscape. Stare decisis is a foundational principle against which other legal rules are gauged. This position of stare decisis was described in an earlier quotation as being "higher" than the specific cases whose precedential force stare decisis determines.[37] The term *higher* was there used to convey the transcendent nature of stare decisis vis-à-vis specific cases. While I concur with this sentiment, I would express it a bit differently. Rather than being considered higher, stare decisis is better conceived as *prior* to the specific cases analyzed according to its requirements. If we view the analysis temporally (as moments of analysis), the word *prior* denotes stare decisis as a standard that must logically exist before specific precedent can be assessed against it; it etymologically reflects the "priority" of stare decisis as a principle of common law judicial process. Viewing the analysis spatially, I prefer to refer to the position of stare decisis as "foundational" rather than "higher," because stare decisis is better conceived as a bedrock principle on which more specific and limited legal rules are built.[38]

As an institutional principle, stare decisis promotes and preserves several values within a common law legal system. The most commonly mentioned are predictability,[39] reliability,[40] equality,[41] and expediency.[42] These four values are closely related to each other and all support the overarching institutional value secured by stare decisis. Walter Murphy and C. Herman Pritchett argue for stare decisis as an instrument of stability:

> Stare decisis is the instrument of *stability* in a legal system. The concept of stability has several important ramifications which may be considered as separate beneficial results of the application of the doctrine, although each is an aspect of stability and each merges almost imperceptibly into the next.[43]

In addition to stability and its constituent principles, courts and commentators also mention adjudicative integrity as another institutional value fostered by stare decisis.[44] The courts are entrusted with the task of "fashioning and preserving a jurisprudential system that is not based upon 'an arbitrary discretion.'"[45] By requiring judges to follow precedent in the absence of any justifiable basis for divergence, stare decisis contributes to the objectivity and impartiality of judicial decision making and legitimates adjudication for litigants and citizens as participants in and observers of the judicial process.[46]

For stare decisis to matter in legal reasoning, a judge must be bound to follow precedent even (or especially) where the judge would otherwise decide differently. Indeed, stare decisis has no genuinely binding effect if it requires courts simply to consult precedent while always remaining free to disregard it should they so choose.[47] Yet it is precisely the binding nature of stare decisis that troubles those writers who believe stare decisis sometimes perpetuates injustice by constraining judges to follow regrettable precedents solely because a wrongheaded or insensitive judge happened to decide the matter first:

> Stare decisis demands that courts conform their decisions to decisions reached by previous courts, and sometimes those previous decisions will have been unjust. Stare decisis, that is, sometimes requires courts to reach unjust decisions. This fact may seem . . . a disturbing anomaly in a system ostensibly devoted to justice.[48]

Various writers have offered theories of stare decisis intended to avoid the anomalies created when adherence to precedent requires perpetuation of injustice. Two efforts in this regard can be classified as the "natural model"[49] of precedent and the "consequentialist model."[50] While superficially appealing, both models suffer from significant deficiencies.

The natural model casts stare decisis as requiring judges to decide cases by seeking the most morally correct rule that will justify a decision, sometimes even where the most morally correct rule conflicts with the rule announced in the precedent that purportedly constrains the deciding judge.[51] While the natural model successfully avoids the injustice-perpetuating difficulties imposed by stare decisis, the baby is out with the bathwater. Simply put, the natural model "is not a model of precedential constraint at all."[52] Stare decisis fosters stability and consistency in common law systems. The natural model sacrifices stability—as well as stare decisis's systemic reasons and functions—in the interests of justice. By single-mindedly seeking justice in (almost) all cases, the natural model would undercut the institutional values of predictability, reliability, equality, expediency, and integrity that engender the larger sense of justice necessary to sustain the legal system itself.[53]

The consequentialist model also stems from theorists' disenchantment with the rigidity of stare decisis. This model instructs courts to consider the results that adherence to stare decisis will produce. If stare decisis requires a judge to reach an unjust result in a given case, then stare decisis must be ignored. Consistent decisions themselves have no inherent value: "Consistency can be nothing more than consequentially valuable; it should be sought only when doing so promotes a just decision. No court ever should fail to do justice in a case before it on grounds of stare decisis."[54] As with the natural model, the consequentialist model is not a model of precedential constraint. Precedent succumbs to (substantive) justice whenever necessary.

There are several problems with the consequentialist model. First, as I already discussed, the principal institutional value promoted by stare decisis is stability. Addressing the consequentialist argument on its own terms, there is every reason to accept that the overall stability of the legal system is a value that, in certain cases, should be promoted even at the expense of some measure of substantive justice. To convince us that judges should do justice in all cases, despite the dictates of precedent, the consequentialist must demonstrate an increase in overall systemic value resulting from the circumvention of precedent. But by decreasing predictability, reliability, equality, and efficiency, pervasive judicial disavowal of precedent would almost certainly decrease the stability of the legal system. More fundamentally, the consequentialist cannot provide any meaningful scale on which these calculations could be made. The consequentialist arguments against precedent do not offer any means of calculating, let alone concluding, that systemic stability would increase or that an increase in some other institutional value would outweigh the loss of systemic stability created by the erosion of stare decisis. Accordingly, the consequentialist model fails on its own terms.

Like all consequentialist theories, the consequentialist model of precedent presupposes an ability to reduce to a common metric all of the values promoted by stare decisis. As a result, the consequentialist model suffers from the incommensurability problems that plague all consequentialist theories.[55] Not all of the institutional values promoted and preserved by stare decisis can be defined in consequentialist terms. For example, equality and integrity, as I have used those terms, cannot be described in a straightforward consequentialist manner. Put differently, there is an inherent value, apart from beneficial results, in treating similarly situated individuals similarly and in creating a judicial process that is legitimated by its evenhanded and impartial treatment of all who submit to it.[56] To address this problem, consequentialist critics of stare decisis tend toward labored, counterintuitive definitions of justice or equality.[57] But whatever other damage these dubious definitions inflict on consequentialist theories, one cannot adequately refute the usefulness and force of stare decisis by attempting to define away its salient characteristics; it must be addressed as it actually exists and functions in the common law world:

> [T]he very existence of a body of precedent is a conservative, stabilizing force . . . A practice of judicial adherence to this body of precedent will further foster conservative values. In the end, therefore, stare decisis reflects a political conception of the nature of our constitutional government, and it must be defended [or criticized] in those terms.[58]

Failure to account adequately for the stabilizing role of stare decisis is the fatal flaw of both the natural model and the consequentialist model. If one wishes to avoid the constraints of stare decisis, one must attempt to find an equally fundamental common law principle that will permit judges to avoid the unjust result that stare decisis would otherwise mandate in particular cases. As I will argue in the next section of this chapter, this principle exists in the common law. Like the critics of stare decisis, I am troubled by certain occasions when stare decisis requires judges to reach unjust results by following precedent. But unlike these critics, I do not attempt to deny the central place or value of stare decisis in common law adjudication. Instead, I argue that stare decisis is a necessary and useful institutional principle that must yield, under certain limited instances of exigent injustice, to a venerable and equally fundamental institutional principle of the common law.

B. Legislative Supremacy

Like stare decisis, legislative supremacy is a fundamental element of the Anglo-American legal system.[59] Stare decisis grounds the judicial obligation to apply the law stated in judicial decisions. The obligation of judges to apply the law contained in statutes is found in the concept of legislative supremacy. Stare decisis applies to trial and appellate courts.[60] Legislative supremacy relates to all Anglo-American courts, including the House of Lords and the Supreme Court.

In fact, though, it is more complicated than this. The United States has never had a doctrine of legislative supremacy that would match the expansive and preclusive doctrine presumed in England.[61] So I propose a more modest definition of legislative supremacy, which might be better expressed as "legislative primacy." I take legislative supremacy to be "the idea that the legislature has legitimate authority to make laws, and that the judiciary must respect that authority in making its decisions."[62] This definition is meant to capture the institutional recognition of the legislature, whether Congress or Parliament, as frequently serving as the primary lawmaker within the American and English constitutional frameworks. It also seems to me that this definition better comports with the genuine function of Parliament in the English constitutional order and practice, and better captures the institutional interrelationships between the English and American judiciary and legislature that are described later in this book by the notion of "deference as respect."[63]

At least since the writing of John Locke,[64] legislative supremacy has been associated with the separation and allocation of governmental powers in constitutional democracies.[65] In this respect, legislative supremacy is unlike stare decisis. Stare decisis is a legal principle of common law systems. Legislative supremacy is a political concept.[66] Stare decisis is an institutional principle; legislative supremacy depicts an institutional relationship. This distinction underscores the fact that stare decisis is a legal doctrine developed by common law judges within common law legal systems. Legislative supremacy is a political doctrine ordinarily associated with democratic governments, which may be found in common law or civil law nations. The difference is between a type of legal system and a form of representative government. I do not mean to suggest that there is no theoretical or practical interaction between the two. On the contrary, legislative supremacy binds common law judges acting within the legal system.[67] I just want to clarify that my interest in legislative supremacy is limited to its constraining force on judges, rather than its political justifications. As with stare decisis, I am interested in examining legislative supremacy's force in common law systems as they exist, not as they might be.

Much of the scholarship concerning legislative supremacy relates to statutory interpretation.[68] Generally speaking, these scholars attempt to do two things. First, they seek the optimal methodology for judicial consideration of legislative language and intention, to assist judges in enforcing or considering whether and how to enforce statutory enactments. These efforts are not, however, my main concern. As I did in the previous section when discussing precedent, I here assume pellucid statutory language that faithfully expresses the legislature's intentions in drafting and enacting the subject statute. This assumption allows me to avoid several corollary issues: the importance, if any, of legislative history;[69] conflicts between statutory language and legislative intention;[70] and problems of discerning collective intent within a single legislative body.[71] Second, scholars of statutory interpretation sometimes attempt to employ statutory interpretation as a collateral basis for judicial avoidance of unjust, undesirable, or obsolete legislation. In doing so, these writers frequently attempt to sidestep what strikes me as the authentic force of legislative supremacy as a matter of the institutional balance of powers in plural democratic government, as well as the delicate and intricate problems raised when a member of the common law judiciary is deeply troubled by the question whether to enforce an unjust statutory product of a representative legislature. I begin to examine these issues in this chapter, and I return to them in the pages to come.

Before turning to these questions, though, I should set aside two issues that I will not examine here. I do not address the disagreements over the normative significance of changes in popular morality for legislative supremacy.[72] Nor do I engage in attempts to differentiate between "strong" legislative supremacy and "weak" legislative supremacy.[73] I prefer the moderate formulation of legislative supremacy with which I began. This formulation is flexible enough to encompass both the English and the American notions of legislative primacy, while evincing an institutional relationship that bespeaks a political allocation of legal powers within a given governmental system. To be sure, legislative authority can be "stronger" (as in England) or "weaker" (as in the United States), but that determination is better made empirically, in reference to a particular political and legal system, rather than through an *a priori* conception.

My interest here is in legislative supremacy as generative of the judicial obligation to apply statutory law. The obligation of judges to apply statutes as the legislature enacted them derives from the allocation of powers to governmental branches and the limitation of these allocated powers. Where the allocation of powers is concerned, the Supreme Court has written:

> Our system of government is, after all, a tripartite one, with each branch having certain defined functions delegated to it by the Constitution. While "it is emphatically the province and duty of the judicial department to say what the law is," . . . it is equally—and emphatically—the exclusive province of the Congress not only to formulate legislative policies and mandate programs and projects, but also to establish their relative priority for the Nation. Once Congress, exercising its delegated powers, has decided the order of priorities in a given area, it is for the

Executive to administer the laws and for the courts to enforce them when enforcement is sought.[74]

The allocation of powers in Anglo-American legal and political systems delegates authority to the legislature to enact statutes and establishes the primacy of the legislature in relation to the judiciary in the sense that the judiciary cannot, absent some extraordinary circumstances,[75] question the propriety of statutes enacted by the legislature. This institutional relationship between the legislature and the judiciary is recognized in judicial opinions[76] and, as judicial statements such as the following often acknowledge, constrains judges when deciding statutory cases:

> The wisdom or propriety of the statute is not a judicial question, but one solely for the Legislature. A statute may seem unwise, it may seem unjust, it may seem unreasonable in its operation upon the rights of the citizen; but that view of the law, in the absence of some conflict with the Constitution, cannot be made the basis of a refusal by the courts to enforce it. If it be deemed thus obnoxious, the complaint should be addressed to the Legislature.[77]

Legislative supremacy forms the basis of the judicial obligation to apply statutory law, because the legislature is allocated unalloyed power to enact statutes and because, according to the doctrine of legislative supremacy, the judiciary must respect and, ordinarily, enforce the laws enacted by the legislature.

The previous quotation acknowledges that legislative supremacy sometimes requires judges to reach unjust results. As with stare decisis, legislative supremacy can only operate as a meaningful judicial constraint if it requires judges to enforce statutes despite their desire to decide differently. As with stare decisis, this binding force of legislative supremacy troubles theorists who believe that legislative supremacy occasionally perpetuates injustice by requiring judges to enforce deplorable statutes.[78] As with stare decisis, several writers have offered theories of legislative supremacy designed to avert the injustices engendered by judicial enforcement of iniquitous statutes. These theories are categorized as "modernist" approaches.[79]

One of these modernist approaches to legislative supremacy is offered by Michael Moore and is styled as a "natural law" theory.[80] Moore's natural law theory provides that legislatures have no inherent authority to bind judges to reach immoral results by enforcing unjust statutes. In a manner reminiscent of his "natural model" of stare decisis,[81] Moore urges judges to interpret and enforce legislation in accordance with "the nature of goodness."[82] Moore's theory is morally attractive but legally fanciful. As his natural model of stare decisis attempted to do for unjust precedent, Moore's natural law conception of legislative supremacy seeks to avoid the strictures of the concept by fundamentally altering it. Moore's version of legislative supremacy denies the doctrine's normative force precisely when it would truly bind judges. This approach is as unpersuasive for legislative supremacy as it was for stare decisis. For legislative supremacy to operate as a constraint, not just a consideration, it must demand more of judges (and theorists). An adequate response to its relevance and importance in judicial decision making must attempt to explain when and why judges can properly (i.e., according to legal principle or legal function) override legislative supremacy as it is, rather than eviscerating the doctrine through reformulation. Moore's natural model of precedent and his natural law vision of legislative supremacy suffer from the same flaw and share the same fate.

Two other modernist theories are labeled "dynamic"[83] and "nautical."[84] Both of these versions argue that the bonds of legislative supremacy weaken as they age. In other words, the older a statute is, the less deference a judge must pay to legislative supremacy and, correspondingly, the more freedom she has to depart from the language or intentions of the legislature.[85] The dynamic and nautical theories propose to "modernize" legislative supremacy by allowing judges to evade clear legislative language and intentions in favor of conformity with changes in prevailing social mores.

Others have already detailed some of the difficulties with the dynamic and nautical models of statutory interpretation.[86] I will concentrate on one: their shared reliance on the age of a statute as a factor mitigating against judicial enforcement of it. This same argument is advanced by others as a reason for judges to avoid following precedent despite stare decisis.[87] As attempts to liberate judges from the fetters of either legislative supremacy or stare decisis, these arguments are unpersuasive for three reasons.

First, legislative supremacy and stare decisis exist to ensure the stability of legal rules across changes in time and circumstance. By relying on the passage of time as a litmus test for judicial avoidance of statutory rules, these theories simply deny the value that the legal system seeks to protect. Consequently, the dynamic and nautical approaches attempt indirectly what Moore sought directly: a fundamental recharacterization of the very nature of legislative supremacy. It will not do to try to make legislative supremacy into some other, far less meaningful constraint to free judges from its actual force and effect. Any argument that judges can legitimately avoid the otherwise determinative influence of legislative supremacy must proceed from a faithful recognition of its real importance. Anything less is bound to be unconvincing.

Second, the passage of time cuts both ways. The dynamic and nautical approaches claim that time erodes the strength of statute law. But others argue that the older a statute or precedent is, the less inclined a court should be to disturb that settled rule of law. The passage of time, on this view, ensures the reliability of statutes and precedents that have withstood the test of time.[88] So it seems that, contrary to the dynamic and nautical views, the age of a statute might just as easily be taken as a factor that should induce judges to preserve and enforce the legislation as it is and has been for many years.

Finally, by asserting that the passage of time enervates statutory rules, the dynamic and nautical approaches are guilty of the same error as those who argue that the passage of time imbues statutes or precedents with some added luster. The passage of time, standing alone, is immaterial.[89] Some statutes and precedents are monstrously unjust when they are written. Leaving aside all of the lawyer's typical "slippery slope" questions (e.g., how long is long enough—fifty years, twenty years, five years?), why, following the dynamic or nautical approach, should a court be forced to wait any length of time before frankly disavowing the iniquitous rule? Or, conversely, if a powerfully unjust rule has endured for centuries, why should that fact alone convince a court to prolong iniquity?[90] When invoking the test of time, one must remember that what matters is not time itself but what time tests.

The dynamic and nautical approaches invoke the judicial function of statutory interpretation to overcome legislative supremacy and thereby restructure the institutional balance of powers between the legislature and the judiciary. This strikes me as "a naked usurpation of the legislative function under the thin guise of interpretation."[91] As I will argue later, there is a legal basis for judges to refuse to enforce unjust legislation. I just do not believe that this refusal can be couched as "interpretation." We must instead ask difficult questions about the systemic necessity of legislative supremacy as that institutional relationship is currently understood.[92] My argument is noninterpretive: "it does not offer a technique of statutory interpretation, but rather offers criteria for when statutory nullification is appropriate."[93] Like stare decisis, legislative supremacy is a fundamental concept of Anglo-American legal systems. And like stare decisis, legislative supremacy can yield only to a similarly foundational legal principle that permits judges to refuse to enforce unjust statutes without circumventing legislative supremacy via statutory interpretation.

4. The Conceptual Argument for the Judicial Obligation to Apply the Law

My first two arguments for the judicial obligation to apply the law are source-based. Stare decisis and legislative supremacy find their legal source in the practice of common law judges. Stare decisis requires judges to apply the law found in cases. Legislative supremacy requires judges to apply the law found in statutes. An independent basis for the judicial obligation to apply the law also exists, which relates not to judicial practice but, instead, to judicial function. Rather than focus on what judges do when deciding cases, this argument concentrates on the judicial role in common law systems. In other words, for a legal system to be a common law system, judges must fulfill this law-applying function, at least much of the time.

In ordinary cases, judges apply a preexisting legal rule (precedential, statutory, or constitutional) to the facts of a dispute and arrive at a resolution to which the parties are bound.[1] Of course, lawyers and judges frequently disagree about precisely what result the rule requires or even what rule should apply. But the important point for my purposes is that lawyers, judges, and litigants all agree that it is the judge's role to determine which rule applies, to apply that rule to the situation, and to resolve the legal dispute.

My reference in the previous paragraph to the agreement of participants in the judicial process as evidence of the judicial function may lead a Dworkinian to wonder whether I have been semantically stung.[2] I believe I remain unbitten, however, because I do not claim that the bald fact of agreement, standing alone, creates the judicial function that most participants in the judicial process would agree judges fulfill. Instead, I argue that part of the point of adjudication[3] is the resolution of legal disputes and that part of the point of common law adjudication requires judges to resolve disputes through particular methods of legal reasoning.[4] These methods of reasoning require that judges consult authoritative legal sources, such as precedent, and resolve disputes in accordance with these sources or, in their absence, in accordance with accepted methods of reasoning (e.g., analogical reasoning). Dworkin agrees. He recognizes that any minimally accurate account of common law adjudication must account for the authoritative force of precedent in judicial reasoning.[5] Dworkin also accepts that judges must either follow precedent or justify their departure from it according to appropriate methods of legal reasoning.[6] The agreement of participants in the judicial practice about the judicial function within that practice is persuasive evidence—though not necessarily conclusive proof—of the judge's role. But if we accept that (part of) the point of common law adjudication is the resolution of legal disputes through principled judicial decision making, supported by justificatory written opinions that are intended to serve as precedent for the future consideration of lawyers, judges, and citizens,[7] then we can begin to evaluate the nature of the judicial role in common law systems without running afoul of Dworkin's semantic cautionary tale.

Ordinarily, of course, there will be no legitimate justification for a judge to depart from the law as stated in an authoritative source. If we assume that a particular, unobjectionable legal rule governs a given dispute in a certain way, then a judge must arrive at a determinate result. Neil MacCormick explains:

> If in any case one party to litigation establishes that the other party is legally liable to him in damages, then the judge must give judgment in favour of the successful litigant . . . What makes [this] so seemingly obvious is that it recites what is on the face of it an almost tautological proposition about the judicial function. Behind it there lies what some people would consider basic presuppositions of legal thinking; that there are rules of law, and that a judge's job is to apply those rules when they are relevant and applicable . . . So what we are in effect presupposing or postulating is that—on this view of the judicial function or the judge's job—every judge has in virtue of his office a duty to apply each and every one of those rules which are rules of law whenever it is relevant and applicable to any case brought before him.[8]

Professor MacCormick recognizes that the judicial function carries with it normative duties, which judges may or may not fulfill—that is, that judicial function and judicial obligation are interrelated. Judges do not simply happen to apply legal rules in certain ways; they must do so. MacCormick rightly appreciates and emphasizes this connection between judicial role and judicial responsibility:

> That "must" is not the "must" of causal necessity or of logical necessity. It is the "must" of obligation. The judge has a *duty* to give that judgment. It is merely banal to observe that his having a duty so to give judgment does not mean or entail that he does or that he will give, or that he has given, such a judgment . . . All that strictly follows is that the judge would be acting in an unjustifiable way if he failed so to give judgment . . . The judge's issuing an order is an act which he performs or does not perform, and in so acting he either fulfils or does not fulfil his duty.[9]

In this passage, MacCormick notes that the judicial function itself carries with it a legal obligation for judges to apply the law. If a judge disregards the law, she disregards her role and her responsibilities.[10]

Dworkin endorses this view. He expresses this point by maintaining that a particular plaintiff or defendant establishes a right to a favorable judicial decision through the mechanisms and process of litigation.[11] Moreover, Dworkin accepts that in many cases it will be "obvious and uncontroversial" that a litigant has "a right to a judicial decision in his favor."[12] So where the law is clear and the legally determined result is straightforward, Dworkin argues that one litigant has a right to prevail in court and that the judge has a duty to resolve the dispute by validating and enforcing that right.

Dworkin disagrees, however, with the account of legal sources that I presented earlier.[13] Although he accepts that precedents, statutes, and constitutions are indispensable to any minimally accurate account of Anglo-American law and legal reasoning,[14] he believes that these texts do not fully determine an individual's legal rights and duties. In other words, while Dworkin accepts the importance of legal sources for legal reasoning, he would not accept that the "limited domain" of materials relevant to legal reasoning and judicial decision making is as limited as I have rendered it. For Dworkin, when judges attempt to determine what legal decision should be reached in a given case, they must take account of all relevant data of political decision making; the texts of cases and statutes are a necessary, but not an exclusive, part of this process. According to Dworkin's account, when judges determine what the law is in a particular case, their determination is the product of a particular interpretive method and attitude that requires them to construct the law as they reason, and this construction requires judges to consider not only textual materials but also legal tradition, institutional practice, social history, cultural norms, political morality, and so on.[15]

Deep-seated as this disagreement may be, it is beyond the scope of this book. For my present purposes, I want to note Dworkin's belief that judges must identify what the law is. I also want to note that the judicial identification of the law must take account of (among other things) the limited domain of legal sources (as I have used that term) and that judges are typically obliged to apply the law as they find it in these textual sources.

Although they may disagree about many things, Dworkin and MacCormick agree that when judges decide cases, they must consult the textual materials. Moreover, they agree that judges fail to meet their legal duties if they neglect or refuse to consult these materials. Of course, judges will disagree about what the legal sources require in a given case, and they may sometimes disagree about which legal sources bear on a particular decision. I want to emphasize here the central importance of the sources for the common law method and the constraints the sources place on the common law judicial obligation to apply the law.[16]

Deriving the judicial obligation to apply the law from the judicial function leads to two further points. First, the connection between judicial obligation and judicial function should always be understood in the context of a type of legal system. Common law judges are obligated to apply the law because that is an integral and irreducible aspect of their role within a common law system. Stated differently, part of what it means for someone to be a judge in a common law system is that she must ordinarily apply the law, and part of what it means for something to be a common law system is that its judges are required ordinarily to apply the law. Moreover, the common law requires its judges to provide the reasons for their decisions, and their reasoned decisions provide the basis for future judicial reasoning and rulings in other cases.[17] The failure of common law judges on trial or appellate courts to explain adequately the reasons for their decisions often results in the invalidation of these defective decisions.[18] Judicial functions differ in different types of legal system, and these differences reflexively relate both to judges and to the legal systems in which they function.[19] Second, the fact that the nature of the judicial function gives rise to a judicial obligation to apply the law does not mean that this is the exclusive judicial obligation in the common law setting. Judges and lawyers frequently make this mistake, viewing the judicial obligation to apply the law as exhaustive of the judicial function.

The United States provides a useful example, though this choice might seem curious at first glance. American judges are often considered to have the widest discretion and the broadest judicial authority in the legal world.[20] American judges interpret statutory language and legislative intent and, most important, review legislation to ensure its consistency with the dictates of the U.S. Constitution. This is precisely why I have chosen the United States, with its tradition of an extraordinarily powerful judiciary, as my example.

My concern here is unjust laws. As I have already explained, I am not interested in statutory interpretation as a tool that might assist judges in avoiding the patently unjust results countenanced by a particular statute. I also am not interested in courts invalidating unjust statutes as violative of a written constitution. I accept that a canonical document, such as the U.S. Constitution, will in many cases afford judges with a legitimate legal basis for invalidating unjust statutes.[21] But not all unjust statutes are necessarily unconstitutional.[22] Well-known examples from the United States are statutes permitting state-sanctioned racial discrimination that (arguably) did not violate the U.S. Constitution.[23] The question that interests me is, what legal grounds are there, if any, for a judge to refuse to enforce a statute that is unmistakably clear, concededly constitutional, and manifestly unjust?

Almost all American judges would respond that there is nothing they can do, as the U.S. Supreme Court stated in *Chung Fook v. White:*

> The words of the statute being clear, if it unjustly discriminates . . . or is cruel and inhuman in its results, as forcefully contended, the remedy lies with Congress and not with the courts. Their duty is simply to enforce the law as it is written, unless clearly unconstitutional.[24]

These are not the resigned remarks of a timid lower court; this is the statement of a notably powerful tribunal. This passage expresses the widespread view among American judges that once statutory interpretation and judicial review are eliminated, judicial authority recedes, and the judicial function reduces to unvarnished application of the law. Underlying this view is the deferential attitude, discussed earlier, of U.S. judges toward the legislature and its enactments.[25] This judicial deference is the product of commonly held beliefs among judges and lawyers concerning the separation of powers in the United States. The powers allocated to judges, even augmented by statutory interpretation and judicial review, are bottomed on the obligation to apply the law as it is, no matter how unjust it may be. Complaints of injustice, however severe, must be directed to the legislature.

The misstep in this thinking lies in the view that the judicial obligation to apply the law is the sole obligation derived from the judicial function. If a judge perceives her role and the scope of her delegated authority as exhausted by law application, she will naturally conclude that there is nothing more she can do when presented with a clear and constitutional statute that happens to be glaringly unjust. The courts of the United States have repeatedly and unreflectively maintained this outlook, as in the following quotation from a Supreme Court decision:

> We begin, of course, with the presumption that the challenged statute is valid. Its wisdom is not the concern of the courts; if a challenged action does not violate the Constitution, it must be sustained: "Once the meaning of an enactment is discerned and its constitutionality determined, the judicial process comes to an end."[26]

This is not, in fact, the end of the judicial process. Where my argument is concerned, it is just the beginning.

The common law judicial function does not generate only a judicial obligation to apply the law, and it should not be conceived so narrowly. The view that the role of judges in the absence of avenues for interpretation or judicial review is solely one of law application unnecessarily restricts and inaccurately depicts their institutional position and authority.[27] Of course, in most cases, where the law is fair and clear, judges must apply the law. But this does not mean that where a law is patently unjust yet constitutional, the judicial role requires judges to close their eyes, wring their hands, and apply a reprehensible law. A common law judge has an institutional and historical authority to articulate and defend, through reasoned opinions, her best understanding of the social values—as expressed in legal principles—that animate her polity. As I explain in the following chapters, these principles and values will frequently be expressed in constitutional form. But this form should not be mistaken for their nature. The textual and conceptual bases for judicial articulation and protection of fundamental common law principles and of common law constitutionalism inheres in the institutional role and responsibilities of the common law judiciary.[28] Just as the judicial obligation to apply the law can be found in legal sources and in the judicial function, an equally fundamental obligation to develop the law can be found in Anglo-American legal sources and in the richness of the common law judge's systemic function. I begin my effort to establish this obligation in the next chapter.

5. The Source-Based Argument for the Judicial Obligation to Develop the Law: Part I (England)

A. *Dr. Bonham's Case* and the Common Law That Controls Acts of Parliament

Just as I did in discussing the judicial obligation to apply the law, I begin with legal sources in my attempt to establish the judicial obligation to develop the law. The first of these sources is Edward Coke's famous decision in *Dr. Bonham's Case.* The facts of the case can be limned briefly. King Henry VIII authorized the Royal College of Physicians to grant licenses and to oversee the practice of medicine in London. This royal grant was later reaffirmed by parliamentary enactment. The College was empowered to adjudicate violations of its regulations and to impose sanctions, including fines and imprisonment. Any fines the College collected were shared equally with the Crown. Thomas Bonham received his medical degree from Cambridge University (Coke's alma mater), not the Royal College of Physicians, and he practiced medicine in London without the College's certification. The College tried him for unauthorized practice of medicine and fined and imprisoned him. Upon his release, he sued the College for unlawful imprisonment.

Determining that the College's charter and its subsequent parliamentary reaffirmation violated the common law principle that no one can act as judge in his own case, Coke ruled in favor of Dr. Bonham and wrote these famous words:

> And it appears in our books, that in many cases, the common law will controul Acts of Parliament, and sometimes adjudge them to be utterly

void: for when an Act of Parliament is against common right and reason, or repugnant, or impossible to be performed, the common law will
controul it, and adjudge such Act to be void.[1]

This language seems clear, and its meaning appears plain enough. Nevertheless, much has been written, and little settled, about precisely what
these words mean. Some writers claim that Coke meant what he said [when
a statute violates fundamental principles of the common law, the courts
may declare the offending statute void.[2] Others assert that Coke simply
proposed a technique of statutory interpretation, such that courts must always attempt to harmonize statutes with the common law.[3] I will refer to
the former view as the "strong reading" of *Bonham* and to the latter view as
the "weak reading."

I will defend the strong reading.[4] The vagaries of history and the vague-
ness of language prevent us from ever conclusively determining what Coke
intended by his statement in *Bonham*. And I am neither presumptuous nor
delusional enough to believe that I will overcome these obstacles. Nonetheless, the strong reading is bolstered by the political climate of Coke's day,
watershed events in Coke's life, analysis of case law, and the subsequent
influence of *Bonham*. Through these four categories, I will explain that
Coke contemplated and should be understood to have countenanced the
strong reading.[5]

1. The Political Climate

At the time Coke authored *Bonham*, Britain was still meaningfully a monarchy, and Parliament was still called a court.[6] Although today the seat of
British political power resides in Parliament, Coke wrote *Bonham* almost
eighty years before the Glorious Revolution of 1688.[7] King James I was a
powerful force in British government. [Today, Parliament is a legislative
body.[8] In the early seventeenth century, however, Parliament also functioned in a judicial capacity.[9] At that time and for the next eighty years, the
monarchy, the legislature, and the courts struggled to assert and maintain
their respective spheres of authority in British government. Primarily, however, Parliament and the courts were attempting to wrest control from the
king.[10] Parliament and the courts seldom competed directly with each
other. In fact, Parliament and the courts frequently viewed their roles as
mutually supportive.[11] Nevertheless, the seventeenth century was a formative period in which political struggles bore constitutional repercussions

for modern understandings of governmental organization and allocation of powers. *Bonham* must be read in light of this atmosphere:

> What was significant about *Bonham* was its timing. It was decided at the very moment when it was becoming possible to distinguish three aspects of the governmental system: the activity of the King in Parliament, the activity of the King outside Parliament, the activity of the King's courts. The prolonged constitutional struggle of the seventeenth century would throw into relief three corresponding institutions—Parliament, the King and the courts—and the problem of the constitutional relationship between them.[12]

At this time, Coke was a common law judge. The Crown and Parliament posed a constant threat to the autonomy of the institution in which he functioned and to the body of law he treasured. [As a judge, Coke devoted himself to maintaining the independence and unique authority of the common law courts as both the expositors and the repository of the common law.] At a time when contemporary ideas of separation of powers had not yet developed, when the three traditional branches of government were struggling to establish themselves against encroachment by the others, Coke's statement in *Bonham* begins to acquire its full resonance. For Coke, supremacy of the common law must be understood as both a legal principle and a structural feature of plural government:

> The question at issue [in *Bonham*] then was not so much whether the courts had the right to render acts of Parliament inoperative in certain details or in full in certain cases, but as to what courts had the power to do it. Did the power reside in the Common Law courts, and hence must acts of Parliament coincide with the general principles of Common Law, or did the power reside in the High Court of Parliament itself, or did it reside with the King in Council? . . . Coke presumed a power in the Common Law courts *alone* and that it was the reason of the Common Law judges which prevailed.[13]

Common Law directly influenced the courts.

As I will argue later, the first sentence of the preceding quotation underestimates the importance of *Bonham* as the conceptual progenitor of what is now called judicial review. The quotation does, however, emphasize a central point about *Bonham* that is often overlooked. Coke was in the unhappy position of carving out and defending the territory of common law courts as against the then entrenched idea of a supreme monarch and against the then embryonic idea of a supreme Parliament.[14] Coke sought to secure the exclusive jurisdiction of common law courts and believed that this was a zero-sum game. For the courts to maintain their unique position as guardians of the common law, they had to resist incursions by the other branches of government. The courts' defender in this political struggle was found in the person of Coke. [He protected the common law courts' baili-wick against encroachments by Parliament and the King.] As Lon Fuller points out, this is the proper perspective from which to read *Bonham:*

> Today this pronouncement [in *Bonham*] is often regarded as the quin-tessence of the natural law point of view. Yet notice how heavily it em-phasizes procedures and institutional practices . . . It may seem odd to speak of repugnant statutes in a context chiefly concerned with the im-propriety of a man's acting as judge in his own cause. Yet for Coke there was here a close association of ideas. Just as legal rules can be repugnant to one another, so institutions can be repugnant. Coke and his associ-ates on the bench strove to create an atmosphere of impartiality in the judiciary, in which it would be unthinkable that a judge, say, of Com-mon Pleas should sit in judgment of his own cause. Then came the King and Parliament sticking an ugly, incongruous finger into this effort, cre-ating a "court" of physicians for judging infringements of their own monopoly and collecting half the fines for themselves. [When Coke as-sociated this legislative indecency with repugnancy he was not simply expressing his distaste for it; he meant that it contradicted essential pur-posive efforts moving in an opposite direction.[15]]

I will later address my dissatisfaction with the simplistic natural law reading of *Bonham* to which Fuller alludes in the first sentence of the pre-ceding quotation.[16] The salient point for my present purposes is Fuller's ap-preciation of *Bonham* as undergirded by and expressive of Coke's view of in-stitutional integrity and competence. [To Coke, the common law was the highest articulation of practical reasoning to which human minds and in-stitutions could aspire. And the common law was the courts' domain]. If the legislature or the king attempted to violate the principles of the common law or the courts' position with respect to it, the courts were required to serve as a foil to the overreaching of the other branches. In *Bonham,* Coke seized the opportunity to articulate his commitment to judicial autonomy and to the judicial authority to curtail abuses of institutional power by the legislature.

For Coke, the common law judiciary was a coordinate, coequal branch of government. [By construing *Bonham* as merely a statement of statutory construction, the weak reading devalues or overlooks the "separation of powers" undercurrent of the case and fails to grasp the political milieu in which it was written.]' Indeed, the weak reading invites the question, what should a judge do when a statute cannot be reconciled with the common law? If the weak reading means simply that judges should take all possible steps to harmonize statutes with the common law and, where this is impossible, that the common law should override irretrievably inconsistent legislation, then the weak reading collapses into the strong reading at the moment of real theoretical interest and practical importance.[18] If, however, the weak reading is committed, as it seems to be, to the view that legislation should predominate over the common law where the two are irreconcilable, then the weak reading is entirely inconsistent with Coke's vision of the integrity and independence of the common law judiciary. The weak reading would sometimes force judges to sacrifice the common law to legislative will, thereby permitting the legislature to supervene upon the common law judiciary. While a judge, Coke would never endorse this result.

So far, I have described my disagreement with the weak reading of *Bonham*. But I do not only disagree with those who claim that *Bonham* stands merely for a rule of statutory construction rather than a conception of constitutional allocation of governmental powers. I also disagree with those, such as Edward Corwin, who accept that "Coke was not asserting simply a rule of statutory construction" and that *Bonham* "uncovers one of the indispensable premises of the doctrine of judicial review," while they simultaneously deny that *Bonham* incorporates some notion of "the principle of separation of powers."[19] This is internally inconsistent. The strong reading of *Bonham* necessitates certain corresponding claims about the constitutional position of the judiciary vis-à-vis the legislature and the executive.[20] [If courts can review legislation and sometimes declare it invalid, then courts cannot be wholly subordinate to the legislature.] Those who argue that Coke intended the strong reading of *Bonham* but that he did not thereby intend any claim about the constitutional ordering of government simply misapprehend the consequences of the strong reading. The strong reading carries with it a conception of the judiciary's place in the constitutional order as an independent branch of government capable of curtailing abuses of power by the legislature or the executive.

Fuller realized that the strong reading of *Bonham* necessitates an autonomous judiciary capable of constraining abuses of power by the monarch or Parliament. This was Coke's precise goal.[21] The strong reading of *Bonham* coincides with Coke's convictions and conceptions of the common law judiciary as possessing an especial expertise, through education and experience, in the only body of legal rules and principles capable of overriding acts of the Crown or Parliament. Furthermore, a judiciary uniquely qualified and positioned to review royal or parliamentary acts for compliance with the common law must exist on a plane alongside (not below) these other, coordinate organs of government. The strong reading of *Bonham* entails a conception of separation of powers that is manifest in Coke's struggle to secure this role and authority for his brethren on the common law bench.

[margin note: Common Law needs that regulatory force]

As I explain in the next section, Coke suffered during his lifetime for his convictions, and events defeated his efforts in England. But he would ultimately, if only posthumously, succeed in achieving his vision in the New World.[22] Against this background, *Bonham* is properly regarded as a flash point in Anglo-American common law history, rather than as the inconsequential footnote to which the weak reading would relegate it.

2. Events in Coke's Life

Two watershed events, one shortly before and one not long after *Bonham*, situate the case within Coke's life and thought and further illuminate the full import of the decision. Less than two years prior to *Bonham*, Coke and the common law judges were embroiled in a conflict with the ecclesiastical courts over the scope of the common law courts' jurisdiction over temporal matters that touched on affairs of the church. On 13 November 1608,[23] King James summoned the bishops and the judges to Whitehall Palace so that he could arbitrate their dispute. As James sat and presided, the bishops and judges stood before him. Coke's position, on behalf of the judges, was that the ecclesiastical courts had jurisdiction over all spiritual matters relating to the church, but only these. He argued that the common law courts were the exclusive forum for all secular cases, even those "of clearly ecclesiastical nature."[24] Archbishop Bancroft pressed the point with Coke. Noting that the judges sat as the king's delegates, the archbishop argued that the king could simply reappropriate these cases from the judges and decide them himself. According to the archbishop (and King James), the royal power was divinely granted.[25]

[margin note: Coke always argued for more power to judges]

Coke disagreed. Tactfully, he reminded His Majesty that "the King may sit in the Star-Chamber; but this was to consult with the justices . . . and not *in judicio* . . . the King cannot take any cause out of any of his Courts and give judgment upon it himself."[26] King James responded that he would defend "to the death" his prerogative to call judges before him for consultation and that he would "ever protect the common law."[27] To this, Coke replied that the common law protects the king. Furious, King James leapt from his chair, shook his fist, and thundered at Coke that this was "a traitorous speech . . . The King protecteth the law, and not the law the King!"[28] Coke fell to his knees and begged the king's mercy. This apparently appeased James. Having regained his composure, "the King said, that he thought the law was founded upon reason, and that he and others had reason, as well as the Judges."[29] Coke replied:

> [T]rue it was, that God had endowed His Majesty with excellent science, and great endowments of nature; but His Majesty was not learned in the laws of his realm of England, and causes which concern the life, or inheritance, or goods, or fortunes of his subjects, are not to be decided by natural reason but by the artificial reason and judgment of law, which law . . . requires long study and experience, before that a man can attain to the cognizance of it: that the law was the golden met-wand and measure to try the causes of the subjects; and which protected His Majesty in safety and peace.[30]

Needless to say, it came as something of a surprise for His Majesty to learn from Coke that he did not fully understand the laws of his realm. Flushed with indignation, King James reiterated that it was treason for Coke to claim that His Majesty was under the law. Quoting Bracton, Coke responded: *"quod Rex non debet esse sub homine, sed sub Deo et lege."*[31]

In the mind's eye, we can envision this scene. Facing a wrathful King James, Coke met His Majesty's eyes (albeit from his knees) and told him that although James was the king, the law was Coke's sovereign. Coke defended the independent, exclusive province of the common law courts. His second fateful encounter with the king would be equally dramatic, and Coke would not emerge unscathed.

Six years after *Bonham*, in April 1616, Coke began to hear arguments in the *Commendam Case*.[32] The case involved a suit by Messrs. Colt and Glover against the bishop, claiming that the funds collected by the bishop on the authority of the king, *in commendam*, were rightfully theirs. Plaintiffs' counsel boldly argued that the king lacked any inherent power to grant *commendams*.[33] Counsel's argument was reported to King James. Upon learning of this temeritous argument, James instructed Francis Bacon—Coke's longtime rival who had recently achieved his lifelong ambition of appointment to the Privy Council—to command Coke to adjourn the proceedings pending a conference with His Majesty. Coke refused, citing the necessity to hear this instruction from the King's Attorney rather than the chief justice.[34] Bacon then dispatched eleven separate letters to the common law judges of the Court of King's Bench, the Court of Common Pleas, and the Court of Exchequer, demanding that they halt the case. In response, Coke drafted the following missive, dated 27 April 1616 and signed by himself and the other eleven judges with whom Bacon had corresponded:

> Most dread and gracious Sovereign[:]
> We, your Majesty's Justices of the courts of Westminster . . . hold it our duties to inform your Majesty that our oath is in these express words: That in case any letters come unto us contrary to law, that we do nothing by such letters, but certify your Majesty thereof, and go forth to do the law, notwithstanding the same letters. We have advisedly considered the said letter of Mr. Attorney [Bacon] and with one consent do hold the same to be contrary to law, and such as we could not yield to do the same by our oath. . . . And therefore knowing your Majesty's zeal to do justice, we have, according to our oaths and duties (at the day openly prefixed the last term) proceeded, and thereof certified your Majesty; and shall ever pray to the Almighty for your Majesty in all honour, health and happiness long to reign over us.[35]

Again, Coke resisted the king's attempt to interfere with the jurisdiction and operation of the courts. King James responded with a letter that made it clear that His Majesty was still smarting from Coke's impertinent lecture, eight years earlier, about the king's ignorance of the laws of his realm:

> Trusty and well-beloved councillor, and trusty and well-beloved, we greet you well[:]
> Ye might very well have spared your labour in informing us of the nature of your oath. For although we never studied the common law of England, yet are we not ignorant of any points which belong to a King to know. . . . But we cannot be contented to suffer the prerogative royal of our crown to be wounded through the sides of a private person: We have no care at all which of the parties shall win his process in this case, so that right prevail. . . . We are therefore to admonish you, that since the prerogative of our crown hath been more boldly dealt withal in Westminster-Hall during the time of our reign than ever it was before in the reigns of divers princes immediately preceding us, that we will no longer endure that popular and unlawful liberty.[36]

Coke and his brethren on the bench were summoned to Whitehall to appear before the Privy Council and the king.

On 6 June 1616, the twelve judges stood before the seated Privy Council, Archbishop Abbot, and the bishop of Winchester. The king then swept into the room and seated himself at the head of the table. At the king's direction, the bishop recited the "record" in this trial: the arguments of the plaintiffs' counsel in *Commendam,* Bacon's letter to Coke, Coke's reply, the letter of the judges to King James, and the king's reply. The king then demanded of the judges why they had not "checked and bridled 'impudent lawyers' who encroached not only on the prerogative but 'on all other courts of justice'?"[37] The king excoriated the judges for their letter, calling it "a new thing, very undecent and unfit for subjects to disobey the king's commandment, but most of all to proceed in the meantime and to return to him a bare certificate."[38] His Majesty then tore their letter in two. All twelve judges kneeled and begged the king's pardon. Coke, however, quickly lifted his head and told James that the king's requested stay of proceedings would have resulted in a delay of justice, contrary to the law and their judicial oath. James asked Lord Chancellor Ellesmere for his opinion concerning Coke's claim. After initially deferring to Bacon as a representative of the King's Attorneys and witnessing a heated exchange between Bacon and Coke concerning the true meaning of the judges' oath, Ellesmere opined that the delay requested by His Majesty did not infringe on the judicial oath. *Coke stood up to King James's intrusion.*

To settle the matter conclusively, James asked the judges individually for their opinions, asking them "Whether, if at any time, in a case depending before the Judges, which his Majesty conceived to concern him either in power or profit, and thereupon required to consult with them, and that they should stay proceedings in the meantime, they ought not to stay accordingly?"[39] Each of the judges, in turn, recanted the written statement and responded that he would accede to His Majesty's request in accordance with his duty. Finally, all eyes turned to Coke. Again on his knees, again facing His Majesty, Coke replied that "when the case should be, he would do that which should be fit for a judge to do."[40]

Coke's frank, solemn, singularly noble statement ended the session but not the issue. It was the harbinger of the demise of his career on the bench. On 30 June 1616, the king again summoned Coke to Whitehall. The king suspended Coke from the Privy Council, forbade him from serving as a justice of assize that summer, and ordered him to review his *Reports,* "wherein, as his Majesty is informed, be many extravagant and exorbitant opinions set down and published for positive and good law. If, in reviewing and reading thereof, he find anything fit to be altered and amended, the correction is left to his discretion."[41] Having no alternative, Coke humbly withdrew.

Coke understood what James desired. James was affording Coke a final opportunity to maintain his judgeship by forfeiting his most forceful judicial statements of his most deeply held beliefs about the common law. And Coke knew where to find, in the over five hundred cases contained in his eleven-volume *Reports,* the decisions that James wanted changed. As he well knew, Coke need not look any further than *Bonham* itself.[42] But Coke had no intention of changing one meaningful word of the *Reports,* to which he had dedicated his legal life.[43]

Coke returned to London after the summer with his "amended" *Reports.* He was ordered to appear with the emendations before Ellesmere, Bacon, and two other men. He explained, tongue firmly in cheek, that with so many cases, one must expect certain errors. He handed Ellesmere one sheet of paper listing five errata. Every acknowledged error was a trifle. Bacon forwarded Coke's short list to King James. James delayed decision, likely due to his distaste at humbling a man who had served him well for many years. Bacon, however, was relentless. On 13 November 1616, eight years to the day after Coke's first dispute with King James, Bacon sent James this note:

> May it please your excellent Majesty,
>   I send your Majesty a form of discharge for my Lord Coke from his place of Chief Justice of your Bench. I send also a warrant to the Lord Chancellor for making forth a writ for a new Chief Justice, leaving a blank for the name to be supplied by your Majesty.[44]

The next day, Coke received the king's writ discharging him from his office as chief justice: "Taking the scroll in his hand, Coke read it, then bowed his head and wept."[45]

Coke's struggle with King James is legendary. In addition to the compelling human drama, though, is a point about the proper context for reading *Bonham.* The weak reading underestimates *Bonham*'s importance by misunderstanding the man who wrote it. As these two vignettes from Coke's life reveal, the weak reading is inconsistent with Coke's attitude toward the common law, the judicial role, his oath, and his *Reports.*

Some writers have argued that even if Coke intended the strong reading of *Bonham* when he wrote the opinion, he subsequently reconsidered his view. These writers note an apparent inconsistency between Coke's statement in *Bonham* and his later claims, made mainly while he was a member of Parliament, about the power of Parliament to alter the common law,[46] suggesting that this vacillation demonstrates Coke's implicit recantation of his strong statement in *Bonham*.[47] There are three responses on Coke's behalf. First, these criticisms misapprehend Coke himself. Second, these criticisms confuse different meanings of the common law. Third, these criticisms misconstrue the nature of a judicial opinion.

Coke was, to the bottom of his soul, a common lawyer and a trial lawyer.[48] He was steeped in a tradition of zealous advocacy of the cause for which one is arguing. And as is the case with many determined advocates, detached counsel often hardens into avowed belief. Even today, it is quite common for lawyers who are, at first, somewhat dubious about their client's claims to grow gradually more sanguine until genuinely convinced of their contentions by the time of trial. This was Coke's mind-set.[49] To a person unfamiliar with the psychology of advocacy, this might seem disingenuous. But it is not or, at least, need not be.

Moreover, the claims of Coke's intellectual inconsistency seem exaggerated. What unites his thought and action as a judge and as a parliamentarian is a sustained effort to constrain the royal prerogative[50] and a wholehearted belief in a fundamental common law to which all are subject—courts, king, and Parliament.[51] When he was a judge, Coke fought for the power of the courts as protectors of the common law; when he returned to Parliament after his removal from the bench, he fought for this power in Parliament. His methods changed with the means available to him, but what remained steadfast was his unstinting effort to preserve England's common law.[52] Of Coke's different vocations, his lasting influence was as a judge and a thinker whose ideas permanently shaped the development of the common law in England[53] and the United States.[54] Now we can begin to appreciate that Coke's purported inconsistencies either are explained by his advocatory mentality or dissipate within deeper congruencies in his life's pursuits.[55]

In addition, the criticisms of Coke's alleged inconsistencies confuse the common law as a body of particular legal rules in different areas of law with the common law as the embodiment of legal principles of justice, legitimacy, impartiality, equal treatment, and fair procedure, used by judges to evaluate official conduct and to curtail abuses of public power. More simply put, these objections confuse the common law as the rules of law (made by judges) with the common law as the rule of law (preserved by judges).[56] While Parliament can, as Coke (sometimes grudgingly) acknowledged, change specific rules of tort, contract, and so on. Parliament cannot fundamentally abrogate the common law as a system of fundamental principles of justice according to which the specific common law rules were developed and against which legislative and executive action was and is subjected to legal validation through the judicial process.[57] Of course, some may doubt that the common law functions at this more recondite and foundational level,[58] but it is most likely that Coke did not share these doubts. In any event, his concession that Parliament could alter common law rules is not evidence that he did.

The previous paragraphs notwithstanding, even if Coke were inconsistent in his beliefs, this means nothing to the ongoing viability of his expressions in *Bonham.* Judicial opinions do not depend for their existence on the continued adherence of their authors. Once written, a judicial opinion takes on a life of its own as a legal source. Absent an explicit reversal of a prior decision in a subsequent ruling, a judge's extrajudicial statements about the soundness of his own decision are immaterial to the decision's status as a source of law.[59]

Coke never expressed, in any of his judicial opinions, any formal disavowal of *Bonham.* Coke's statements while a member of Parliament, even if they were somehow shown to be inconsistent with *Bonham,* are just that: statements of a member of Parliament. They do not directly address *Bonham,* and they have no effect whatsoever on its standing as a legal source.

3. Case Analysis

A. COMMON LAW AND NATURAL LAW

An additional, conspicuous consistency in Coke's thought and writing, which further deflates the assertions of his alleged wavering discussed in the previous section, was Coke's belief in the "artificial reason" of the common law. This idea, which formed the fulcrum of Coke's feud with James, remained constant throughout his tenure as a judge and was expressed in his *Institutes* in language strikingly reminiscent of Coke's earlier response to the king:

> [R]eason is the life of the Law, nay the common Law itself is nothing else but reason, which is to be understood as an artificial perfection of reason, gotten by long study, observation, and experience, and not of every man's natural reason . . . This legal reason, *est summa ratio.* And therefore if all the reason that is dispersed into so many several heads were united into one, yet could he not make such a Law as the Law of

England is, because by many successions of ages it has been fined and refined by an infinite number of grave and learned men, and by long experience grown to such a perfection, for the government of this Realm.[60]

With this idea firmly in mind, we can begin to analyze the case itself as supportive of the strong reading.

The language Coke chose is the proper place to begin, and the straightforward meaning of the words chosen by Coke supports the strong reading. Some have suggested that we cannot impose contemporary understandings on words that are several hundred years old.[61] While this seems true enough, it is likewise the case that we ought not to assume words have drastically changed in meaning simply because many years have passed since they were written. [After all, we still read and understand the words Shakespeare wrote, even if we must resort to annotations for some phrases whose meaning has been obscured by time.] Someone who wants to convince us we are mistaken in the patent meaning we ascribe to Coke's words "the common law will controul Acts of Parliament, and sometimes adjudge them to be utterly void" should present some pretty persuasive reasons to believe that our understanding differs demonstrably from Coke's own. And the task the linguistic evolutionist sets for himself becomes especially daunting, if not insurmountable, once we consider that Coke's contemporaries understood him to mean just what we think he means. For example, in his pointed criticism of *Bonham*, Ellesmere wrote:

> And for novelty in *Dr. Bonham's case*, the Chief Justice [Coke] having no precedent for him, but many precedents against him, yet doth he strike in sunder the bars of government of the College of Physicians: and, without any pausing on the matter, frustrate the patent of King Henry VIII, whereby the college was erected, and tramples upon the Act of Parliament, 14 & 15 H. 8. whereby that patent was confirmed, blowing them both away as vain, and of no value.[62]

Unless those who defend the weak reading on grounds of linguistic evolution can somehow establish that "strike in sunder," "frustrate," "tramples," "blowing away," "vain," and "of no value" mean something entirely different today from what they meant when Ellesmere used them, [it becomes evident that Ellesmere shared our reading of the plain language Coke used in *Bonham*.[63]]

Most defenders of the weak reading realize the futility of attempting to attack the language of *Bonham* itself. Instead, they take another route. One of the most influential of these comes from Samuel Thorne, who challenges defenders of the strong reading this way:

> Coke seems to be asserting that there were acts of Parliament void *ab initio* since they conflicted with common right and reason, but if this interpretation of his words is adopted one has difficulty in explaining both the absence of the familiar passages in *Doctor and Student*, and elsewhere, that might have been usefully cited, and his references in the same sentence to repugnant statutes and acts impossible to be performed. Such acts he likewise considered "void," but clearly that section of an act which is inconsistent with another portion of it need only be considered ineffective, nor need the authority and validity of a statute that it is impossible to apply be impugned.[64]

I will not dwell on Thorne's ancillary question concerning Coke's reference to statutes being void as against common right and reason, or for repugnancy, or due to the impossibility of performance. Here, again, the age in which Coke wrote is important, and "there is little or no evidence that the distinction drawn between void *ab initio* and 'ineffectiveness' played an appreciable role in Coke's time."[65] In addition, it seems likely that Coke viewed violations of common right and reason, repugnancy, and impossibility of performance along a spectrum of ineffective statutory enactments, all of which would be void *ab initio*.[66] I will concentrate on Thorne's reference to the omission of any citation to *Doctor and Student*[67] in *Bonham*.[68] This is the crux of Thorne's challenge to the strong reading's defenders.

Thorne's mention of *Doctor and Student* is thoughtful. As he rightly notes, these "familiar passages" had been discussed by Coke only two years earlier, in *Calvin's Case*.[69] *Calvin* was the most celebrated case of its day.[70] The case concerned whether the plaintiff, Robert Calvin, who was born in Edinburgh, Scotland, after James's succession to the throne, could inherit English lands as an English citizen. The specific legal question was whether Calvin was an alien. If so, he was precluded from pursuing a claim for property in England.[71] Pleading and plaintiff aside, however, the case was, at bottom, initiated by King James himself. After Parliament defeated James's plan for the union of Scotland and England, His Majesty sought, through *Calvin*, to secure property rights for the Scots in England.[72]

Trying to respond to Thorne's challenge, Raoul Berger has suggested two rejoinders. First, Berger suggests that Coke neglected to cite *Doctor and*

Student in *Bonham* because "he might well [have felt] no need to repeat citations for a proposition so generally accepted [and so recently reiterated in *Calvin*]."[73] This answer is unavailing. As several commentators have noted, the precedents Coke cited in *Bonham* were rather tenuous support for the conclusion he reached.[74] Coke surely knew this. Furthermore, Coke commented on the importance of *Calvin* in his report of that case.[75] It is doubtful that Coke failed to cite *Doctor and Student* because he believed he had a wealth of impressive authority available to support him.

Second, Berger proposes that Coke chose not to cite *Doctor and Student* in *Bonham* because "it may . . . be inferred that he employed 'reason' [as used in *Bonham*] as equivalent to the law of nature, for that Dialogue [*Doctor and Student*] stated that 'The law of nature . . . is also called the law of reason.'" Berger continues, "In the circumstances a 17th century lawyer might reasonably assume that Coke's 'against common right and reason' [as used in *Bonham*] was a familiar version of against the 'law of nature' [as used in *Doctor and Student*]."[76] Berger does not explain why, if Coke intended seventeenth-century lawyers to draw this inference, he did not simply cite *Doctor and Student* to ensure that his opinion in *Bonham* would be properly understood. Beyond this, however, I will argue that the inference Berger proffers—that Coke intended "common right and reason" in *Bonham* to be understood as equivalent to "the law of nature" in *Doctor and Student*—is precisely the inference Coke hoped to avoid and that this is why Coke deliberately omitted any reference to *Doctor and Student* in *Bonham*.

Contrary to Berger, I believe that the best answer to Thorne's challenge lies in Coke's desire to maintain a clear distinction between common right and reason and the law of nature.[77] Long before, during, and long after Coke's lifetime, natural law has been equated or conflated with divine law.[78] Although certain writers, notably John Finnis, have painstakingly endeavored to demonstrate natural law's conceptual and historical distance from divine law,[79] contemporary writers continue to search for connections between them.[80] Natural law and divine law were frequently linked in Coke's time.[81] In fact, not long before *Bonham*, King James himself authored a tract espousing, as Harold Berman puts it, "the interrelationship of divine law, natural law, and positive law."[82] As *Calvin* relies specifically and repeatedly on *Doctor and Student*, this thinking pervades *Calvin*:

> The law of nature is that which God at the time of creation of the nature of man infused into his heart, for his preservation and direction; and

this is *lex aeterna,* the moral law, also called the law of nature. And by
this law, written with the finger of God in the heart of man, were the
people of God a long time governed, before the law was written by
Moses, who was the first reporter and writer of law in the world . . . And
the reason hereof is, for that God and nature is one to all, and therefore
the law of God and nature is one to all. By this law of nature is the faith,
ligeance, and obedience of the subject due to his Sovereign or superior
. . . This law of nature, which indeed is the eternal law of the Creator, in-
fused into the heart of the creature at the time of his creation, was two
thousand years before any laws written, and before any judicial or municipal laws.[83]

[*Calvin* equates natural law with divine law and then derives positive law
from these sources.] It accepts that the "law of nature is part of the laws of
England."[84] From here, it is a short step to the ruling in *Calvin:*

Seeing then that faith, obedience, and ligeance are due by the law of nature, it followeth that the same cannot be changed or taken away . . .
[T]he very law of nature itself never was nor could be altered or changed
. . . [T]he Parliament could not take away that protection which the law
of nature giveth . . . Wherefore to conclude this point (and to exclude
all that hath been or could be objected against it) if the obedience and
ligeance of the subject to his sovereign be due by the law of nature, if
that law be parcel of the laws, as well of England, as of all other nations,
and is immutable . . . and we of England are united by birth-right, in
obedience and ligeance (which is the true cause of natural subjection)
by the law of nature; it followeth that Calvin the plaintiff being born
under one ligeance to one King, cannot be an alien born.[85]

The subtler thinkers of Coke's day were aware of the problematic entanglements of natural law, divine law, and positive law.[86] But *Calvin* did
not avoid this snare. It is a natural law *cum* divine law decision that repeatedly elides natural law and divine law, and relies heavily on *Doctor and Student,* with its emphasis on the "law of nature." Coke deliberately declined
to cite *Doctor and Student* in *Bonham* because he wanted *Bonham* to rest
solely on a common law basis, separated from any troublesome associations with natural law and natural law's problematic association with divine law.[87] He left it to others to debate natural law's divine source. For
Coke, the common law was based on human reason—the "artificial reason" of which he spoke both from his knees to King James and in his *Insti-*

tutes.[88] This brings us back, then, to the beginning of this section. Natural law and natural reason were, according to *Doctor and Student,* dependent on or derived from the divine wisdom of the Creator. The common law and common right and reason were, as Coke emphatically maintained, "an artificial perfection of reason, gotten by long study, observation, and experience, and not of every man's natural reason."[89] Indeed, the very phrase Coke chose, "artificial reason," pointedly differentiates the concept from natural reason and distinguishes common law from natural law.[90]

John Underwood Lewis offers the most succinct and direct explanation of why Coke did not cite *Doctor and Student* in *Bonham:*

> [A]lthough this may be shocking to those who see in his [Coke's] work the continuation of the traditional notion of natural law displayed in the works of medieval thinkers and in Saint Germain's *Dialogue Between the Doctor and the Student* (c. 1531) . . . Coke does not use the concept of "reason" the way the medievals did . . . [U]nlike them, he does not equate "fundamental law" with the orthodox sense of "higher" or "natural" law.[91]

Coke appeals to levels of law

Had Coke cited *Doctor and Student* in *Bonham,* the natural law core of the former would have bled into the latter. To ensure that *Bonham* rested solely on common law sources and legal arguments[92] and to avoid any confusing entanglements with natural law, Coke eschewed any reference to *Doctor and Student* whatsoever. The reason Coke declined to cite *Doctor and Student* was that the higher law discussed in *Doctor and Student* (natural law) was not the law against which he wanted judges to measure statutes (common law).[93] Glenn Burgess explains that "'judicial review' was, for Coke, not conducted in the name of natural law or natural equity, but in the name of the fundamental common law of England."[94] Coke said "common law" in *Bonham,* and St. German said "natural law" in *Doctor and Student.* These were very different things to Coke, and he wanted to keep them distinct in *Bonham.* The reason Coke did not cite *Doctor and Student* was because it involved a different matter.[95] Coke knew what he was doing and meant what he said.

Coke was not pointing to a greater power

B. LEGAL SOURCES

Consideration of the sources on which Coke based *Bonham* leads to the second reason Coke refrained from citing *Doctor and Student.* Coke was greatly troubled by the haphazard and slipshod method of referring to cases that prevailed in English courts at the time. He intended his *Reports* to rectify this problem:

> The ancient order of Arguments by our Serjeants and Apprentices of Law at the Bar is altogether altered. 1. They never cited any Book Case or Authority in particular . . . 2. Then was the Citing general, but always true in particular; and now the Citing is particular, and the Matter many times mistaken in general. 3. In those days few Cases in Law were cited but very pithy and pertinent to the purpose . . . and now in so long Arguments with such a Farrago of Authorities, it cannot be but there is much refuse, which ever doth weaken or lessen the weight of the Argument. This were easily holpen, if the Matter (which ever lieth in a narrow roomth) were first discerned, and then that every one that argueth at the Bar would either speak to the purpose, or else be short. But seeing my desire is, and ever hath been, that the Counsel learned, and consequently the Parties might receive satisfaction, for which cause all the Counsel that have argued in the Case to be adjudged, ought to give diligent attendance and attention on those days when the Judges do argue . . . I have for that purpose (the pains being mine own, and the Matter not without some fruit) in the Cases of greatest consequence made the larger Report . . . I will add as a Caveat to all the Professors of the Law, that seeing their Arguments should tend for the finding out of the true Judgment of Law, for the better execution of Justice, that therein they commit not manifest Injustice; for I am of Opinion that he that wresteth or misapplieth any Text, Book or Authority of the Law against his proper and genuine Sense, yea though it be to confirm a Truth, doth against distributive Justice, which is to give to every one his own.[96]

Coke's *Reports* comprised the first comprehensive, authoritative, standardized source for citation to case law.[97] Coke fully appreciated their importance in this respect; he recognized that his *Reports* were legal sources (as I have been using that term).[98] He expected and desired the *Reports* to be read and cited carefully.

As I just mentioned, *Doctor and Student* derives natural law from a divine source. Coke derived the common law from a human, legal source. Coke's exchange with Archbishop Bancroft demonstrates that Coke carefully distinguished between divine matters properly decided in ecclesiastical courts and legal matters properly decided in common law courts.[99] This thinking carried over to Coke's distinction between sources of divine doctrine and sources of legal doctrine. Just as he saw his own court as a legal tribunal in which legal disputes were decided by legal means, Coke saw his *Reports* as containing a faithful record of legal proceedings and legal rulings that might later be used by lawyers and judges as sources of common law doctrine.[100] For Coke, any citation in *Bonham* to *Doctor and Student* would have introduced an extralegal, divinely derived source into an otherwise exclusively legal decision.

As I mentioned earlier, some writers have suggested that the cases Coke cited in *Bonham* were inapposite.[101] Even if this is true, it further proves my point. Coke well knew that the cases on which he relied were not ideal. He also knew that a citation to *Doctor and Student,* which figured so prominently in *Calvin,* could have lent great weight to *Bonham.* But this would have sacrificed the pristinely legal reasoning of Coke's opinion. Coke preferred to rely on legal sources, even fragile ones, rather than on sweeping references to the divine. As James Stoner puts it, "the law Coke is concerned with is English law, especially English common law, not universal law."[102] Therefore, Coke declined to cite *Doctor and Student,* in part, because of its notoriety at the time. He wanted *Bonham* to rest only on a common law basis. As a matter of legal reasoning, he did not want a citation to *Doctor and Student* to confuse the issue.

C. *LEX LOQUENS*

The final reason Coke refrained from any citation to *Doctor and Student* in *Bonham* concerns its connection to Ellesmere's arguments in *Calvin.* Ellesmere was the lord chancellor of the Court of Equity and a committed monarchist. Unlike Coke, he believed that King James's royal power was divinely granted and that the monarch maintained an absolute right to adjudicate in any court of the realm. Ellesmere's arguments in *Calvin* accentuated everything Coke abhorred about the political thinking of the time:

> Ellesmere spoke last; the gist of his oration centred upon neither Calvin nor Scotland . . . Certain new-risen philosophers, said Ellesmere scornfully, looked upon the common law as above the monarch, even daring to declare that "kings have no more power than the people from whom they take their temporal jurisdiction." . . . Near treason! said Ellesmere warmly. "The monarch *is* the law. *Rex est lex loquens,* the king is the law speaking." In his place nearby, Coke must have heard it with gloom and revulsion. "Our constitution," Ellesmere went on indignantly, "is to be obeyed and reverenced," not bandied by persons walking in Paul's aisle or sitting in ordinaries "drowned with drink, blown away with a whiff

of tobacco!" Such "busy questionists" cited Plato and Aristotle on the
framing of states and commonwealths. In Ellesmere's opinion, Plato
and Aristotle were men "lacking knowledge of God, born in popular
states, mislikers of monarchies" and no more fit to give laws "than Sir
Thomas More's *Utopia* and such pamphlets as we have at every mart." It
was a typical expression of a point of view. And the Lord Chancellor,
without referring openly to the court of Common Pleas [in which Coke
sat], had employed the oratorical trick of classifying thoughtful, purposeful men all in one lump with popular demagogues—and by the use
of More's name, with "popery" too. Ellesmere added a three-column
definition of the English common law that must have well-nigh curdled
Coke's blood. Pronouncing the word *moreover* like an ejaculation, he
fired a parting shot: "Moreover! Had *Calvin's Case* proven difficult, his
Majesty himself should have decided it—the most religious, learned and
judicious king that ever this kingdom or island had!" Such a statement,
made officially in an English courtroom—and by the Lord Chancellor
himself—was a slap in the face of Edward Coke and all who held his
ideas on government.[103]

As I hope is manifest by now, Ellesmere's diatribe was anathema to
Coke. So much so, that in his report of the decision in *Calvin*, Coke wrote,
"*judex est lex loquens*," "the judge is the law speaking."[104] This was a keen-
edged riposte to Ellesmere, deliberately replacing Ellesmere's word with
Coke's own. Coke's replacement of Ellesmere's chosen term encapsulates
Coke's tenacious belief in both the purpose of common law judges in common law systems and the place of an independent judiciary within the
larger governmental structure. This also further clarifies Coke's refusal to
cite *Doctor and Student* in *Bonham*. In light of *Doctor and Student*'s inescapable connection to *Calvin*, Coke sensibly avoided any reference to a
book so strongly relied on by those with whom he fundamentally and vehemently disagreed about the place and force of the common law.

4. Subsequent Influence

I have thus far offered three reasons that explain the absence of any citation to *Doctor and Student* in *Bonham* and serve as responses to Thorne's
challenge. First, in contradistinction to Raoul Berger, I demonstrated that
Coke distinguished between the common law and natural law or divine
law. Against Berger, I argued that Coke very much wanted to prevent the
inference—which a citation to *Doctor and Student* would have fostered—
that the common law and common right and reason were "equivalent to

the law of nature."[105] Second, I have shown that Coke's understanding of legal argument based on legal sources led him to avoid any citation in *Bonham* to any extralegal source, such as *Doctor and Student*. Third, I demonstrated that Coke wished to steer clear of any reference to a source cited frequently and prominently in *Calvin* to support a claim Coke found antipathetic.

The final reason I offer in support of the strong reading over the weak reading of *Bonham* is the influence of the decision since its publication. As I have already mentioned, Coke's contemporaries understood him to intend the strong reading.[106] Beyond this immediate impact, however, *Bonham* is widely understood to be the conceptual foundation for the modern doctrine of judicial review, particularly as developed in the United States.[107] My discussion of *Bonham*'s influence on the development of judicial review in colonial and post-Revolutionary America appears in the next chapter. At this point, I want only to underscore that the recognition of *Bonham* as the progenitor of judicial review is entirely consistent with and supportive of the strong reading.

The early American case that exemplifies the weak reading of *Bonham* and stands for the proposition that statutes should be construed wherever possible to comport with the common law[108] is *Brown v. Barry.*[109] If the weak reading were the proper reading of *Bonham*, then *Bonham* would long ago have vanished into the obscurity in which *Brown v. Barry* languishes. Instead, *Bonham* is remembered as a critical decision in a seminal period in common law history[110] and is regarded as underpinning such decisions as *Marbury v. Madison.* The weak reading is entirely incompatible with the subsequent importance of the decision as understood in Coke's day and thereafter. Of course, proponents of the weak reading can always assert that everyone from Ellesmere up to and including current legal scholars simply misconstrued Coke's meaning in *Bonham*. But this response is thoroughly unpersuasive, once one realizes that the strong reading was shared by Coke's contemporaries, was invoked by early Americans when fashioning their doctrine of judicial review, and best reflects the political climate of Coke's day, critical events in his life, and analysis of the cases that he argued, decided, and reported. Needless to say, the fact that American colonial lawyers later read *Bonham* in one way does not prove that this is the way Coke meant *Bonham* to be read. But this fact, coupled with the consistent reading of *Bonham* by Coke's colleagues, makes it difficult to accept the weak reading.

In chapter 2, I noted Roscoe Pound's citation of *Bonham* for the prin-

ciple of "supremacy of law," which Pound called one of the two fundamental doctrines of the common law. Supremacy of law is the idea that
common law judges possess the authority to review legislative or executive
actions to ensure that all branches of government act according to law,
without exceeding the boundaries of their authority. This is what I have
called the "strong reading" of *Bonham*. My previous analysis and discussion
of *Bonham* can therefore be seen as an extended demonstration of the accuracy of Pound's reading of Coke's opinion. In any event, I believe the
strong reading is the correct reading of *Bonham*, and I adopt that reading of
the decision for the rest of this book.

B. *Omychund v. Barker* and the Common Law That Works Itself Pure

Although *Bonham* was cited (or implicitly endorsed) by some of Coke's
colleagues on the bench[111] and remained viable at least through the mid-
eighteenth century,[112] one cannot deny the disfavor into which it fell in
England during the nineteenth century.[113] Nevertheless, one of the eighteenth-century cases that was faithful to the spirit of *Bonham* engendered a
well-known concept whose richness has not yet been fully explored. In
that case, *Omychund v. Barker*,[114] Lord Mansfield coined a phrase that has
stirred common lawyers and judges ever since:

> [A] statute very seldom can take in all cases, therefore the common law,
> *that works itself pure* by rules drawn from the fountain of justice, is for
> this reason superior to an act of parliament.[115]

In this passage, Mansfield adverts to the common law's nature as a system
of legal reasoning and as a body of legal principles. I will discuss the
methodological aspect of *Omychund* as support for my conceptual argument later on.[116] At this stage, I am concerned with *Omychund's* relevance
in linking a doctrinal point I raised earlier to its historical roots.

In my general discussion of the common law, I explained that the common law method applies in all legal contexts within common law systems.
This means that the common law method applies not just to cases that involve precedential law but also to cases involving constitutional and statutory law.[117] The legal issue and the arguments presented in *Omychund* provide an excellent illustration of the historical and doctrinal connection
among constitutional law, statute law, and common law.

The question in *Omychund* was whether the depositions of Indian witnesses, who had sworn oaths in accordance with their "Gentoo" (Hindu)
religious beliefs, could be read as evidence in an English court[The objection by the defense to the admission of this deposition testimony was that
by virtue of their religious beliefs, Hindus were incapable of taking the
Christian oath and were therefore incompetent as witnesses in an English
court.] Defense counsel relied heavily on Coke's statements in his *Institutes*
and elsewhere to the effect that "an infidel is not to be admitted as a witness; the consequence whereof would be that a Jew who only owns the Old
Testament, could not be a witness."[118] The gist of this argument was that if
a Jew, who accepted the Old Testament but not the New Testament, could
not be a witness, then *a fortiori* a Hindu, who accepted neither, could not
be a witness. Plaintiff's counsel responded to this argument with the following:

> The only authority of consequence cited [by the defendant], is a saying
> of Lord Coke's . . . That an infidel cannot be a witness. This saying is not
> warranted by any authority, nor supported by any reason, and lastly
> contradicted by common experience. Lord Coke meant Jews, as em-
> phatically Infidels by shutting their eyes against the light. He hardly
> ever mentions them without the appellation of Infidel Jews . . . and thus
> this noble king (meaning Edward the First) banished for ever these
> infidel usurious Jews: therefore Lord Chief Justice Hale was not mis-
> taken when he understood Lord Chief Justice Coke meant Jews for
> Infidels as well as others.[119]

The subtext of the plaintiff's argument intimated that Coke allowed his
apparent prejudice to color his evaluation of the law. This subtlety in the
plaintiff's argument was not lost on the court. In his speech, Lord Chief Justice Willes embraced and expanded on the plaintiff's argument:

> The defendant's counsel are mistaken in their construction of Lord
> Coke, for he puts the Jews upon a footing with stigmatized and infa-
> mous persons: this notion, though advanced by so great a man, is con-
> trary to religion, common sense, and common humanity; and I think
> the devils themselves, to whom he has delivered them, could not have
> suggested any thing worse . . . Lord Coke is a very great lawyer, but our
> Saviour and St. Peter are in this respect much better authorities, than a
> person possessed with such narrow notions, which very well deserves all
> that Lord Treby has said of it . . . Maddox's History of the Exchequer

clears it up beyond all contradiction, that Jews were constantly sworn, and from the 19 Car. 1, to the present time, have never been refused.[120]

In rejecting the defendant's arguments, overruling the defendant's objection, and admitting the testimonial evidence, the *Omychund* court corrected a legal error perpetuated by Coke's inaccurate insistence—motivated by an evidently injudicious attitude—that Jews were incapacitated as witnesses because of their religious beliefs. It is especially appropriate that in the case where the idea of the common law working itself pure originated, one can actually observe the common law working itself pure. It is important for my argument, however, that common law sources were not all that the defendant's counsel relied on in *Omychund*.

In attempting to forestall introduction of the witnesses' deposition testimony, Barker's counsel also relied on an act of Parliament that required strangers (aliens) to swear their allegiance to the crown "upon the holy evangelists."[121] Harold Berman states that this "statute of Parliament required the oath [in *Omychund*] to be taken on the Gospels."[122] If this were the case, the *Omychund* court's decision would effectively have countermanded this statute. Despite the support Berman's claim offers my argument, I think it seems slightly too strong. The statute cited by Barker's counsel in *Omychund* and discussed by Berman did not specifically address testimonial oaths in court proceedings. The statute provided an analogy, rather than a direct authority, to support Barker's position. The analogy was intended to proceed this way: since Parliament required aliens to be sworn according to the English (Christian) oath when declaring their loyalty to the king, the witnesses in *Omychund* should be expected to swear similarly when providing testimony in an English court.

Counsel's reliance on this statute demonstrates the incorporation of analogical arguments based on statutes in a common law decision. In Mansfield's time, just as today, lawyers do not rigidly compartmentalize their arguments. This is because cases do not always come nicely packaged in the convenient boxes in which people today sometimes attempt to classify them. Frequently, cases raise issues that touch on decisional law, statutory law, and constitutional law; and lawyers often blend these different authoritative sources together into a single coherent argument or use them to make related arguments.[123] If a common law precedent or principle, a statute, and a constitutional provision are relevant to an argument in a particular case, all will be cited, and some may be mutually dependent or related. Obviously, I do not deny the differentiation of constitutional law, statutory law, and case law. But this differentiation sometimes obscures a crucial aspect of common law reasoning and argument.

Furthermore, the issue at stake in *Omychund* would now be classified as one of constitutional law. We would now think that the refusal to permit a witness to testify because of his religious beliefs violates constitutional principles of religious freedom and equal protection.[124] But Mansfield— and Coke before him—did not impose this distinction. As *Omychund* demonstrates, case law, statute law, and constitutional law were not bracketed off from one another. Precise or rigid distinctions were not drawn between constitutional and common law or between public and private law.[125] What Mansfield and the *Omychund* court saw as an improvement in the common law would today be viewed as a development in constitutional law. And given that Mansfield viewed the common law as encompassing issues and principles that we would now think of as constitutional law, it is important to recall that the idea of the common law working itself pure was not limited to the more narrowly conceived body of case law that we sometimes label the "common law." When invoking this idea, I use it as Mansfield did.

For Coke and Mansfield, the common law represented the application of human reason in the pursuit of legal justice. John Underwood Lewis was sensitive to this affinity in the thought of the two men:

> After Coke's time, his conception of law moved through history in the thought of such men as Lord Mansfield (1705–93), whose decisions as Chief Justice of the Court of King's Bench ensured the continuity of the common law's development . . . *Omychund v. Barker* . . . and his continual references to notions like "eternal justice," as in *Towers v. Barrett* (1786), were . . . high-minded ways of talking about "what is reasonable."[126]

Reading *Bonham* and *Omychund* together, then, we find a consistent theme. The common law is an ongoing enterprise of human reason, conceived as practical, "artificial" reason. So any law that conflicts with reason controverts the common law,[127] and unjust laws are, in this strict sense, unreasonable.[128]

This historical and doctrinal connection between common law and constitutional law is evident in the incorporation of *Bonham* into early American law and in its maturation into what would come to be called judicial review. As this concept flourished in the United States, we can see the crucial connection between Coke's thought and Mansfield's as expressed in their decisions in *Bonham* and *Omychund:* sometimes the only way for the common law to work itself pure is to adjudge a statute void. The common law works itself pure over time by purging the law of unjust statutes and precedents that contravene the principles of reason and justice embodied in common law. This is the purpose that would ultimately explain the emergence of judicial review in the United States, the subject to which I now turn.

6. The Source-Based Argument for the Judicial Obligation to Develop the Law: Part II (United States)

A. The Origins of Common Law Review in the State Courts

Americans today think of judicial review as the process by which judges review legislation to ensure compliance with the U.S. Constitution and, on occasion, to invalidate laws determined to violate the Constitution. The *locus classicus* for this authority is Chief Justice John Marshall's decision in *Marbury*.[1] But as one scholar writes, "well before *Marbury v. Madison,* there were instances of state court judges announcing the power of courts to annul unconstitutional legislation."[2] Many of these state court decisions[3] do not base judicial review on any canonical text; instead, they use common [law principles as the basis for the authority of judges to review legislation.] In this respect, these state court cases are the direct descendants of Coke's decision in *Bonham.* In fact, *Bonham* is cited in some of these cases as legal authority for the result reached. For a thorough understanding of the development of judicial review in the United States, these state court cases are indispensable.

To broaden current understandings of judicial review so that they accurately reflect the historical development of the doctrine, I must distinguish the current conception of judicial review from the alternative version that coexisted with it in eighteenth- and nineteenth-century America. To refer to the version of judicial review established by *Marbury,* I will use the term *constitutional review.*[4] This term is intended to refer only to review of legislative action to ensure compliance with the dictates of the U.S. Constitution (or the constitution of any other legal system). To refer to the review of legislative action to ensure compliance with the principles of the common law, I will use the term *common law review.* As with *constitutional review,* I choose the term *common law review* to emphasize the body of legal principles against which legislative action is evaluated.[5] I will continue to use the term *judicial review* to refer generically to judicial authority to review legislative action without reference to the underlying body of law invoked in the evaluative process. As a corollary to this argument, I will explain that prominent colonial lawyers and judges recognized a doctrinal and theoretical distinction between common law and natural law as bodies of principle and bases for judicial decision. The influence of common law (rather than natural law) as a foundation for extraconstitutional judicial review provides a basis in Anglo-American legal sources for the exercise of review as a legal (rather than extralegal) power of the common law judiciary.

In an effort to clarify this discussion, I should define the terms *natural law* and *common law* as used here. Natural law is the legal theory that certain rights or values are inherent in or universally cognizable by virtue of human reason or human nature. Natural law theory is characterized also by a metaethical commitment to moral realism.[6] In this way, whether something falls within the domain of the concept "law" is, for a natural lawyer, at least partially or nominally determined by reference to an extralegal standard or norm.[7] Common law is the legal tradition that certain rights or values are legally cognizable by virtue of judicial recognition or articulation. By legally cognizable, I mean capable of assertion by individuals through participation or representation in the legal process. Whether something falls within the domain of the concept "law" is, for a common lawyer, determined by legal standards and norms—the particular methods and sources of that legal tradition. Unlike natural law, the common law itself has no necessary metaethical or extralegal preconceptions.[8]

This conceptual distinction of common law from other "unwritten" or fundamental law was well known to certain early American lawyers and judges.[9] I do not mean to suggest that all American judges always carefully observed the distinction. But some did. And it is worth seeing the coherent expression of this intellectual orientation in these early American cases.

The mention of extraconstitutional judicial review and legal sources leads to another point. There is some question about what, precisely, the Constitution contains as a legal source.[10] Is the Constitution the text alone, the text supplemented (or supplanted) by judicial interpretations of it, or the text as constructed by considerations of historical, social, and institutional context and moral justification? My claim is only the (I hope) uncontroversial assertion that the language of the Constitution maintains a unique and inescapable role in formulating constitutional doctrine. The constitutional text, however expansively or restrictively construed, is a source of law distinct from other sources of "unwritten" law, even if certain unwritten legal sources may possess a constitutional dimension. More specifically, as a matter of historical detail, legal theory, and constitutional law, the fact that the U.S. Constitution and various state constitutions were written was and is thought to differentiate constitutional documents from the common law. Evidence of this differentiation may be found in the cases I will discuss in this chapter, because judges repeatedly referred to the common law and constitutional charters as independent (yet related) sources of fundamental law.

In this chapter, I will focus on carefully chosen phrases from certain judicial opinions as support for my argument that the judges I discuss based their reasoning and decision making on the common law. It might initially seem that this emphasis on particular phraseology is somewhat facile and haphazard, particularly in reference to cases decided two centuries ago. But as Forrest McDonald explains, the chosen terms and phrases of the time in which these decisions were written are especially important to a historically accurate understanding of these judicial writings, because these repeated and related terms and phrases were often then and now should be associated "with particular ideologies or bodies of thought."[2] Following McDonald, then, I intend to show that the phrases I highlight were and should be associated with an intellectual orientation that favored the common law as the basis for legal reasoning and judicial decision making.

I have three principal goals for this chapter. First, I hope to sharpen and clarify the doctrinal analysis of some early American case law about which scholars continue to disagree. I offer a historically grounded and theoretically integrated account of certain important decisions that helped to shape institutional relationships in the United States for the centuries to come. Second, I provide an account of judicial review that might help theorists better evaluate the genuine legal and historical meaning of American constitutionalism, in terms of the nature of the written U.S. Constitution and its implications for legislative authority, judicial autonomy, and individual rights. Third, I trace the distinctive contours of different sources of "unwritten" fundamental law. In particular, I draw attention, at certain points, to distinctions between common law and natural law as bodies of legal principle to which lawyers and judges appealed for support when arguing and deciding cases.

Some scholars today believe that American lawyers in the eighteenth and nineteenth centuries drew no distinctions among these various sources of unwritten law. Others who accept that some Americans drew these distinctions read the cases I discuss here as providing the exercises of judicial review during this period with an underpinning based in natural law. Indeed, this natural law reading of these early cases is so widely accepted that people rarely pause to consider the matter. Both views are mistaken. Instead, I argue that the common law was the principal source of fundamental law on which several influential early American jurists relied as legal authority for judicial review. Appreciating this distinction and its implications is essential for a proper understanding of this case law, the authentic conceptual origins of judicial review and constitutionalism, and methods of legal reasoning and judicial decision making.

There is a long-standing and ongoing debate among American scholars of constitutional law, theory, and history about the authentic legal, theoretical, and historical basis for judicial review in the United States. The purpose of this chapter is to demonstrate that there is a legal, theoretical, and historical basis that does not depend on the written Constitution or on natural law and that still provides a unique but limited authority for common law courts to preserve the rule of law in the United States. In other words, a complete understanding of the origins of judicial review and American constitutionalism requires an examination of more than constitutional review alone, because there may be another basis for judicial authority to review legislative action and to ensure conformity with legal principle.

My argument diverges, then, from those made by such scholars as Wil Waluchow, William Treanor, Sylvia Snowiss, and Suzanna Sherry. Waluchow seeks to apply common law processes of reasoning and adjudication to the constitutional morality intrinsic in charter documents.[13] In contrast, I argue that the conceptual and historical legitimacy of judicial review in the common law tradition is exogenous to the existence or nature of a (written)[14] constitution, in part because constitutions themselves reflect and instantiate (but do not supersede) preexisting common law principles.[15] Treanor argues very persuasively that there is important historical evidence to support an expansive, antiliteralist (to use his term) conception of judicial review during the founding period of the United States.[16] Treanor's interest lies in examining attitudes toward constitutional review during the late eighteenth century. Treanor's arguments are therefore tangential—or perhaps parallel—to my own. I am interested in studying early doctrinal support for judicial review during the period following the Revolution, but unlike Treanor, I focus on the doctrinal foundations for this authority aside from (but sometimes alongside) constitutional review. In this respect, my focus is more closely aligned with the work of Snowiss and Sherry. They, too, are interested in examining the doctrinal support for extraconstitutional judicial review during the colonial and post-Revolutionary period.[17] But they cite natural law as the extraconstitutional basis for judicial review at this time. As I describe in detail later in this chapter, common law—not natural law—was the most authentic basis for extraconstitutional judicial review during the late eighteenth and early nineteenth century in the United States.

I should add two further clarifications. First, in the previous paragraphs, I refer to judicial review of legislative action. While this is my principal interest at this point, constitutional review is understood in the United States to extend to judicial review of actions of the executive (as well as the legislative) branch of government,[18] and I intend my discussion of common law review to extend similarly. Second, I also intend my discussion of common law review to encompass judicial review of prior judicial decisions.[19]

1. Paxton's Case, *Unreported Decisions, and Careful Citations*

The earliest prominent argument in favor of common law review by an American lawyer occurred in *Paxton's Case of the Writ of Assistance* in 1761.[20] James Otis resigned as Advocate General of Admiralty so that he could challenge the writs.[21] Otis argued for a power of judicial review grounded specifically on the common law (complete with a citation to Coke's decision in *Bonham*):

> As early as 24 February 1761 he [Otis] attacked the Writs of Assistance as being "against the fundamental principles of law" . . . "and if an Act of Parliament should be made in the very words of this petition it would be void. The executive Courts must pass such acts into disuse." Here was an explicit espousal of the doctrine of judicial review, and Otis based it on Coke, for he added: "8 Rep. 118 from Viner. Reason of the common law to control an Act of Parliament."[22]

Otis's reliance on *Bonham* in *Paxton* would have an important and discernible influence on the development of judicial review by state courts in the period following the Revolution.[23]

The next three decades of American legal history saw the increasing influence of *Bonham* on state courts that based their power of judicial review on the common law.[24] In the thirty years following Otis's argument in

Paxton, state courts would assert, in several cases, a common law authority to invalidate statutory enactments. In reviewing these state court decisions, I restrict myself to cases in which state courts refer explicitly to the common law as the legal standard for reviewing legislative action to draw particular attention to the invocation of the common law as a basis for judicial review independent from either natural law or a written constitution.[25]

Gordon Wood recognized the influence of common law constitutionalism on post-Revolutionary conceptions of judicial review and of the legal restraints on legislative will. Unfortunately, however, the case Wood cites most prominently as the clearest expression of "this Cokean conception" is *Rutgers v. Waddington* In addition to *Rutgers,* Wood mentions *Trevett v. Weeden* and *Bayard v. Singleton*[26] as developing the account of judicial review authority advocated by Otis and others.[27] The problem with these citations is that none of these cases rests exclusively on a common law foundation. As Wood himself acknowledges, *Rutgers* rests, at least in part, on a possible violation of the New York state constitution. To be sure, the court also seems to consider the conflict between the state legislation and the common law. But it is never clear precisely which body of legal principle the court deems controlling. In addition and perhaps most important, the court explicitly disclaims any authority to reject the clearly expressed will of the legislature (as Wood also acknowledges). *Trevett* primarily involved appeals to natural law along with common right and reason, while *Bayard* stands solely on a determination of unconstitutionality. Wood's reliance on these cases reinforces the importance of distinguishing carefully among the cases cited as support for different modes of early American legal thought and doctrine. These details of the opinions Wood cites leave me in the position of agreeing with his conclusion but suggesting that the doctrinal support for that conclusion can be better found in the cases I examine here rather than in the cases Wood selected.

2. Ham v. M'Claws

Ham v. M'Claws[28] was the first reported case in which a state court ruled that legislation contrary to common law principles was void. Refusing to enforce the forfeiture statute at issue and incorporating arguments of counsel, the South Carolina court, consisting of Judges Grimke, Waties, and Drayton, wrote:

> It was, therefore, the duty of the court, in such case, to square its decision with the rules of common right and justice. For there were certain fixed and established rules, founded on the reason and fitness of things,

which were paramount to all statutes [and if laws are made against those principles, they are null and void.] For instance, statutes made against common right and reason, are void. 8 [Co.] Rep. 118 . . . It is clear, that statutes passed against the plain and obvious principles of common right, and common reason, are absolutely null and void, as far as they are calculated to operate against those principles.[29]

Even without the overt citation to *Bonham,* the influence of Coke's decision is manifest in *Ham.* The South Carolina court's verbatim incorporation of the language from *Bonham* confirms the importance of Coke's decision to the court's ruling.

3. Bowman v. Middleton

Three years later, in 1792, [*Bowman v. Middleton*[30]] was decided by Judges Grimke and Bay of the South Carolina court. *Bowman* involved a 1712 statute that transferred property ownership from one party to another. The plaintiffs inherited the land from the beneficiary of the 1712 enactment. Middleton had agreed to purchase the land from the plaintiffs. Middleton later refused to consummate the purchase, claiming that a portion of the property still belonged to the heirs of the original owner and not to the plaintiffs [The plaintiffs asserted complete ownership rights as derived from the 1712 act.] Despite the passage of eighty years since the putative transfer of ownership rights pursuant to the statute, the court ruled for Middleton and voided the 1712 statute as violative of common law principles:

> [T]he plaintiffs could claim no title under the act in question, as it was against common right, as well as against Magna Charta, to take away the freehold of one man and vest it in another, and that, too, to the prejudice of third persons, without any compensation, or even a trial by the jury of the country, to determine the right in question. That the act was, therefore, ipso facto void. That no length of time could give it validity, being originally founded on erroneous principles.[31]

As with *Ham,* the court in *Bowman* tracks Coke's own language. Coke used the phrase "common right and reason" in *Bonham.* The *Bowman* court used the truncated term "common right." Coke himself sometimes used the abbreviated term as a reference to the common law:

> [T]he common law of England sometimes is called right, sometimes common right, and sometimes *communis justitia.* In the grand charter the common law is called right . . . And all the commissions and char-

ters for execution of justice are, *facturi quod ad justitiam pertinet secundum legem et consuetudinem Angliae*. So as in truth justice is the daughter of the law, for the law bringeth her forth. And in this sense being largely taken, as well the statutes and customs of the realm, as that which is properly [called] the common law, is included within *common right*.[32]

Bowman involved a statute enacted by the South Carolina colonial legislature. For this reason and to avoid any possible retroactivity concern, the Court's decision can be read as applying common law principles in effect when the statute was enacted. So, standing alone, *Bowman* does not settle the question of whether the state constitution and common law principles were viewed as distinct sources of fundamental law against which the 1712 statute was evaluated. The case would provide more certain guidance on this question if the statute at issue had been enacted after ratification of the state constitution.

4. Lindsay v. Commissioners

The South Carolina court reiterated the importance of the common law as a basis for evaluation of legislation in *Lindsay v. Commissioners*,[33] which involved a takings issue. Specifically, the court was asked to determine whether property owners whose unimproved land was appropriated by the state for public use in constructing a street were entitled to compensation. After unanimously acknowledging the authority of the state to acquire the property, the court divided 2–2 on the state's obligation to provide compensation.

Two aspects of this case are especially noteworthy for my argument. First, even though the judges disagreed about the proper disposition of the case, they all relied on common law principles as the legal basis for their reasoning and resolution. For example, Judge Thomas Waties concluded, along with Judge Aedanus Burke, that the legislation should be overridden and that compensation should be provided to the owners by the state. Judge Waties clarified the legal basis for his conclusion as follows:

> He [Judge Waties] admitted the right of the state to take the property of an individual . . . but in exercising this power, it was essential to its validity, that a full compensation should be provided at the time, for every injury that the individual might suffer . . . The common law of England, which has also recognized this power, does it always with the same restriction . . . The rights of our citizens are not less valuable than those of

the people of England: we have besides a constitution, which limits and controls the power of the legislature, the 9th article of which, declares, that no freeman shall be divested of his property, but by the judgment of his peers, or the law of the land. On a former occasion, . . . he said, he had gone into a long investigation of the technical import of the words *lex terrae,* and therefore should only state here, that they meant the common law . . . He said he understood, therefore, the constitution to mean, that no freeman shall be deprived of his property, but by such means as are authorized by the ancient common law of the land . . In what way, then, does the common law authorize the power of taking private property for public uses? "by providing," says Mr. Blackstone, "a full indemnification for it." This is the condition on which the valid exercise of this power depends.[34]

Judges John Grimke and Elihu Bay, who disagreed with Judge Waties about the compensation question, nevertheless agreed with him that the common law was the legal source against which the subject legislation should be evaluated, as well as the legal limitation on the state's legislative power. As they put it:

They considered the act in question as authorized by the fundamental principles of society . . . [T]he legislature of South Carolina, had exercised this power and authority [to make and maintain public thoroughfares], from the first establishment of civil government in it, to the present day. They therefore considered it, as much a part of the common law of South Carolina, as any other part of that great and valuable system.[35]

Second, a more subtle point of agreement between Judges Grimke and Bay and Judge Waties concerned the relationship between the common law and the South Carolina Constitution. On this point, Judges Grimke and Bay wrote:

That it was neither against *magna charta,* nor the state constitution, but part of the *lex terrae,* which both meant to defend and protect. The so much celebrated *magna charta* of Great Britain . . . was therefore only declaratory of the well known and established laws of the kingdom. So, in like manner, the 2d section of the 9th article of our state constitution, confirms all the before-mentioned principles. It was not declaratory of any new law, but confirmed all the ancient rights and principles, which had been in use in the state.[36]

With their explicit statement that the South Carolina Constitution "was not declaratory of any new law," Judges Grimke and Bay indicated their adherence to the view of many early American lawyers and judges that written constitutions reaffirmed the rights and principles of the common law.[37] Moreover, this common law foundation of written constitutions informed the judges' interpretations of these constitutions, as is evident in the previously quoted extract from Judge Waties's opinion.

Lindsay demonstrates that these South Carolina judges viewed written constitutions as derivative of the common law and that, even though they might mention both as legal sources against which legislative acts could be measured, this differentiation was not considered as ordinal or hierarchical.[38] Both the common law and a written constitution might be used concurrently to evaluate legislation, but these judges did not consider a constitution to be "higher" or more fundamental than the common law. Judges Grimke and Bay (who had decided *Bowman*) agreed with Judges Waties and Burke that the South Carolina Constitution was declaratory of preexisting common law principles. This does not mean that the state constitution and the common law were necessarily coextensive with or entirely duplicative of one another, although they were interpreted in that way in this case. Moreover, my analysis of *Ham, Bowman,* and *Lindsay* suggests that judges on the South Carolina court, like Judge Carrington of the Virginia court in *Jones* (which I discuss next) apparently viewed the common law and constitutions as distinct (mutually reinforcing) bodies of fundamental law and as conceptually distinct bases for judicial review.[39]

5. Jones v. The Commonwealth

Another example of a state court discussing common law review and constitutional review side by side occurs in *Jones v. The Commonwealth*.[40] *Jones* involved the attempt to impose joint fines on several defendants who had been convicted of assault. In negating the fines, Judge Carrington noted their inconsistency with the common law principle that one person "ought not to suffer for the fault of another." Judge Carrington then concluded:

> Therefore, whether I consider the case upon . . . the doctrines of the common law, *or* the spirit of the Bill of Rights and the act of Assembly, I am equally clear in my opinion, that the District Court should have required the jury to discriminate; and, having failed to do so, that their judgment is erroneous, and must be reversed.[41]

In *Jones,* which was decided after the ratification of the federal Bill of Rights and before *Marbury,* we find the Virginia Supreme Court of Appeals articulating parallel doctrines of common law review and constitutional review.

6. Holmes v. Walton *and the Absence of Hierarchy in Legal Sources*

Some scholars who recognize the early legal and conceptual distinctions between common law and written constitutions assume that these sources of law were ranked hierarchically in the minds of American lawyers and judges. These scholars believe that common law principles existed on a plane below statutory law and constitutions.[42] This is a natural assumption for contemporary readers of dated legal materials to make, but it inaccurately renders the legal thought of the period. For example, Wayne Moore points out that in perhaps the first example of judicial review in American legal history, a state court articulated parallel doctrines of common law review and constitutional review. In *Holmes v. Walton,* the New Jersey Supreme Court apparently invalidated state legislation providing for trials in certain cases before six-person juries rather than twelve-person juries. The New Jersey court stated that the six-person jury provision in the statute was contrary to "the Law," "the constitution of New Jersey," and "the Constitution, practices and Laws of the Land." As Moore indicates, the court's reference to the "Law" seems to be a reference to common law and statute law, as distinct from the court's separate reference to New Jersey's written constitution.[43]

Moore goes on to claim that, as he sees it, the constitution of New Jersey established "a tri-partite hierarchy," in which common law and statutory law then existing were at the bottom, statutory law enacted subsequent to the New Jersey Constitution's ratification was in the middle, and the state constitution was at the top. The difficulty in *Holmes* was that the New Jersey Constitution did not stipulate a specific number of jurors, so "the judges could not rely on the common law to invalidate a trial by six jurors, but had to rely on the constitutional text or other (unwritten) norms of higher authority than ordinary legislation."[44]

There are two problems with Moore's analysis. First, early American lawyers and judges did not draw sharp or categorical distinctions between common law and constitutional law.[45] As I mentioned in my discussion of *Lindsay,* the common law provided the substantive and procedural bases for American federal and state constitutions.[46] Lawyers and judges of the time recognized the political importance of committing to writing their fundamental charters of government, but they did not believe that these charters were, by virtue of being written, necessarily exhaustive or transformative expressions of legal rights.[47] Second, where a fundamental common law right was concerned, such as trial by jury in *Holmes,* the common law could continue to function as, in Moore's words, an unwritten norm of higher authority than ordinary legislation. In their reception and integration of English common law into American jurisdictions, American lawyers retained Coke's view "that Magna Carta together with traditional common law made up a body of fundamental law" and that fundamental common law principles could "guard against the slightest inroads on traditional constitutional guarantees . . . [such as] the threat to trial by jury."[48]

In other words, not all common law rights were created equal. There is no doubt that a legislature could alter certain existing common law rights (e.g., in the law of contract). But it is another thing altogether to say that the legislature could statutorily alter (or abrogate) more cherished and fundamental common law rights, such as the right to a jury trial or the ownership of private property. Put differently, the recognition of the judiciary as a coequal branch of government in America—in reaction to the English tradition of parliamentary sovereignty—meant that the courts were charged with the constitutional responsibility to preserve fundamental rights (e.g., the right to a jury trial) and to ensure that the legislature acted in accordance with fundamental law (common law or constitutional text). Although the constitutional doctrine of sovereignty would occupy many British legal minds during this period, the Cokean conception of common law constitutionalism was fully embraced by their American counterparts in the latter half of the eighteenth century.

Scholars who assume that the common law was ranked below statutory or constitutional law in the minds of early American lawyers and judges miss the intrinsic differences among common law rights. Some common law rights, such as the right to trial by jury, were frequently mentioned explicitly in constitutional texts. But this was primarily an effort to reaffirm a political and legal commitment to this right. When called on to determine the qualities and contours of the right, as the New Jersey Supreme Court was in *Holmes,* it is unsurprising that the court would mention the common law and the state constitution as separate, independent, equally meaningful foundations for that right. The common law did not cease to exist as a basis for grounding the existence of the right to a jury trial or as a basis for determining the specific procedural requirements of that right, simply because the importance of that right was accentuated by the drafters of the New Jersey Constitution. As George Anastaplo puts it, fundamental common law rights "were always considered by early Americans to be constitutionally available to them, independent of what any document might say from time to time."[49] The twelve-person jury was a cherished, ancient common law right.[50] When confronted with legislation that conflicted with this right, the New Jersey court was not deterred by the state constitution's silence or the legislation's recent enactment. The *Holmes* court cited common law and constitutional law as parallel bases for judicial review precisely because both sources of law remained operative in locating and defining fundamental rights.

Today, Americans assume that "judicial review is synonymous with constitutional review."[51] But this misconceives the development of judicial review in early American legal history. Judicial review and constitutional review are not coextensive. As *Ham, Bowman, Lindsay,* and *Jones* demonstrate, common law review existed alongside constitutional review during the formative period of American constitutional thought.[52] Early American state courts instituted a doctrine of judicial review founded not solely on a constitutional text but also on the common law. As I will show in the next section, during this same period, the U.S. Supreme Court and Chief Justice John Marshall himself continued to refer to common law principles as a basis for evaluating legislative action independent of and parallel to the text of the Constitution, even after Marshall established constitutional review through his famous decision in *Marbury.*[53]

B. The Origins of Common Law Review in the Supreme Court
1. Calder v. Bull

Before and after *Marbury,* the U.S. Supreme Court invalidated legislative action on the basis of common law principles along with (or instead of) constitutional provisions. In this way, the Supreme Court endorsed the practice of common law review in much the same way, and during the same period, that the state courts had[The first example of common law review in the Supreme Court is *Calder v. Bull.*[54]]

Calder involved a will dispute in Connecticut. The Connecticut probate court that heard the case invalidated the will. In response to the court's decision, the state legislature abrogated the court's ruling and ordered a new trial.[At the second hearing, the probate court upheld the will.] The heirs, Caleb Bull and his wife, who would have recovered by intestacy had the will remained invalid, appealed the probate court's second ruling, claiming that the legislature's action violated the *ex post facto* provision in Article I, section 10, of the U.S. Constitution.[55] The Supreme Court refused to override the Connecticut legislature's act. In his seriatim opinion, Justice Samuel Chase expressed his belief that the prohibition against *ex post facto* laws obtained only in the criminal context. As a result, he ruled that the civil nature of *Calder* rendered the *ex post facto* clause inapplicable.[56]

Though *Calder's* holding is somewhat forgettable, *Calder* contains two justices' seminal statements of competing views concerning the characteristics of a written constitution and its implications for the scope of judicial review and the balance of governmental powers. [Simply put, one view (held by Justice Chase) maintains that the rights and principles found in the Constitution's text are not exhaustive of the rights and principles to which judges may appeal when reviewing the legality of governmental actions.] The second view (taken by Justice James Iredell) is that the rights and principles to which judges may refer when reviewing exercises of public power are delimited by the text of the Constitution. In his famous enunciation of the first view, Chase wrote:

> There are acts which the Federal, or State, Legislature cannot do, without exceeding their authority. There are certain vital principles in our free Republican governments, which will determine and over-rule an apparent and flagrant abuse of legislative power; as to authorize manifest injustice by positive law . . . The genius, the nature, and the spirit, of our State Governments, amount to a prohibition of such acts of legislation; and [*the general principles of law and reason forbid them* .] . To maintain that our Federal, or State, Legislature possesses such powers, if they would not be expressly restrained; would, in my opinion, be a political heresy, altogether inadmissible in our free republican governments . . . [But] if I ever exercise the jurisdiction I will not decide any law to be void, but in a very clear case.[57]

Iredell responded to Chase with the following:

> If, then, a government, composed of Legislative, Executive and Judicial departments, were established, by a Constitution, which imposed no limits on the legislative power, the consequence would inevitably be, that whatever the legislative power chose to enact, would be lawfully enacted, and the judicial power could never interpose to pronounce it void. It is true, that some speculative jurists have held, that a legislative

act against natural justice must, in itself, be void; but I cannot think that, under such a government, any Court of Justice would possess a power to declare it so . . [In order, therefore, to guard against so great an evil, it has been the policy of all the American states, which have, individually, framed their state constitutions since the revolution, and of the people of the United States, when they framed the Federal Constitution, to define with precision the objects of the legislative power, and to restrain its exercise within marked and settled boundaries.]If any act of Congress, or of the Legislature of a state, violates those constitutional provisions, it is unquestionably void; though, I admit, that the authority to declare it void is of a delicate and awful nature, the Court will never resort to that authority, but in a clear and urgent case. If, on the other hand, the Legislature of the Union, or the Legislature of any member of the Union, shall pass a law, within the general scope of their constitutional power, the Court cannot pronounce it to be void, merely because it is, in their judgment, contrary to the principles of natural justice.[58]

[Chase and Iredell agreed on many things. Least important, they agreed that the prohibition against *ex post facto* laws extended only to criminal cases.[59] They also agreed that the U.S. Constitution and its system of government were intended to avoid the perceived imbalances of the English style of government, especially those occasioned by parliamentary sovereignty.[60] Furthermore, they agreed that judges should assert the authority to review legislation only in very clear cases. Finally, they agreed that the Constitution furnished a body of legal principle that judges could invoke in reviewing legislative action. But, of course, they disagreed vehemently about whether the Constitution furnished the exclusive body of principle for this purpose; and accordingly, they disagreed about the instances in which judges could appropriately exercise this authority.

Obviously, I fall on Chase's side of the fence. My specific purpose here, though, is not to defend Chase's position against Iredell's concerns (my entire project is devoted to that effort).[Instead, I want to explore the precise meaning of Chase's opinion.]

Chase's reference to "the general principles of law and reason" is a reference to the common law.[61] Some writers claim that Chase's decision in *Calder* asserts a natural law basis for judicial review of legislation.[62] This claim is curious, if not utterly baseless, given the common law's prominent role in Chase's opinion[63] and the conspicuous absence of any reference to natural law, natural rights, or the law of nature anywhere in Chase's opinion (or in the opinion of any other justice who decided *Calder*). Moreover, as Leonard Levy explains, unenumerated positive rights "deriving from the social compact that creates government" were distinguished from natural rights in the minds of American lawyers and jurists of this period.[64] Taking this distinction into account helps to illuminate Chase's well-known but not well-understood statement in *Calder* that legislative acts "contrary to the great first principles of the social compact, cannot be considered a rightful exercise of legislative authority."[65] These legislative acts were void, according to Chase, because they conflicted with the positive rights protected at common law (as distinct from natural rights).[66] Positive rights were derived by reference to legal sources (common law, constitutional, or statutory), while natural rights were claimed by virtue of human dignity. Chase's reference in *Calder* to legislative acts that conflicted with the social compact is best understood not as an allusion to natural rights or natural law but, instead, as a statement about judicial authority to review legislation that contradicted positive rights grounded in acknowledged sources of law.

One scholar troubled by the tendency to read natural law into Chase's *Calder* opinion is Matthew Franck. In responding to the natural law reading of Chase's opinion, Franck argues that Chase was not invoking any judicial authority to refer to nonconstitutional fundamental law when reviewing legislative enactments. Instead, Franck says, Chase's well-known statements "turn out to be little more than an aside in political theory [of limited government derived from the social contract] with, practically speaking, no juridical significance."[67]

There are two problems with Franck's argument. First, as Franck himself notes, Chase explicitly refers in *Calder* to "'certain vital principles' [that] will 'overrule' a legislature when it 'authorize[s] manifest injustice by positive law.'"[68] As Franck also concedes, the examples Chase uses to exemplify such injustices "were forbidden by either the statute law or common law of England, precisely the sources from which Connecticut's charter derives its limits on legislative power."[69] Franck then refers to one of the examples of injustice selected by Chase—"the principle that no man should be judge in his own case"—and concludes that this places Chase "squarely in the tradition of Blackstone . . . which is probably where Chase derived the example."[70] Of course, as I have tried to show, Chase's opinion (and the example Franck cites) place Chase squarely in the tradition of Coke and *Bonham,* which is more likely to be the source from which Chase derived the example. Due to the overwhelming inclination to assume that the issue in *Calder* is whether Chase's opinion is or is not derived from natural law reasoning and principles, Franck is a victim of asking the wrong question. He is right about the widespread misreading of Chase's opinion as based on natural law, but rather than looking to an alternative source of fundamental law, he attempts to construct a reading of Chase's opinion that resembles a political tract more than a judicial opinion. This results in the yeoman's effort by Franck to avoid or reconstruct the explicit language of Chase's opinion and leads directly to the second problem with Franck's conclusion.

To his credit, Franck appreciates that his attempt to debunk "the orthodox *Calder* myth" necessitates an explanation of Iredell's pointed (apparent) retort to Chase in his opinion. Franck cites certain historical speculations (i.e., perhaps Iredell did not hear Chase's opinion, or perhaps Iredell's apparent response to Chase was instead directed toward arguments of counsel) as potential support for doubting that Iredell's opinion was intended as a response to Chase.[71] In addition, Franck says that Iredell "was not a legal positivist who rejected the existence of natural law."[72] Rather, Franck says, Iredell "does not deny either the existence or the moral force of natural law as a standard for the positive."[73] But of course, this just begs the question. The issue in *Calder* is not whether natural law existed as a body of legal principle familiar to lawyers and judges trained in the eighteenth century. The question is whether this familiar body of extraconstitutional fundamental law (or some other) could be employed by judges to review legislative acts. For good reason, *Calder* is widely understood as a disagreement between Chase and Iredell about the nature of a written constitution and the basis of judicial authority. Franck's attempt to challenge this widespread understanding leads him to reinterpret Chase's opinion, downplay the apparent theoretical dispute between Chase and Iredell, and entirely recast the meaning and import of the decision.

Finally, Franck says that the "speculative jurists" to whom Iredell refers in his opinion were not Chase and those who might agree with him about extraconstitutional judicial review but, rather, the theorists studied by lawyers of the day (Blackstone, Pufendorf, Vattel). He suggests that Iredell actually should be read as subscribing to the views of the speculative jurists he mentions.[74] Leaving aside the incongruity of this reading with the language and structure of Iredell's opinion, two aspects of Franck's list of jurists are noteworthy. First, Franck's list consists of three natural lawyers. By omitting Coke from this list, Franck fails to acknowledge a powerful influence on Anglo-American legal education and thought at this time.[75] Second, as I will explain in the next section, Franck's attempted reading of

Iredell in *Calder* does not cohere with Iredell's other judicial opinions (e.g., *Chisholm*) or with Iredell's broader intellectual focus on recognized, definitive legal sources (e.g., a written constitution).

Other scholars suggest that any attempt to seek a coherent distinction between common law and natural law in early American legal thought is hopeless, because early American lawyers were hopelessly muddled about the matter.[76] But I am more sanguine. For my purposes, the issue is not whether some early American lawyers and judges conflated common law and natural law. I only intend to argue that some early American lawyers and judges did not. Although there was confusion about the doctrines in America as there had been in England, common law and natural law were recognized by certain early American lawyers to be distinct bodies of principle. Other early Supreme Court opinions and the arguments of counsel presented to the Court in these cases offer support for this claim.

2. Chisholm v. Georgia

The first opinion to support the claim that common law and natural law were recognized as distinct by certain early American lawyers is Justice Iredell's opinion in *Chisholm v. Georgia*.[77] The question raised in *Chisholm* was whether a private party resident of one state could bring suit against a sister state in federal court for violation of state law.[78] The *Chisholm* majority held that a state could be sued in a federal forum, in an appropriate case, by a resident of another state. The principal bases for the majority decision were: the plain language of Article III of the U.S. Constitution,[79] the practical necessity of enforcing the Constitution's provisions against the states,[80] and the states' implicit consent to suit by virtue of each state's ratification of the Constitution.[81] The Supreme Court's decision in *Chisholm* resulted in the enactment of the Eleventh Amendment, which precludes federal jurisdiction over claims by private parties against individual states.

Iredell dissented in *Chisholm*. Perhaps realizing the futility of contesting the language of Article III prior to the enactment of the Eleventh Amendment, Iredell instead focused on the Judiciary Act of 1789 in maintaining that a state was immune from private suit in federal court. In his analysis of the statutory language, Iredell took the phrase "the principles and usages of law" in the Judiciary Act to mean "the common law."[82] Iredell's reading of the Judiciary Act is important for three reasons.

First, Iredell's understanding of the general statutory language as a reference to the common law shows that early American lawyers differentiated common law from natural law and that they viewed the common law as the body of doctrine relevant to judicial reasoning. When considering the possibility of disparities in the law of different states and the value of continuity in the law of the United States, Iredell grasped the need to recognize and establish a coherent body of legal principle applicable to all states in the union. He found that body of principle in the common law:

> The *only* principles of law, then, that can be regarded are those common to all the States. I know of none such, which can affect this case, but those that are derived from what is properly termed "the common law," a law which I presume is the ground-work of the laws in every State in the Union, and which I consider, so far as it is applicable to the peculiar circumstances of the country, and where no special act of Legislation controuls it, to be in force in each State, as it existed in England.[83]

Later in his opinion, Iredell reaffirmed his exclusive reliance on the common law as the determinative legal source on which he based his opinion:

> [W]e have no other rule to govern us but the principles of the pre-existent laws, which must remain in force till superceded by others, then it is incumbent upon us to enquire, whether previous to the adoption of the Constitution (which period, or the period of passing the law, in respect to the object of this enquiry, is perfectly equal) an action of the nature like this before the Court could have been maintained against one of the States in the Union upon the principles of the common law, which I have shewn to be *alone* applicable.[84]

Iredell continued to refer to the common law throughout the remainder of his opinion,[85] and it was only after establishing the common law as the exclusive body of principle relevant to the decision in *Chisholm* that Iredell mentioned natural law in passing.[86] Iredell's *Chisholm* opinion represents a compelling example of an early American jurist distinguishing the common law from natural law and confirming the prominence of the former in judicial decision making.[87]

Second, the reference to "the principles and usages of law" in the Judiciary Act discussed by Iredell in *Chisholm* is markedly similar to the phrase "the principles of law and reason" used by Justice Chase in *Calder*. Here, again, we find the influence of the identification of common law principles with the principles of (right) reason.[88] Despite their theoretical disagreement in *Calder*, Chase and Iredell would both have understood such a general phrase as "the principles of law" to refer to the common law (as Iredell did in *Chisholm*).[89] Chase and Iredell would both have understood Chase's phrase "the principles of law and reason" to refer to the reason and principles of the common law.

Third, Iredell's *Chisholm* opinion takes on added significance given Iredell's consistent recognition of the importance of authoritative legal sources. As a result of his opinion in *Calder*, his argument in *Bayard*, and other written remarks, many scholars highlight Iredell's fondness for written statements of law, particularly the written U.S. Constitution.[90] This is undoubtedly an accurate assessment of Iredell's intellectual perspective as a lawyer and a judge. But *Chisholm* suggests that Iredell also viewed the common law as a uniquely important legal source, even in cases of constitutional significance. The salient point seems to be that Iredell focused on definitive legal articulations of rights and constraints on legislative power. These expressions of law need not be limited, however, to a written constitution or (for Federalists, such as Iredell) by a bill of rights.[91] Iredell believed in the importance of law as an external limitation on legislative power intrinsic to genuine constitutionalism, but the rule of law was not necessarily, ultimately, or exclusively confined to the text of the Constitution itself; the rule of law was preserved by judges applying accepted legal principles and processes to restrain the government and to ensure the liberties of the people.[92] For Iredell and certain other early American jurists, the common law provided these authoritative legal principles and processes, while natural law did not.

3. McIlvaine v. Coxe's Lessee

Another, contemporaneous case that exemplifies early American reliance on common law rather than natural law as the authoritative source of judicial determination is *McIlvaine v. Coxe's Lessee*.[93] *McIlvaine* involved an inheritance claim founded on the property rights of an individual born in New Jersey who supported Britain during the Revolution. The most interesting aspect of the case, for my argument, is that counsel for both the plaintiff and the defendant relied on principles of common law rather than natural law as support for their arguments. For example, plaintiff's counsel noted that "natural allegiance, i.e. the allegiance due from birth, is the only kind which by the rule of the common law, cannot be shaken off."[94] Defense counsel's argument was even more explicit in rejecting natural law in favor of the common law as uniquely relevant to legal argument and judicial decision: "[W]hatever might be the principles of natural law . . . by the principles of common law, Daniel Coxe had a right to inherit lands in New-Jersey."[95] [Counsel raised natural law only to discard it in favor of the common law.] Although the Supreme Court's opinion turned on its interpretation of New Jersey's state sovereignty and relevant legislation, it is noteworthy that the Court expressly mentioned "the principles of the common law," while making no reference to natural law anywhere in its opinion.[96] As in *Chisholm*, the Court and counsel in *McIlvaine* based their reasoning only on common law principles (or statutory law).

Common law ideas of sovereignty and sovereign immunity in colonial and post-Revolutionary America were influenced by the growing mistrust of English ideas of absolute legislative supremacy. It comes as no surprise, then, that judges and lawyers working in this legal and political atmosphere should look to the common law as the legal basis for controlling threatened abuses of legislative power. American lawyers linked common law with right reason, distinguished common law from natural law, and relied on the common law (rather than natural law) in formulating and amplifying legal doctrines that touched on the most fundamental aspects of the nascent federal system of government and its balanced separation of powers, which eschewed English parliamentary sovereignty and embraced a judiciary with accepted powers of judicial review.

4. Fletcher v. Peck

Calder was decided five years before *Marbury*. But *Marbury*'s establishment of constitutional review in America did not end the Supreme Court's reliance on the common law as an alternative basis for judicial review[In *Fletcher v. Peck*,[97] decided seven years after *Marbury*, Chief Justice Marshall continued to invoke common law principles as a basis for judicial review apart from review by exclusive recourse to constitutional provisions]

Fletcher involved the conveyance of land in Georgia from John Peck to Robert Fletcher by deed. Unfortunately, however, some of the Georgia state legislators who originally voted in favor of the grant by which Peck's predecessor, James Gunn, acquired title to the property were bribed.[98] The Georgia legislature subsequently annulled the earlier, tainted act and rescinded the land grant. The problem presented in *Fletcher* centered on the ability of the Georgia legislature to annul the original land grant to Gunn, thereby stripping Peck of his ownership interest and Fletcher of his purchase.[99]

The Supreme Court refused to acknowledge the subsequent act of the Georgia legislature, relying on two grounds for its decision. First, Marshall referenced the common law rule that *bona fide,* innocent purchasers of land for valuable consideration acquire good legal title.[100] Second, Marshall indicated that the act of the Georgia legislature purporting to vitiate the original land grant was tantamount to a law impairing the obligation of contracts in violation of Article I, section 10, of the U.S. Constitution.[101] Combining these two rationales for the Court's ruling, Marshall wrote:

> It is, then, the unanimous opinion of the court, that, in this case, the estate having passed into the hands of a purchaser for a valuable consideration, without notice, the State of Georgia was restrained, either by general principles which are common to our free institutions, *or* by the particular provisions of the constitution of the United States, from passing a law whereby the estate of the plaintiff in the premises so purchased could be constitutionally and legally impaired and rendered null and void.[102]

In this passage, Marshall indicates two parallel bases for the Court's invalidation of the Georgia legislature's action. According to Marshall, the act of the Georgia legislature was subject to invalidation either for violating general principles or for violating the Constitution itself. Commentators have recognized Marshall's reliance on these dual grounds of constitutional and extraconstitutional review of legislative action in *Fletcher.*[103] These commentators have also noted that the general principles referenced by Marshall in *Fletcher* are the same principles discussed by Chase in *Calder.*[104]

As with Chase in *Calder,* Marshall's reference to general principles in *Fletcher* is a reference to the principles of the common law. Accordingly, *Calder* and *Fletcher* stand for the proposition that the principles of the common law provide a legal basis for judicial review of legislative action independent of (and along with) a written constitution. Moreover, as in the proper reading of *Bonham,*[105] the power of common law review cannot be divorced from its attendant implications for the relationship among the branches of plural government. Marshall seemed to recognize this in *Fletcher:*

> It is the peculiar province of the legislature to prescribe general rules for the government of society; the application of those rules to individuals in society would seem to be the duty of other departments. How far the power of giving law may involve every other power, in cases where the constitution is silent, never has been, and perhaps never can be, definitely stated.[106]

Marshall wisely and cautiously left the door open in *Fletcher*. He might well have believed that common law principles had to be maintained as an independently viable basis for judicial review, because he did not yet know what the political and legal fate of constitutional review would be.[107] Of course, constitutional review would soon be accepted as a part of the constitutional structure of American government.[108] And as constitutional review became widely accepted, common law review was gradually forgotten,[109] until we have today reached a point where American lawyers and judges believe that the only available basis for judicial review is by reference to the Constitution.[110] But as *Calder* and *Fletcher* demonstrate, this does not seem to be what Marshall or Chase foresaw.

Additional support for this argument and for the focus on the precise language of certain key passages in these judicial opinions may be also be found in *Marbury* itself. Marshall's chosen phrasing—"the constitution controls any legislative act repugnant to it . . . an act of the legislature, repugnant to the constitution, is void"[111]—seems to echo Coke's language in *Bonham*.[112] In *Marbury*, Marshall concentrated his attention on the written Constitution; but his later decision in *Fletcher* makes it clear that he did not believe, even when he wrote *Marbury*, that the written Constitution was the exclusive legal basis on which courts could invalidate abuses of legislative power. In his opinions in *Marbury* and *Fletcher*, in his private writings,[113] and in his less famous judicial opinions,[114] Marshall indicated that the common law was anterior to and incorporated in the substantive guarantees of the Constitution and that the common law continued to exist as an independent body of fundamental law binding on the government and the people after the Constitution's ratification. Throughout the founding period of the United States, American judges and lawyers viewed the common law as a legal constraint on governmental power, echoing and incorporating the common law's long-standing link, in English constitutional thought, to the rule of law and to common law constitutionalism—a link that had largely been forgotten in the England of that day, with its constitutional commitment to parliamentary sovereignty.[115]

The reliance by the Supreme Court and counsel on the common law as the predominant method and source for legal argument and decision making continued well after *Fletcher*.[116] Other cases from the first quarter of the nineteenth century indicate the postcolonial American preference for common law (rather than natural law) as a source of legal authority.[117] The cases I cite and discuss here are (and can only be) suggestive of American legal attitudes and practices at this time. To be sure, other cases could be found in which natural law seemed to play the principal role, and still more cases could be found in which courts or counsel might seem to refer to common law and natural law carelessly, if not synonymously. But my effort here is not to establish that all American lawyers during this period maintained a precise and pristine distinction between common law and natural law. I only aim to show that some lawyers and judges did appreciate this distinction and that some of these lawyers and judges recognized the common law as forming the legal and theoretical basis for an alternate practice of judicial review that did not necessarily derive from the text of the Constitution.

The development of common law review in the Supreme Court mirrored the state court experience. Common law review was first articulated, to some extent, in isolation. Here, *Calder* can be equated with *Ham* and *Bowman*. But quickly, as evidenced by the Virginia Supreme Court in *Jones* and Marshall's opinion in *Fletcher* (and less explicitly by the South Carolina court in *Lindsay* and Iredell's opinion in *Chisholm*), American judges realized that common law review and constitutional review could stand alongside one another, providing complementary bases for judicial evaluation of legislative and executive action.

how common law interact w/ constitution.

C. Common Law and Natural Law, Again

Although many of the cases cited and discussed in this chapter have received far less scholarly attention than they deserve, most have received some. Now that I have explained my reading of these cases and their conceptual connections, I should respond to the work of some scholars who also have studied these cases. I cannot here fully address all of the points raised by these writers, but some remarks seem especially pertinent. For the most part, I am concerned here to correct a common misreading of these cases as being grounded on natural law principles rather than on principles of common law. I do not argue that common law and natural law were (or are) entirely irreconcilable. On the contrary, certain common law principles were understood as reflective of natural law precepts. My case analysis is intended to demonstrate, however, that the more general relationships between common law and natural law did not necessarily filter down to their reception by courts as authoritative sources of legal doctrine. In deciding cases, certain American judges distinguished common law and natural law as sources of law, and this is where the distinction matters for my purposes—as a theoretical and doctrinal foundation for the exercise of judicial review.[118]

[Before turning to some specific remarks about the cases themselves, I should respond to a preliminary point]John Phillip Reid is quite dismissive of the influence of natural law on the recognition of specific rights during the colonial and post-Revolutionary period. In fact, he states that "natural law was never the dominant source of law, and perhaps not even a significant one."[119] It is fair and accurate to say, as Reid and McDonald do, that natural law was disfavored by some lawyers and politicians of the time, because it was taken to be too amorphous and evanescent a foundation on which to ground law or rights.[120] But it is also true, as Reid sometimes concedes, that natural law did serve as authority for legal claims and rights in judicial decisions, legislative acts, and legal pronouncements.[121]

It seems to me that the frequent references to natural law in judicial opinions and elsewhere cannot be dismissed entirely as mere rhetorical flourishes,[122] given the doctrine of precedent and the character of legal sources in the common law tradition. [It seems unavailing and unnecessary to deny that some early American lawyers treated natural law as a source of principles available to judges in the recognition of legal rights and the assessment of legislative enactments.] This is the reason that I focus so carefully on the cases I have chosen and the language I have cited. The crucial point, I think, is to see that certain early American lawyers and judges carefully distinguished natural law from common law and referred to the latter as the basis for legal argument and judicial decision. The cases I discuss are indicative of an important and distinct perspective in American legal thought, a perspective according to which common law appeared as singularly authoritative. [This is entirely sensible, considering that in the period on which I focus, American judges were beginning to assert an institutional authority and autonomy grounded in English legal tradition but nevertheless unfamiliar to English constitutional structure and orthodoxy (at least as it was then and is now commonly understood).[123]]

To some important American lawyers and judges reared in the English legal tradition, the common law did not suffer from the specific conceptual and legal weaknesses that seemed to undermine natural law. While natural law was viewed by some common lawyers as too tenuous a legal basis for grounding concrete rights and governmental limitations, the common law represented a body of historically and legally established concepts and doctrines (e.g., due process, jury trials, liberty and property rights) that defined

the institutional position of the judiciary and its obligation to preserve individual rights.] Whatever its moral force might be, natural law was not a
recognized legal source (as common law was).[124] Reconsidering the cases
discussed in this chapter will, I hope, help to reorient the study of early
American judicial review and clarify the distinctive evolution of public law
in the United States.

Two scholars who have considered some of the same cases I discuss but
who read them differently are Sylvia Snowiss and Suzanna Sherry.[My disagreements with Snowiss about these cases are less stark and less comprehensive than my disagreements with Sherry.]In her discussion of *Lindsay*,
Snowiss states that the case represents an amalgam of natural law and positive law.[125] Snowiss then goes on to stress that judges on both sides of the
legal outcome based their reasoning on the common law, and she notes
Judge Grimke's acknowledgment that the state constitution reaffirmed preexisting legal rights and principles rather than creating new ones.[126] She
concludes by observing that the *Lindsay* court evaluated the subject legislation in light of both the South Carolina Constitution and common law
principles, suggesting that these served as independent bases of review for
the court.[127] [Given the prominence of the common law in her analysis of
Lindsay, Snowiss's initial reference to natural and positive law might just be
a seemingly minor linguistic slip, but as I argue in this chapter, this sort of
imprecision may allow us to miss subtleties in the thought and language of
certain eighteenth- and nineteenth-century American judges concerning
the sources of judicial authority and the development of American constitutionalism.]

I agree with some of what Snowiss says about *Fletcher* as well. She recognizes, for example, that *Fletcher* provides "alternate grounds" for judicial
renunciation of legislation.[128] Unfortunately, though, she believes Marshall
treated natural law as the extraconstitutional foundation for the decision.[129] As I have already explained, the language and reasoning of Marshall's opinion do not support a natural law reading of *Fletcher*.[130] In contrast to Marshall's own opinion, however, Justice Johnson's concurrence in
Fletcher does rest on natural law grounds, mainly due to his pointed effort
to distinguish his reasoning from Marshall's, through his reference to "a
principle which . . . will impose laws even on the deity."[131] In fact, Johnson's decision to write a separate opinion based on natural law actually reinforces the common law reading of Marshall's opinion. Snowiss accepts
this to a degree. She considers Johnson's opinion "strikingly different"
from Marshall's.[132] But she and I see the difference differently. For Snowiss,

the difference turns on Johnson's vision of government limited by natural law and natural rights as compared with Marshall's reliance on the exposition of constitutional text to invalidate legislation. To me, the language of *Fletcher* indicates that Marshall understood the legal limitations on legislative power as inhering in more than the Constitution's text alone. In contrast with Johnson's reliance on natural law as the extraconstitutional restraint on government power, Marshall relied, at least in part, on the common law in support of the same end.

[The connection of the state court cases to the Supreme Court cases in the development of common law review raises another issue]. I have already mentioned that some scholars interpret Justice Chase as invoking natural law, rather than common law, as the basis for extraconstitutional review in *Calder*. Sherry, for example, sees *Fletcher* and the state court cases I have discussed as based on natural law, rather than common law.[133] According to Sherry, in "*Fletcher v. Peck* . . . the written constitution vied with unwritten principles of natural law for pride of place among the sources of fundamental law."[134] Similarly, where the state court cases are concerned, Sherry claims: ["[T]he judicial enforceability of natural law in South Carolina is best illustrated by two early cases. [In] *Ham v. M'Claws* . . . [and] three years later, in *Bowman v. Middleton* . . . [where] the court went further and actually invalidated a statute on the basis of unwritten law."[135] Sherry makes these assertions despite quoting the *Ham* court's references to "common right" and "common reason"[136] and the *Bowman* court's references to "common right" and "Magna Charta"[137] and despite the fact that not a single reference to natural law or the law of nature appears anywhere in *Fletcher*, *Ham*, or *Bowman*.

It is difficult to know what to make of Sherry's apparently indiscriminate references to natural law, rather than common law, as the extraconstitutional fundamental law invoked by the courts in *Fletcher*, *Ham*, and *Bowman*. Sherry may provide the answer, though [Despite appearances, she is ostensibly cognizant of subtle differences among the different sources she categorizes as unwritten law.] Sherry writes:

> [T]he written constitution [w]as only one of several sources of fundamental law. Other sources, all unwritten, included the laws of God, the common law . . . the law of nature, and natural law . . . "The law of nature" and "natural law" were related but distinguishable in the period I am discussing: the former was grounded in observation and human sentiment, while the latter was founded upon abstract reason. For purposes

importance of unwritten law [margin annotation]

of this article, the differences among the various unwritten sources of higher law are irrelevant. Therefore, I will use "unwritten law," "natural law," and "law of nature" interchangeably.[138]

I am troubled by several aspects of this statement, all of which I will not pursue at length here. Especially worrying for my present purposes is Sherry's indifferent gloss over the several sources of unwritten law.[139] [Sherry says that the differences among the laws of God, the common law, and natural law are irrelevant for the purposes of her article.] But one of the purposes of her article is to analyze the historical and theoretical bases for extraconstitutional review of legislative action in late eighteenth-century and early nineteenth-century American law. The theoretically disparate foundations of common law and natural law (to say nothing of divine law) cannot be more relevant to this project. If the basis of extraconstitutional judicial review were natural law, this might raise genuine concerns about the legal source of the authority at issue and about the desultory and unconstrained nature of the enterprise.[140] If the basis of extraconstitutional judicial review is the common law, however, then judges remain bounded by the authoritative methods, concepts, and sources established and recognized within the Anglo-American legal tradition. These are, it seems to me, two drastically different things. Particularly for Sherry's (and my) purposes, the distinction between natural law and common law cannot be discounted.

Others have noted some of these deficiencies in Sherry's analysis.[141] Christopher Eisgruber, for one, identifies the problems with Sherry's treatment of *Fletcher* and highlights the common law (as opposed to natural law) basis of Marshall's opinion.[142] But the aspect of Sherry's work that is most problematic from my perspective is her citation of *Bonham* as support for her argument.[143] Even worse than simply citing *Bonham*, Sherry goes on to claim, "[T]he Cokean and continental notion of fundamental principles and the more Lockean idea of fundamental rights are two sides of the same coin: both were grounded on unwritten natural law."[144] Leaving aside the doctrinal and historical differences between Cokean and continental notions of fundamental principles, [Coke's notion of fundamental principles and Locke's idea of fundamental rights are not both grounded on natural law,[145] and it is misleading to suggest that they are two sides of the same coin.] They are very different coins. They may, however, sometimes be found together in the same pocket.

The problems with Sherry's position have both a theoretical and a practical dimension. At the theoretical level, to a legal positivist and even to some natural lawyers, fundamental rights cannot be confidently claimed as legal rights until they are articulated at the level of common law (or by some other authoritative means in a common law system).[146] Sherry does not adequately differentiate the status of natural law and common law as sources of authoritative legal principle and doctrine that could be and were relied on by judges in some of the cases she discusses. At the practical level, natural law conceptions of fundamental rights generally maintain that these rights inhere immutably in human beings, irrespective of their recognition within a particular legal order; they do not depend for their existence on positive law, and they cannot be abrogated or altered by legislative or judicial action. Common law rights, even for Coke, were generally defeasible by legislative action.[147] By equating Cokean fundamental legal principles with Lockean fundamental rights and then claiming that both are derived from natural law, Sherry jumps from general theoretical commitments to specific systemic analysis while ignoring the practical and theoretical differences between natural law and common law conceptions of fundamental rights.

In eliding natural law and common law and in relying on *Bonham* as putative support for a natural law conception of fundamental legal principles, Sherry does more than misread some case law. She threatens to undermine the proper doctrinal basis of extraconstitutional judicial review in the United States. In her failure to differentiate common law from natural law, Sherry has committed the same error as Berger,[148] and it has led them both to misconceive the authentic significance of the common law as legal authority for judicial evaluation of legislative action.[149]

D. The Source-Based Judicial Obligation to Develop the Law

In the previous chapter and in this one, I set out to establish the existence of Anglo-American legal sources that support the common law judicial authority to refuse to enforce unjust laws, even where those laws do not necessarily violate a written constitution. That is the proposition for which the cases I have discussed in these chapters stand. And these decisions—*Bonham, Omychund, Ham, Bowman, Lindsay, Jones, Calder, Chisholm, McIlvaine,* and *Fletcher*—should be appreciated for what they are: a discrete, coherent, and cohesive line of reported case law articulating a common law principle and a body of legal thought that reflect the distinctive authority and responsibility of common law judges to develop the law by eliminating instances of injustice from the law, a principle and a conception that have endured throughout Anglo-American common law history. This is the legal basis, derived from legal sources, for judges to refuse to enforce unjust laws.

As it turns out, this is what Coke had in mind all along:

> In this stand for the right to give the Common Law priority in general principles . . . Parliament must not go beyond the general principles of the Common Law or beyond its general reasonableness. This would place statute law in a subordinate place to the Common Law if pressed to its logical conclusion, and give at least to the Common Law courts a superior position as the interpreter of statute law. It would in many cases result in the will of the framers of statutes being set aside or at least modified by the judges of the Common Law courts. It would, in short, create a practice of judicial criticism or judicial review of statutes by the Common Law judges . . . [I]n Bonham's case he [Coke] contended there was a *legal,* not an extra-legal, power in the courts to do this very thing.[150]

Coke's emphasis in *Bonham* on a legal (as opposed to an extralegal) power of the courts to refuse to enforce unjust laws undercuts the moral-formal dilemma and its overly narrow presuppositions about judicial obligation and authority in common law systems. The judge's obligation to develop the law is not, as the moral-formal dilemma would have us believe, limited to a choice between legal and moral obligations. Common law judges have a legal obligation, grounded in case law, to refuse to enforce unjust laws. This is not to suggest that this is not also a moral obligation.[151] I am simply arguing that the judge's legal obligations extend into the sphere that the moral-formal dilemma designates as "moral" (and thereby extralegal). My point is that a judge's legal obligations in these cases are triggered by and track her moral reactions and obligations.[152]

The moral-formal dilemma erects a false dichotomy between the judge's moral and legal obligations. In so doing, the moral-formal dilemma assumes or accepts that a judge's moral obligation may be to corrupt the integrity of the judicial process:

> [M]orality requires or prohibits some solutions, in which case the law, interpreted conventionally, might get it wrong. In that case, the judge's *legal* duty . . . is to uphold the conventional understanding of the law whether or not the legal system is generally just. The loyal and dutiful judge in a wicked legal system is fully complicit in its wickedness and

deserves to be criticized, perhaps harshly. That judge's *moral* duty may be to resign or to engage in disobedience from the bench, throwing monkey wrenches into the works at every opportunity.[153]

To my mind, this is a disturbing, distorted view of a judge's genuine legal obligations, evidencing the powerful hold maintained by the moral-formal dilemma on the conventional Anglo-American understanding of the alleged rift between a judge's moral and legal duties. This stunted view of judicial responsibility conflicts directly with the common law vision, which requires judges to exercise their legal powers in accordance with their legal obligations. This was the vision of judicial authority that was carried across the Atlantic, where it finally found fertile soil. A brief return to the period of its planting will help me make this point.

St. George Tucker, a preeminent early American judge and jurist, wrote the following commentary regarding the *Case of Josiah Philips,* sometimes considered one of the earliest American cases in which the doctrine of judicial review was discussed:

> In May, 1778, an act passed in Virginia, to attaint one Josiah Philips unless he should render himself to justice within a limited time; he was taken after the time had expired and was brought before the general court to receive sentence of execution pursuant to the directions of the act. But the court refused to pass the sentence and he was put upon trial according to the ordinary course of law. This is a decisive proof of the importance of the separation of the powers of government and of the independence of the judiciary; a dependent judiciary might have executed the law, whilst they execrated the principles upon which it was founded.[154]

Very early, as Judge Tucker's remarks show, American lawyers understood the importance of an independent judiciary and the relevance that the judicial authority to refuse to enforce an unjust act of the legislature or the executive held for the separation of governmental powers.[155] Moreover, as Tucker recognized, an independent judiciary must exercise independent judgment, because there are certain circumstances in which a judge ought not simultaneously to execute and to execrate a law. If a legislative act is sufficiently deplorable, the judge may legitimately, within the bounds of his legal authority, refuse to enforce it. That is the motivating concern of common law review as revealed through careful consideration of the cases in which this principle was incorporated into Anglo-American law and legal tradition. Some early American judges realized the importance of an independent but legally restrained judiciary and its central place in maintaining the rule of law in accordance with the Anglo-American tradition of common law constitutionalism.

Early American judges were not the only important legal thinkers of the time who stressed the importance of an independent judiciary whose obligation to protect legal rights against abuses of public power, sometimes by refusing to enforce unjust laws, was neither created nor circumscribed by a written constitution. Certain framers of the Constitution indicated that judicial influence and authority should not be limited by the document they drafted. For example, in a less-frequently quoted passage from *Federalist* No. 78, Hamilton wrote:

> [I]t is not with a view to infractions of the constitution only, that the independence of the judges may be an essential safe-guard against the effects of occasional ill humours in the society. These sometimes extend no farther than to the injury of private rights of particular classes of citizens, by unjust and partial laws. Here also the firmness of the judicial magistracy is of vast importance in mitigating the severity and confining the operation of such laws. It not only serves to moderate the immediate mischiefs of those which may have been passed, but it operates as a check upon the legislative body in passing them.[156]

I have here attempted to demonstrate the existence of a source-based legal obligation for judges to develop the law by repudiating unjust legislative or executive action. So far, I have tried to show that judges may refuse to enforce unjust laws. But the judicial obligation in these cases is stronger. Common law review does not just permit judges to develop the law in this fashion; it requires them to do so. The parallel here between common law review and constitutional review is again useful: "the rule [is] that a law repugnant to the Constitution is void and that it is not only the right but the duty of a court so to declare when the violation unequivocally appears."[157] Just as constitutional review does not just permit but requires judges to invalidate statutes that violate the Constitution, common law review does not just authorize but obligates judges to refuse to enforce certain statutes that contravene common law principles. This robust conception of judicial obligation is entirely consistent with the tradition—based in English common law thought—that animated Coke's beliefs and informed his decision in *Bonham*.[158]

Bonham is widely accepted as the Anglo-American legal basis for the doctrine of constitutional review. But only by extension was *Bonham* the theoretical justification for constitutional review. After all, Coke was not espousing a doctrine of constitutional review in *Bonham*. He could not. There was no written constitution to which he could appeal. So while *Bonham* is the indirect progenitor of constitutional review, it is the direct lineal authority for common law review: *importance of   Bonham*

> It was Coke's version of the supremacy of the common law principles as exemplification of rules of reason and of justice, that served as . . . precedent when American justices were confronted with the demand that limits must be placed on legislative powers in order to safeguard individual rights and privileges.[159]

Traced back through its legal ancestry, common law review seeks a fully formed conception of a common law judge's legal obligations and of the place of an independent judiciary in a system of plural government. This is the authentic common law tradition we have inherited from Coke, Mansfield, Chase, and Marshall. We should take care not to forget the long history, in the common law tradition, of an independent judiciary applying common law principles to ensure that the government remains within and accountable to the law. [Constitutionalism does not require a Constitution.]

7. The Conceptual Argument for the Judicial Obligation to Develop the Law

In the previous two chapters, I discussed the legal sources that ground a legal obligation for common law judges to develop the law by refusing to enforce unjust laws. In addition to the source-based argument, a conceptual argument based on the nature of the common law judicial function supports judges developing the law in this manner. I call this argument "conceptual" because it is based on the concept of the common law judicial function.[1]

The term *common law judicial function* refers to a quadripartite concept, with each of the four words in the term designating a particular concept. For this chapter, each part of the concept is important. It is important to my argument that we are discussing judges, the people who are in the business of making judgments. It is important that we are discussing those judges who make judgments about or according to law, as opposed to those who reach ecclesiastic or aesthetic judgments. The particular judicial function that is important here is the deciding of cases through the articulation of published, justificatory written opinions. It is important to my argument that we are discussing judges whose decisions are understood as being justified according to law and legal reasoning. And it is important that we are discussing this judicial function in the context of the common law tradition. Of the components of this compound concept, the last is the most important. The common law tradition places particular importance on judicial decisions and decision making, and according to this tradition, common law judges are central to the development of the law.

To sum up the conceptual argument in one sentence, the common law is designed to develop over time in the direction of justice; judges are the primary institutional actors designated by the common law system to guarantee that this development takes place; and when they fail to meet that obligation, serious negative consequences ensue. In this chapter, I divide the argument into four sections, broken down in accordance with its progression. First, I offer an argument to explain how the common law's developmental design can be seen. Second, I explore the relationship between common law judges and justice. Third, I examine some conflicting understandings of the judicial function and defend the one that best incorporates the full measure of common law judicial authority and responsibility in ensuring the common law's doctrinal development. Finally, I examine some of the damage done when common law judges fail to ensure the common law's development. In an effort to reduce the abstraction of the argument, I will refer to a famous improvement in American law regarding racial segregation as a leitmotif of the issues I discuss. Before turning to the four prongs of the conceptual argument, though, I begin, in the next section, with a short explanation of the complexion of the obligation for which I will argue.

A. Role Obligations

When one agrees to assume the role of a judge, one assumes certain responsibilities attendant to that role. "Since no one *has* to be a judge," writes Kent Greenawalt, "those who assume official positions implicitly agree to perform the duties of those positions."[2] The question is, what duties has a judge implicitly agreed to perform when she assumes her role as a judge?[3] I have already explained that one responsibility of the judicial role is the faithful application of the law. I have also already mentioned that this is not the only responsibility engendered by the judicial role.

The responsibilities that attach to one's role are sometimes referred to as "role duties"[4] or "role obligations."[5] To avoid repetitiousness, I will use both terms, but I will omit the word *role,* with the qualification that when I use the terms *duty* and *obligation* in this chapter, I always only refer to duties that are inherent in or derivative of the common law judicial role and function. Whichever term is used, my argument adapts the idea as it is described by Greenawalt:

> A duty attaches to a particular position or to one's status as a human being; one speaks of the duties of judges and parents and of people gener-

ally. In this usage, one can speak of moral obligations and duties, but one can also speak of obligations and duties that are other than moral. These nonmoral duties, or obligations, may carry moral weight—"it is morally right that judges perform their legal duties"—but moral argument is needed to link the nonmoral duty to what one morally ought to do.[6]

In my conceptual argument for a judicial duty to develop the law by refusing to enforce an unjust law, I invert the progression suggested by Greenawalt. I do not assume the nonmoral (legal) duty of judges and propose a moral argument to link the nonmoral judicial duty to what one morally ought to do. Instead, I assume (as most people do) that a judge morally ought to refuse to enforce an unjust law,[7] and I propose an argument to link the moral duty to what a judge legally ought to do. This is because I am interested in challenging the prevailing assumption, which underlies the moral-formal dilemma, that a judge's moral and legal duties conflict in cases involving unjust laws. As I will argue in this chapter and in the two chapters that follow it, the link between a judge's moral duty not to enforce unjust laws and her legal duty not to enforce unjust laws is found in certain fundamental common law principles, which are relied on by English and American judges when evaluating the legality of government action in both systems.

B. Disagreements about the Law: Dissenting Opinions and the Design of the Common Law

In discussing Lord Mansfield's statement in *Omychund* that the common law works itself pure, I mentioned the methodological and doctrinal components of this concept. In chapter 5, I discussed the doctrinal aspects of *Omychund*. But Mansfield was not, it seems to me, just advancing a legal argument based on the facts and issues of that case. He was identifying an intrinsic feature of common law legal systems. Fundamentally, the idea and the image of the common law working itself pure are attempts to depict the common law's nature. The common law is designed to develop over time. We should not, however, allow Mansfield's evocative phrase to overshadow the fact of the matter: the common law does not work itself pure; it is worked pure by judges.[8] In this aspect of the common law judicial function, we find the central place of the judicial process in the common law system and the central place of the common law judge in the judicial process.[9] The common law is designed to develop over time and develops through judicial effort and experience. This development is usually incremental and gradual but occasionally dramatic. However it happens, the point remains the same. The common law system assigns the role of developing the common law to its judges.

The common law method requires judges to state the reasons for their decisions so that the decisions can be justified to the litigants involved and used as authority in later cases.[10] The paramount importance that this method gives to judicial opinions—as records of judicial reasoning and justifications for judicial rulings—can hardly be overstated. Simply put, the way judges write their opinions matters, for the litigants and for the law:

> The opinion thus engages in the central conversation that is for us the law, a conversation that the opinion itself makes possible. In doing these things it makes two claims of authority: for the texts and judgments to which it appeals, and for the methods by which it works. These things can be done well or badly in virtually every dimension . . . It is important that they be done well, not only because it is important that the parties be shown that their case has been treated with intelligence and respect, but because the way the opinion is written has large consequences for the future. It deeply affects and shapes the way we think and argue and, in so doing, constitute ourselves through the law. If an opinion is narrow-minded or unperceptive or dishonest or authoritarian, it will trivialize the experience of those it talks about, and it will trivialize the law too. If it is open and generous, full of excitement at the importance it gives to the events and people it speaks of, and to its own treatment of them as well, it will dignify the experience of those it talks of, and in so doing it will dignify the law itself. It may even be touched with nobility.[11]

The way opinions are written is important even, or especially, when judges disagree about the law.[12] When judges agree about the proper result in a case but disagree somewhat about the proper rationale for reaching that result, concurring opinions permit judges the opportunity to provide their best understandings of the legal justification for the result reached. Dissenting opinions provide judges who disagree about the proper result in a case the opportunity to explain the legal justification for the divergent results they reach.

As a common law innovation and a heuristic device, dissenting opinions serve as symbolic and tangible evidence that the common law is designed to develop over time. In some notable instances, we can actually observe this development through the law's adaptation of what began as a dissenting opinion into a majority opinion and, eventually, into settled legal doctrine. Perhaps the most famous example of this, at least in the United States, is the progression of American law from Justice Harlan's dissenting opinion in *Plessy*[13] to the unanimous decision in *Brown*,[14] with Harlan's prescient prediction in his *Plessy* dissent of the ignominy into which the majority decision in that case would finally descend.[15]

Someone might object that *Plessy* and *Brown* are poorly chosen as illustrations of the influence of dissenting opinions on legal development. After all, Chief Justice Earl Warren went out of his way not to cite Harlan's *Plessy* dissent in *Brown*. In addition, the point is sometimes made that, in *Brown*, the Supreme Court never expressly overruled *Plessy*.[16] Far from rendering these cases inapt as an example of dissenting opinions influencing the development of the law, however, these aspects of *Brown* highlight the common law's developmental design and the relevance of dissenting opinions to it, because *Brown* reveals judges working the law pure while either failing to give a candid account of their reasons for doing so or failing to rely on the right sorts of reason.

First, let me address the claim that *Brown* did not overrule *Plessy*. While this claim is accurate (so far as it goes), it seems a bit hypertechnical.[17] As a result of *Brown*, racial segregation in the sphere of public education is prohibited beyond cavil in the United States.[18] Furthermore, *Brown* effectively eradicated *Plessy*'s "separate but equal" doctrine from American law,[19] despite arguments that *Brown* was limited solely to education by its facts and by its failure to overrule *Plessy* frankly, in its entirety.[20]

Even more important, though, are the reasons given in the *Brown* opinion as the ostensive justification for the Court's decision. For reasons related to the politics of the time and to Chief Justice Warren's desire to maintain unanimity among the justices, the *Brown* decision was written in temperate tones.[21] These social and political pressures may have led the Court to mischaracterize the genuine foundations of its decision. Warren founded the *Brown* decision on social science data demonstrating the deleterious effects of racial segregation on black children.[22] To a segregationist for whom Jim Crow laws were a welcome fact of life in the 1950s, it might have been more tolerable to hear that the Supreme Court concluded segregation was harmful to schoolchildren than to hear that the Supreme Court determined segregation was fundamentally unjust. The Supreme Court knew that its *Brown* decision might meet with strident—even violent—reactions. The Court may have done what it thought it should to minimize the extremity of these reactions.

But even if one can understand the reasons why Warren wrote *Brown* as he did, it was a mistake to shrink from the principled legal decision that should have been written. The legal principle for which *Brown* stands is that separate, racially segregated facilities are "inherently unequal" and therefore violate the Fourteenth Amendment to the U.S. Constitution.[23] Lawyers might disagree about whether *Brown* stands for the narrow legal principle that racially segregated educational facilities are unconstitutional or for a broader legal principle prohibiting any state-sanctioned disparate treatment of American citizens based on race. Whichever understanding of *Brown* one favors, however, the Court should have decided that segregation was illegal in the United States simply because it violates the Constitution, not because of possible psychic harm to schoolchildren:

> [T]he Court's attempts to avoid overruling *Plessy*'s permission for racial discrimination on the ground that *Plessy* did not involve education . . . undermined the relatively simple, clear, and defensible justification for the decision with which the Court started: the Fourteenth Amendment should be interpreted as "proscribing all state-imposed discrimination against the Negro race." To depart from this justification was unnecessarily to provide arguments for opponents of the decision and handicap its defenders . . . [T]he justification for a decision is, like all explanations, a matter of adequacy rather than of absoluteness . . . No principle is more generally accepted, appealing on its face, or basic to American ideals than that a human being or, at least, an American citizen in America should not be disadvantaged by government because of his race or ancestry. It is no use to pretend that even this principle is an absolute, that it answers all racial questions and obviates the need for further thought, but it may be as close to a useful absolute as any we have. If one accepts this principle, as nearly all do, no more is required to justify the *Brown* decision . . . than to show that the individuals involved were in fact disadvantaged by school segregation. No resort to psychology is necessary to show this . . . An individual is necessarily disadvantaged when he is confined to association with only a part of the society.[24]

Social science data are irrelevant to the legal conclusion that segregation, or segregated educational facilities, violates American legal principles. By basing its decision in *Brown* on social science studies, the Court weakened the force of its legal contribution.[25] The unavoidable problem with the Court's reliance on these data is that the conclusions to be derived from the data are debatable.[26] The fact that the scientific data may remain inconclusive, however, does not mean that the legal issue should as well. The Court's reliance on scientific data will always leave open the spectre of the converse question: what if it did not harm the self-image of black children to be educated in segregated schools?[27] Should segregation suddenly be legalized?[28] The problem with *Plessy* and the point of *Brown* is that, as a matter of legal principle, the U.S. Constitution does not permit the government to use race as a reason for treating individuals disparately.[29] Why people react as they do to racial differences and what harm is visited on individuals as a result of those reactions are fascinating psychological, sociological, and anthropological questions. But the debates surrounding those issues are not principally relevant to the legal question, and it was a mistake for the *Brown* Court to enter into those debates. Whatever the Court may have thought about the social science support for its conclusion, its ruling in *Brown* should rest squarely, unambiguously, and unmediatedly on legal reasoning drawn from legal sources and principles. That is what the common law obligation to justify legal decisions requires of judges. And this obligation exerts its force most acutely when a judge's legal decision is most likely to be controversial and even unpopular, as the *Brown* decision surely was.

The obligation imposed on judges by the common law to explain the reasons for their decisions necessitates that the proffered explanations be complete and candid. The value of a judge's statement of reasons for a decision is lost if the judge does not state those reasons accurately: "The danger is that this duty of exposition can be evaded. It requires candor from judges in addressing the strongest arguments against their views . . . The duty of exposition seeks to remind the judge that the power to do something is not the same as the right to do it—that right can be earned, if at all, through reason."[30] Justly celebrated as the outcome is, the *Brown* Court failed to do all it could in its decision to purge segregation from American society as a matter of legal principle. The point of *Brown* is (or should be) that American law prohibits racial segregation because segregation violates constitutional (or other legal) provisions and principles, not because segregation may (or may not) damage the self-image of the people subjected to it.

Notwithstanding my misgivings about the Court's reasoning in *Brown,* the outcome represents a paradigmatic example of judges working the law pure. The criticisms of the *Brown* opinion highlighted in the previous paragraphs demonstrate that outcomes alone are not enough, however: to meet fully their obligations in the common law tradition, judges must offer reasons that justify outcomes, no matter how justified the outcome may appear when standing alone. Nevertheless, *Plessy* and *Brown* are a fitting demonstration of the influence that reason and principle and a dissenting opinion can have on the law's later development.[31] *Brown* and *Plessy* are, of course, just one famous (yet flawed) example of judges improving the law and of the influence of dissenting opinions on that process. The common law is replete with myriad examples of dissenting opinions serving as the groundwork for what would later become the law.[32]

Dissenting opinions evince the common law's commitment to improvement over time. Dissenting opinions demonstrate that the common law is designed to improve and that it does improve through the efforts of judges to articulate the reasons that they think best justify the result reached in a given case.[33] The common law requires judges to justify their decisions as explanations to the individual litigants of the law's treatment of them and to serve as precedential authority for later judges and lawyers to reason about the law. This common law practice depends on the candor and comprehensiveness of the judges' justificatory explanation.[34] Anything less impairs the litigants' understanding of their own case, the public perception of the integrity of the judicial process, and later consideration of the rule and rationale announced in a particular precedent, whether by the majority or in dissent.[35]

Brown and *Plessy* represent an object lesson in all of these features of the common law. First and foremost, *Brown* is a source of pride for Americans as a judicial achievement in the cause of justice. *Brown* also built on—even if it did not explicitly cite—the courageous example of judicial integrity manifest in Harlan's dissenting opinion in *Plessy*. Harlan's dissent shows that when judges candidly state their reasons for refusing to enforce unjust laws, they meet their obligations as common law judges to assist the ongoing process of legal development, even if they are prevented from achieving their desired result in the case at hand.[36] The dissenting judge contributes to the corpus of available precedent and helps—as much as a judge can within the role assigned to her by the common law—to develop the law.[37]

C. Judges and Justice

When examining the connections in Coke's and Mansfield's thought, I noted the connections in the common law between reason and justice.[38]

The idea that the common law works itself pure expresses the common law's commitment to seek justice in the process of adjudication through the application of judicial reason to human experience and legal dispute. An essential part of the business of common law courts is, on this account, to strive toward justice. At times when judges find themselves faced with an unjust law, the obligations placed on them by their role within common law systems requires them to develop the law in the direction of justice:

> The connection of justice to law, on this view, turns out to be indirect and non-exclusive. It comes of the combination of two facts: first, that adjudicative institutions should be just above all; secondly, that adjudicative institutions are, in a sense, the linchpin of all [common law] legal systems . . . If they are to be just, the courts should still not surrender to a rule that cannot be justly applied; in that case, justice would have the courts either change the rule . . . or depart from the rule.[39]

The idea that adjudicative institutions should be just above all connects judges and the judicial process to justice. Where a legal rule cannot be applied justly, the judge's duty to seek justice requires the judge to change or depart from the unjust legal rule. This is what common law review requires of judges.

This is a teleological view of the common law judicial process, with justice as its telos. Justice is what the judicial process is proceeding toward.[40] This is, it seems to me, exactly what Mansfield had in mind when he spoke of the common law working itself pure. The design of the common law to develop over time dovetails with and depends on the common law judicial method of reasoning by referring to, relying on, and sometimes reevaluating established legal doctrine.[41] This ongoing judicial reevaluation of existing law is the common law's insurance that the law will never stagnate or ossify.

Judges will ordinarily find that the law is fine as it is. But when they find that it is not, the common law tradition intends for them to do something about it. The common law insists on the active application of judicial reason as a necessary part of the aspiration to justice. As Justice William Brennan has written:

> I am convinced that law can be a vital engine not merely of change but of other civilizing change. That is because law, when it merits the synonym justice, is based on reason and insight. Decisional law evolves as

litigants and judges develop a better understanding of the world in which we live. Sometimes, these insights appear pedestrian, such as when we recognize, for example, that a suitcase is more like a home than it is like a car. On occasion, these insights are momentous, such as when we finally understand that separate can never be equal. I believe that these steps, which are the building blocks of progress, are fashioned from a great deal more than the changing views of judges over time. I believe that problems are susceptible to rational solution if we work hard at making and understanding arguments that are based on reason and experience.[42]

In a system where justice is a public value, as it is in every existing common law system, judges must apply their reason and experience in the attempt to achieve justice, at times by rectifying or eliminating injustice. That is their role and their responsibility—to the law, to the judicial institution, to the public, and to the litigants.[43]

The idea that the obligation to achieve justice is a fundamental element of the judicial role is hardly novel.[44] Yet few people seem to appreciate that, in common law systems, this element of the judicial role is imposed or presupposed by the legal system itself. People resist the claim that common law judges may, by virtue of their role and responsibility as judges, refuse to enforce unjust laws. Such refusal will result, so the argument goes, in (unelected, unrepresentative, and unaccountable) judges unreservedly imposing their subjective moral beliefs onto litigants and into the law "by fiat." But this is what the common law has always expected.[45] Moreover, as a practical matter, the law's relationship with politics might also help to explain why the common law has always expected its judges to engage in value judgments when rendering their legal judgments. In part, this is an unavoidable aspect of positioning an independent judicial system within a larger representative governmental structure; it is a means of restraining judicial action in relation to other branches of government.[46] To argue that judges must evaluate the law without recourse to their personal values and convictions is not merely to suggest a cautious and prudent circumscription of otherwise dangerously elastic judicial discretion. It is, in fact, to argue against the common law as a legal system.[47] Some have, from time to time, taken this position.[48] This view is not incoherent, but it should be recognized for what it is; and those who adopt it should realize what their argument requires and suggest the type of legal system they would prefer as a replacement. We must understand that our epistemological conceptions and preconceptions concerning the judicial role relate directly to our onto-logical notions of a legal system.

As a legal system, a legal tradition, a legal method, a mode of legal thought, and a body of legal principle, the common law functions at both structural and substantive levels. Structurally, if a legal system is a common law system, the common law—in every sense of that term—is relevant to the organization of government, the powers of government, the limita-tions of government, and the responsibilities of government. If a legal sys-tem is a common law system, the common law functions at a constitu-tional level, organizing and allocating power among the organs of government. This is an important part of the meaning of common law con-stitutionalism.[49] In referring to common law constitutionalism, I mean that the common law serves as a principal source for determining what are considered constitutional rights and fundamental values and that the com-mon law method applies to the articulation, evaluation, and interpretation of the (written or unwritten) constitution. According to common law con-stitutionalism, the common law must, at some level and in some fashion, constrain abuses of state power.

Here structure meets substance, the common law system's form meets the common law judge's function. In any healthy common law system, the judiciary must exercise some meaningful measure of independence and in-terdependence. Common law judges must be independent, because many of the fundamental rights and principles maintained at the level of com-mon law were first recognized or formulated by judges and because the common law depends on its judges jealously to preserve and protect them.[50] As Ruth Bader Ginsburg has observed, "[common law] judges [also] play an interdependent part in our democracy . . . [insofar as] they do not alone shape legal doctrine but . . . they participate in a dialogue with other organs of government, and with the people as well."[51] In their indepen-dence and their interdependence, judges bear institutional obligations to preserve the principles inherent in the common law. Common law judges cannot separate their role from their responsibilities.

One of the fundamental principles of the common law is justice, and one of the fundamental values of a common law legal system is the pursuit of justice.[52] Common law constitutionalism is, then, a version of justice-seeking constitutionalism.[53] Even those who would restrict the common law judicial function concede justice's place as a fundamental common law principle.[54] As I explained in chapter 1, the fundamental principle of justice in the common law should not be understood, for purposes of my argument, as an abstract principle. The principle of legality, which I discuss in chapter 9, and the principle of access to the courts, which I cite in chapter 8, are two concrete contemporary expressions of fundamental common law principles of this type, operating to maintain legal constraints on public power in accordance with the rule of law.[55]

The common law serves as the structural basis of the judicial authority to review legislative and executive action and provides a substantive standard against which this action is assessed.[56] By requiring all common law judges, by virtue of their position and status as judges, to develop the law, sometimes by refusing to enforce unjust legislative or executive action, common law review simply acknowledges a truth about the common law's systemic effort to attain justice and the judges' obligations in that process:

> [T]he common law should be understood as a body of principle which makes constant appeal to the requirements of justice, it must invite continuous debate and deliberation about questions of political morality. Properly understood, the common law serves the ideal of the rule of law by incorporating such deliberation within its ordinary process of evolutionary change and development.[57]

Without judges constantly and continuously appraising the law through the lights of their reason, the common law has no hope of achieving justice. The common law depends on the dynamic, recurrent exercise of judicial reasoning in the evaluation of the law, the resolution of disputes, and the issuance of decisions.[58] It is not just irresponsible for a common law judge to suspend her reason and silence her voice when deciding a case; it is perfidious for the common law judge to deprive the common law of the benefit of her reason and her unique contribution to the cause of justice:

> For my own part, with all becoming deference to the great minds, whose province it is not only to enlighten, by their wisdom and learning, but sometimes to enslave, by their authority, my reason will not allow me to give my sanction, as a public officer, to doctrines so subversive, in my humble judgment, of the principles and theory of our republican, constitutional governments. It would be an abandonment of duty as well as reason, were I, under such circumstances, to resign my right and obligation of independent thought and opinion, which, I may add, it is not the least commendation of the noble profession of the law, that it inspires, encourages, demands.[59]

Reluctant as I am to offer any essentialist account of the common law or common law systems, there is one integral feature of all common law systems, and a legal system lacking this feature cannot accurately be designated a common law system. This feature is a judiciary whose obligation is to resolve legal disputes in an honest effort to achieve justice, through justificatory written opinions that serve as guidance to lawyers, judges, and citizens in subsequent reasoning and decision making. It is not just a coincidence that we find this sort of judiciary in every common law legal system; it is what makes these legal systems common law systems.

D. Disagreements about the Judge's Role: Interpreting the Judicial Function

Judges disagree about their role, and so judges disagree about their responsibilities. As I have already explained, some judges assume that their role is strictly limited to the enforcement of the law as it is. These judges believe that they exceed their authority if they refuse to enforce a law that is constitutional, no matter how unjust the law might be. Other judges see things differently. These judges consider their role and their responsibilities to be more capacious.

Common law review requires judges to take the broader outlook. The common law has always required its judges to bring their moral faculties and convictions to bear on their legal decisions, as an essential contribution to the common law's ongoing development. This is true not only in the uncontroversial areas of common law adjudication. It is also appropriate, and most important, in what are now called "constitutional cases." Of course, as I have already explained, the attempt to distinguish common law adjudication from constitutional adjudication is not well founded historically or doctrinally. But even those judges who seem to presuppose the distinction recognize the importance of the intersection between their moral evaluations and their legal determinations. These judges recognize the value of their values when deciding common law cases[60] and constitutional cases.[61]

The disagreement about whether the role of judges limits them to the enforcement of a law irrespective of the law's injustice touches inevitably on judicial attitudes toward the "part played by a judge's own values and sense of justice"[62] when deciding cases. Some judges deem their own moral faculties to be entirely irrelevant to their duties as judges to enforce the law.[63] Other judges understand that their individual moral convictions and reactions are a necessary element of the legitimate judicial decision-making process. In his lecture in honor of Justice Benjamin Cardozo, Justice William Brennan declared his (and Cardozo's) membership in the latter camp:

> It is my thesis that this interplay of forces, this internal dialogue of reason and passion, does not taint the judicial process, but is in fact central to its vitality. This is particularly true, I think, in constitutional interpretation . . . Having admitted and demonstrated that judges inevitably confront value choices, Cardozo did not shrink from the implications of that admission. He rejected the prevailing myth that a judge's personal values were irrelevant to the decision process, because a judge's role was presumably limited to application of existing law, a process governed by external, objective norms.[64]

As Cardozo had before him, Brennan rejected the idea that the judicial role requires a judge to disengage his moral values when adjudicating legal disputes. On the contrary, Brennan decided that this moral engagement between the judge and the law was an unavoidable and beneficial part of the judicial process.

In stark contrast with the view shared by Cardozo and Brennan, Judge Robert Bork sees his role very differently: "[W]here the Constitution does not apply, the judge, while in his robes, must adopt a posture of moral abstention."[65] Needless to say, common law review is predicated on the rejection and refutation of Bork's claim. But for now, I am interested in looking at the fact of this disagreement about the proper understanding of the judicial role, rather than discussing its resolution.

Ronald Dworkin's theory of constructive interpretation provides an interesting analytic framework for considering this disagreement about the judicial function.[66] Dworkin's two dimensions of interpretation, fit and justification,[67] are frequently applied to determine what the law is at a given time in a given place. In fact, Dworkin himself applied his theory to explain the result in *Brown*.[68] But we can step back from the immediacy of a particular legal question and apply Dworkin's interpretive theory to the practice of judging.[69] In Dworkinian parlance, we may reasonably conclude that both Bork's and Brennan's competing views of the judicial role sufficiently fit the Anglo-American common law judicial tradition.[70] The question then becomes, which interpretation best justifies the judicial function by portraying the judicial role in the best light?[71]

It seems to me that Brennan's view does. Unlike Bork's ideal of a moral abstentionist judge, Brennan's view of the judicial function permits judges to exercise their moral faculties while wearing their robes and when formulating and evaluating legal rules found in statutes and precedents. This vision better conveys the judiciary's role as an institutional counterweight against a majoritarian legislature, whose members must occasionally shield individuals and minority groups from legislative encroachments on their liberties. The Borkian quietist judge represents a portrait of a judiciary that reads its own responsibilities so narrowly as to vanish at the point when they are most needed, allows the law to remain static when change is urgently sought, and perpetuates injustice in the name of judicial restraint or deference.

Most of the arguments for judicial restraint and originalism, in their various forms, boil down to arguments that the absence of explicit references to judicial review in the U.S. Constitution undermines—theoretically and historically, if not practically—the exercise of that power by American courts. But the institutional functions of the common law judiciary call into question the significance of that omission for purposes of establishing autonomous judicial authority in reliance on legal tradition and legal sources. The scope and nature of judicial authority and institutional independence in the common law tradition were not initially and should not now be conceived as created or completely circumscribed by a charter document. A common law foundation has long existed for the inherent judicial authority—irrespective of a constitutional text—to evaluate governmental action. In the United States, this means that resolution of the countermajoritarian problem—if judicial review is truly countermajoritarian and if that is a problem—need not and ultimately cannot be resolved by reference to particular modes of constitutional interpretation (e.g., originalism) or by inveighing against the activism of the judiciary. In England (and elsewhere in the common law world), as I explain in chapter 9, this means that efforts to reconcile parliamentary sovereignty and the rule of law[72] cannot be accomplished solely by resort to the *ultra vires* doctrine.

The vision of judges whose moral values are necessary, worthwhile, and legitimate components of the judicial process is the vision embraced by common law review, because this is the vision intrinsic to the common law. This is the vision that best allows judges to prevent injustice by acting on their strongest and deepest convictions. The risk to the integrity of the judicial process and to the public esteem of the judicial institution is far greater when judges fail to bring their convictions to bear on their adjudication. That is what the common law has always expected of them: "[T]he danger is not that judges will bring the full measure of their experience, their moral core, their every human capacity to bear in the difficult process of resolving the cases before them. It seems to me that a far greater danger exists if they do not."[73]

The proper interpretation of the judicial function is not solely an academic exercise. Judges who disagree about the scope of their role and their duties will sometimes reach very different decisions in a given case. In considering different interpretations of the judicial function and the effect of these different interpretations on judicial reasoning and decision making, there are four basic categories into which interpretations of the judicial function fit. The first category consists of judges whose functions and obligations are limited exclusively to applying the law as it is. On this account, the judicial role is minimally interpretive or evaluative; it is almost entirely instrumental. Of course, even judges in this first category must engage in some interpretation or evaluation when determining whether a statute or precedent should apply to a given set of facts. But this interpretation or evaluation is not supposed to be especially reflective or creative. I will call this interpretation of the judicial function "instrumentalist."

The second category adds something important, but limited, to the first conception. In addition to determining what the law is, these judges reckon that they must ensure that the law complies with the prescriptions of a constitution as understood by its framers. If, and only if, a particular law violates the original understandings of those who framed a constitution, then these judges determine they have the authority to refuse to enforce the offending legislation. If the law cannot reasonably be said to violate the provisions of the constitution, as those provisions would have been understood by those who originally considered them, then the judge has no alternative but to enforce the law as it is. I will call this interpretation of the judicial function "originalist." Originalist judges concede that they have some interpretive function when deciding what the constitution's authors intended and whether a law contravenes those intentions, but this interpretive function is narrowly and somewhat rigidly confined.

In the third category are judges who agree that they must ensure that particular laws comply with the constitution, but these judges do not assume that the constitution's meaning is fixed by the intentions or understandings of those who wrote it. These judges believe their function requires them to interpret the constitution in accordance with contemporary legislators' or citizens' prevailing beliefs about social and political morality. I will call this interpretation of the judicial function "interpretivist."

The fourth category consists of those judges who agree with the interpretivists about the nature of the judicial function with one exception. When deciding whether to enforce a particular statute or precedent, they evaluate the law in the light of constitutional directives. But in cases of extreme injustice, these judges are willing to refuse to enforce certain laws, even where the law violates no particular constitutional provision. In extreme cases, these judges rely on their own individual moral convictions (in preference to those of the community) when evaluating and developing the law. I will call this interpretation of the judicial function "individualist."[74] Individualist judges would still view the constitution as the first and (usually) the last stop in the judicial evaluation of the enforceability of legislation or precedent. They also believe, however, that the constitution is not the exclusive legal basis against which a judge might evaluate a particular law and that in certain cases where the constitution does not preclude some egregious injustice, there may be some other legal basis for judicial intervention. I argue that the common law provides this alternative basis for judicial invalidation of unjust government action.

The first category represents the stereotypical civil law judicial function (as well as the position of some common lawyers and common law judges).[75] The second and third categories encompass versions of constitutional review. And the fourth category is common law review as I envision it. Judges in each of these categories believe that they are deciding cases in accordance with their role and responsibilities as judges:

> I should say that most depends upon the judge's unspoken notion as to the function of his court. If he views the role of the courts as a passive one, he will be willing to delegate the responsibility for change, and he will not greatly care whether the delegated authority is exercised or not. If he views the court as an instrument of society designed to reflect in its decisions the morality of the community, he will be more likely to look precedent in the teeth and to measure it against the ideals and the aspirations of his time.[76]

To the litigants whose lives will be directly affected by the court's decision and to the citizens who will live under the law established by the court's decision, the way a judge interprets his role and his responsibilities is a question of the gravest importance when it determines the outcome of a momentous case.

Judges are responsible for their view of their role and its repercussions.[77] The relationship among judicial role, judicial responsibility, and judicial ruling affects the way judges see one another and the way we see the judiciary as an institution. This relationship can best be seen through the example of actual cases, such as *Plessy* and *Brown*.

Let us assume that both *Plessy* and *Brown* fit American social and legal history and practice when they were decided.[78] It is difficult to deny that *Brown* portrays American law in a better moral light and is a better justification and interpretation of American law than *Plessy*.[79] But now let us assume that originalist judges will view segregation only as it was viewed by the framers of the U.S. Constitution,[80] while interpretivist judges will evaluate segregation in accordance with contemporary social morality. If we can accept that these two interpretations of the judicial function might lead to different judicial decisions and that the latter interpretation of the judicial function will permit a better judicial decision, then this reveals the connection between the interpretation of the judicial role and the formulation of judicial rulings. The interpretation of the judicial function that permits the better interpretation of a society's law is the better interpretation of the judicial function.

Common law review simply takes this argument one step further. Common law review fits Anglo-American common law traditions, methods, and sources and affords the greatest operative latitude for the judge's personal values when faced with unjust laws. Individualist judges, with their proposed interpretation of the judicial function, come to better decisions in certain cases when engaging in common law review than judges who adopt other interpretations of the judicial function. By permitting the judge *qua* judge to develop the law in cases where other interpretations of the judicial function would not, common law review best justifies the judicial practice and process of adjudication.[81] Consequently, according to Dworkin's theory,[82] common law review incorporates the best interpretation of the common law judicial function.

The belief that the judicial function is exhausted by enforcing existing law is, then, just one interpretation of the judicial function. Similarly, the belief that judges must adopt a "posture of moral abstention" is likewise an interpretation of the judicial function. Moreover, as I have explained, these are interpretations at odds with the traditional common law conception. Common law judges were never supposed to be the factotums of the legislature and were never expected to disengage their moral faculties when they put on their robes. The common law always understood that inside those robes are human beings. Common law judges have always been expected to bring the full panoply of their moral sensibilities and life experiences with them to the bench while exercising independent judgment about the laws they are asked to enforce.[83]

It is worth pausing here to make a clarification. In this discussion, one must distinguish among three factors: (1) the legal basis and authority for a judicial power recognized within a legal system, (2) the form of that power, and (3) judicial attitudes toward the exercise of that power. Take constitutional review as an example: one must determine where that power comes from, what that power allows judges to do, and when judges may properly exercise that power. All of these are contingent facts about particular legal systems, and all are grist for debate and disagreement.

People disagree about the legitimacy and foundation of constitutional review in America. People could also disagree about what constitutional review empowers judges to do. In America, when judges declare statutes unconstitutional, they are eliminated from the body of viable law. But this need not be the case. As in discussions of *Bonham* where people argue about what it means "to adjudge a statute void," it is a potentially open question (settled in the United States) whether constitutional review automatically empowers judges to remove constitutionally offensive statutes from the law. I will discuss this issue relative to common law review later. Most important for my current discussion, the existence of constitutional review in a legal system does not necessarily dictate anything about the occasions when judges may appropriately exercise that power. Judges who agree that they possess the power of constitutional review may (and do) still disagree about whether they should exhibit restraint or activism in their exercise of that power. The same holds true for common law review. I am now arguing only for the existence of the power. Later, I will argue for the form I believe that power should take. I will also argue later that the proper judicial attitude toward the exercise of common law review is one of care and restraint. At the risk of belaboring the obvious, I should stress that one may accept the existence of common law review but disagree with me about the proper form of that power, the appropriate judicial attitude toward it, or the correct instances of its application.

E. Consequences of Judicial Failure to Develop the Law

To analyze the consequences of judicial failure to develop the law by refusing to enforce unjust laws, I place these consequences into three categories: (1) legitimation, (2) social and legal harm, and (3) complicity and accountability. While there is some considerable overlap among these categories, they are distinct from one another and worth considering separately.

1. *Legitimation*

Writers sometimes refer to the "legitimation" of statutes enforced by the courts.[84] The idea, usually associated with constitutional review, is that judges endorse, at least implicitly or indirectly, those statutes that they conclude do not violate a constitution. To be sure, the simple determination by a judge that a statute is not unconstitutional need not indicate any measure of judicial approbation. But as a practical matter, it frequently is taken to do so.[85] Furthermore, even though the courts in these cases only permit actions taken by other governmental actors, the courts are often the chosen targets for public anger and outrage.[86] Although one might assume that most hostility is directed at instances of judicial "activism," in which the courts strike down legislation, it is usually the other way around. The harshest and most extreme reactions often come when judges fail to invalidate challenged legislative or executive action.[87] I think, as I will explain presently, that people react so angrily to these incidents of judicial inertia because they expect more of judges and the judiciary in combating injustice than they expect of the more representative branches of government. At this point, though, I want to compare legitimation in constitutional review with legitimation in common law review.

In much the same way and with the same qualifiers that attach to legitimation as a corollary of constitutional review, judges who enforce unjust laws help to legitimate the iniquitous actions or relations permitted or encouraged by those laws. Despite whatever language the judge may use to distance himself from his decision, the result for the litigants and the public is that the judge has determined that their nation's law permits this atrocity. No language can place enough distance between the judge and this ruling.

Judges do not write unjust statutes. But judges do decide whether to enforce them and are ultimately responsible for the laws they enforce.[88] We can take *Plessy* as an example once again. Judges did not invent segregation. But as Herbert Hovenkamp argues, the judges who upheld statutes permitting segregation must share some of the responsibility for the racism that their rulings helped to legitimate and perpetuate:

> The courts must bear a heavy share of the burden of American racism. An outpouring of recent historical scholarship on racism and the American law reveals the outrageous and humiliating extent to which American lawyers, judges and legislators created, perpetuated, and defended racist American institutions. Legal rules recognized and justified racism. More importantly, legal rules enforced racism by making segregation

and the other degradations of racism a legal duty rather than an act of individual free will. In the process they cleared the consciences of white Americans by relieving them of any sense of responsibility for racist practices.[89]

The perception of absolution is perhaps the most insidious element of the judicial legitimation of unjust laws. Notwithstanding any judicial protestations to the contrary, the stamp of legality and the air of credibility lent to unjust laws through judicial enforcement sends an unmistakable message to the law's proponents and to its victims: the courts cannot or will not prevent the practice the law permits. Moreover, those who favor an unjust law that is upheld are not responsible to the victims, because the courts will not hold them responsible for their actions; the courts have told them that, legally speaking, they have done nothing wrong.

2. Social and Legal Harm

Legitimation only opens the door. The further consequences of judicial enforcement of unjust legislation are often much more dire. *Plessy* and *Brown* serve as historical evidence of the damage done by judges who fail to develop the law where they should. The damage done is legal and social.

Addressing the legal damage, "*Plessy* planted the doctrine of separate-but-equal more firmly than before in American law and particularly in the Constitution . . . [T]he case embedded a still more pernicious principle into constitutional law: that separation without reference to equality met the test of the Reconstruction Amendments."[90] *Plessy* paved the way for "the first wave of *legislated* transportation segregation, enacted between 1887 and 1892."[91] This had two immediate results: black travelers who sought accommodations in white railway cars were no longer just denied access but were subject to criminal prosecution, and railway carriers could no longer choose not to provide segregated accommodations but were forced to provide them.[92]

The social damage precipitated by *Plessy* was incalculable. Buoyed by *Plessy*, Jim Crow laws flourished in the American South:

> From hospitals before birth to cemeteries after death, separate-but-equal set the legal status of blacks. Fifty-four years after *Plessy*, one commentator found laws and decisions extending the doctrine "to every type of transportation, education, and amusement; to public housing, restaurants, hotels, libraries, public parks and recreational facilities, fraternal

associations, marriage, employment, and public welfare institutions. It ha[d] pursued the negro even into prisons, wash houses in coal mines, telephone booths, and the armed forces." The separation extended as well to inanimate objects, as in Florida where school textbooks which had been used by one race were to be stored separately from those used by the other race . . . After 1896, *Plessy* provided judicial authority for this degradation.[93]

The human cost of a judge's decision to enforce an unjust law can never be calculated, but that does not mean it cannot be considered. America and Americans still suffer from the damage done by the Court in *Plessy*.[94] And *Plessy* is hardly the lone instance of judges enforcing unjust government action that legally authorized racial discrimination. *Prigg v. Pennsylvania*,[95] *Dred Scott*,[96] *Hirabayashi*,[97] and *Korematsu*[98] all represent sad chapters in the history of judicially enforced racism in America. All of these cases demonstrate the consequences of judicial inaction. These are the consequences that common law review seeks to avoid.

When a judge fails to develop the law where she should, she does not only fail those who appear before her and the institution she helps to constitute. She fails the common law system itself.[99] She retards the progress she is supposed to ensure, and she further embeds the injustice she has been asked to rectify, making the task even more daunting for her successors, to whom she has left it.

3. Complicity and Accountability

For the two reasons I have just discussed, among others, we are often piercingly disappointed when judges enforce unjust laws and impede the law's development. While reactions to *Brown* were sharply divided when the decision was announced, most Americans now revere the decision as a very positive step for American law. Likewise, most Americans deride *Plessy* as a blight on American legal history. Two factors explain these reactions, and each of these factors reflects, in one form or another, one of the most fundamental aspects of the common law judicial function, expressed by Owen Fiss as follows: "[T]he function of the judge, which is both a statement of social purpose and a definition of role, is not [just] to resolve disputes but to give the proper meaning to our public values."[100]

First, every judge is a constituent member of the judicial institution. As is true of any institution, the judiciary is understood by its participants as having a particular character or purpose.[101] Officials of an institution have a duty to "protect the character" of the institution.[102] One irreducible element of the common law judicial institution is its relationship with the effort to achieve justice. Many of the public values we associate with the law and the judiciary—equality, liberty, impartiality, and so on—help to comprise the more expansive public value of justice. So when a judge preserves equality or liberty, we see this as promoting justice. We claim our more specific, derivative rights (to equal protection, freedom of speech, due process, etc.) through the common law judicial process; and judges recognize, promote, and defend these rights in their legal rulings. When a judge acquiesces in injustice (for whatever reason), that judge fails in his duty to protect the character of the judicial institution. When a judge fails us, we believe that the courts, as an institution, have failed us. By failing to give the proper meaning to our public values, the judge has betrayed the character of the judicial institution. The disappointment we feel on these occasions is, at some level, personal: we live in this society; these are our courts; this is our law; we expect more of our institutions than this. We expect more of our judges expressly because of their role, its responsibilities, and its relationship to justice. Judges are, in this respect, accountable to all of the members of the nation whose law the judge interprets, enforces, and expounds.[103]

Second (and related to the first point), judges are accountable to every litigant who appears before them. In a passage that would have pleased his grandfather, especially because it was written in dissent, Justice John Marshall Harlan II wrote:

> If a "new" constitutional doctrine is truly right, we should not reverse lower courts which have accepted it . . . Anything else would belie the truism that it is the task of this Court, like that of any other, to do justice to each litigant on the merits of his own case. It is only if each of our decisions can be justified in terms of this fundamental premise that they may properly be considered the legitimate products of a court of law, rather than commands of a super-legislature.[104]

Harlan's statement demonstrates the felt obligation, at least on the part of some judges, to gauge their results by the ultimate test of substantive justice. It may well be true, as Justice Brandeis said, that "it is usually more important that a rule of law be settled, than that it be settled right."[105] But this is not so in cases involving unjust laws. These are occasions when nothing is more important than that the law be settled right. When judges are asked to enforce an unjust law, they have no greater obligation to the litigants (and to the judicial institution) than the concerted effort to develop the law and to realize the most just result.[106] Only in this way can a judge look in the eyes of each litigant who appears before her and bear the conscientious assurance that she has done everything she can—in her power and within her role—to infuse our public values with their most noble content. As I explain in the discussion of the relationship between common law review and stare decisis in the next chapter, unjust laws present a situation where the concerns of formal justice (stability, predictability, continuity) must yield to the demands of substantive justice (fairness, rightness, dignity).[107]

Judges are accountable to their institution, to the litigants who appear before them, and to the public that lives with and by their rulings. When judges enforce unjust laws, out of excessive deference to the legislature or a stunted view of their own function, they become complicit in the injustice that their office exists to prevent.[108] Once again, *Plessy* serves as a historical reminder of this relationship between judicial duty and public values and of judicial accountability and complicity. As Gerald Postema puts it:

> Segregation, then, was not merely a matter of the private opinions or attitudes of whites in post-Reconstruction America. It was the public expression of a structure of domination, and part of a systematic denial of the standing of blacks as full and equal members of American society . . . It is not surprising, then, that Justice Brown [writing for the *Plessy* majority] and Justice Harlan paid scant attention to the question of whether the separate travelling accommodations were in fact equal in their separate quality; and why Brown sought to deny, and Harlan to assert, the law's complicity in the structure of social inequality . . . The most important lesson of *Plessy*, as I read it, lies in Justice Harlan's articulation of the fundamental evil of segregation . . . We cannot responsibly deny that it [racism] still exists, but equally we cannot responsibly accept that it is just "in the nature of things." We commit the morally unconscionable error of the *Plessy* majority yet again if we contend that law can and must do nothing to remove its sting.[109]

By claiming that judges must give the proper meaning to public values, I do not mean that judges must necessarily enforce and reinforce their society's prevailing social norms. On the contrary, when a judge refuses to enforce an unjust law, she will, almost by definition, frustrate the wishes of many people who support the law, not least those who have sought its enforcement in her court. The Louisiana statute at issue in *Plessy* was, after all, the product of a majoritarian legislature.[110] Reprehensible though the statute was, we expect legislatures to act in the interests of the majority. And if it proves nothing else, history amply demonstrates that the majority will frequently want things detrimental to the minority.[111] For this reason, among others, the common law has, at least since Coke's disputes with King James, placed the courts in a position independent and insulated from the political pressures and accountabilities endemic to the politically representative branches of government.[112] Judges are accountable to something less tangible but no less important.

In response to Ronald Dworkin's claim that "the United States is a more just society than it would have been had its constitutional rights been left to the conscience of majoritarian institutions,"[113] Jeremy Waldron questions whether judicial review is necessary as an institutional antidote against legislative injustice. Waldron even wonders whether *Brown* itself was necessary to discontinue segregation in America:

> Should we accept this as a starting point? I have my doubts. Like any claim involving a counterfactual ("more just than it would have been if . . ."), it is an extraordinarily difficult proposition to assess. As we consider it, we think naturally of landmark decisions like *Brown v. Board of Education*, and the impact of such decisions on desegregation and the promotion of racial equality. But it is not enough to celebrate *Brown*. Verifying the counterfactual would involve not only an assessment of the impact of that and similar decisions but also a consideration of the way in which the struggle against segregation and similar injustices might have proceeded in the United States if there had been no Bill of Rights or no practice of judicial review.[114]

Waldron then goes on to mention two points that he sees as challenges to Dworkin's claim: (1) some countries are as just as the United States even though they lack an established practice of judicial review, and (2) judicial review has sometimes damaged the cause of justice.[115]

To my mind, Waldron's argument misses the point and needlessly complicates a simple issue. Waldron may raise doubts about where Dworkin begins. But it is difficult to dispute where Dworkin finishes. Judicial review has eliminated from American law instances of unjust legislation. *Plessy* declared that segregation by statute was constitutionally permissible in the United States. As a result, segregation flourished in the American South.

Waldron cannot seriously doubt that *Brown* improved the law that *Plessy* helped create.

We can wonder whether segregation would, at some point, have grown so distasteful to those who lived in areas where it was practiced that it would have died a legislative death. But there is nothing in the almost sixty intervening years between *Plessy* and *Brown* to encourage us to think so. More to the point, the issue is not whether legislatures sometimes correct injustice or courts sometimes contribute to it. They do. The important point is that courts sometimes are the only governmental authority capable of resisting and correcting legislative injustices that reflect the prejudices of the majority. Majoritarian legislatures are decidedly unlikely to rescind legislation that continues to represent the interests of the majority, even where those interests are hateful, prejudiced, or ignorant.[116] The common law recognized this long ago. For at least the last three hundred years, the common law has recognized the courts' unique, independent institutional position and capability to correct injustices committed through legislative or executive action.[117] Even Waldron cannot deny that courts have, on some notable occasions of which *Brown* is an example, improved the law by excising unjust legislation.[118]

8. Common Law Review

I have presented two independent arguments—one source-based and one conceptual—that support an ability and an obligation of common law judges to develop the law by refusing to enforce unjust laws. I have called this *common law review*. In this chapter, I will explore in some detail how the theory of common law review might translate into practice. The discussion in this chapter is generic; it holds whichever way common law review is established, conceptually or by case law. In particular, I will do five things in this chapter. First, I will examine some analytic features of the doctrine. Second, I will describe what I take to be the proper form of the power of common law review and the appropriate judicial attitude toward its exercise. Third, I will consider common law review's interaction with stare decisis and legislative supremacy. Fourth, I will relate the exercise of common law review to broader themes of common law constitutionalism. Fifth, I will respond to a classic concern of legal theory regarding unjust laws, to avoid the misapprehension that my argument tracks the so-called Radbruch formula.

Implicit (and at times explicit) in this discussion are my responses to three likely objections to common law review: (1) that the doctrine is an unwieldy and unworkable notion, (2) that there is no room in the law for judges to rely on their own idiosyncratic moral beliefs, and (3) that there is far too much danger of its overuse by undisciplined or irresponsible judges.[1] As I will explain in this chapter and in the one that follows, these concerns might seem acute in the abstract, but they ought not to be considered in the abstract. In the common law tradition, these concerns arise only in the context of specific cases. And in this case-specific context, these concerns are far less pervasive than they might seem. The judicial authority I describe is a feature of all common law systems, although its constitutional description will vary from jurisdiction to jurisdiction and although individuals will rightly disagree about the proper instances of its invocation. Those disagreements, whether expressed in judicial opinions or elsewhere, are a necessary and healthy aspect of the common law's dialogic nature. But those disagreements about when and whether the courts should exercise their review authority in particular cases should not be taken for doubts about whether the courts have that authority at all.

A. Analytic Features

1. The Epistemic Threshold

Stephen Perry introduced an idea called the "epistemic threshold" to help explain the proper balance between judicial deference to precedent and independent judgment:

> [I]f the facts of the present case fell within the scope of her [a judge's] reasoning in an earlier case, she would be bound to decide in the way indicated by her prior reasoning unless her conviction that she had been wrong rose above a certain epistemic threshold. In that event she would be free and indeed obligated to decide in accordance with her present assessment of what the objective balance of reasons requires . . . [T]he point would be to introduce a certain stability into the general legal environment without at the same time sacrificing completely the judge's ability to decide cases according to her own best present judgment.[2]

In the preceding excerpt, Perry discusses the epistemic threshold as it relates to the reassessment of a judge's own prior decision. He explains in a later article that the concept applies with equal force when a judge reviews the reasoning of a different court: "[I]f judges are sufficiently confident that an earlier court was mistaken, then they can, to an extent that will vary with the circumstances, rely on their present moral beliefs to decide the case at bar and, in the process, change the law."[3]

Building on Perry's formulation, the epistemic threshold concept captures three key facets of common law review. First, a judge cannot invoke the power of common law review unless she is sufficiently certain that a mistake was made—or, to repeat Perry's phrasing, unless her conviction rises above a certain epistemic threshold. Second, the epistemic threshold links the judge's moral reasoning to her legal ruling. The mistake with which the epistemic threshold (and common law review) is concerned is a moral mistake and not just a legal error—a moral mistake that has led to or underlies a legal ruling.[4] Third, once the epistemic threshold is crossed, the judge is obligated to reach a legal decision in accordance with her best judgment, informed by her moral beliefs.

It is not entirely clear whether Perry believes the obligation triggered by the epistemic threshold is absolute or supererogatory. In the first passage I quoted, he states that a judge is "free and indeed obligated to decide in accordance with her present assessment of what the objective balance of reasons requires." This suggests that once the epistemic threshold is crossed, the judge must act to correct the perceived error. In the second extract, however, Perry writes that when judges are sufficiently confident of an earlier court's mistake, they "can" rely on their moral beliefs to change the law.

I set out to justify a legal basis for judges to refuse to enforce unjust laws. It would be perfectly consistent with my stated project for me to claim that once the epistemic threshold is satisfied, a judge may refuse to enforce unjust laws, but not that she must. Surely, it would be satisfying for me if I convinced readers that common law review grounds a supererogatory judicial authority to refuse to enforce unjust laws. Nevertheless, I will try to do even more. For reasons I discussed in the previous chapters, I believe the obligation is absolute. Once the epistemic threshold is crossed, a judge not only can but must refuse to enforce an unjust law.

Where common law review is concerned, it seems to me that the epistemic threshold rotates on two axes: certainty and gravity. The axis of certainty, on which Perry's analysis centers, emphasizes the necessity that a judge be sufficiently confident of a prior error before disavowing precedent. For common law review, this is only half of the story. Not only must a judge be sufficiently certain that a mistake was made before refusing to enforce a particular law, but the judge must also be convinced that the issue at stake is grave enough to justify the extraordinary power of common law review. This is the "gravity" axis of the epistemic threshold.[5]

Certainty relates to the confidence that an error was made; gravity relates to the importance of that error. Of course, the idea of certainty pertains to the gravity axis as well insofar as a judge must be certain not only that a mistake was made but also that the mistake involves a matter of sufficient weight to justify the exercise of common law review. I separate certainty and gravity, though, to underscore the fact that a judge can refuse to enforce an unjust law under the aegis of common law review only where the injustice is profound and compelling. Common law review cannot be invoked by judges who wish to correct a trivial detail or even a moderately important mistake made by a legislature or a higher court.[6] Common law review is concerned with iniquity, not inequity. The very idea of an "unjust law" recalls the gravity component of the epistemic threshold and should preclude judicial misinterpretations of the aspect of gravity in the practice of common law review. Common law review requires the judge to be convinced that a mistake has been made and that it is a serious mistake—or, more carefully, that it is a mistake about something serious.[7]

To this point, I have considered the epistemic threshold only in relation to judicial appraisal of existing case law. It applies in the same fashion when judges review and assess the injustice of legislative enactments.[8] My primary interest in the epistemic threshold as it relates to common law review is straightforward: before a judge can properly engage in common law review, she must, after critical and searching reflection, be thoroughly convinced that a particular judicial decision, legislative enactment, or executive action was mistaken and that it involves an issue of the first moral magnitude. When, and only when, the judge is satisfied that both axes of the epistemic threshold have been reached, the judge can and must develop the law by refusing to enforce or endorse the unjust decision, legislation, or action.

The previous paragraphs touch on an important jurisprudential debate that I should pause to address. Exclusive legal positivists, such as Joseph Raz, believe that the law sometimes requires judges to engage their best evaluative moral reasoning when reaching legal determinations, even when changing or developing the law. For these legal theorists, however, the judge's moral evaluations, while necessary to the law's articulation, always remain external to the law itself.[9] In contrast, Ronald Dworkin maintains that the adjudicative process of constructive interpretation always requires judges to engage in moral reasoning when reaching legal determinations and that the judge's moral evaluations are part of and cannot meaningfully be separated from the law itself.[10]

An example may help clarify the relevance of this dispute for common law review. Imagine a case where a plaintiff railroad company has sued a defendant passenger of African descent for refusing to remove himself from a "whites only" railroad car in violation of a statute passed in the wake of *Plessy*. Common law review holds that in a case involving a sufficiently unjust law, such as this one, a judge has a legal obligation to develop the law in accordance with her moral convictions by refusing to enforce the unjust statute against the defendant. I have argued that the legal basis for this judicial obligation can be traced either to common law legal sources or to common law legal concepts. A Razian may prefer sources, and a Dworkinian may prefer concepts, but notice what they agree and disagree about. They agree that judges have a legal obligation in this case to invoke their moral convictions when reaching a legal ruling. So they agree about the fundamental analytic structure and substance of common law review. They disagree, however, about the proper scope and limits of the judge's legal obligation. The Razian would say that the (common) law instructs judges to use their moral faculties when reaching a legal decision but that the decision is ultimately left to the judge's discretion. The Dworkinian would say that the judge's legal obligation runs all the way down to the specific decision reached—that is, that the judge has a legal obligation to engage in moral evaluation and a legal *cum* moral obligation to decide in the defendant's favor.

Given the parameters of the argument for common law review as I have constructed it, even this disagreement is far less stark than it may appear. On Raz's view, the law may require a judge to consult morality, yet the law cannot dictate a particular result in a specific case where a judge has discretion. But for the common law judge who is deeply troubled by the racialist law's injustice, common law review establishes a legal obligation for the judge to decide in accordance with her felt moral convictions, provided that the epistemic threshold has been met. So in this case, for this judge, a Razian who accepts common law review might well accept that the judge must reach a legal decision that coincides with her moral convictions. This is, on Raz's view, one of those situations where the judge's discretion is cabined by law. What is unusual (or perhaps, as I will explain in the next section, not so unusual) is that the judge is legally required to decide the case in accordance with her own moral beliefs.[11] In an early essay, Raz himself explicitly referred to legal norms that instruct or require judges to invoke their moral convictions when deciding cases (and he noted the convergence between legal positivism and Dworkin on this point): "Both [positivism and Dworkin] contend that courts are legally required to apply source-based standards and both claim that they are legally required to follow certain moral standards, even when these are not source-based. Both further agree that the source-based standards determine which nonsource-based standards should be applied by the courts and when."[12] A Dworkinian would still wish to go much further, arguing that in every case, for every judge, if both dimensions of constructive interpretation are satisfied, the correct judicial decision is the one that eliminates injustice from the law (or recognizes that the law, properly understood, did not permit the injustice in the first place). All I want to point out here is that for the specific instances where I claim that common law review is appropriate, a judge's legal obligation to decide in accordance with her moral convictions and evaluations is consistent with a variety of jurisprudential perspectives.

2. Personal Convictions

The epistemic threshold (as I have construed it) and the practice of common law review itself are dependent on the personal convictions of the judge who reviews the law or action at issue. Common law review is dependent on the individual moral convictions of the common law judge. In the previous chapter, I explained that common law review is inconsistent with the belief that a judge's legal deliberations and determinations should be kept isolated and insulated from her moral beliefs. Now I want to consider the claim that a judge should and must consider morality when reaching legal decisions but that the moral beliefs the judge should consider are the community's rather than her own.

This is the view of Benjamin Cardozo, Melvin Eisenberg, Christopher Eisgruber, John Rawls, and others.[13] Although Eisenberg's preoccupation is common law adjudication, he recognizes that the same principles apply broadly in constitutional (and statutory) adjudication as well.[14] While this is an initially attractive position, it fails to account for certain difficulties raised in the previous chapter.[15] The community as a whole may share a moral view that is abhorrent and that has led to abhorrent legislation. Directing a judge to consider the community's moral beliefs will do nothing to correct injustice when those beliefs precipitated the injustice and perpetuate its existence.[16]

Common law review, then, involves the judge's own individual moral convictions. The epistemic threshold, as it operates in common law review, leaves to the judge alone the determination of whether and when the certainty and gravity prongs have been met. In these respects, common law review is quite close to a view expressed by Kent Greenawalt:

> Where authoritative legal sources leave an issue genuinely in doubt, I think a judge properly decides in accordance with firm convictions of moral rightness and social welfare that command wide support, even if these convictions are at variance with the theory that would best justify

existing legal standards. Indeed, if the judge's convictions are very firm and if the issue involved is of great moral or social significance, I think a judge may follow these convictions even if he does not think they are shared by most members of the community. A judge is an agent for change in the law in marginal cases and, just as a legislator, he sometimes may rely on his own strongly held views in preference to those of the community . . . Usually a judge will assume his own perspectives have broad support because his own intensive consideration of a problem may seem to him the best indicia of what others think or would think if they gave the problem equally serious thought. But I believe that a judge is sometimes justified in "striking out on his own" even when he recognizes he has little support. That is appropriate, however, only if his convictions are very firm and the issue involved is of great significance.[17]

Greenawalt and I walk a while together before we part ways. Our only real disagreement, albeit a significant one, is that Greenawalt believes judges should engage in this sort of critical reflection about the law only in "marginal cases," by which he means only those cases "where authoritative legal sources leave an issue genuinely in doubt."[18] I conclude, *pace* Greenawalt, that judges must sometimes engage in this normative evaluation of the law in cases where the law is absolutely clear—and absolutely unjust.

To many, my claim might seem to be contrary to a government based on the rule of law. Some might argue, at the very least, that this places far too much undiluted power in the hands of unelected judges, allowing them to enforce their subjective moral beliefs under the guise of legality. Some might argue further that even well-meaning judges will inevitably misuse this awesome authority. But contrary to these objections, common law review can be a confined, practicable doctrine. A body of case law in the United States established a legal principle and a test that require of judges precisely the sort of analytic process—based on an epistemic threshold derived directly from subjective moral convictions—that I envision for common law review. Moreover, these cases demonstrate that this sort of legal test can be implemented by judges in a principled, responsible manner.

In American law, the leading case that first established this legal concept and standard, known as the "shocks the conscience" test, is *Rochin v. California*.[19] Some factual background is necessary to appreciate fully the *Rochin* holding. The Los Angeles County Sheriff's Department was informed that Antonio Rochin was selling narcotics. Acting on this information, three sheriff's deputies entered Rochin's home on 1 July 1949 and surprised him in his bedroom, where they found two capsules on Rochin's bedside table. One of the deputies asked Rochin, "Whose stuff is this?" In response, Rochin grabbed the capsules and put them into his mouth. The deputies immediately pounced on Rochin and struggled to wrench his mouth open and forcibly extract the capsules before he could swallow them. The deputies were unsuccessful, and Rochin managed to ingest (but not digest) the capsules. The deputies then handcuffed Rochin and brought him to the nearest hospital. Acting on the deputies' instructions, a doctor snaked a tube down Rochin's throat and forced into his stomach an emetic solution that induced vomiting. From the material Rochin regurgitated, the deputies recovered two capsules that proved to contain morphine.[20]

Rochin was convicted of possession of morphine in violation of a California statute. The two capsules were the primary physical evidence against him. His conviction was upheld by the state appellate court, despite the appellate court's observation that the sheriff's deputies "were guilty of unlawfully breaking into and entering defendant's [Rochin's] room and were guilty of unlawfully assaulting and battering defendant while in the room . . . [and] of unlawfully assaulting, battering, torturing and falsely imprisoning the defendant at the . . . hospital."[21] The California Supreme Court denied Rochin's request for a hearing, over the objections of two state justices who likened the forced extraction of physical evidence from Rochin's body to a coerced confession.[22]

Writing for a unanimous Court, Justice Felix Frankfurter (a judge not known for flights of judicial fancy) reversed Rochin's conviction, introducing the "shocks the conscience" standard into American law with the following passage:

> [W]e are compelled to conclude that the proceedings by which this conviction was obtained do more than offend some fastidious squeamishness or private sentimentalism about combatting crime too energetically. This is conduct that shocks the conscience. Illegally breaking into the privacy of the petitioner [Rochin], the struggle to open his mouth and remove what was there, the forcible extraction of his stomach's contents—this course of proceeding by agents of government to obtain evidence is bound to offend even hardened sensibilities . . . Due process of law, as a historic and generative principle . . . say[s] that convictions cannot be brought about by methods that offend "a sense of justice."[23]

The shocks the conscience test is concerned with the moral reactions and convictions of individual federal judges. Governmental action offensive to judges' personal consciences and senses of justice violates the *Rochin* standard.[24] In this respect, the shocks the conscience test differs subtly from the "evolving standards of decency" inquiry used to determine whether a particular form of criminal punishment should be considered cruel and unusual under the Eighth Amendment.[25] The evolving standards of decency assessment requires judges to ascertain the prevailing moral beliefs of the community when determining whether a constitutional violation has occurred. In contrast to the evolving standards of decency inquiry, the shocks the conscience test appeals directly to the judge's personal moral convictions—not to the community's moral beliefs—when evaluating the constitutionality of certain categories of government action.

The shocks the conscience test is a formulation of the substantive due process protections of the Fourteenth Amendment. The test and that amendment are intended "to prevent government 'from abusing [its] power, or employing it as an instrument of oppression.'"[26] As I demonstrated in chapters 5 and 6, this is the same purpose that grounds *Bonham* and *Calder,* and this is the specific goal of common law review.

As established by *Rochin,* substantive due process prevents government from exercising public power in a manner that shocks the conscience. Substantive due process also prohibits government from interfering with rights "implicit in the concept of ordered liberty."[27] I concentrate here on *Rochin,* but it is worth remembering, in the context of the relationship of common law review to broader themes of constitutionalism, that both the shocks the conscience test and the values implicit in the concept of ordered liberty are attempts by the judiciary to articulate principled legal limitations on republican government and to protect the judicial process itself from abuse or misuse.[28] From the beginning, the Supreme Court has articulated the meaning and scope of due process liberties under the Fourteenth Amendment by explicit reference to Anglo-American common law principles and traditions, which concomitantly define fundamental freedoms and prevent undue governmental interference with those freedoms.[29]

The general substantive due process protection afforded by the Fourteenth Amendment relates to and controls governmental actions by both the legislative and the executive branches.[30] Currently, however, the shocks the conscience test is applicable only to abuses of power or egregious actions by agents of the executive branch of government.[31] There is no theoretical or practical impediment, though, to the test's application in the legislative context as well. Even Justice Scalia, a critic of the test,[32] acknowledges its apparent suitability to abuses of legislative power[33] and suggests that the test has on one occasion been referenced by the Supreme Court when reviewing legislative action.[34] In any event, the applicability of the test directly to the judicial evaluation of legislation is a tangential point. Of most interest to me and of most importance to my argument are the ways that the test helps me to counter criticisms of common law review.

To those critics who would assert that common law review is impractical, improperly permits judges to rely on their subjective moral convictions, or would lead inevitably to judicial misuse, I would respond that the shocks the conscience test addresses and deflates all of these concerns. The test has proven to be a flexible and viable doctrine in U.S. law for decades, without evidence of judicial abuse. Furthermore, the criticism that common law review permits judges to rely on their moral convictions when deciding cases fails to recognize that this is and has always been an intrinsic attribute of common law adjudication, even in what we now call constitutional cases. As I have argued at length, the common law has always expected its judges to engage their moral faculties whenever they are judging.[35] The shocks the conscience test overtly integrates this feature of common law adjudication into an explicit legal standard.

The test provides a close analogy for common law review. Like common law review, it is both notional and normative, conjoining a judge's moral convictions and evaluations with her legal obligations and determinations; it expressly incorporates a threshold moral determination into a legal standard against which governmental action is assessed; it requires that this threshold moral determination be made by individual judges in the light of their own moral faculties and sensibilities; and it is an especially stringent legal standard that will be met only in extreme situations.[36] As with common law review, when the test has been satisfied, the offensive governmental action is voided of its legal effect. Also as with common law review, review of government action under the test is uniquely a judicial responsibility: "because ensuring that the government does not trample in an unconscionable manner on individual dignity is a bed-rock duty of judicial officers."[37]

The shocks the conscience test helps me to show that common law review is not the radical or romantic notion it might first appear to be. Common law review can be viewed as an adaptation and application of a legal test for assessing executive abuses of power to the legislative context. Common law review simply transposes the analytic method of the shocks the conscience test to legislative as well as executive action, and where an abuse of governmental power has occurred, common law review affords judges the same authority found in *Rochin*. Common law review says that what binds police officers binds legislators, too.

The analytic method that I argue is appropriate for common law review might initially seem unconventional but is well established and has been widely employed in U.S. courts since long before *Rochin* was decided. Common law review and the shocks the conscience test both leave room in the law for a judge's personal convictions. They both ensure that the law will not permit judges—and judges will not permit the law—to sanction government action deeply offensive to the judge's individual sense of justice:

> Practical considerations can be used to resolve many constitutional issues that do not turn on disagreement over moral or political ultimates. But what about the issues that cannot be resolved so? The judge has two choices. One is to say that if public opinion is divided on a moral issue, courts should leave its resolution to the political process. The other is to say, with Holmes, that while the political process is ordinarily the right way to go, every once in a while an issue on which public opinion is divided so excites the judge's moral emotions that he simply cannot stomach the political resolution that has been challenged . . . That is the position in which the first Justice Harlan found himself in *Plessy v. Ferguson* and in which Holmes found himself from time to time . . . I prefer the second route . . . It leaves a place for conscience . . . [A judge's] refusal to enforce a law "as written" because it violates his deepest moral feelings—is a significant datum.[38]

The preceding quotation leads me to a further response to the objection that common law review leaves judges free to impose their subjective moral beliefs onto and into the law. Judge Henry Friendly once noted that "while the *Rochin* test, 'conduct that shocks the conscience,' is not one that can be applied by a computer, it at least points the way."[39] Friendly's characteristically trenchant observation is well taken. Neither the shocks the conscience test nor common law review can be applied by a computer. Nor should we wish they could be. As I have emphasized throughout my discussion of common law review, common law adjudication requires the infusion of human values into the law through the efforts of judges to reach decisions informed by their own experiences and evaluations, tempered by reason, reflection, and, as stated in the *Rochin* opinion, "the habit of self-discipline and self-criticism, incertitude that one's own views are incontestable and alert tolerance toward views not shared."[40] "[T]hese are," as Frankfurter stressed in *Rochin*, "precisely the presuppositions of our judicial process. They are precisely the qualities society has a right to expect from those entrusted with . . . judicial power."[41] We want judges, not computers, deciding cases.

B. Adjudging a Statute Void: The Form and Exercise of Common Law Review

In the previous section, I mentioned that common law review permits judges to void the legal effect of governmental action. This hearkens back to an issue raised by *Bonham*. What does it mean to adjudge a statute void? Adjudging a statute void amounts to a statement of invalidity, the impact of which varies in different legal systems and in different circumstances within the same legal system.[42] Earlier, I identified this as a contingent fact about the form of this judicial power.[43]

It seems to me that there are three things we might mean when we say that a court has adjudged a statute void. First, we could mean that the court, in its written opinion, declared the statute inconsistent with its nation's body of law and legal principle but did not bind the parties in any fashion or otherwise impair the statute's viability. An example of this sort of authority is found in the power of the English judiciary to issue a "declaration of incompatibility" in accordance with the Human Rights Act of 1998.[44] Second, we could mean that the court refused to apply or enforce the statute against a particular party in a particular case but did not excise the statute from the nation's body of law (although the court's written opinion will then become a part of that jurisdiction's precedential material). Third, we could mean that the court refused to enforce the law in a given case, with the effect that the law has no further legal existence and is eliminated as a legal source, as though the statute never existed. This is the power and effect of constitutional review in the U.S. legal system.[45] I will refer to these three possible meanings of adjudging a statute void as "declaration," "repudiation," and "elimination," respectively.

Common law review (as I conceive it) calls for something more than declaration, because declaration permits judicial enforcement of an unjust statute against the litigants who are before the court. Declaration leaves the obligation to change the law to the legislature, and as I have already explained, this is an unsatisfactory solution to the problems posed by unjust laws.[46] Although elimination is inoffensive to me and not inconsistent with the overall theory, common law review does not necessitate a judicial power of elimination. So long as the judge is legally empowered to refuse to enforce a law that she determines to be intolerably unjust, there is no necessity that her judgment result in the offending law's complete eradication from the corpus of legal sources.

Some might say that even in the absence of an acknowledged power to eliminate offending legislation, a judicial authority to refuse to enforce unjust statutes is itself sufficient to remove the statute from the jurisdiction's body of legal sources.[47] I do not go this far. My goal is only to establish the judicial authority to refuse to enforce unjust laws in particular cases. I am willing to concede that these statutes may retain legal status and force until they are formally repealed or abolished by an authority acknowledged within the given governmental and legal system as possessing that power. The resulting status of these unjust laws following judicial repudiation is not my primary concern (although a judge's explicit refusal to enforce the statute will undoubtedly impair its legal force to some degree). The principal objectives of common law review are to ensure a judge's legal ability and authority to spare parties from the consequences of an unjust law and to allow the judge to contribute a candid written opinion as a source of precedent that explains the reasons for her refusal, without unduly altering the allocation of powers within the governmental system. Accordingly, repudiation is the form of judicial power common law review requires.

C. Applying and Developing the Law: Common Law Review, Stare Decisis, and Legislative Supremacy

Judges, I have argued, have two fundamental legal obligations: to apply the law and to develop the law. Unjust laws bring these obligations into conflict. When a judge is asked to enforce an unjust law, the obligation to develop the law overrides the obligation to apply the law. I will now explain, with more precision, exactly how these two obligations interact. More specifically, I will explain how common law review (as the legal doctrine embracing the judicial obligation to develop the law) can coexist with stare decisis and legislative supremacy (the legal bases for the judicial obligation to apply the law). In addition, I will continue to examine these fundamental judicial obligations in the context of threats to the judiciary as an institution traditionally charged with ensuring that the government acts in accordance with the rule of law. In other words, I will continue to examine how common law review relates to, reinforces, and reflects common law constitutionalism.

A bit later in this chapter, I will discuss a legislative challenge to the judicial obligation to ensure the legality of government action in the form of statutory provisions that attempt to strip the courts of jurisdiction to review acts of the government. In the next section, I consider a perceived threat to the courts' institutional integrity stemming from the decision of a state high court. The case example in the next section also happens to involve the reaction of an appellate court judge to a decision of the high court in his jurisdiction. Regardless of what one ultimately concludes about the ability of lower court judges to resist decisions of high courts, this case also raises important questions about the obligation of judges to maintain the character of the judicial institution against challenges to the judiciary's institutional integrity, whether derived from legislation, executive action, or judicial decision.

1. Stare Decisis

Stare decisis requires judges to enforce precedent, and legislative supremacy (or primacy) requires judges to enforce statutes. The epistemic threshold provides an analytic tool with which judges determine when their obligation to enforce precedents or statutes is overridden by their obligation to develop the law. At least where horizontal stare decisis is concerned, there is no reason to think that common law review's relationship with stare decisis presents any unusual difficulties for high courts and appellate courts beyond those encountered by judges whenever they decide to deviate from precedent. These cases always force judges to balance stability against substance. Ordinarily, social and legal interests in certainty, predictability, and the satisfaction of litigants' expectations will tip the balance in favor of stare decisis and the status quo. Occasionally, however, when a particular precedent strikes judges as importantly mistaken, the balance will tip toward the improvement of the law's substantive merit, the departure from precedent, and the establishment of a new rule.[48]

To be sure, different judges, lawyers, and theorists will conclude that the balance between stability and substance should be measured in different ways. But as a matter of principle, the attempt to achieve this balance has always been at the heart of the common law judicial process:

> [S]tare decisis has never been used . . . as an excuse for judicial inaction that amounts to an abandonment of this court's duty to guide and develop the common law of this State. "Our common law, which is of judicial origin, is comprised of broad, flexible principles that find their source in fundamental values of justice, logic, and common sense, and

is adapted by the judiciary according to the changing demands of our society" . . . "We find no wisdom in abdicating to the legislature our essential function of re-evaluating common-law concepts in light of present day realities. Nor do we find judicial sagacity in continually looking backward and parroting the words and analysis of other courts so as to embalm for posterity the legal concepts of the past." As these principles demonstrate, the rule of stare decisis is not "so static that it deprives the court of all power to develop the law . . . [T]he maintenance of stability in our legal concepts does not and should not occupy a preeminent position over the judiciary's obligation to reconsider legal rules that have become inequitable."[49]

The common law has always permitted horizontal stare decisis to yield to the judicial obligation to develop the law. The area of vertical stare decisis is where problems arise.[50] Here, I embark on the most unorthodox part of my argument. In those extreme circumstances where a judge is firmly convinced that the epistemic threshold has been breached, common law review permits the judge to refuse to enforce precedent of a higher court. Having just written this, I feel the need to take a deep breath. I realize the reactions this claim is likely to elicit. Yet even this claim is not without legal foundation.

There are rare cases where trial and appellate court judges chose not to follow the precedent of the high courts of their jurisdiction.[51] One well-known example is *Barnette v. West Virginia Board of Education*,[52] where Judge Parker, sitting in a three-judge panel, declined to follow the Supreme Court's decision in *Minersville School District v. Gobitis*.[53] In *Gobitis*, the Supreme Court had held that the school district of Minersville, Pennsylvania, could legally prohibit Lillian and William Gobitis (aged twelve and ten) from attending public school, because Lillian and William refused to salute the American flag, in keeping with their religious belief (as Jehovah's Witnesses) that the Bible is the supreme authority and that a gesture of deference toward the flag was forbidden by scripture. Parker refused to follow *Gobitis*. Noting that of the seven sitting members of the Supreme Court who participated in *Gobitis,* four had publicly expressed their belief that the decision was incorrect. Parker also cited a later case in which the majority of the Court declined to rely on *Gobitis* as authority.[54] Parker's decision was vindicated; the Supreme Court upheld his ruling and overruled *Gobitis*.[55]

Helpful as *Barnette* is to my argument, Parker's reliance on critical public statements by sitting justices limits its relevance somewhat for my purposes. Another case provides an even more compelling example of a judge refusing, for reasons of principle and conscience, to follow precedent of a higher court. This case is *Morrow v. Hood Communications, Inc.*,[56] in which the California Court of Appeal addressed the enforcement of a stipulated reversal of judgment.

Unique to California law, stipulated reversals were sanctioned by the California Supreme Court's decision in *Neary v. Regents of University of California*.[57] As authorized by *Neary*, in the absence of "extraordinary circumstances," a stipulated reversal permits litigants to facilitate the settlement of a lawsuit by filing a joint application to an appellate court seeking the *pro forma* reversal of a trial court judgment, without any contention that the trial court judgment is legally deficient in any way. As support for the practice of stipulated reversals, the *Neary* majority relied on the public policy favoring settlement of litigation, the courts' power to control judicial proceedings, the appellate courts' inherent authority to reverse trial court rulings, and the inability of trial courts to establish binding precedent.[58] In reaching its decision, the *Neary* majority reversed the decision of the California Court of Appeal and rejected the reasoning of dissenting California Supreme Court Justice Joyce Kennard.

Fundamental to the *Neary* majority's disagreement with the Court of Appeal and Justice Kennard are two points. First, Kennard and the Court of Appeal shared concerns about the purpose of the judicial process and the judicial system. Kennard argued: "[M]ore than just a dispute resolution service, the judiciary is an integral part of our government. Working in the context of actual disputes . . . when a trial court renders judgment in a particular case, it is not just deciding who wins and who loses, who pays and who recovers. Rather, the ultimate purpose of a judgment is to administer the laws of this state, and thereby to do substantial justice."[59] Second, the Court of Appeal noted the value of the trial court's decision as a source of guidance and precedent for judges and lawyers.[60]

The *Neary* majority challenged both of these points. Regarding the purpose of the judicial institution, the *Neary* majority stated: "[T]he primary purpose of the public judiciary is 'to afford a forum for the settlement of litigable matters between disputing parties' . . . [T]he Court of Appeal's concern for the integrity of trial court judgments is flawed . . . [T]he notion that such a judgment is a statement of 'legal truth' places too much emphasis on the result of litigation rather than its purpose."[61] Where the precedential value of the trial court's decision is concerned, the *Neary* majority reasoned that trial court decisions have no such value, since "trial courts make no binding precedents."[62] Underlying the *Neary* court's view on this point are the nested, unstated premises that a court's opinion must be precedent to have value and that a court's decision must be binding to be precedent. This was not the California Court of Appeal's understanding of precedent, and as I have already explained, it is not mine, either.

With this discussion of *Neary* in mind, we can look at *Morrow*. *Morrow* involved an application by litigants for a stipulated reversal of a trial court judgment. *Morrow* came before the Court of Appeal five years after *Neary* was decided. *Neary* was, under applicable principles of vertical stare decisis, binding precedent for the Court of Appeal. Nevertheless, Anthony Kline, presiding justice of the Court of Appeal, declined to follow *Neary:*

> There are rare instances in which a judge of an inferior court can properly refuse to acquiesce in the precedent established by a court of superior jurisdiction. This is, for me, such an instance. I acknowledge that the opinion of the California Supreme Court in *Neary v. Regents of University of California* requires that the motion before us be granted. I would deny the motion, however, because I cannot as a matter of conscience apply the rule announced in *Neary* . . . based on my deeply felt opinion that the doctrine of stipulated reversal announced in *Neary* . . . is destructive of judicial institutions. The debate in *Neary* pertains to the role of the courts . . . The judicial responsibility is fundamentally public . . . [Judicial] "officials, like members of the legislative and executive branches, possess a power that has been defined and conferred by public law, not by private agreement. Their job is not to maximize the ends of private parties, nor simply to secure the peace, but to explicate and give force to the values embodied in authoritative texts such as the Constitution and statutes: to interpret those values and to bring reality into accord with them" . . . The parties in this case waived a jury and submitted their dispute to the Honorable Harlan K. Veal, Judge of the San Mateo Superior Court. After conducting a public trial, Judge Veal made a variety of factual determinations and on that basis rendered judgment for the plaintiff. For reasons not revealed by the record, the defendants induced the plaintiff to agree to the reversal of that judgment as a condition of settlement. This bargain would have been pointless unless defendants believed our order would cast doubt on the validity or force of the judgment of the trial court. The parties have not, however, even claimed, let alone shown, that the judgment rendered by Judge Veal is erroneous in any way, and it remains presumptively correct. The reversal of such a judgment is either a travesty or a charade. In either case, I refuse to participate . . . My conscientious refusal to acquiesce is not designed to offend our Supreme Court, for which I have the most profound respect. It is constitutionally justified and, I hope, constructive.[63]

Kline's opinion demonstrates that, while rare, it is not unheard of for lower court judges to refuse to enforce higher court decisions as required by vertical stare decisis.[64] In certain exigent circumstances,[65] judges may follow their convictions, rather than precedent. Moreover, these rare circumstances need not undermine the structure or stability of a hierarchical judicial system. Kline went on to observe in *Morrow*: "So long as the lower court may still be reversed by the higher court, there is no interference with either the 'supremacy' of the Supreme Court or with the idea of the rule of law . . . Indeed, quite to the contrary, such 'underruling' may be an essential part of the process of judicial self-correction."[66]

A judge who declines to enforce an unjust precedent in accordance with his deeply felt beliefs and who records the reasons for his refusal in a candid opinion contributes as much as he can within his defined role to the development of the law, even where his opinion is written in dissent or is certain to be reversed on appeal to a higher court.[67] It is incumbent on the judge in the lower court to enunciate for the law his best reasoned opinion as to why he believes his refusal to enforce an unjust law is legally justified, because "society does not have such confidence in the superior wisdom of higher judges that it wants their judicial inferiors to abdicate all independent judgment."[68] What the law ultimately does with the judge's opinion is not up to him. Through his conscientious effort to develop the law, the judge does as much as he can.

A doctrine as powerful and important as vertical stare decisis may succumb, in a very narrowly circumscribed set of cases, to the dictates of a judge's conscience and to his countervailing obligation to contribute to the law's development. Moreover, the hierarchical structure of the courts must be considered as a feature of the institutional nature and purpose of the judiciary. In *Morrow*, Kline concluded that the integrity of the judicial process was his paramount consideration, even when viewed from his place within the judicial hierarchy, because ultimately the hierarchical structure of the courts exists to maintain the integrity of the institution. In the extraordinary circumstances of *Morrow*, Kline ultimately determined that his obligation to the integrity of his institution outweighed even his place within the hierarchy of that institution. Even though judges cannot bind courts above them in the hierarchy, this does not mean that the judges' decisions are without worth or influence: "decisions of . . . [lower] courts may persuade other courts by the force of the supporting rationale."[69]

As I argued in the previous chapter, judges at every level of the hierarchy owe to the law and to the public the benefit of their rationale. This is true of trial court judges and judges writing in dissent. This is true even where a judge finds himself alone in his convictions, with an opinion that is likely to be little more than a still small voice in the legal wilderness.[70] In fact, these may be the most important occasions for a judge to record his reasons. He is speaking not to his colleagues but to his successors; he is speaking to the future.[71] Neither horizontal nor vertical stare decisis can overcome the judge's obligation to develop the law in those rare cases where a judge concludes, after careful reflection, that the law undermines the institutional integrity of the court or is otherwise fundamentally unjust. Once the epistemic threshold has been reached, "a decided case is worth," as one opinion puts it, "as much as it weighs in reason and righteousness, and no more."[72]

Though issued in dissent, Kline's principled refusal to follow *Neary* met with heated resistance.[73] The California Commission on Judicial Performance filed judicial misconduct charges against him that could have resulted in censure or removal from the bench.[74] But Americans overwhelmingly understood that he should not, as a judge, be subjected to disciplinary action for registering his opinions about the law and his legal responsibilities.[75] In fact, in response to the commission's action against Kline, the California legislature passed two statutes, one of which would prohibit the commission "from disciplining judges for issuing opinions that are legally incorrect or issuing dissents that do not follow the precedent of a higher court."[76]

The California legislature was not finished, however. No doubt due in part to Kline's opinion in *Morrow*, the California legislature significantly limited the practice of stipulated reversal in California courts. The statute that took effect on 1 January 2000 stated:

> An appellate court shall not reverse or vacate a duly entered judgment upon an agreement or stipulation of the parties unless the court finds both of the following: (A) There is no reasonable possibility that the interests of nonparties or the public will be adversely affected by the reversal. (B) The reasons of the parties for requesting reversal outweigh the erosion of public trust that may result from the nullification of a judgment and the risk that the availability of stipulated reversal will reduce the incentive for pretrial settlement.[77]

The influence of Kline's and Kennard's dissents is manifest in this statute. The factors delineated in the statute are evident throughout the opinions of both justices.[78] Kline and Kennard wrote their dissenting opinions in a concerted effort to improve California law. Kline's dissent in *Morrow* went even further. Out of respect for the judicial institution and the public interest, and despite the strong pull of vertical stare decisis, Kline refused to follow a higher court precedent. Now Kline's opinion is itself a source of guidance and legal reasoning to which other judges can turn in the future, when their consciences call to them to forestall injustice or unfairness, to improve the law.

2. Legislative Supremacy

The dialogue between California's courts and its legislature about the efficacy and equity of stipulated reversals, resulting in the legislature's statutory enactment, is a good illustration of courts and legislature working together to ensure the law's overall fairness. The California example is just one instance of cooperation between courts and legislatures in their joint responsibility to ensure that the law is as just and fair as possible. The courts and the legislature operate with the awareness that "ultimately, common law and statute law coalesce in one legal system."[79] Although there are, without question, occasions of friction between governmental branches, the judiciary and the legislature are not engaged in an internecine battle to grab and maintain the lion's share of legal power. Generally speaking, each views and treats the other's legal pronouncements with deference and respect.

The reciprocal deference and respect of legislatures and judiciaries in common law jurisdictions helps to illustrate that judicial review, in its constitutional or common law incarnation, need not undermine the legal or political authority of the legislature. When a court refuses to enforce a statute, the legislature will usually accept that the court is acting out of its best judgment about the law and will frequently alter or amend the statute in response to the courts' concerns.[80] For their part, courts are circumspect in exercising this power, because they recognize that the legislature acts, most of the time, out of its best judgment about the interests of the nation and the majority of its citizens.[81] The relational structure of our governmental institutions imparts the principal lawmaking function to the legislature, in any event. This is what I have called legislative primacy. Moreover, the judiciary's respect for legislative primacy is not inconsistent with a recognized legal power of judicial review:

> [I]t is as much our inclination, as it is our duty, to receive with all possible respect every act of the Legislature, and that we never can find ourselves in a more painful situation than to be obliged to object to the ex-

ecution of any [act] . . . But . . . we are under the indispensable necessity of acting according to the best dictates of our own judgment, after duly weighing every consideration that can occur to us.[82]

This balance between legislative primacy and judicial responsibility is aptly expressed in David Dyzenhaus's notion of "deference as respect." As Dyzenhaus describes it, this notion invokes not the idea of deference "in its primary Oxford English Dictionary meaning of submission to the commands of an authority" but, rather, "deference according to the secondary meaning, deference as respect—a judicial attitude of respectful attention to the reasons which are or could be offered in support of a legal authority's decision."[83] The notion of deference as respect requires judges not to countermand legislation unless (1) there is no formulation or interpretation of the statute that can save it from its defects and (2) there is no other basis on which the case could be decided.[84] When legislation cannot be saved, however, it falls to the courts to renounce it, and deference must yield to duty. As Chief Justice Marshall noted in *Fletcher,* judges must be reluctant to exercise their authority to interfere with legislative pronouncements yet unafraid to meet their duty when absolutely necessary:

> The question, whether a law be void for its repugnancy to the constitution, is, at all times, a question of much delicacy, which ought seldom, if ever, to be decided in the affirmative, in a doubtful case. The court, when impelled by duty to render such a judgment, would be unworthy of its station, could it be unmindful of the solemn obligations which that station imposes. But it is not on slight implication and vague conjecture that the legislature is to be pronounced to have transcended its powers, and its acts to be considered as void. The opposition between the constitution and the law should be such that the judge feels a clear and strong conviction of their incompatibility with each other.[85]

With its references to the judge's necessarily "clear and strong conviction" that cannot be satisfied by "slight implication and vague conjecture" and to the "solemn obligations" that the judge's "station imposes," the preceding passage appropriately characterizes the judicial attitude that underpins common law review's epistemic threshold. Common law review permits a judge to refuse to apply a statute only when no other avenue (apart from enforcement, resignation, or prevarication) is left open to him. In its application to common law review, the notion of deference as respect does not threaten the authority of the legislature. In all but the most extraordinary cases, judges will enforce the law as the legislature has enacted it: "Judges must, except when exercising the power of judicial review, defer to the decisions of legislatures."[86] But deference as respect and common law review indicate that deference does not demand undeviating subservience. Just as deference and judicial independence are not mutually exclusive, neither are deference and legislative primacy.[87]

The need to balance stability and substance in the legal system requires courts and legislatures to respect each other's decisions, even though they will sometimes disagree. The need to balance stability and substance in the law requires judges to offset their respectful deference toward the decisions of the legislature or another court against their independent assessment of the law's fairness and ongoing development.[88] In the end, balancing stability and substance demands that judges must weigh their obligations to apply the law and to develop the law. In most cases, the doctrines that contribute to the law's stability—stare decisis and legislative supremacy—will carry the day. In some cases, however, a judge will conclude that something weightier sits on the other side of the scales. In these cases, the judge's obligation is to contribute what he can to the law's development, to work the law pure. When balancing the obligation to apply the law against the obligation to develop the law, common law review attempts to free judges from an excessively formalistic perception of legal doctrines, such as legislative supremacy and stare decisis. According to common law review, "judges would frankly recognize both that legislative supremacy does not entail that courts *always* follow legislative rules, and that faithfulness to higher courts does not entail that lower courts *always* follow their rules."[89]

D. Common Law Principles and Rule-of-Law Values: The Example of Ouster Clauses

In thinking about how common law review would operate in practice, it might be helpful to explore in more detail some concrete contemporary situations in which common law review is appropriate. In the next chapter, I will examine a specific example of a common law principle of constitutional dimension that operates to maintain constitutional limitations on government action.[90] In this chapter, I will consider an example of judges maintaining the constitutional relationship of government organs in response to legislative attempts to alter that relationship. Judges in England and the United States frequently refuse to enforce statutory provisions that purport to divest the courts of jurisdiction to review certain administrative determinations and other uses of public power. These statutory provisions that attempt to exclude certain government actions from judicial evaluation are referred to as ouster clauses, privative clauses, or jurisdiction-stripping clauses. As with Justice Kline in *Morrow,* these cases involve judges reacting to what they perceive to be a fundamental threat to the integrity of the judiciary as an institution, to their obligations as judges, and to the constitutional commitments of their government.

The most famous English case involving an ouster clause is *Anisminic.*[91] In *Anisminic,* the House of Lords addressed the Foreign Compensation Act of 1950. The act contained an explicit ouster clause in section 4(4): "the determination by the [Foreign Compensation] Commission of any application made to them under this Act shall not be called in question in any court of law."[92] The Foreign Compensation Commission argued that the language of the statute was transparent and not open to interpretation. The appellants argued that the word "determination" in section 4(4) could refer only to a substantively valid determination rather than to a compromised determination that lacked any legal weight or import. They claimed, "[I]f you seek to show that a determination is a nullity you are not questioning the purported determination—you are maintaining that it does not exist as a determination."[93]

The House ruled in the appellants' favor. According to Lord Wilberforce, the commission misapplied the requirements of the 1950 act:

> [A]rticle 4 should be read as if it imposed three conditions only on satisfaction of which the applicant was entitled, under statutory direction, to have his claim admitted, namely—(a) that his application related to property in Egypt referred to in Annex E; (b) that he was the person referred to in Annex E paragraph (1)(a) as the owner of the property; (c) that he was a British national at the specified dates. As, ex concessis, all these conditions were fulfilled to the satisfaction of the commission, the appellants' claim was in law established; the commission by seeking to impose another condition, not warranted by the Order, was acting outside its remitted powers and made no determination of that which alone it could determine.[94]

The commission incorrectly imposed a condition on the appellants that was not statutorily required, namely, that their successor in title must be a British national.[95] Although Anisminic could not satisfy this condition, Wilberforce noted that the 1950 act did not require Anisminic to do so. In other words, the commission applied a legal test to Anisminic that the commission was not empowered to apply.

The commission could not, Wilberforce concluded, avoid judicial review of its decision under the 1950 act simply by calling its decision a determination: "The respondents' argument that the commission has only to make a self-styled 'determination' in order to enjoy automatic protection is thus at once seen to be unsustainable."[96] Wilberforce accepted the appellants' argument that some "determinations" of the commission were legal nonentities; they were nullities with no legal merit or meaning, and the ouster clause did not prevent the courts from reviewing these administrative decisions to ensure that they complied with the law. Despite the apparent clarity of section 4(4), the House refused to permit Parliament to oust its jurisdiction over an otherwise justiciable matter.[97]

Anisminic is substantial evidence for the claim that English courts will, when pressed sufficiently, refuse to enforce parliamentary legislation that is deemed to undermine the very foundation of the English judiciary's institutional competence and constitutional obligations.[98] In its support for the proposition that English courts will sometimes refuse to enforce parliamentary legislation for reasons of principle and to maintain the rule of law, *Anisminic* also supports the principle of common law review.

Similarly, U.S. courts resist perceived legislative incursions into their jurisdiction. In general, federal courts differentiate between legislative preclusion of statutory claims and legislative preclusion of constitutional claims.[99] And while federal courts will usually accede to legislative preclusion of review of statutory claims, they are much more resistant to statutory attempts to preclude judicial review of substantial constitutional claims. *Webster v. Doe*[100] is a characteristic example in this regard. *Webster* involved an employee of the Central Intelligence Agency who was dismissed due to his sexual orientation. Doe sued the agency, in the person of the director, for statutory and constitutional violations. The agency responded that section 102(c) of the National Security Act[101] precluded judicial review of the director's termination decision under the Administrative Procedure Act. Specifically, section 701(a) of the APA stated: "This chapter applies, according to the provisions thereof, except to the extent that—(1) statutes preclude judicial review; or (2) agency action is committed to agency discretion by law."[102] The agency argued that the National Security Act, read in conjunction with section 701(a) of the APA, precluded any court from reviewing Doe's statutory and constitutional claims.

The Supreme Court accepted the agency's argument that Doe's statutory claims were precluded from review. But the Court rejected the agency's claim that "no matter what the nature of respondent's constitutional claims, judicial review is precluded by the language and intent of § 102(c) . . . [because] all Agency employment termination decisions, even those based on policies normally repugnant to the Constitution, are given over to the absolute discretion of the Director, and are hence unreviewable under the APA."[103] Writing for the Court, Chief Justice Rehnquist refused to view section 102(c) as ousting its jurisdiction over Doe's claims of constitutional violation:

> We do not think § 102(c) may be read to exclude review of constitutional claims. We emphasized [in several cases] . . . that where Congress intends to preclude judicial review of constitutional claims its intent to do so must be clear. We require this heightened showing in part to avoid the "serious constitutional question" that would arise if a federal statute were construed to deny any judicial forum for a colorable constitutional claim.[104]

Rehnquist's opinion in *Webster* bears, in many respects, a strong family resemblance to such English decisions as *Anisminic*. In these cases, the Supreme Court and the House of Lords seem to be saying that Congress and Parliament might assert the theoretical authority to extinguish any judicial review of the legality of certain administrative actions. However, these cases also indicate that Congress and Parliament cannot entirely strip the judiciary of its constitutional role and institutional authority to ensure that the government acts in accordance with the law.[105]

Despite the presence of legislative supremacy and the absence of a written constitution in England and the absence of legislative supremacy and the presence of a written constitution in the United States, English and American courts respond to statutory ouster clauses in strikingly similar ways. These judicial responses to legislative attempts to circumvent or eliminate the courts' traditional constitutional role demonstrate the commitments of the Anglo-American legal tradition to the rule of law and to an independent judiciary that maintains legal limitations on government through the recognition and enforcement of fundamental rights and principles.[106] These commitments are actually more meaningful indicators of the nature of the Anglo-American legal and political structure than either the existence of a written constitution or references to parliamentary sovereignty. I explore the relationship between common law constitutionalism and legislative power (and the *ultra vires* doctrine) in more detail in the next chapter. For now, my point is that the decisions of courts in England

and the United States demonstrate that judges will not lightly permit their jurisdiction to be ousted and their constitutional obligations to be extinguished by legislative provisions. To maintain constitutional commitments to rule-of-law values, the courts of the United States and of the United Kingdom recognize fundamental principles through which those commitments are enforced in court. A useful example, taken from English law, of a specific fundamental common law principle that functions at a constitutional level to ensure the maintenance of rule-of-law values is the right of access to the courts.[107] I discuss another of these principles in chapter 9.

In chapter 5, I considered the connection between the correct reading of *Bonham* and the coequal position of the organs of government in common law systems. The refusal of English and American judges to permit ouster clauses to undermine their institutional authority to ensure that public power is exercised only within legal constraints is another reflection of this constitutional balance and relationship of powers. English and American cases establish that in the view of judges, their power to review the constitutionality of government action is intrinsic to the Anglo-American commitment to the rule of law. English judges and American judges use different terms to describe the fundamental rights and principles involved when individuals raise constitutional challenges to the actions of government. However the principles are described, though, the consistency of the courts' reactions and the shared refusal of English and American judges to accept legislative preclusion of their jurisdiction is a noteworthy demonstration of the realization of common law constitutionalism in the preservation of jurisdiction to review the legal legitimacy of government action.[108]

E. Responding to Radbruch

Before concluding my discussion of the analytic features and practical applications of common law review, I should try to preempt a possible misunderstanding. In previous chapters, I described some distinctions between common law and natural law in the analysis of English and U.S. case law. I should also explain an important and related distinction at a more theoretical level. In the wake of World War II and the fall of the National Socialist government in Germany, Gustav Radbruch renounced legal positivism as partially to blame for the acquiescence of so many German lawyers and officials in the atrocities committed by the Nazis in the name of law.[109] In their famous exchange in the *Harvard Law Review,* H. L. A. Hart and Lon Fuller debated the accuracy of Radbruch's conclusion that positivism was partly responsible for the legal injustices of the Third Reich.[110] Rather than enter into the debate over Radbruch's claim that positivism engendered submission to the Nazi subversion of German law, which is not my concern here, I want to address a possible response to my argument that relates to the discussion of Radbruch by Hart and Fuller.

Radbruch was a German legal theorist writing about a period in German legal history. Despite this distance from the common law tradition, considerations of Nazi law unavoidably influence almost any contemporary analysis of unjust laws. Moreover (and more to the point), some might think that my argument about judicial resistance to injustice in the common law tradition draws on or substantially reproduces claims made by Radbruch. This is the possible misapprehension that I want to prevent. In his renunciation of positivism, Radbruch developed an orientation toward unjust laws that is now referred to as the "Radbruch formula." Robert Alexy explains that this formula has two parts. The first part is the claim "that positive law loses its legal validity when its contradiction with justice reaches an 'intolerable level.'"[111] The second part of the formula states that positive law is denied legal status when equality is deliberately disavowed in its enactment or, in other words, when "justice is not even aimed at."[112] Alexy restates the formula more straightforwardly: "appropriately enacted and socially effective norms lose their legal character or their legal validity when they are extremely unjust," or "extreme injustice is no law."[113] Julian Rivers notes that by denying the legal validity or character of powerfully unjust laws, Radbruch's formula "is none other than a modern day version of Augustine's *lex iniusta non est lex,* with the gloss that the *iniusta* must be extreme."[114]

Given the emphasis earlier in this chapter on the severity of the injustice involved as a dispositive criterion for the exercise of common law review through the epistemic threshold and on the obligation of common law judges to refuse enforcement of egregiously unjust laws via what I have called repudiation, it might seem that my argument tracks Radbruch's formula. This is not the case, however, for two reasons. First, I do not argue that law loses its legal validity when it reaches an intolerable level of injustice. On my account, unjust laws are still laws. In fact, my argument about judicial function and obligation within the common law tradition requires that unjust laws retain their character as laws no matter how unjust they might be. To take a famous example, if Parliament enacted a statute requiring the execution of all blue-eyed babies,[115] simply denying that the law possessed any validity *ab initio* as law would misrepresent and oversimplify the problems created by that law. The purpose of my argument is to acknowledge that such an intolerably unjust law possesses legal validity and then to consider whether any systemic response to such a law is available within the common law tradition. Rather than attempt to convert common law tradition into natural law theory, I attempt to offer an argument grounded in the doctrine and nature of the common law itself.

Second, I do not claim that enacted law loses its legal status whenever a deliberate disavowal of equality or failure to aim at justice occurs during the legislative process. Again, I assume the opposite. I assume that the proposed law against blue-eyed babies would retain its status as law even if Parliament deliberately disavowed equality and did not attempt to aim at justice during its enactment. Radbruch's formula is an attempt to avoid the problems posed by unjust laws by denying that they are laws. My argument is an attempt to address the problems posed by unjust laws by exploring these problems within the legal sources and concepts of the common law tradition. My argument is not a general argument about the nature of law; it is a contextual argument about the doctrines and concepts of the common law. Of course, very few natural lawyers have ever accepted the *lex injusta* formula endorsed by Radbruch.[116] Part of the reason for this is that saying unjust laws are not laws will not make them go away. An attempt to address the difficulties raised by unjust laws must begin with the recognition that they are laws. The neutralization of unjust laws requires that an institution within a legal tradition respond based on legal arguments from within that tradition's sources, concepts, and history.

Rivers attempts to integrate Radbruch's formula into a common law framework by relying on theories of interpretation.[117] According to Rivers, such integration would mean that we do not have to deny entirely the legal validity of unjust laws. Instead, he argues, we could place the possible interpretations of an unjust law on the scale of political morality and conclude that the adoption of "an interpretation that deviates grossly from that indicated by conventional canons of interpretation, requires a very strong appeal to abstract justice if it is to be legitimate."[118]

For the reasons I explained in chapter 3, I do not believe that theories of interpretation can extricate us from the quandaries created by unjust laws. For similar reasons, Rivers's effort to resuscitate Radbruch's formula by turning to interpretation is unpersuasive. In the end, no appeal to abstract justice, however compelling, can legitimate a desired result that is fundamentally groundless in a given legal system. Natural lawyers can be common lawyers—John Finnis is one—but Radbruch's *lex injusta* formula cannot be harmonized with the common law's sources, method, and history.

Rivers seems to concede this point, to some extent. In the following passage, he contrasts the challenges unjust laws pose for judges during and after the existence of an evil regime:

> In one sense, adjudication becomes easier under an evil regime. The requirements of fairness are weakened in the case of laws passed by undemocratic tyrannies, so the radical reinterpretation of such laws in accordance with standards of abstract justice is proportionately more legitimate. But the practical stakes for the conscientious judge whose conception of justice puts him at odds with the government are much higher. Certainly, he does not have to resign in advance, but he is more likely to be dismissed, or worse. Adjudication in the aftermath of an evil regime reverses the difficulties. It is politically easier, but intellectually more complex . . . [C]ourts adjudicating in the aftermath of an evil regime are only observers of an historically completed process. They cannot legitimise unfair readings of statutes in the name of integrity by appealing to the consequent reconciliation of justice and fairness within the law that their interpretation achieves.[119]

Rivers argues that it is legitimate for conscientious judges under an evil regime to reinterpret unjust laws radically in the pursuit of abstract justice. Rivers's way of expressing this form of "radical reinterpretation" seems dangerously close to what Dworkin identified as a judge lying about what the law is and saying that "the legal rights are different from what he believes they are."[120] Even if we assume that this is not what Rivers means here, I want to consider the cases where radical reinterpretation of this sort is unavailable. As I indicated in chapter 1, I do not believe that an appeal to "abstract justice"—no matter how well intentioned or morally desirable— is adequate to justify a reinterpretation of the law that lacks any foundation in common law sources. On this point, Rivers's reference to the circumstances of adjudication in the aftermath of an evil regime recalls the case of *Oppenheimer v. Cattermole.*[121]

In *Oppenheimer,* the House of Lords was forced to confront a 1941 Nazi law that deprived German Jews of their citizenship and facilitated the confiscation of their property. The House was, of course, deciding a case in the aftermath of an evil regime of a foreign nation. Nevertheless, choice-of-law doctrine required the House to consider the applicability of this Nazi law in England. The House declined to enforce the Nazi statute, concluding that it conflicted with other sources of law binding in England.[122] More specifically, there is a principle in English common law that creates an exception to the general enforcement of foreign law when the enforcement of foreign law would violate "basic principles of justice and fairness which the courts seek to apply in the administration of justice in this country."[123] *Oppenheimer* reinforces my claim that principles of justice can be invoked by judges to preclude the enforcement of unjust laws. But unlike Rivers, I argue that these principles of justice are only those articulated in common law sources, not principles of abstract justice.

F. Summing Up

I have identified eight features of common law review as it might operate in practice within an existing common law legal system. First, the epistemic threshold applicable to common law review sets exacting standards of certainty and gravity, which ensure that no judge can properly invoke common law review unless she is as certain as she can be that a mistake was made by a prior court or a legislature and that this mistake concerns a matter of grave social importance that violates the judge's deepest convictions. Second, the convictions with which common law review is concerned are the judge's own, not the judge's assessment of society's prevailing beliefs. Third, the judge alone must determine, with reference to her personal beliefs and ideals, when the epistemic threshold has been crossed. Fourth, the judge must undertake careful and comprehensive reflection and analysis before concluding that a particular law meets the epistemic threshold and triggers common law review. Fifth, if the judge finally concludes that the exercise of common law review is warranted, this authority overrides any conflicting legal principle, including stare decisis and legislative supremacy, and requires the judge to develop the law by refusing to enforce the law deemed to be unjust. Sixth, common law review empowers judges to refuse to enforce an unjust law only in particular cases; common law review does not demand that this refusal have the legal effect of striking a precedent or statute out of the body of existing law in a jurisdiction (unless the court in question is the high court of a jurisdiction whose rulings are understood to have that effect). Seventh, common law review is consistent with judicial respect for doctrines of legal stability, such as stare decisis and legislative supremacy, which are overridden only in the most drastic circumstances.[124] Finally, common law review allows the courts to resist threats to its institutional integrity and reinforces the judiciary's institutional obligation to maintain constitutional restrictions on the government and to ensure the legality of all government action.

Given all of the restrictions this conception places on the practice of common law review and given all of the other institutional constraints inherent in the judicial process,[125] there is little worry (notwithstanding the complaints of certain likely critics)[126] that common law review would leave us, adrift and listing, on a sea of judicial whim and doctrinal instability. On the contrary, the principle I have defended is narrowly confined by the epistemic threshold and the case-specific form of the common law review power. There is no reason to suppose that judges would treat this authority with any less care than they do their other responsibilities. Indeed, there is every reason to believe that judges would view this as their most solemn duty, to be exercised only with the utmost consideration and restraint and only in the rarest of cases. Rather than viewing legal authority as a scarce resource for which the legislature and the judiciary compete, common law review fits within a picture of legal authority that is shared by coordinate and cooperative governmental entities, seeking to secure, through their own institutional capacities, a body of law and a legal system that are as fair as possible to those governed by them. According to this picture, the law is limitless in its potential to achieve justice. In its realization of that potential, the law is limited only by the reason, vision, compassion, and imagination of those to whom its expression is entrusted.

9. Common Law Review in Two Common Law Systems

A. England

In this chapter, I intend to show that common law review can operate not just in the abstract but in actual common law legal systems. Given the prominence of American cases in the previous chapter's discussion, it might be tempting to think that if common law review can work anywhere, it can work only in the United States. This is incorrect. Common law review may fit most smoothly and easily (although certainly not without objection) into U.S. legal culture and practice. But common law review can fit even within the English legal tradition.

The English common law system has the most restrictive notion of stare decisis, the most monolithic conception of legislative supremacy, and the least powerful judiciary in the common law world. The confluence of these factors has led one jurisprudential provocateur to allege that England is more truly a civil law than a common law nation.[1] While this goes too far, it is one of the great ironies of legal history that the nation of the common law's birth has been perceived historically as the common law nation with the most anemic common law judiciary.[2] Of all existing common law systems, England's appears to be the least hospitable to the principle and practice of common law review. Nevertheless, I will argue in this chapter that common law review can adapt even to the English environment, and if common law review can work there, it can work anywhere (where there is an existing common law system).

I should begin by explaining, just in case it is not already apparent, why

I will not discuss the Human Rights Act of 1998 and its explicit incorporation into English law of the European Convention for the Protection of Human Rights and Fundamental Freedoms. As I have indicated, I am interested in examining common law review, not constitutional review; that is, my arguments address the common law's intrinsic constraints on abuses of legislative or executive authority, rather than those of a written constitution. So to the extent that the Human Rights Act and the European Convention represent an English Bill of Rights, they are immaterial for my purposes. Moreover, even though certain English judges apparently believe (or perhaps believed) that the absence of a written English constitution, such as the Human Rights Act and the Convention might provide, presents an impediment to their exercise of vigorous judicial review,[3] many English judges view the Human Rights Act and the Convention as largely superfluous, because English common law long ago articulated and protected the fundamental rights, principles, and values identified in the Convention.[4]

England's unwritten constitution is, in other words, a common law constitution,[5] which subjects the government to the rule of law and protects individual rights and fundamental values from infringement through abuses of power. Demonstrating that common law review can operate in England requires overcoming the doctrines of stare decisis and legislative supremacy as they are currently understood by English lawyers and judges. I will begin with stare decisis.

1. Stare Decisis

Since the issuance of the *Practice Statement of 1966,*[6] there is no question that the English House of Lords may depart from its own precedent. Therefore, horizontal stare decisis would present no extraordinary barrier for the House's acceptance of common law review. The matter is less clear where the Court of Appeal is concerned. Following the House's decision in *Davis v. Johnson,*[7] most English lawyers assume that the Court of Appeal is bound to follow its previous decisions in all civil cases.[8] But as Sir Rupert Cross and Professor James Harris explain,[9] whether the Court of Appeal is absolutely bound by its prior rulings depends on one's view of stare decisis as a legal rule prescribed by the House of Lords or as a legal rule defined by judicial practice.[10] Both views find support in English law and legal tradition.[11]

Cross and Harris point out that "the rule that the Court of Appeal is, in general, absolutely bound by its past decisions is the product of th[e mid-twentieth] century."[12] In fact, the Court of Appeal did not consider itself invariably bound by its own prior rulings for much of the twentieth century.[13] The exceedingly austere version of horizontal stare decisis found in England today is of relatively recent vintage. If stare decisis is a legal norm whose source is judicial practice, as I have argued earlier,[14] then England's version of stare decisis need not be so sclerotic. Only the conceit of the present prevents English judges and lawyers from embracing the more supple and discriminating view of precedent that prevailed in the not-too-distant past.[15] So a judge of the English Court of Appeal can find a legitimate basis in English law and legal tradition for departing from a previous Court of Appeal decision. As with the House of Lords, horizontal stare decisis need not present an insuperable obstacle to endorsement of common law review by the Court of Appeal or, at least, one of its judges.

I promised to apply common law review to common law systems as they actually exist today. One might object that by arguing that the Court of Appeal could rely on older case authority, rather than prevailing current understandings, I am sidestepping the issue. But this misapprehends the meaning of judicial practice as the basis for stare decisis as a legal standard. It is true that it would be a change in current practice for a Court of Appeal judge to depart from a Court of Appeal precedent, but judicial practices (and practice-based legal doctrines) can change only through judicial innovation. To say that this would be a change in judicial practice is not to say that the change would be improper or legally unfounded. Moreover, the presence of legal sources that support this change only strengthens the basis for the new practice; in fact, as I just discussed, this is not a new practice at all, it is a return to a previous practice, improvidently discontinued.

Horizontal stare decisis and the current practice of lockstep adherence to its own precedent need not, then, prevent the Court of Appeal from adopting common law review. What about vertical stare decisis? In its own subdued way, the Court of Appeal has occasionally declined to follow decisions of the House of Lords. For example, in *Schorsch Meier G.M.B.H. v. Hennin*,[16] the Court of Appeal reconsidered the long-standing rule in English common law that an English court could award a judgment for money damages only in pounds sterling. *Hennin* involved a claim by the plaintiff, a German corporation, for the balance of an account owed by the defendant for goods delivered to the defendant in England. The defendant had made a partial payment to the plaintiff in deutschmarks, the currency stipulated in the contract. When the defendant failed to pay the balance owed to the plaintiff, the plaintiff sued the defendant in England and sought the payment in deutschmarks, in accordance with the contract. Relying on the

English common law rule, the trial court ruled that it could not award damages to the plaintiff in any currency other than sterling.

On appeal, the plaintiff argued that article 106 of the Treaty of Rome,[17] which was incorporated into English law via the European Communities Act of 1972, required English courts to give judgments for creditors residing in other member states in the creditors' home currency.[18] Although the Court of Appeal agreed with the plaintiff about the effect of the treaty, the court began its decision and spent most of its discussion addressing the common law rule. Recognizing that the English rule requiring that judgments be given only in pounds dated back at least to the early seventeenth century,[19] and acknowledging that the rule had been reaffirmed by the House of Lords in *Re United Railways of Havana and Regla Warehouses Ltd.,*[20] the Court of Appeal nonetheless refused to apply the traditional common law rule and awarded judgment to the plaintiff in deutschmarks. In reaching this result, the Court of Appeal relied on an even older common law principle: "*Cessante ratione legis cessat ipsa lex.*"[21]

The House of Lords was sharply and predictably critical of the Court of Appeal's refusal in *Hennin* to follow *United Railways of Havana.* In *Miliangos v. George Frank (Textiles) Ltd.,*[22] Lord Wilberforce chided the Court of Appeal, saying, "It has to be reaffirmed that the only judicial means by which decisions of this House can be reviewed is by this House itself, under the declaration of 1966."[23] This rebuke notwithstanding, Wilberforce and the rest of the House then went on to overrule *United Railways of Havana* and affirm the rule announced by the Court of Appeal in *Hennin.*[24]

Hennin and *Miliangos* are not the end of the story. Over a decade after *Miliangos* was decided, the Court of Appeal again declined to follow a decision of the House of Lords. In *Pittalis v. Grant,* the Court of Appeal refused to apply a rule established by the House almost one hundred years before.

> [W]e hold that the rule in *Smith v. Baker & Sons* [1891] A.C. 325 ought no longer to be applied. We are conscious that it may seem a strong thing for this court to hold thus of a rule established by the House of Lords . . . But where it can see that the decision of the higher court has become obsolete, the lower court, if it is not to deny justice to the parties in the suit, is bound to say so and to act accordingly.[25]

The House of Lords has not, to date, responded to the Court of Appeal's statement in *Pittalis.*

As Cross and Harris rightly observe, the rare refusal by an English lower court to follow a decision of a higher court is not the death knell for England's common law system: "On two recent occasions the Court of Appeal has declined to follow decisions of the House of Lords and the House has reacted in an appropriately admonitory manner, but the common law is intact."[26] Cross and Harris provide a healthy dose of historical and doctrinal perspective concerning the operation of vertical and horizontal stare decisis in the English legal tradition. Along with the decisions in *Hennin* and *Pittalis,* they demonstrate that not all English judges and lawyers turn paroxysmal at the suggestion that English judges might exercise their own best independent judgment in extreme cases where the enforcement of existing precedent would lead to an unjust result, even when this means that a lower court judge might refuse to follow a higher court precedent. In other words, English law provides a basis for the acceptance of common law review at all levels of the English judicial hierarchy, even in the face of a restrictive understanding of vertical and horizontal stare decisis.

I have tried to show that common law review is a viable legal doctrine with a basis in English law and judicial practice, which can overcome horizontal and vertical stare decisis, even in their most rigid manifestations. I have argued that England, like the United States, permits its judges, including its lower court judges,[27] a meaningful measure of independent judgment and a theoretical ability (sometimes evident in practice) to refuse to follow precedent that leads to untoward results. For those who remain unconvinced or who reject the source of stare decisis in judicial practice, the Court of Appeal could not reject its own prior decisions or the decisions of the House of Lords in the exercise of common law review. For these contrary-minded individuals, common law review would be available only to the House of Lords. Even these individuals must concede, however, that nothing in the English doctrine of stare decisis prevents the House from refusing to follow its own precedent, if a precedent struck one or more of its members as powerfully and irretrievably unjust.

2. Legislative Supremacy

In England, legislative supremacy is called parliamentary sovereignty. This is because, in England, to be sovereign was to be supreme, and to be supreme was to be uniquely powerful. As Jeffrey Goldsworthy explains, this part of the English cultural subconscious was formed over centuries in which the same idea was repeated as a legal litany. Traced through hundreds of years, the idea is this: "There must be absolute, unlimited, and uncontrollable power lodged somewhere in every government . . . [T]he question then is only this, where is its most safe resting? . . . [I]n England it was lodged in the King, Lords and Commons in Parliament."[28] The English predisposition to view governmental power as necessarily localized in a singular governmental body evolved, almost certainly, from its monarchic legal and political history, as Goldsworthy carefully documents.[29] What was once lodged in the person of the monarch came to be lodged in the body of Parliament. And it follows from this conception of parliamentary sovereignty that "the judiciary was therefore subordinate to the legislature."[30]

England's legal history translated directly into its legal and political theory. Thomas Hobbes's claim that every legal system necessarily presupposes a sovereign lawmaker[31] and John Austin's "command theory of law"—the concept of law as the commands of an uncommanded commander[32]—are evident in the thought and language of England's proponents of Parliament's sovereignty as unique and unassailable. Here is an example: "[A] sovereign power necessarily existed at the apex of any legal system . . . '[It] must have necessarily a fountain that derives it to all others, and receives it not from any . . . therefore a well-spring it follows there is, and a supreme head of justice, whereunto all are subject, but itself in subjection to none.'"[33] This is Austinian legal positivism.[34] The antecedents of this commitment to a legally limitless sovereign power can be found in Bodin's writings,[35] and its torch was passed and carried into contemporary English thought by Dicey.[36]

While the Bodinian-Austinian-Diceyan conception of parliamentary sovereignty dominates English legal minds today, it does not control them all. Some judges and theorists have raised criticisms of parliamentary sovereignty as a political and legal doctrine and as an allegedly ineluctable fact of English political and legal history.[37] For example, Trevor Allan argues: "Dicey's [Austinian] positivist assumptions—and those of his adherents—have skewed our wider constitutional vision, and the confused condition of contemporary theory seems to be the consequence. It is a question of the nature of public law and the legitimacy of the judicial function."[38] As Allan goes on to explain, the continuing debate among scholars and judges about the proper conception of judicial review and the *ultra vires* doctrine in English constitutional law and theory is linked directly to an underlying disagreement about the historical and theoretical basis for absolute parliamentary sovereignty in English legal thought and practice. This continuing debate and this underlying disagreement echo the dispute over the proper reading of *Bonham,* as either a version of statutory construction or a vision of judicial review (and the view of the separation and allocation of governmental powers that attends each reading of *Bonham*).

On the Diceyan model, judicial review of legislation in England is limited to an effort to realize legislative intentions. In the lexicon of English constitutional theory, this is called the *ultra vires* model of judicial review. According to the *ultra vires* model, judges may examine the actions of administrative bodies only to ensure that they have not exceeded their delegated authority. If the administrative agency has acted within the scope of the power granted by Parliament, English judges are powerless to review that agency's action, because to do so would be to usurp the absolute sovereignty of Parliament.[39] Those who defend the *ultra vires* model claim, following Dicey, that judicial review can be justified solely by the judicial attempt to enforce parliamentary intentions.[40] In contrast to the *ultra vires* model, other theorists defend a common law model of judicial review that is justified without reference to legislative intention or authorization.[41] By this brief summary, I do not mean to create the impression that there is only one version of the *ultra vires* model or the common law model or, indeed, that these are the only two models of judicial review available in English constitutional theory.[42]

Vires-based models of review proceed from the assumption that English courts cannot invalidate primary legislation; they are limited to the interpretation and enforcement of legislation in an effort to apprehend and effectuate parliamentary intention. Common law theories, especially as espoused by the so-called strong critics of *vires*-based models, do not accept this basic premise; these theories and theorists might permit judicial invalidation of parliamentary statutes, on rare occasion.[43] Furthermore, as Allan notes, even if one accepts the *vires*-based models' premise that courts cannot invalidate primary parliamentary legislation, English courts could still refuse to apply unjust or unconstitutional statutes in particular cases.[44] This is completely consistent with the distinction between elimination and repudiation, which I discussed earlier,[45] and with common law review's commitment to the latter.

Allan emphasizes that the view of fettered judicial authority and autonomy presupposed by the *ultra vires* conception of judicial review undermines "the traditional role of the courts in defence of individual rights."[46] In fact, according to Allan, the attenuated role of common law courts assumed by current English legal practice threatens the constitutional legitimacy of England's governmental order:

If there were ultimately no limits to legislative supremacy, as a matter of constitutional theory, it would be difficult to speak of the British polity as a constitutional state grounded in law. Although the form of the separation of powers may vary between constitutions, the independence of the superior courts from government and legislature seems fundamental to the rule of law. It follows that if we deny all restrictions on legislative competence—even in respect of the adjudication of particular cases—we thereby reject constitutionalism.[47]

Absolute parliamentary sovereignty and correlative judicial subordination are neither historically inevitable nor constitutionally desirable.

For over three hundred years, the independence of the English common law judiciary has allowed it to develop and maintain English public law doctrines and values.[48] England's authentic common law heritage has always recognized that judges must be capable of and amenable to an exercise of independent review of legislative and executive action to ensure the preservation of the rule of law. Allan argues for just this sort of English judicial independence, and his writing offers strong and quite specific support for the principle of common law review as I have presented and defended it:

It is hard to see how judges, in a constitutional democracy, can escape the responsibility to settle the limits of legislative power. They must, of course, employ the tools at hand: some constitutions are more aptly framed than others; a written constitution of some kind is generally better than none. In the end, however, a court must decide whether or not it is a constitutional court, in the sense that it acts under, and exists to safeguard, a constitution, in which powers are reasonably distributed between the different organs of government. The grant of unlimited powers to the legislature, even in relation to specific individuals, amounts to the abnegation of constitutionalism and therefore to a renunciation, in all but the most arid and formal sense, of the rule of law ... Moreover, this is not merely an abstract constitutional logic: it is the logic of the common law. It is through the development and experience of the common law that we know the ingredients of a fair criminal trial, and discern the point at which a retrospective penal statute strikes unacceptably at the heart of judicial power. It is not, of course, in the common law tradition to define such a point conclusively in advance; but it is the responsibility of common law judges to reserve the right to reject a statute which is sufficiently abhorrent.[49]

To Allan's specific arguments and observations, I will add two further reactions. The first is that sovereignty and supremacy strike me as remarkably tendentious and unhelpful concepts when attempting to understand the relationships among organs of government in healthy constitutional democracies.[50] As Mark Walters explains, the nature of Parliament's authority is described better as "omnicompetence" than as omnipotence or absolute supremacy.[51] Contrary to the rudimentary notion of legal power evident in Austin's theory of law, there is no need for a single source of legal power, and there is no necessity that this source be legally boundless. As I have already mentioned, in healthy governments, the legislature and the judiciary are not engaged in a war of wills to grasp and maintain legal and political power over the populace. Powers are shared and exercised according to institutional aptitude and constitutional allocation. The idea of absolute parliamentary sovereignty sometimes seems to be dogmatically superimposed on the genuine state of affairs in English constitutional structure and then subsequently rationalized or reconfigured. In England, as in all common law nations, legal power resides in different governmental organs with different legal and political roles and responsibilities. It would be well for English lawyers, judges, and theorists to remain open to a different, more accurate conception of parliamentary and judicial powers as those powers are actually exercised and experienced.[52]

Some suggest that this process of reconceptualization has already begun. According to these writers, the English constitutional paradigm of absolute parliamentary sovereignty is shifting to "a bi-polar sovereignty of the Crown in Parliament and the Crown in the courts."[53] To be sure, many English neoparliamentarians would disagree, cleaving to the status quo. But my point here is to stress that the idea of a more balanced, plural English government, with an independent, robust judiciary, is not a picture unfamiliar to English legal history, theory, or practice. The changes I suggest are not revolutionary, even in the Kelsenian sense. Or if they are, then they represent a reactionary revolution. What I mean by this oxymoron is that this revolution would return England's legal system and culture to its roots, rather than plant an entirely new tree.[54]

My second reaction also begins by recalling my discussion of absolute parliamentary sovereignty as having its theoretical basis in Austinian legal positivism. If legal theory can ever assist political and constitutional theory, perhaps here is an opportunity. Legal philosophers widely and routinely dismiss as simplistic and misleading Austin's conception of an absolute sovereign, unbounded by legal constraints on the exercise of its power.[55] Meanwhile, a version of just this sort of sovereignty persists in Britain as the prevailing conception of Parliament's legal authority. If Austin's notion of a legally unlimited sovereign is objectionable in theory, why is it so vigorously defended in practice by so many English lawyers, judges, and scholars? The answer seems to be some combination or variation of history and tradition. It might seem that the idea of Parliament as able to, as William Blackstone put it, "do every thing that is not naturally impossible"[56] has become irretrievably imbedded in the collective psyche of the English legal community. Nevertheless, as I have tried to explain, views among contemporary scholars differ on this issue. When we consider it as a historical matter, there is reason to doubt the necessity of viewing parliamentary sovereignty as absolute sovereignty. When we consider the issue as a theoretical and practical matter, the doubts only intensify. This debate will continue for as long as Parliament continues, but English lawyers can no longer respond to doubts about parliamentary sovereignty with bromides about the way it has always been or must be.[57]

An English lawyer might object that the previous discussion of parliamentary sovereignty is purely academic. Although some prominent English judges have argued that they should have the power to invalidate legislation as American judges do,[58] they have not made this claim from the bench. Parliamentary sovereignty is a feature of England's constitutional architecture, and English judges do not possess the power to invalidate parliamentary legislation.[59] Whatever the arguments against sovereignty or in favor of judicial review may be, I promised to discuss common law review in the context of the English legal system as it exists today, and a critic might object that I have not yet done so. While it seems to me that this objection ignores the thrust of Allan's (and others') arguments, I accept, for the purposes of argument, that I have more to do. And I can do more.

Support for common law review can be found in decisions of the House of Lords or, at least, in the speeches of some of their lordships. A frequently cited modern starting point for discussing English judicial independence and resistance to absolute parliamentary sovereignty is the House's *Anisminic* decision, which I discussed in the previous chapter.[60] *Anisminic* is not, however, the only available support for a doctrine of common law review derived from decisions of the House of Lords. Even stronger support can be found in *Simms*.[61]

Simms involved prison inmates convicted of murder who, while incarcerated, met with journalists interested in investigating and publicizing the prisoners' continued protestations of innocence. After learning of the reasons for the journalists' visits, the prison officials prohibited the journalists from visiting the prisoners unless the journalists agreed in writing that they would not use for professional purposes any information obtained. The legal basis for the prison officials' position was Prison Service Standing Order 5, section A, paragraph 37 (1996), which was issued pursuant to rule 33 of the Prison Rules (1964) under authority granted by the Prison Act of 1952, section 47(1). The journalists refused to sign and were denied further access to the prisoners.[62]

The trial judge granted an application for judicial review of the Secretary of State's decision to require journalists to waive in writing their professional interests prior to being granted meetings with prisoners. The trial judge determined that a blanket prohibition against any journalistic use of information obtained during a visit with a prisoner amounted to a violation of the prisoner's right to freedom of expression and, consequently, that paragraphs 37 and 37A of Prison Service Standing Order 5 were unlawful. The Court of Appeal reversed the trial judge's determination, but the House of Lords reversed the decision of the Court of Appeal.

Lord Steyn's speech is most important to my argument. After reviewing the facts and arguments of the parties, Steyn began his legal analysis with the right to freedom of expression. In Steyn's opinion, this right is the primary right in a democracy (without which "an effective rule of law is not possible"),[63] and freedom of expression is a common law right[64]—one of those fundamental common law rights recognized by English judges to be of constitutional dimension.[65] This common law constitutional right of freedom of expression is crucial, according to Steyn, in exposing and curtailing abuses of governmental power:

> The free flow of information and ideas informs political debate . . . It acts as a brake on the abuse of power by public officials. It facilitates the exposure of errors in the governance and administration of justice in this country . . . The applicants argue that in their cases the criminal justice system has failed, and that they have been wrongly convicted. They seek with the assistance of journalists, who have the resources to do the necessary investigations, to make public the wrongs which they allegedly suffered . . . The prisoners are in prison because they are presumed to have been properly convicted. They wish to challenge the safety of their convictions. In principle it is not easy to conceive of a more important function which free speech might fulfil.[66]

Steyn understood the importance of a common law right in restraining abuses of state power and in preventing or correcting injustice, specifically in rectifying the (possible) wrongful conviction of an innocent person, probably the greatest injustice of which a legal system is capable. At the conclusion of his speech, in which he provides his opinion as to the proper legal disposition of the case, Steyn authored the following striking passage:

> It is now necessary to examine the correctness of the interpretation of paragraphs 37 and 37A, involving a blanket ban on interviews, as advanced by the Home Secretary. Literally construed there is force in the extensive construction put forward. But one cannot lose sight that there is at stake a fundamental or basic right, namely the right of a prisoner to seek through oral interviews to persuade a journalist to investigate the safety of the prisoner's conviction and to publicise his findings in an effort to gain access to justice for the prisoner. In these circumstances even in the absence of an ambiguity there comes into play a presumption of general application operating as a constitutional principle . . . This is called "the principle of legality[.]" Ample illustrations of the application of this principle are given in the speech of Lord Browne-Wilkinson, and in my speech, in *Reg. v. Secretary of State for the Home Department, Ex parte Pierson* [1998] A.C. 539, 573G–575D, 587C–590A. Applying this principle I would hold that paragraphs 37 and 37A leave untouched the fundamental and basic rights asserted by the applicants in the present case. The only relevant issue in the present proceedings is whether paragraphs 37 and 37A are ultra vires because they are in conflict with the fundamental and basic rights claimed by the applicants. The principle of legality justifies the conclusion that paragraphs 37 and 37A have not been demonstrated to be ultra vires in the cases under consideration . . . Declarations should be granted in both cases to the effect that the Home Secretary's current policy is unlawful, and that the governors' administrative decisions pursuant to that policy were also unlawful.[67]

Steyn's speech is a fine example of a judicial opinion that demands and repays close, careful study. To begin with, it is impossible to appreciate completely the force of the preceding passage without reading the portions of Steyn's speech in *Pierson* to which he refers in *Simms*. There Steyn wrote:

> Parliament does not legislate in a vacuum. Parliament legislates for a European liberal democracy founded on the principles and traditions of the common law and the courts may approach legislation on this initial

assumption. But this assumption only has prima facie force. It can be displaced by a clear and specific provision to the contrary. These propositions require some explanation. For at least a century it has been "thought to be in the highest degree improbable that Parliament would depart from the general system of law without expressing its intention with irresistible clearness" . . . Dicey explained the context in which Parliament legislates, "By every path we come round to the same conclusion, that Parliamentary sovereignty has favoured the rule of law, and that the supremacy of the law of the land both calls forth the exertion of Parliamentary sovereignty, and leads to its being exercised in a spirit of legality." But it is to Sir Rupert Cross that I turn for the best modern explanation of the "spirit of legality," or what has been called the principle of legality . . . "One function of the word 'presumption' in the context of statutory interpretation is to state the result of this legislative reliance (real or assumed) on firmly established legal principles. There is a 'presumption' that mens rea is required in the case of statutory crimes, and a 'presumption' that statutory powers must be exercised reasonably. These presumptions apply although there is no question of linguistic ambiguity in the statutory wording under construction, and they may be described as 'presumptions of general application' . . . These presumptions of general application not only supplement the text, they also operate at a higher level as expressions of fundamental principles governing both civil liberties and the relations between Parliament, the executive and the courts. They operate here as constitutional principles which are not easily displaced by a statutory text."[68]

Steyn's mention in *Simms* of the principle of legality as "a presumption of general application operating as a constitutional principle" is a direct reference to his earlier discussion in *Pierson*.

In *Pierson*, Steyn explained that certain fundamental legal principles operate as presumptions of general application. As such, these fundamental principles are not simply interpolated into statutory texts by implication; they supervene upon the constitutional organization of government and the recognition of fundamental rights and values. In *Simms*, Steyn explained further that the common law principle of legality is one of the fundamental legal principles that operates as a presumption of general application and that the right to freedom of expression is one of the civil liberties governed by this principle.[69] Moreover, Steyn stated unequivocally in *Simms* that "even in the absence of an ambiguity" in a particular statutory text, the principle of legality operates as a constitutional principle and a presumption of general application.[70]

Steyn's dissociation from the rubric of ambiguity in *Simms* is exceptional. In the minds of many English judges, the judicial role vis-à-vis parliamentary legislation consists solely in enforcing or interpreting statutes, and interpretation depends on some ambiguity, real or contrived, in parliamentary intention or statutory language.[71] By rejecting ambiguity as a prerequisite to judicial action, Steyn rejects this narrow view of judicial authority and responsibility.

I have tried to accentuate the relationship between common law review, on the one hand, and the constitutional order and balance of the different branches of government, on the other. I have also tried to show that the common law necessitates a particular conception of this constitutional order and balance and a particular conception of judicial authority and responsibility, which I have called, respectively, common law constitutionalism and common law review. The principle of legality as defined and discussed by Steyn in *Simms* supports common law review and common law constitutionalism in three ways. First, the principle of legality is a common law principle that serves to protect fundamental rights and interests (in *Simms*, the freedom of expression) from encroachment by the legislative or executive branches. Second, English courts enforce the principle of legality not just to interpret an arguably ambiguous statute but irrespective of ambiguity. Third, when viewed this way, the critical inquiry in applying the principle of legality is not whether a particular legislative, executive, or administrative act was *ultra vires;* the proper judicial inquiry is whether "there is at stake a fundamental or basic right" and whether the act in question infringes or interferes unduly with this fundamental or basic right.[72] If so, the principle of legality requires the court to safeguard the fundamental right.

I believe this is why Steyn writes, at the end of his *Simms* speech, that the paragraphs relied on by the prison officials "leave untouched the fundamental and basic rights asserted by the applicants in this case," even though the acts of the prison officials "have not been demonstrated to be *ultra vires.*" Steyn held in *Simms* that even in the absence of a demonstration that the prison officials' acts were *ultra vires* and even in the absence of any textual ambiguity, the prison officials' acts should still be declared unlawful for violation of the principle of legality, which operates, in that case, to secure the prisoners' fundamental and basic right to freedom of expression. The prison officials may have had the authority to draft and interpret the rules as they did (they were not *ultra vires*), but whatever those rules might say, the prison officials have no authority to infringe on the fundamental rights of the prisoners (the prison rules "leave untouched" the prisoners' fundamental rights). This is what Steyn means when he says that the principle of legality operates as a presumption of general application: it is always operative, and it always operates as a higher-order principle against which governmental action is assessed.

This is common law review. The principle of legality is a principle of English common law that is invoked by English judges to ensure that common law rights of constitutional dimension are protected against infringement by abuses of governmental power. And this common law principle operates at the constitutional level, organizing and balancing the relationships and responsibilities of the organs of government. Steyn's quotation from Rupert Cross in *Pierson* highlights the dual functions of common law principles, as fundamental legal principles and as constitutional presumptions of general application. Moreover, these functions cannot be divorced from one another. Common law review and common law constitutionalism go hand in hand. The principle of legality is a concrete manifestation of the common law's commitment to the preservation of the rule of law. As a common law principle, the principle of legality is a legal standard for judges to apply when reviewing actions taken by other government bodies. As a presumption of general application, the principle of legality requires judges, at all times, to secure fundamental rights and to maintain the equilibrium of the English constitutional framework.

I do not want to overstate matters. Steyn does not claim in *Simms* that English judges may apply the principle of legality to avoid results required by unjust primary legislation. *Simms* involved the validity not of a statute but of statutorily derived regulations and statutorily delegated discretionary powers. Nevertheless, Steyn's opinion in *Simms* supports the key elements of common law review, and his opinion represents a purposeful step away from an English judiciary (or at least a House of Lords) wholly captivated and captured by the dogma of absolute parliamentary supremacy, toward an independent English judiciary fully prepared to accept the mantle of its common law ancestry.

The issue of judicial invalidation of primary legislation was not directly raised in *Simms*. However, Steyn indicates in *Simms* that delegated administrative discretion is subject to the common law principle of legality operative as a presumption of general application at the constitutional level. If I have read Steyn's speech correctly, this is more than enough to link the reasoning and the result of *Simms* to the principle and practice of common law review.

Judicial review in England proceeds from the principle that administra-

tive decisions are subject to judicial oversight to guarantee the proper consideration of fundamental values in the administration of justice.[73] At the
moment when the law intersects with the individual through the exercise
of administrative discretion, the government's decisions are always subject
to the rule of law as enforced through judicial review according to fundamental common law principles.[74] That the primary legislation may remain
viable is, on this account, immaterial.[75] What matters is that the courts
must, at all times, even in the absence of any ambiguity, act to uphold the
rule of law by ensuring that the government acts in accordance with it. And
when the court determines that the government has abused its power, the
court can overturn the government's exercise of discretion. As an articulation of legal principle that embraces English common law constitutionalism, Steyn's decision in *Simms* can reasonably be read as the doctrinal and
theoretical progeny of Coke's ruling in *Bonham*. In both judgments, common law principles are affirmed as maintaining fundamental values of justice that apply, without exception, to all exercises of public authority.

In English administrative law, a little ambiguity goes a long way. This is
because, according to the prevailing understanding of judicial review
within the context of parliamentary sovereignty, ambiguity permits the
courts to review decisions based on delegated discretion, without under-
mining or challenging Parliament's unfettered authority to legislate:

> Just as the courts' construction of legislation dealing with, say, personal
> liberty is rationalised in terms of a legislative endeavour that is funda-
> mentally shaped by constitutional principle, so the courts' approach to
> legislation which creates discretionary powers may be conceptualised as
> an interpretive process which is normatively premised on those values
> which make up the rule of law. Consequently, when Parliament enacts
> legislation which (typically) confers wide discretionary power and
> which makes no explicit reference to the controls which should regulate
> the exercise of the power, the courts are constitutionally entitled—and
> constitutionally right—to assume that it was Parliament's intention to
> legislate in conformity with the rule of law principle. This means that
> Parliament is properly to be regarded as having conferred upon the de-
> cision-maker only such power as is consistent with that principle. It fol-
> lows from this that, in the absence of a very clear contrary provision,
> Parliament must be taken to withhold from decision-makers the power
> to treat individuals in a manner which offends the rule of law . . . [T]he
> task of transforming this general intention . . . into detailed, legally en-
> forceable rules of fairness and rationality is clearly a matter for the

courts . . . Parliament thus leaves it to the judges to set the precise limits of administrative competence.[76]

This is the modified *ultra vires* model of judicial review,[77] which is an attempt by some theorists to balance the rule-of-law values preserved through judicial review against the assumption that parliamentary sovereignty demands that these values must yield to the supremacy of Parliament's apparent or expressed legislative intentions. The modified *ultra vires* model incorporates into English constitutional and administrative law the familiar judicial presumption that Parliament always intends to legislate in accordance with the rule of law; and this presumption authorizes courts to resolve perceived tensions between parliamentary enactments and the rule of law by attempting to reconcile the former with the latter. The lingering problem, however, as the previous quotation indicates, is that parliamentary sovereignty still seems to necessitate that Parliament remain capable of legislating in contravention of the rule of law, provided that its intention is expressed in an unmistakably and inescapably clear provision. In such an instance, even the modified *ultra vires* model would require judges to abandon the rule of law and enforce the legislation. Predicating judicial review on the endeavor to ascertain and enforce parliamentary intentions, as the modified *ultra vires* model does, means that the modified model cannot disavow the dogma of sovereignty and the sacrifice of legal principle to a sufficiently clear manifestation of legislative will.

In *Simms*, Lord Steyn says that a lot of clarity can go only so far. In his departure from the ambiguity precondition, Steyn determines that even in the presence of a very clear contrary provision, Parliament cannot contravene the rule of law in the delegation of administrative authority, nor can the administrative agency do so in its exercise of that authority. To make this point clearer, it might help to suppose that *Simms* involved a "substantive privative clause." A substantive privative clause is a statutory "provision which precludes judges from relying on particular principles of the rule of law as grounds of review."[78] We might imagine that rather than the broad and undefined authority at issue in *Simms*, the enabling legislation specifically provided that the prison officials' discretion could be exercised without concern for the prisoners' right to the freedom of expression or the relationship between that right and the administration of justice.[79] According to Steyn, the judicial obligation in such a case is to preserve fundamental rule-of-law values contained in the common law, by refusing to permit the violation of the individual's fundamental rights. The rule of law applies to and governs all governmental action, and all governmental action is evaluated subject to this prior judicial obligation. Whatever the enabling statute may say, the courts' jurisdiction over the substance of core English constitutional values cannot be ousted by legislative means. The conception of judicial authority and responsibility that underlies Steyn's speech in *Simms* is entirely consistent with the House's ruling in *Anisminic*.

The full portent of Steyn's *Simms* speech can best be appreciated by contrasting his opinion with Lord Hoffmann's. Although indicating his agreement with Steyn's reasoning, Hoffmann thought it necessary to "add only a few words of [his] own about the importance of the principle of legality in a constitution which, like ours, acknowledges the sovereignty of Parliament."[80] Hoffmann discreetly qualified his own adherence to Steyn's claim that the principle of legality operates even in the absence of statutory ambiguity:

> In the absence of express language or necessary implication to the contrary, the courts therefore presume that even the most general words were intended to be subject to the basic rights of the individual. In this way the courts of the United Kingdom, though acknowledging the sovereignty of Parliament, apply principles of constitutionality little different from those which exist in countries where the power of the legislature is expressly limited by a constitutional document.[81]

Here we find Hoffmann's quiet disagreement with Steyn. Hoffmann is not yet willing to agree that the principle of legality operates to prevent the infringement of basic rights even in the absence of ambiguity. Evidently, Hoffmann continues to assume that the courts' authority to prevent the infringement of basic rights is limited, at least in theory, by an expression of Parliament's intention to do so "with irresistible clearness."

This is why Steyn's opinion in *Simms* is so extraordinary. Read carefully, Steyn's decision provides that even in the absence of any ambiguity, even with irresistible clearness, the government cannot act in violation of the principle of legality. Put differently, there are fundamental common law principles of justice and fairness that operate at a constitutional level; they are always present, always significant, and the government's actions are always subject to them through the exercise of judicial review. In *Simms*, then, Steyn seems to accept the nucleus of common law review and common law constitutionalism. The English government is, at all times and at every level, a government limited by law.

Even if I have read Steyn's speech in *Simms* correctly, most English judges would still agree with Hoffmann's restrained gesture toward parliamentary sovereignty. Some things still must change for common law review to be accepted even only in the House of Lords. More things must change for common law review to be accepted in the Court of Appeal. And even more things would have to change for common law review to be embraced by English trial court judges. These changes, however, are principally attitudinal, because, as Professor Wade explained, legislative supremacy is based finally on the attitudes of judges rather than on the pronouncements of Parliament.[82]

I have endeavored to show in this chapter that these changes are not nearly as revolutionary as English lawyers and judges might assume. English judges need only claim their birthright. Indeed, English judges sometimes obliquely refuse to enforce parliamentary statutes that conflict with their most fundamental moral convictions.[83] Additionally, as others have argued, English courts already engage in a practice of judicial review under the euphemism of statutory interpretation, which involves the search for or construction of Parliament's implied or imputed intention.[84] One might consider this simply a matter of calling a rose by another name. But in this instance, it seems to me that the rose does not smell as sweet.[85] In the garden of English law, there is value to calling a rose only by its name, because the law grows best without pretext or manure. There is no room in England's majestic legal heritage for fig leaves or fairy tales.[86]

B. United States

Things are a bit easier for my argument in the United States. My discussions in previous chapters contain detailed references to American law, and I will not repeat those arguments and citations here. Suffice it to say that the American doctrines of horizontal and vertical stare decisis are not nearly as rigid or restrictive as the current English versions.[87] And there is no doctrine of legislative supremacy in the United States.[88] The model of English legal culture built into the American governmental framework was located in "a unique legal-historical tradition which guaranteed the fundamental rights and positive liberties of free-born English" citizens rather than the blinkered vision of the "inns of court men who . . . had largely lost touch with this liberal strain of the common law tradition."[89] Judicial deference to the federal and state legislatures in the United States follows something much closer to the model of deference as respect, which I discussed earlier.[90] This respectful deference, however, was never conceived, in the United States, as the absolute sovereignty of the legislature or the subjugation of the judiciary:

> It is not particularly useful to say that the Constitution assigns "ultimate" authority to any single institution. And although the institutions and procedures established by the Constitution collectively attempt to implement the ideal of government by the people, they hardly could have been intended simply to ensure that government power is exercised by elected officials . . . [The] structure of government set up by the Constitution negates any assertion that democracy, in our [American] constitutional system, can be reduced to the simple notion of legislative supremacy.[91]

From this, however, one should not get the idea that the critical difference between the United States and England concerning ideas of legislative supremacy and judicial deference lies in the distinction between the former's written Constitution and the latter's unwritten one. Judicial review does not depend, logically or legally, on a written constitution, because the power of judicial review is neither granted nor created by a constitution.[92] This means that England does not need a written constitution as a precondition to the recognition of a power of judicial review (in the American sense).[93] This also means that judicial review in the United States need not be understood solely as constitutional review. As I have argued at length, this assumption betrays a legal and historical mistake. The written American Constitution and the unwritten English constitution are both derived directly from the common law.[94] "[O]ur constitutional law," as Sir William Holdsworth put it, "is simply a part of the common law."[95] Where the organization of government and the competency, authority, and responsibility of its institutions are concerned, the common law foundation of both nations' legal and governmental systems is their most salient defining characteristic.[96] The U.S. Supreme Court established long ago that the common law must inform the interpretation and evaluation of all legislation, including the Constitution.[97]

This is also the reason that efforts to differentiate judicial authority and interpretive paradigms in the United States and England—in the context of the debate about the "unwritten constitution," by the presence of parliamentary sovereignty in England, or because of the presence of a written constitution in the United States—are misguided.[98] Whatever the historical or theoretical pedigree of parliamentary sovereignty in England or constitutional review in the United States, the shared common law foundations of both the English and American constitutions require the realization that one cannot seriously doubt the presence of an unwritten common law constitution in either nation, even if Americans chose to codify certain common law antecedents in their charter document. Moreover, the common law foundations of the English and American constitutions entrench the common law, in both nations, as the conceptual foundation for the exercise of judicial review, as well as a body of legal principle against which government action may be judicially evaluated.[99]

For many American lawyers and judges, however, the Constitution, not the common law, is the defining feature of the American legal and governmental system. The Constitution has become the sacred text of a secular religion.[100] But this sometimes seems to blind the faithful. Just as it is a mistake to suppose that constitutional review is the only form of judicial review found in American law and legal history, it is a mistake to think that the Constitution is more fundamental than its common law underpinnings.[101] The common law, as the legal system operating within a governmental structure, helps to define that governmental structure. In other words, saying that a country has a common law legal system is necessarily saying something about the constitutional organization of its government.[102] Declaring that a nation is a "constitutional democracy" tells us nothing about its legal system and little about its political and governmental scheme. Constitutional democracies can and do exist with common law, civil law, and hybrid legal systems. Saying that a nation is a "common law democracy" tells us much more. It tells us something useful about its legal system and, relatedly, something meaningful about the organization of its government.[103] Saying that a country has a common law legal system is necessarily saying something about the constitutional order of its government, because wherever one finds the common law, one finds legal principles that act to constrain abuses of state power. Wherever one finds the common law, one finds common law constitutionalism.

The debate within the Anglo-American tradition about the proper, or preferred, allocation of governmental powers will continue. But when engaging in this debate, we ought not to allow a preoccupation with democratic political processes to obscure the importance, in England and the United States, of the combination of these processes with common law processes, principles, and traditions. It is a mistake to ignore or devalue the relationship between the legal system and the political system, where a common law system exists within a democratic polity. The legislature's authority must be balanced against the historical, legal, and political import of the common law courts' place as a salutary influence on the government and the governed. The legislature does not cede power to the judiciary.[104] The judiciary possesses that power as a coequal branch of plural government. This is what Coke sought and Marshall secured.

The textual and conceptual bases for common law review provide independent justifications for judicial review as reflective of the coordinate position of the common law judiciary within the constitutional organization of governmental and legal institutions. The problems posed by unjust laws help to highlight the unique position, authority, and responsibility of common law judges to ensure the law's development by refusing to enforce unjust laws. The common law judges' position, authority, and responsibility are relevant to the disposition of particular cases and in the organization and allocation of governmental powers. This dual nature of common law judicial decision making is the signal feature of common law adjudication and common law constitutionalism. In common law legal systems and in the governments of which they form a part, a particular case can help to shape an entire government; as judges develop the law by deciding cases, the law they develop limits what the government can do in accordance with the rule of law.

As a coda to my argument, I want to mention one aspect of common law review that I have not yet raised. Common law review requires of judges a certain combination of qualities: they must have the moral compass and sensitivity to recognize injustice and feel its sting; and they must have the strength of character and will to act on their convictions, even when they must act alone. Not everyone has these attributes. But some do, and they are some of the finest judges of the common law tradition.[105] The remarks of two of these judges, fittingly one Briton and one American, exhibit the disposition I have in mind. The first words are Lord Mansfield's:

> I will not do that which my conscience tells me is wrong, upon this occasion; to gain the huzzas of thousands, or the daily praise of all the papers which come from the press: I will not avoid doing what I think is right; though it should draw on me the whole artillery of libels; all that falsehood and malice can invent, or the credulity of a deluded populace can swallow . . . Once and for all, let it be understood, "that no endeavours of this kind will influence any man who at present sits here."[106]

The second passage comes from Justice Holmes:

> Law is the business to which my life is devoted, and I should show less than devotion if I did not do what in me lies to improve it, and, when I perceive what seems to me to be the ideal of its future, if I hesitated to point it out and to press toward it with all my heart.[107]

10. Conclusion

A. Types of Injustice

Injustice comes in many forms, most of which do not arise within the domain of law. But some injustices are legal injustices. When expressed in legal form, these injustices must be corrected by legal means—that is, the means recognized within the common law tradition. Those means classically involve political, electoral, legislative, and judicial processes. In democratic systems of government, questions of who gets what, when, and how—and of the relative fairness of these social and economic allocations and relations—are often best left to the former processes.[1] However, when an alleged injustice involves constitutional organization, institutional obligations, fundamental rights, and certain other normative constraints on government power, the common law tradition has allocated the responsibility of correcting this sort of injustice to the courts.[2] In these instances, the political processes of government themselves must be regulated by the rule of law, enforced by judges in accordance with common law constitutionalism.

Many citizens and officials (including judges) assume that the authority of the judiciary to correct certain legal injustices is necessarily subordinate to the democratic processes of government. Judges, so the story goes, are charged with interpreting the law and perhaps with articulating the law, but not with challenging or changing the law made by representative and politically accountable branches of government. Judges must apply the law as it is. This was the assumption of certain judges during the period of legalized slavery in the United States; this is the assumption of many American judges and theorists today; and due to the doctrine of parliamentary sovereignty, this is the assumption of many judges and theorists in England. But it is important to be careful in determining what type of injustice is at issue, because when an injustice is expressed in a legal source, it is the judges' institutional responsibility to attempt to correct that type of injustice. It is just as much a mistake to assume that judges are powerless to correct injustices inside the legal domain as it is to assume that judges can correct injustices outside that domain. Within the legal domain, the common law tradition empowers and obligates judges not only to enforce the law as it is but also to correct injustice and develop the law. There are limitations here, as well, however. Not all moral outrage at a perceived legal injustice can honestly be traced to and expressed in a source recognized as law by the common law tradition. For common law judges to correct injustice through the judicial process, the moral evaluation and proffered correction of injustice must, at every stage, be amenable to expression in a judicial ruling supported by a reasoned opinion.

B. An Alternative

Common law judges do more than simply apply the law. Common law judges also develop the law. These are, I have argued, their two fundamental obligations. These two obligations can be legally grounded in two ways, textually or conceptually. I have presented source-based and conceptual arguments for the judicial obligation to apply the law, and I have presented source-based and conceptual arguments for the judicial obligation to develop the law.

The source-based arguments for the judicial obligation to apply the law center on stare decisis and legislative supremacy. Stare decisis, through its use in judicial practice, requires judges to apply case law. Legislative supremacy, through its recognition in judicial practice, requires judges to apply statutory law. At times, the constraining force of these doctrines seems to demand that judges reach unjust results in certain cases. This has led some theorists to reconstruct the doctrines, in the hope of allowing judges to avoid their occasionally untoward effects. It seems to me, though, that we demonstrate more respect for the authentic importance of these doctrines in the common law tradition if, in response to the injustice they sometimes appear to require, we attempt to locate an equally fundamental countervailing obligation that legally justifies judicial refusal to enforce unjust laws, rather than promoting reformulations of stare decisis and legislative supremacy that would merely enervate their genuine impact on judicial decision making.

The conceptual argument for the judicial obligation to apply the law acknowledges that an irreducible part of the common law judicial function is the application of settled law in the resolution of legal disputes according to accepted practices of legal argumentation and decision making. Put differently, for a common law system to be a common law system, its judges must frequently, as part of their institutional role, apply the law as they find it to the situations brought before the court for resolution. The judicial obligation to apply the law is, however, only part of the story.

I have also argued that common law judges have a legal obligation to develop the law, sometimes by refusing to enforce unjust laws. This obligation derives from common law principles articulated in case law and from the nature of the common law system, method, and tradition. The common law cannot be divorced from its commitments to constitutionalism and the rule of law. In other words, in a common law system, fundamental principles exist that constrain abuses of power by other branches of government. One of these principles, which I discussed at length in chapter 9, is the principle of legality. Another principle, which I mentioned in chapter 8, is the right of access to the courts. Injustice—whether legislatively directed, executively attempted, or judicially indicated—is always subject to the subsequent review and evaluation of the common law judiciary. As I have described this process here, that evaluative review and its consequences differ in different jurisdictions. But those differences do not alter the existence and importance of the judicial power and process at issue.

Common law review, as I have called this judicial authority and responsibility, can be traced either to legal sources or to legal concepts. I have here examined sources (i.e., case law and judicial practices) from England and the United States. *Bonham* and *Omychund* demonstrate that the evaluative judicial role and corrective judicial process have long and deep roots in Anglo-American legal history and doctrine. And such cases as *Anisminic* and *Simms* show that the burgeoning of parliamentary sovereignty has not swept from the English legal landscape either these fundamental aspects of the common law judiciary or the importance of fundamental common law principles of justice. Whatever terms they happen to use, many English judges remain steadfast in their efforts to protect fundamental rights and institutional values against the legislature's and the executive's overstepping—via ouster clauses or administrative discretion—of their rightful exercise of political power.

In the United States, *Calder, Chisholm, McIlvaine,* and *Fletcher,* together with *Ham, Bowman, Lindsay,* and *Jones,* establish that judicial review was not and need not be conceived only in terms of a constitutional document. Before and after constitutional review was introduced into American law, common law principles were used as an independent, alternative basis for judicial review of legislative action. Moreover, as with *Anisminic* and *Simms* in the English context, *Rochin, Webster,* and *Morrow* (among others) demonstrate that judges in the United States will ensure the legality of government action and will defend their institutional integrity and authority against challenges of various sorts, regardless of whether those challenges originate in executive action, legislative provision, or judicial decision.

Legal sources are not the only means, however, by which a common law judicial obligation to develop the law can be defended. I have argued that the nature of the common law itself, as a legal system and a legal tradition, grounds a legal obligation for common law judges to refuse to enforce unjust laws. Through its design to develop over time toward substantive justice, the judges' integral role in that process, and the consequences of judicial failures to fulfill that role, the obligation to develop the law is understood to be intrinsic to the common law judicial function. Simply put, for a legal system to be a common law system, its judges must possess the institutional authority to develop the law.

Substantively and structurally, common law review reveals an inherent institutional relationship in all common law legal orders. The developmental refinement of existing law and the evaluative review of governmental action cannot be decoupled in the common law tradition. The common law judiciary's institutional independence has long been recognized as an intrinsically valuable feature of the legal system and the larger constitutional architecture in which it fits. Indeed, this is one of the fundamental values of the rule of law and the subjection of governmental power to legal limitation. This is, in other words, the connection between common law review and common law constitutionalism.

To those who view judicial review of any stripe as worrisome,[3] common law review will doubtless seem an ill-advised expansion of what already is tantamount to judicial hegemony. For the most part, though, these worries are overblown. Historically, theoretically, and doctrinally, common law review is a long-standing, workable, and circumscribed aspect of the common law judiciary's authority. But it is nevertheless an aspect of that authority. Those who find it objectionable must explain the basis of those objections and appreciate the ramifications of them, because those of us who prize this part of the common law's heritage will need very persuasive reasons to relinquish it.

C. Unsatisfying Answers

My arguments in favor of common law review and, more generally, in support of the common law judicial obligation to develop the law are motivated by the desire to explain more fully and accurately the real scope of the common law judiciary's authority and responsibility. In particular, I hope to expand the three truncated alternatives suggested by those who have considered a judge's options when asked to enforce an unjust law. It may be that in some places, at certain times, under particular circumstances, all a judge can do when faced with an unjust law is resign, misrepresent himself, or enforce the law as it is.[4] But this is not all a judge can do in England, the United States, or any contemporary common law system. Judges have another legal option and another legal obligation.

Common law judges who find themselves in this situation have a legal obligation to develop the law by refusing to enforce an unjust law. This is their obligation to the legal system, the judicial institution, the public, and the litigants who appear before them. It is their contribution to the proper articulation of public values and to the integrity of the judicial process.

D. The "Moral-Formal Dilemma"

The three unsatisfying options of resignation, misrepresentation, and enforcement derive from and depend on the "moral-formal dilemma," with its myopic vision of the judiciary. Once we see that the legal side of the dilemma is not limited to a stunted, mechanistic image of the common law judiciary, we begin to appreciate the true nature of the dilemma posed by unjust laws. Unjust laws do not present judges with a moral-formal dilemma at all. They present a legal-legal dilemma, a conflict between the judge's fundamental obligations to apply the law and to develop the law. Given the exigency of the situation and provided that the judge is satisfied after careful reflection and consideration that the epistemic threshold has been reached, the judge's obligation to develop the law outweighs the (in this case) conflicting obligation to apply the law.

E. Unjust Laws

As long as people need laws to govern themselves and as long as these laws are made by people, some of these laws will be unjust. As long as the threat of unjust laws persists, people will and should consider how judges ought best to address that threat and its occasional actualization. To this point, consideration of these problems has left judges with only three possibilities. But mendacity, abnegation, or acquiescence are not the only options. The common law tradition and legal principles permit and require more of judges. Judges must develop the law. That, too, is a fundamental aspect of their legal obligations. Sometimes, as in cases involving unjust laws, development demands that judges subject government action to the rule of law. This should not elicit fear or frustration. The common law has always functioned this way, and common law judges have always, in one form or another, fulfilled this function. The common law tradition recognized long ago what we sometimes still lose sight of today: only when the waters are pure can we hope to see down to the riverbed.[5]

Table of Authorities

Cases Cited

Statutes Cited

UNITED KINGDOM

UNITED STATES

Other Sources

EUROPEAN UNION

UNITED STATES

Notes

Chapter 1

1. *See, e.g., Loving v. Commonwealth,* 206 Va. 924, 147 S.E.2d 78 (1966) (enforcing a statute that prohibited interracial marriage), *rev'd sub nom., Loving v. Virginia,* 388 U.S. 1, 87 S.Ct. 1817, 18 L.Ed.2d 1010 (1967).

2. *See, e.g., Plessy v. Ferguson,* 163 U.S. 537, 16 S.Ct. 1138, 41 L.Ed. 256 (1896) (enforcing a statute that permitted racial segregation on railroads).

3. *See, e.g., In re Yick Wo,* 68 Cal. 294, 9 P. 139 (1885) (upholding the conviction of a laundry owner for violation of a San Francisco ordinance requiring consent of the board of supervisors prior to operation of a laundry in any building not constructed of brick or stone, which was enforced only against Chinese laundry owners), *rev'd sub nom., Yick Wo v. Hopkins,* 118 U.S. 356, 6 S.Ct. 1064, 30 L.Ed. 220 (1886). *See also* John Rawls, *A Theory of Justice* (Harvard University Press, 1971), 235.

4. I use the term "law" here to refer broadly to exercises of public authority, because my argument applies to all forms of government action taken under color of law: precedents, statutes, executive action, administrative directives, and so on.

5. By this sentence, I do not intend to express a view about the legality or justness of differential treatment intended to benefit a disadvantaged group, perhaps to enhance diversity or as a remedy for past discrimination against a racially segmented underclass.

6. *See infra* pp. 153–57, 159–63, 178–87.

7. For an example of a characteristic, but inadequate, discussion of these issues, *see* Edgar Bodenheimer, *Jurisprudence: The Philosophy and Method of the Law* (rev. ed.) (Harvard University Press, 1974), 350–57. Bodenheimer carefully and correctly differentiates certain issues raised by unjust laws, in terms of legal sources, judicial interpretation, and judicial responsibility. But his attempt to resolve the problems unjust laws pose for judges resorts to two unpersuasive positions. First, Bodenheimer argues for the disavowal of unjust laws as legal sources, almost to the point of embracing something like the maxim *lex injusta non est lex,* which is disclaimed these days by (almost) all natural lawyers. *See id.* at 357 ("There may be types of laws so utterly repugnant to the postulates of civilized decency that the judge has a right to treat them as non-laws."). I return to this point later in my discussion of Radbruch. *See infra* pp. 163–66. Second, Bodenheimer characterizes the judicial refusal to enforce unjust laws as employing principles of justice against or contrary to law. *See* Bodenheimer, *Jurisprudence,* 357 ("[R]esort to elementary considerations of justice *contra*

legem should not necessarily . . . be regarded as a transgression of judicial authority.")". While I agree that judicial refusal to enforce unjust laws should not necessarily be regarded as a transgression of judicial authority, it is deeply misleading to say that judges who refuse to enforce such laws are employing principles of justice "*contra legem.*" As I will explain, I assume the formal validity of unjust laws as legal sources and argue that the purported conflict between principles of justice and principles of law misapprehends the nature of common law principles and the common law judicial process.

8. *See, e.g.,* Steven J. Burton, *Judging in Good Faith* (Cambridge University Press, 1992), 207.

9. *See* Robert M. Cover, *Justice Accused: Antislavery and the Judicial Process* (Yale University Press, 1975), 197–225.

10. *Id.* at 228.

11. *Id.* at 229–36.

12. *Id.* at 236–38.

13. *See* Ronald Dworkin, *The Law of the Slave-Catchers,* Times Literary Supplement (5 Dec. 1975), at 1437. For an interesting take on Dworkin's review of *Justice Accused* (and a claim that John Marshall subscribed to the moral-formal dilemma—described as the "jurist-moralist" distinction), *see* Sanford Levinson: "Hercules, Abraham Lincoln, the United States Constitution, and the Problem of Slavery," in Arthur Ripstein, ed., *Ronald Dworkin* (Cambridge University Press, 2007).

14. *See* Cover, *Justice Accused,* 85 (describing the use of natural law principles by judges during this period). *See also* Christopher L. Eisgruber, *Justice Story, Slavery, and the Natural Law Foundations of American Constitutionalism,* 55 U. Chi. L. Rev. 273, 288 n. 51 (1988).

15. Anthony J. Sebok, *Judging the Fugitive Slave Acts,* 100 Yale L.J. 1835, 1837 (1991). *See* Cover, *Justice Accused,* 258 ("Antebellum jurisprudence was positivist and preoccupied with refuting the Jacksonian myth of judicial lawmaking run amuck. As a result, the universe of responses available for the judge in the moral-formal dilemma posed by the Fugitive Slave law tended to include and stress formulations of self-denial and mechanical limits.").

16. *See infra* pp. 163–66.

17. Eisgruber, *Justice Story,* 289.

18. *See* Dworkin, *Law of the Slave-Catchers,* 1437.

19. *See* Sebok, *Judging the Fugitive Slave Acts,* 1839–40.

20. *See id.* at 1844–54.

21. (1772) 98 Eng. Rep. 499.

22. But not the slave trade. That was not abolished by law until the Slave Trade Act, 47 Geo. III 1, c. 36 (1807).

23. *See* Anthony J. Sebok, "The Case of Chief Justice Shaw," in David Dyzenhaus, ed., *Recrafting the Rule of Law: The Limits of Legal Order* (Hart Publishing, 1999), 116–17, 141–42.

24. *Id.* at 138–39. Sebok also relates this reference to authoritative sources to broader claims about legal positivism as the theoretical orientation of these early judges. I do not address these claims here.

25. Ronald Dworkin, *Law's Empire* (Harvard University Press, 1986), 219. *See also id.*

at 106. Dworkin's other statements on the subject are all to the same effect. *See* Ronald Dworkin, *Justice in Robes* (Harvard University Press, 2006), 18–19; Ronald Dworkin, "A Reply by Ronald Dworkin," in Marshall Cohen, ed., *Ronald Dworkin and Contemporary Jurisprudence* (Rowman and Allanheld, 1983), 256–57; Ronald Dworkin, *Taking Rights Seriously* (Harvard University Press, 1978), 326–27, 341–42. *See also* Kent Greenawalt, *Law and Objectivity* (Oxford University Press, 1992), 57; Lon L. Fuller, *Positivism and Fidelity to Law: A Reply to Professor Hart,* 71 Harv. L. Rev. 630, 648 (1958).

26. *See, e.g.,* H.L.A. Hart, *Essays on Bentham: Studies in Jurisprudence and Political Theory* (Oxford University Press, 1982), 150–53; Allan C. Hutchinson, *Indiana Dworkin and Law's Empire,* 96 Yale L.J. 637, 658–60 (1987).

27. *See* Burton, *Judging in Good Faith,* 203–4.

28. *See id.* at 197; Kent Greenawalt, *Policy, Rights, and Judicial Decision,* 11 Ga. L. Rev. 991, 1050 (1977) ("[T]he judge might be morally justified either in resigning his office or subverting the law.").

29. (1610) 8 Co. Rep. 107a, 77 Eng. Rep. 638.

30. By "independent," I mean that the arguments rely on different premises to reach the same conclusion—that is, that judges have legal obligations to apply and to develop the law.

31. Elsewhere in this book, I italicize foreign language phrases. But the term *stare decisis* appears so frequently that I have chosen to forgo this convention in its case.

32. (1744) 1 Atk. 22, 26 Eng. Rep. 15.

33. *Marbury v. Madison,* 5 U.S. (1 Cranch) 137, 2 L.Ed. 60 (1803).

34. *Cf.* Hans-Georg Gadamer, *Truth and Method* (2nd ed.) (Continuum, 1989), 318 ("[T]he situation of the person 'applying' law is quite different. In a certain instance he will have to refrain from applying the full rigor of the law. But if he does, it is not because he has no alternative, but because to do otherwise would not be right. In restraining the law, he is not diminishing it but, on the contrary, finding the better law.").

35. *See generally* Dworkin, "Reply by Ronald Dworkin," 256; Hart, *Essays on Bentham,* 160–61.

36. *See* David Dyzenhaus, *The Constitution of Law: Legality in a Time of Emergency* (Cambridge University Press, 2006), 4–5; Mark D. Walters, "The Common Law Constitution and Legal Cosmopolitanism," in David Dyzenhaus, ed., *The Unity of Public Law* (Hart Publishing, 2004), 431; T.R.S. Allan, *Constitutional Justice: A Liberal Theory of the Rule of Law* (Oxford University Press, 2001), 4 ("A general commitment to certain foundational values that underlie and inform the purpose and character of constitutional government, at least as it has been understood in [common law] democracies, imposes a natural unity on the relevant jurisdictions, allowing us to draw close parallels between them and identify common legal characteristics at a fundamental level.").

37. *See* Thomas R. Kearns and Austin Sarat, "Legal Justice and Injustice: Toward a Situated Perspective," in Austin Sarat and Thomas R. Kearns, eds., *Justice and Injustice in Law and Legal Theory* (University of Michigan Press, 1996), 12.

38. *See* Dworkin, "Reply by Ronald Dworkin," 269.

39. *See id.*

40. *See id.*

41. *See, e.g.,* Dworkin, *Law's Empire*, 88, 97–98, 255, 401; Dworkin, "Reply by Ronald Dworkin," 256 ("Legal rights are different from the rights we call moral, when we have that distinction in mind, because legal rights are rights based in the political history and decisions of the community and have special institutional force against judges in litigation.").

42. *Cf.* Judith N. Shklar, *Legalism: Law, Morals, and Political Trials* (Harvard University Press, 1964), 119 ("It might be suggested that political or ultimate social justice lies in giving their 'due' to all conflicting moral and political claims and ideologies whether they be legalistic or not. There is no need to doubt that the realization of personal justice is infinitely more likely in a society which thus honors freedom and equality. However, the three are not, for all that, identical. Justice presupposes an identifiable rule and the disposition to follow it . . . [I]t is the thread that ties legalistic morals, legal institutions, and legal politics into a single knot.").

43. *Bradlaugh v. Gossett,* (1884) 12 QBD 271, 285 (Stephen, J.). *See also Reynolds v. Sims,* 377 U.S. 533, 624, 84 S.Ct. 1362, 1414, 12 L.Ed.2d 506 (1964) ("[not] every major social ill in this country can find its cure in some constitutional 'principle'") (Harlan, J., dissenting). *Cf. Marbury,* 5 U.S. at 164 (bracketing off from judicial consideration "that class of cases which comes under the description of *damnum absque injuria*—a loss without an injury").

44. *Cf.* Ronald Dworkin, *Freedom's Law: The Moral Reading of the American Constitution* (Harvard University Press, 1996), 11 ("Nor could a judge plausibly think that the constitutional structure commits any but basic, structural political rights to his care. He might think that a society truly committed to equal concern would award people with handicaps special resources, or would secure convenient access to recreational parks for everyone, or would provide heroic and experimental medical treatment, no matter how expensive or speculative, for anyone whose life might possibly be saved. But it would violate constitutional integrity for a judge to treat these mandates as part of constitutional law.").

45. *See, e.g., Exodus* 20:13 ("Thou shalt not kill.") (King James); *Romans* 12:19 ("Avenge not yourselves, but rather give place unto wrath: for it is written, vengeance is mine . . . saith the Lord.") (King James).

46. The most often cited constitutional provision is, of course, the Eighth Amendment. *See* U.S. Const. amend. VIII ("nor cruel and unusual punishments inflicted").

47. Some might argue that this statement is incorrect, because Judeo-Christian biblical texts and traditions are the moral groundwork of the anglophone legal tradition. This claim is simply mistaken as a legal and historical matter. *See, e.g.,* Paul Finkelman, *The Ten Commandments on the Courthouse Lawn and Elsewhere,* 73 Fordham L. Rev. 1477, 1500–1516 (2005).

48. *Cf.* Dworkin, *Justice in Robes,* 15 ("[I]t would not be a competent justification of contemporary legal practice to say that it serves the value of enforcing a god's will as this is revealed in some specified biblical document. Even if that were a legitimate and important goal for legal practice to adopt, we cannot claim that it is the goal of our legal practice because that claim would not even begin to fit what lawyers and judges actually do.").

49. William J. Brennan, Jr., "The Constitution of the United States: Contemporary

Ratification," in David M. O'Brien, *Judges on Judging: Views from the Bench* (2nd ed.) (CQ Press, 2004), 192.

50. *See, e.g., Walton v. Arizona,* 497 U.S. 639, 110 S.Ct. 3047, 111 L.Ed.2d 511 (1990) (Brennan, J., dissenting); *Demosthenes v. Baal,* 495 U.S. 731, 110 S.Ct. 2223, 109 L.Ed.2d 762 (1990) (Brennan, J., dissenting); *Saffle v. Parks,* 494 U.S. 484, 110 S.Ct. 1257, 108 L.Ed.2d 415 (1990) (Brennan, J., dissenting); *Blystone v. Pennsylvania,* 494 U.S. 299, 110 S.Ct. 1078, 108 L.Ed.2d 255 (1990) (Brennan, J., dissenting); *Stanford v. Kentucky,* 492 U.S. 361, 109 S.Ct. 2969, 106 L.Ed.2d 306 (1989) (Brennan, J., dissenting); *Penry v. Lynaugh,* 492 U.S. 302, 109 S.Ct. 2934, 106 L.Ed.2d 256 (1989) (Brennan, J., concurring in part and dissenting in part); *McCleskey v. Kemp,* 481 U.S. 279, 107 S.Ct. 1756, 95 L.Ed.2d 262 (1987) (Brennan, J., dissenting); *Tison v. Arizona,* 481 U.S. 137, 107 S.Ct. 1676, 95 L.Ed.2d 127 (1987) (Brennan, J., dissenting); *Glass v. Louisiana,* 471 U.S. 1080, 105 S.Ct. 2159, 85 L.Ed.2d 514 (1985) (Brennan, J., dissenting); *Wainwright v. Witt,* 469 U.S. 412, 105 S.Ct. 844, 83 L.Ed.2d 841 (1985) (Brennan, J., dissenting); *Strickland v. Washington,* 466 U.S. 668, 104 S.Ct. 2052, 80 L.Ed.2d 674 (1984) (Brennan, J., concurring in part and dissenting in part); *Pulley v. Harris,* 465 U.S. 37, 104 S.Ct. 871, 79 L.Ed.2d 29 (1984) (Brennan, J., dissenting); *Maggio v. Williams,* 464 U.S. 46, 104 S.Ct. 311, 78 L.Ed.2d 43 (1983) (Brennan, J., dissenting); *Gregg v. Georgia,* 428 U.S. 153, 96 S.Ct. 2909, 49 L.Ed.2d 859 (1976) (Brennan, J., dissenting).

51. *See* Brennan, "Constitution of the United States," 192–93.

52. Brennan, "Constitution of the United States," 193 (emphasis supplied).

53. Allan C. Hutchinson, *Evolution and the Common Law* (Cambridge University Press, 2005), 119.

54. *Id.*

55. *Id.*

56. *See, e.g., Lindsey v. Normet,* 405 U.S. 56, 74, 92 S.Ct. 862, 874, 31 L.Ed.2d 36 (1972) ("We do not denigrate the importance of decent, safe, and sanitary housing. But the Constitution does not provide judicial remedies for every social and economic ill. We are unable to perceive in that document any constitutional guarantee of access to dwellings of a particular quality . . . Absent constitutional mandate, the assurance of adequate housing and the definition of landlord-tenant relationships are legislative, not judicial, functions.").

57. *Cooper v. Wandsworth Board of Works,* (1863) 14 CB (NS) 180, 194, 143 Eng. Rep. 414, 420. *See also Wiseman v. Borneman,* [1971] AC 297, 309; *Ridge v. Baldwin,* [1964] AC 40, 69.

58. *R. (on the application of Wooder) v. Feggetter* , [2002] EWCA Civ 554, [44], [2003] QB 219.

59. *See* Dawn Oliver, "Review of (Non-statutory) Discretions," in Christopher Forsyth, ed., *Judicial Review and the Constitution* (Hart Publishing, 2000), 322.

60. *See, e.g., Raymond v. Honey,* [1983] 1 AC 1, 13–14; *Pyx Granite Co. Ltd. v. Ministry of Housing and Local Government,* [1960] AC 260, 286; *R. (on the application of G) v. Immigration Appeal Tribunal,* [2004] EWHC 588, [9], [2004] 1 WLR 2953, 2959; *R. v. Lord Chancellor, ex parte Witham,* [1998] QB 575, 584–86; *R. v. Secretary of State for the Home Department, ex parte Leech,* [1994] QB 198, 210; *R. v. Secretary of State for the Home Department, ex parte Anderson,* [1984] QB 778, 793–94; *Commissioners of Customs and Ex-*

cise v. Cure & Deeley, Ltd., [1962] 1 QB 340, 370; *Chester v. Bateson,* [1920] 1 KB 829, 833, 836–37.

61. *See Boddie v. Connecticut,* 401 U.S. 371, 374–75, 91 S.Ct. 780, 784–85, 28 L.Ed.2d 113 (1971) (violation of constitutional right of due process); *Witham,* [1998] QB at 581, 587 (violation of common law right of access to the courts).

62. *See Douglas v. California,* 372 U.S. 353, 83 S.Ct. 814, 9 L.Ed.2d 811 (1963) (assistance of counsel on appeal); *Gideon v. Wainwright,* 372 U.S. 335, 83 S.Ct. 792, 9 L.Ed.2d 799 (1963) (assistance of counsel at trial). Assistance of counsel for defendants accused of felonies has also been required by statute in English law since 1836 (and for much longer for defendants accused of misdemeanors). For the current statutory scheme, *see* the Access to Justice Act 1999.

63. Lon L. Fuller, *The Morality of Law* (rev. ed.) (Yale University Press, 1969), 171.

64. Fuller, *Morality of Law,* 171. *See also id.* at 176 ("[W]e must face the plain truth that adjudication is an ineffective instrument for economic management and for governmental participation in the allocation of economic resources.").

65. *Id.* at 184.

Chapter 2

1. *See* H. Patrick Glenn, *Legal Traditions of the World: Sustainable Diversity in Law* (2nd ed.) (Oxford University Press, 2004), 224 ("The only avenue for a Norman legal order, common to the realm, was through a loyal judiciary. This immediately marks off a common law tradition from all others.").

2. Roscoe Pound, *The Spirit of the Common Law* (Marshall Jones Company, 1921), 1. *See also id.* at 40, 42.

3. Roscoe Pound, "What Is the Common Law?" in Roscoe Pound, ed., *The Future of the Common Law* (Peter Smith, 1965), 7–8.

4. *Id.* at 8.

5. *See* John Chipman Gray, *The Nature and Sources of the Law* (Ashgate/Dartmouth, 1997), 54 ("[Judges] seek the rules which they follow not in their own whims, but they derive them from sources often of the most general and permanent character, to which they are directed, by the organized body to which they belong, to apply themselves.").

6. *See* Joseph Raz, *The Authority of Law* (Oxford University Press, 1979), 47–48 ("A 'source' is here used in a somewhat technical sense (which is, however, clearly related to traditional writings on legal sources [such as Pound's and Gray's]). A law has a source if its contents and existence can be determined without using moral arguments . . . The sources of law are those facts by virtue of which it is valid and which identify its content. This sense of 'source' is wider than that of 'formal sources' which are those establishing the validity of a law.").

7. *See* Gray, *Nature and Sources of the Law,* 78 ("The other sources from which courts may draw their general rules are fourfold—judicial precedents, opinions of experts, customs, and principles of morality (using morality as including public policy).").

8. *See* Gray, *Nature and Sources of the Law,* 78 ("[I]f a court should frame a rule based on the principle that infanticide was not immoral, that rule would not be the Law.").

9. Inclusive positivism, also called "incorporationism" or "soft positivism," is the view that moral principles "can count as part of a community's binding law in virtue of their status as moral principles provided the relevant rule of recognition includes a provision to that effect" (Jules Coleman, "Authority and Reason," in Robert P. George, ed., *The Autonomy of Law* (Oxford University Press, 1996), 287–88). *See also* H.L.A. Hart, *The Concept of Law* (2nd ed.) (Oxford University Press, 1994), 269.

10. *See, e.g.,* Hart, *Concept of Law,* 254 (citing Joseph Raz, *Dworkin: A New Link in the Chain,* 74 Cal. L. Rev. 1103 (1986)); Martin Lyon Levine, *Forward to Symposium: The Works of Joseph Raz,* 62 S. Cal. L. Rev. 731, 738 (1989).

11. Raz, *Authority of Law,* 199–200.

12. *See* John Finnis, *Natural Law and Natural Rights* (Oxford University Press, 1980), 319–20 ("[L]egal science . . . reasonably insists both that legal obligation be understood as invariant and that legal obligation (whether or not it is also a form of moral obligation) be sharply distinguished from all those moral (or other) obligations which would subsist apart from or in the absence of the law. The last mentioned demand or insistence of legal thought is not of interest only to 'positivists.' A 'natural law' jurist can also make the demand, and can observe that it is satisfied . . . This step expresses the fact that, wherever it reasonably can, legal thought looks to distinct sources for legal rules and obligations, viz. to the acts which lawyers treat as authoritative.") (emphasis deleted). *See also* John Finnis, "Natural Law and Legal Reasoning," in Robert P. George, ed., *Natural Law Theory* (Oxford University Press, 1992), 142, 151 (discussing the "authoritative sources" of law). I include Finnis to underscore the widespread agreement among lawyers and legal theorists about the nature of legal sources and their importance in legal reasoning.

13. My present concern is with textual sources. Judicial practice also can function as a source of law. *See infra* pp. 29–30, 170–71. As I explain there, this does not necessarily mean that these legal sources are exhaustive of the legally relevant materials that might be interpreted by judges through the adjudicative process.

14. *See, e.g.,* Gerald J. Postema, "Law's Autonomy and Public Practical Reason," in Robert P. George, ed., *The Autonomy of Law: Essays on Legal Positivism* (Oxford University Press, 1996), 83; Frederick Schauer and Virginia Wise, *Legal Positivism as Legal Information,* 82 Cornell L. Rev. 1080, 1093–99 (1997). Schauer and Wise believe further that the "limited domain" thesis is unique to legal positivism (*id.* at 1081–82). As my citations to Finnis's book and essay in n. 12 *supra* are intended to show, this seems inaccurate. My point here, however, is to express my agreement with Schauer and Wise's central claim that "the feature that explains law's differentiation is the information set on which legal argumentation and legal decisionmaking relies" (Schauer and Wise, *Legal Positivism,* 1082).

15. *See, e.g.,* Frederick Schauer, *Easy Cases,* 58 S. Cal. L. Rev. 399, 410 n. 34 (1985).

16. Melvin Aron Eisenberg, *The Nature of the Common Law* (Harvard University Press, 1988), 97.

17. *See generally* Kent Greenawalt, *Law and Objectivity* (Oxford University Press, 1992), 88, 255 n. 60.

18. Eisenberg does not specify which courts he refers to in his definition. The most likely consequence of this is that he means that all courts are free to rely on the decisions of all other courts as persuasive, even if not binding, authorities. Even read-

ing Eisenberg's definition very narrowly, however, he must, at a minimum, be writing from the implicit position of an intermediate appellate court. In his definition, Eisenberg refers to cases decided by "lower or parallel courts" as official legal sources. If we suppose that Eisenberg intended to write his definition from a high court perspective, his reference to "parallel courts" would be nonsensical. A high court in a given legal system has no parallel tribunal. Similarly, if we assume that Eisenberg wrote his definition from the trial court perspective, his reference to "lower courts" is likewise nonsensical. There is no court lower than a trial court on the three-tier model. Even read very technically, the judicial perspective from which Eisenberg's reference always makes sense is that of an appellate court.

19. *Cf.* Jerome Frank, *Courts on Trial: Myth and Reality in American Justice* (Princeton University Press, 1949), 4, 222–23. Judge Frank was not concerned with the specific question of trial court decisions as legal sources. He was, however, keenly aware of the overwhelming importance of trial courts in a common law system. To my mind, Frank's realist sensibilities and iconoclastic bent led him to overemphasize the trial courts' fact-finding function at the expense of their legal rulings. His fetish for facts notwithstanding, Frank rightly reminded common lawyers of the central role of trial courts within the larger judicial framework.

20. *See, e.g.,* Theodore Eisenberg and Stewart J. Schwab, *What Shapes Perceptions of the Federal Court System?,* 56 U. Chi. L. Rev. 501, 517–18 (1989).

21. *See, e.g., Terry v. Adams,* 345 U.S. 461, 73 S.Ct. 809, 97 L.Ed. 1152 (1953).

22. *See generally Reich v. Continental Casualty Co.,* 33 F.3d 754, 757 (7th Cir. 1994) (Posner, J.), *cert. denied,* 513 U.S. 1152, 115 S.Ct. 1104, 130 L.Ed.2d 1071 (1995) (noting that it is ordinarily the duty of lower courts to be guided by higher court dicta as "the best, though not an infallible, guide to what the law is").

23. *See, e.g., Sierra Club v. EPA,* 322 F.3d 718, 724 (D.C. Cir. 2003).

24. *See U.S. v. Carolene Products Co.,* 304 U.S. 144, 152 n. 4, 58 S.Ct. 778, 783, 82 L.Ed. 1234, 1241 (1938).

25. Samuel J. Konefsky, *The Legacy of Holmes and Brandeis: A Study in the Influence of Ideas* (Collier Books, 1961), 100–102 (citation omitted). *See also* Benjamin N. Cardozo, *The Nature of the Judicial Process* (Yale University Press, 1921), 79 ("It is the dissenting opinion of Justice Holmes [in *Lochner v. New York,* 198 U.S. 45, 25 S.Ct. 539, 49 L.Ed. 937 (1905)], which men will turn to in the future as the beginning of an era. In the instance, it was the voice of a minority. In principle, it has become the voice of a new dispensation, which has written itself into law.").

26. *See generally* John P. Kelsh, *The Opinion Delivery Practices of the United States Supreme Court, 1790–1945,* 77 Wash. U. L.Q. 137, 161 (1999) (noting the "increased sense," beginning in the mid-nineteenth century, "that dissents were a legitimate and important source of law").

27. *Cf.* Richard A. Posner, *The Problems of Jurisprudence* (Harvard University Press, 1990), 98 ("The point to be particularly emphasized is that in a system of precedent it is the later court that has the whip hand, not the earlier court.").

28. Pound, *Spirit of the Common Law,* 65. In this quotation, Pound also mentioned trial by jury as the third characteristic common law institution. Jury trials are irrelevant to my discussion here.

29. *Id.* at 182. Like Pound, Dicey also views the supremacy of law as a fundamental aspect of the (English) common law tradition, although Dicey preferred the phrase *rule of law* to *supremacy of law*. Writing in (or defining) the orthodox English perspective, Dicey believed that the other fundamental doctrine of the English common law system was parliamentary sovereignty. *See* A.V. Dicey, *Introduction to the Study of the Law of the Constitution* (10th ed.) (Macmillan, 1959), ch. 4.

30. Pound, *Spirit of the Common Law,* 64–65, 74–75.

31. *Id.* at 75 (quoting *Dr. Bonham's Case,* (1610) 8 Co. Rep. 107a, 77 Eng. Rep. 638).

32. *See generally* A.W.B. Simpson, "The Common Law and Legal Theory," in A.W.B. Simpson, ed., *Oxford Essays in Jurisprudence* (2nd ser.) (Oxford University Press, 1973), 77 ("[T]he elaboration of rules and principles governing the use of precedents and their status as authorities is relatively modern, and the idea that there could be binding precedents more recent still. The common law had been in existence for centuries before anybody was very excited about these matters."). Henry II is generally credited with laying the institutional groundwork, in the twelfth century, for the common law courts and common law system, which would take identifiable shape, in the thirteenth century, as the historical precursor to the modern common law system, through the emergence of the *coram rege* as a part of the *curia regis.* The Court of Common Pleas and the Court of King's Bench would later develop from the *coram rege. See generally* R.C. van Caenegem, *The Birth of the English Common Law* (2nd ed.) (Cambridge University Press, 1988), 22–23; S.F.C. Milsom, *Historical Foundations of the Common Law* (2nd ed.) (Butterworths, 1981), 31–33, 52–55; 1 Frederick Pollock and Frederic William Maitland, *The History of English Law* (2nd ed.) (Cambridge University Press, 1968), 136–67. Judicial deference to precedent began in the fifteenth century at the earliest; *see* Robert A. Sprecher, *The Development of the Doctrine of Stare Decisis and the Extent to Which It Should Be Applied,* 31 A.B.A. J. 501, 502 (1945). A genuine doctrine of stare decisis did not arise until the eighteenth century; *see* Simpson, "Common Law and Legal Theory," 77. The doctrine of supremacy of law traces its ancestry back to *Bonham* in the early seventeenth century.

33. *See, e.g.,* Frederick Schauer, *Is the Common Law Law?* 77 Cal. L. Rev. 455 (1989).

34. *See* W.J. Waluchow, *A Common Law Theory of Judicial Review: The Living Tree* (Cambridge University Press, 2007), 204; Allan C. Hutchinson, *Evolution and the Common Law* (Cambridge University Press, 2005), 200; Michael J. Perry, "What Is 'the Constitution'? (and Other Fundamental Questions), in Larry Alexander, ed., *Constitutionalism: Philosophical Foundations* (Cambridge University Press, 1998), 132; Cass R. Sunstein, *Legal Reasoning and Political Conflict* (Oxford University Press, 1996), 79–83; Richard A. Posner, *The Federal Courts: Challenge and Reform* (Harvard University Press, 1996), 309; Laurence H. Tribe and Michael C. Dorf, *On Reading the Constitution* (Harvard University Press, 1991), 114–17; Harry H. Wellington, *Interpreting the Constitution* (Yale University Press, 1990), 77–88; Paul Craig and Nicholas Bamforth, *Constitutional Analysis, Constitutional Principle, and Judicial Review,* [2001] Pub. L. 763, 767; David A. Strauss, *Common Law Constitutional Interpretation,* 63 U. Chi. L. Rev. 877 (1996); Ernest Young, *Rediscovering Conservatism: Burkean Political Theory and Constitutional Interpretation,* 72 N.C. L. Rev. 619, 688–97 (1994); Schauer, *Is the Common Law Law?* 470 n. 41; Paul Brest, *The Misconceived Quest for the Original Understanding,* 60

B.U. L. Rev. 204, 228–29 (1980); R.L. Brilmayer, *Judicial Review, Justiciability and the Limits of the Common Law Method,* 57 B.U. L. Rev. 807, 809–21 (1977); Thomas C. Grey, *Do We Have an Unwritten Constitution?* 27 Stan. L. Rev. 703, 715 (1975).

35. *See* Sunstein, *Legal Reasoning and Political Conflict,* 83–90; Guido Calabresi, *A Common Law for the Age of Statutes* (Harvard University Press, 1982), 101–19, 161–66; Edward H. Levi, *An Introduction to Legal Reasoning* (University of Chicago Press, 1949), 27–57; Note, *Intent, Clear Statements, and the Common Law: Statutory Interpretation in the Supreme Court,* 95 Harv. L. Rev. 892, 913–15 (1982). *Cf. National Society of Professional Engineers v. U.S.,* 435 U.S. 679, 688, 98 S.Ct. 1355, 1363, 55 L.Ed.2d 637 (1978).

36. *See generally* Strauss, *Common Law Constitutional Interpretation,* 889–90.

37. *See* R.C. van Caenegem, *European Law in the Past and the Future: Unity and Diversity over Two Millennia* (Cambridge University Press, 2002), 41–42.

38. By this I mean that a common law case may raise constitutional issues and, conversely, that a constitutional case might be resolved by recourse to a common law principle.

39. *See infra* pp. 74–78, 87–88, 89–91, 188–90. *See also* sources cited in n. 34 *supra.*

40. *See* Strauss, *Common Law Constitutional Interpretation,* 887–88.

41. *See infra* pp. 163, 178–87.

42. *See, e.g.,* Raz, *The Authority of Law,* 39–40 ("A jurisprudential theory is acceptable only if its tests for identifying the content of the law and determining its existence depend exclusively on facts of human behaviour capable of being described in value-neutral terms, and applied without resort to moral argument.").

43. *See, e.g.,* Hart, *Concept of Law,* 204 ("In some systems, as in the United States, the ultimate criteria of legal validity explicitly incorporate principles of justice or substantive moral values."); Coleman, "Authority and Reason," 295 ("The incorporation thesis claims that in virtue of their truth or correctness certain of a community's moral principles can be incorporated into law through the rule of recognition: the rule of recognition asserts, in effect, that certain moral principles are law provided they express the certain demands of morality or justice.").

44. *See* Ronald Dworkin, *Taking Rights Seriously* (Harvard University Press, 1978), 39–45.

45. *See* Ronald Dworkin, *Law's Empire* (Harvard University Press, 1986), 65–68, 230–31.

46. *See id.* at 66.

47. *See* Ronald Dworkin, *Justice in Robes* (Harvard University Press, 2006), 9–21.

48. *Id.* at 21.

49. *See id.* at 223–27; Dworkin, *Law's Empire,* 37–46, 68–76.

50. *See* Dworkin, *Justice in Robes,* 9–12, 152–55, 224–25; Dworkin, *Law's Empire,* 87–88.

51. *See* Nicos Stavropoulos, *Objectivity in Law* (Oxford University Press, 1996), 141–42.

52. *See id.* at 187–88.

53. *See, e.g.,* Dworkin, *Justice in Robes,* 6 ("In Anglo-American legal systems . . . the truth or falsity of propositions of law depends on past judicial decisions as well as statutes."); Dworkin, *Law's Empire,* 88, 99.

54. *See* Dworkin, *Law's Empire,* 255 ("Convictions about fit will provide a rough threshold requirement that an interpretation of some part of the law must meet if it is to be eligible at all . . . That threshold will eliminate interpretations that some judges would otherwise prefer, so the brute facts of legal history will in this way limit the role any judge's personal convictions of justice can play in his decisions . . . [I]f his threshold of fit is wholly derivative from and adjustable to his convictions of justice, so that the latter automatically provide an eligible interpretation—then he cannot claim in good faith to be interpreting his legal practice at all."). *See also id.* at 401 ("[L]aw is a matter of rights tenable in court. This makes the content of law sensitive to different kinds of institutional constraints, special to judges, that are not necessarily constraints for other officials or institutions . . . Strict doctrines of precedent, which require some judges to follow past decisions of other judges even when they think these are mistaken, are a familiar instance . . . [L]egislative supremacy is another institutional constraint, and this normally embraces all courts . . . If Hercules had decided to ignore legislative supremacy and strict precedent whenever ignoring these doctrines would allow him to improve the law's integrity, judged as a matter of substance alone, then he would have violated integrity overall. For any successful interpretation of our legal practice must recognize these institutional constraints.").

55. For more on this point, *see* Nicos Stavropoulos, "Hart's Semantics," in Jules Coleman, ed., *Hart's Postscript: Essays on the Postscript to* The Concept of Law (Oxford University Press, 2001).

56. For more on the debate between exclusive and inclusive positivists, *see, e.g.,* Brian Leiter, "Legal Realism, Hard Positivism, and the Limits of Conceptual Analysis," in Coleman, *Hart's Postscript.*

57. *Cf.* Dworkin, *Justice in Robes,* 228–29 ("Two lawyers [or judges] who disagree sharply about what the law requires in various circumstances could nevertheless both have equally well mastered the concept of law. One of them, at least, is wrong about the law, but he is wrong because his legal arguments fail, not because he understands the concept of 'how the law is on a particular point' less well than his rival. So we cannot say that legal theory should identify the essential nature of what lawyers, exhibiting their mastery, converge on identifying as law. Analytic doctrinal positivism points out that lawyers' opinions normally do overlap to a considerable degree: there is generally a large area of source-based law that is for a time uncontroversial among them. It then hails that area of overlap as exhausting the extension of the doctrinal concept of law and announces that the essential nature of law so identified is source-based.").

Chapter 3

1. *See generally* Ruth Gavison, *The Implications of Jurisprudential Theories for Judicial Election, Selection, and Accountability,* 61 S. Cal. L. Rev. 1617, 1646 (1988).

2. *See, e.g.,* Philip Soper, *A Theory of Law* (Harvard University Press, 1984), 41 ("[T]here is virtually no literature on the question of the judge's obligation to apply the law, although there is a huge body of literature on the question of how a judge determines the law and thus fulfills this obligation.") (emphasis deleted).

3. *See* Larry Alexander, *Constrained by Precedent,* 63 S. Cal. L. Rev. 1, 1 (1989) ("The notion that courts ordinarily should follow precedent in deciding cases is one of the core structural features of adjudication in common-law legal systems.").

4. *See, e.g.,* Evan H. Caminker, *Allocating the Judicial Power in a "Unified Judiciary,"* 78 Tex. L. Rev. 1513, 1542–43 (2000).

5. *See generally* Michael C. Dorf, *Dicta and Article III,* 142 U. Pa. L. Rev. 1997, 2024–25 (1994).

6. *See, e.g., Allegheny General Hospital v. NLRB,* 608 F.2d 965, 969–70 (3d Cir. 1979), *overruled on other grounds by St. Margaret Memorial Hospital v. NLRB,* 991 F.2d 1146, 1155 (3d Cir. 1993) (equating the doctrine of precedent with horizontal and vertical stare decisis).

7. *See Patterson v. McLean Credit Union,* 491 U.S. 164, 172, 109 S.Ct. 2363, 2370, 105 L.Ed.2d 132 (1989) ("Stare decisis is a basic self-governing principle of the Judicial Branch."). *See also* Neil MacCormick and Robert S. Summers, eds., *Interpreting Precedents: A Comparative Study* (Ashgate/Dartmouth, 1997), 327 ("There is no statute law governing the use or citation of precedent in the UK. This is an aspect of common law which has developed itself purely by common law methodology."). For this reason, I do not participate in the interesting (but, it seems to me, unavailing) attempts to locate a textual source for the doctrine of stare decisis. *See generally* M.B.W. Sinclair, *The Semantics of Common Law Predicates,* 61 Ind. L.J. 373, 389 (1986) (explaining that the rule of stare decisis cannot be traced to a statute or case in England or the United States).

8. Rupert Cross and J.W. Harris, *Precedent in English Law* (4th ed.) (Oxford University Press, 1991), 105. *See also* Joseph Raz, *The Authority of Law* (Oxford University Press, 1979), 68 ("[T]he rules practised by the courts of a legal system are rules of that system . . . [T]he courts' practice is what makes the rule a legal rule and is thus its source.").

9. *See generally Patterson,* 491 U.S. at 172–73, 109 S.Ct. at 2370 ("Considerations of stare decisis have special force in the area of statutory interpretation, for here, unlike in the context of constitutional interpretation, the legislative power is implicated, and Congress remains free to alter what we have done.") (citations omitted).

10. *See generally Burnet v. Coronado Oil & Gas Co.,* 285 U.S. 393, 406–8, 52 S.Ct. 443, 447–48, 76 L.Ed. 815 (1932), *overruled by Southern Pacific Co. v. Gallagher,* 306 U.S. 167, 59 S.Ct. 389, 83 L.Ed. 586 (1939) ("[I]n cases involving the Federal Constitution, where correction through legislative action is practically impossible, this Court has often overruled its earlier decisions. The Court bows to lessons of experience and the force of better reasoning, recognizing that the process of trial and error, so fruitful in the physical sciences, is appropriate also in the judicial function.") (Brandeis, J., dissenting) (citations and footnotes omitted).

11. *See* Rafael Gely, *Of Sinking and Escalating: A (Somewhat) New Look at Stare Decisis,* 60 U. Pitt. L. Rev. 89, 108–10 (1998) (discussing the rationale for the sliding stare decisis scale in American law).

12. The House of Lords rejected this reasoning in *Farrell v. Alexander,* [1977] AC 59.

13. *See, e.g.,* Frank H. Easterbrook, *Stability and Reliability in Judicial Decisions,* 73 Cornell L. Rev. 422, 426–27 (1988) (criticizing the rationale underlying heightened statutory stare decisis by noting that "the failure of a different [Congressional] body to act hardly shows that the interpretation of what an earlier one did is 'right'").

14. England does not have a sliding scale of stare decisis. There is no heightened statutory stare decisis, and there is no relaxed stare decisis in constitutional cases. Where the doctrine binds, it binds all courts with equal stringency. *See* Cross and Harris, *Precedent in English Law,* 6 ("Every court is bound to follow any case decided by a court above it in the hierarchy, and appellate courts (other than the House of Lords) are bound by their previous decisions.").

15. An objection to including trial courts on this list is the claim that trial courts never issue precedent, because their decisions are never binding on any later court, not even another trial court. This objection overlooks the distinction between precedent as persuasive or binding. Trial court decisions are never binding precedent, but they are frequently considered as persuasive precedent. This is my reason for including trial courts on this list.

16. Some judges and theorists indicate that a distinction should be drawn between ordinary precedent and "superprecedent" or between ordinary stare decisis and "super stare decisis." *See, e.g., Richmond Medical Center for Women v. Gilmore,* 219 F.3d 376, 376 (4th Cir. 2000) (Luttig, J.). The issue of whether certain paradigm cases should be treated as more constitutionally embedded or entrenched than others raises important questions about the normative force of precedent both horizontally and vertically, but I do not consider those questions here.

17. For arguments favoring the presumptive model, *see* Maxwell L. Stearns, *Standing Back from the Forest: Justiciability and Social Choice,* 83 Cal. L. Rev. 1309, 1356 n. 140 (1995); Henry P. Monaghan, *Stare Decisis and Constitutional Adjudication,* 88 Colum. L. Rev. 723, 757–58 (1988). For two examples endorsing the rule model, *see* Alexander, *Constrained by Precedent,* 17–28, 53; Frederick Schauer, *Precedent,* 39 Stan. L. Rev. 571, 593–95 (1987).

18. I do not consider whether precedent is "relevant." Relevance is redundant. If the prior case is a precedent in the instant case, it must be relevant. The real question is whether the precedent is "binding" and, if so, whether the judge has any legitimate latitude to disregard it. *Cf.* A.W.B. Simpson, "The *Ratio Decidendi* of a Case and the Doctrine of Binding Precedent," in A.G. Guest, ed. *Oxford Essays in Jurisprudence* (1st ser.) (Oxford University Press, 1961), 148, 165–67.

19. *See generally Webster v. Fall,* 266 U.S. 507, 511, 45 S.Ct. 148, 149, 69 L.Ed. 411 (1925) (questions never ruled on by the court cannot "be considered as having been so decided as to constitute precedents") (citing cases); *Wright v. Regan,* 656 F.2d 820, 839 n. 1 (D.C. Cir. 1981) (Tamm, J., dissenting), *rev'd sub nom., Allen v. Wright,* 468 U.S. 737, 104 S.Ct. 3315, 82 L.Ed.2d 556 (1984) (noting that a case cannot properly be considered precedent unless it directly addressed the issue raised in the subsequent proceeding). Of course, many cases do not involve only one discrete legal issue. This just means that there will typically be a wider array of precedent for a judge to consider and on which she may base her decision. Moreover, judges and lawyers may and frequently do disagree about what the dispositive issue in a case is; accordingly, they frequently disagree about which cases are precedent and which of these the court should follow. *See, e.g., State v. Rees,* 748 A.2d 976, 980–81 (Me. 2000) (Saufley, J., dissenting).

20. *See generally* Richard Bronaugh, "Persuasive Precedent," in Laurence Goldstein, ed., *Precedent in Law* (Oxford University Press, 1987), 236–37.

21. *See supra* pp. 24–25.

22. As lawyers and judges use the term, a case can be "persuasive" precedent even if the judge is not ultimately persuaded by it.

23. Another category of cases that might be considered persuasive precedent involves cases addressing analogous or related issues that a judge might consider useful in resolving the pending matter. It seems to me that these cases are not, strictly speaking, "precedent" decisions. I recognize, however, that many attorneys and judges would be inclined to include these cases within the ambit of persuasive precedent, and I have no strong objection to expanding my definition, where necessary, to include these cases.

24. *Cf.* Richard A. Wasserstrom, *The Judicial Decision: Toward a Theory of Legal Justification* (Stanford University Press, 1961), 53. The implicit premise here is that a judge must have a sufficient reason for departing from precedent. Ordinarily, this reason will serve as part or all of the justification for the departure.

25. *See Black's Law Dictionary* (6th ed.) (West, 1990), 1406 (defining *stare decisis et non quieta movere* as "to adhere to precedents, and not to unsettle things which are established").

26. *Arizona v. Rumsey,* 467 U.S. 203, 212, 104 S.Ct. 2305, 2311, 81 L.Ed.2d 164 (1984) (citations omitted).

27. The Southern District of New York is one of the Second Circuit's constitutive districts and federal trial courts. The Second Circuit is the federal appellate court for the geographic area comprising the states of Connecticut, New York, and Vermont. The Second Circuit is directly above the Southern District in the federal judicial hierarchy of the United States.

28. In the interests of full disclosure, I should mention that the Southern District judge was reversed on appeal to the Second Circuit. *See Chelsea Square Textiles, Inc. v. Bombay Dyeing and Mfg. Co., Ltd.,* 189 F.3d 289 (2d Cir. 1999). Some might claim this as proof that the Southern District judge was bound by the Second Circuit's precedent after all. But that claim misrepresents the situation. The Southern District judge did not follow certain binding Second Circuit precedent in making his decision. Where stare decisis is concerned, that is the moment at which the binding force of precedent matters, and that is why I believe my definition of binding precedent most accurately reflects judicial practice and legal doctrine. *Cf.* Edward H. Levi, *An Introduction to Legal Reasoning* (University of Chicago Press, 1949), 2–3 ("It is not what the prior judge intended that is of any importance; rather it is what the present judge, attempting to see the law as a fairly consistent whole, thinks should be the determining classification.").

29. This capacious conception of binding precedent is also faithful to the historical development of the doctrine. *See, e.g.,* Gerald J. Postema, *Classical Common Law Jurisprudence (Part II),* 3 Oxford U. Commonwealth L.J. 1, 17 (2003).

30. Eisenberg expresses this point as the distinction between a precedent's bindingness and a precedent's force. As he puts it, a precedent may be formally binding and yet be so "drained of normativity" as to lack any legal force. *See* Melvin Aron Eisenberg, *The Nature of the Common Law* (Harvard University Press, 1988), 152–53.

31. When discussing situations where a court is absolutely bound to follow particular cases, judges and lawyers sometimes refer to those cases as "controlling." As my definition applies in the United States, then, all controlling precedent is binding

precedent, but not all binding precedent is necessarily controlling. I should also emphasize that in the United States and all common law jurisdictions, most binding precedent is controlling. For a remarkably forthright statement along these lines from a Supreme Court justice in a reported opinion, *see Kimel v. Florida Board of Regents,* 528 U.S. 62, 97, 120 S.Ct. 631, 653, 145 L.Ed.2d 522 (2000) ("Despite my respect for *stare decisis,* I am unwilling to accept *Seminole Tribe* as controlling precedent.") (Stevens, J., dissenting).

32. Another category of cases in which lower courts sometimes decline to follow binding precedent involves cases where the lower court determines that the higher court would reach a result contrary to precedent if the higher court revisited the issue. See, *e.g., Vukasovich, Inc. v. C.I.R.,* 790 F.2d 1409, 1416–17 (9th Cir. 1986); *U.S. v. City of Philadelphia,* 644 F.2d 187, 191–92 (3d Cir. 1980); *Spector Motor Service v. Walsh,* 139 F.2d 809, 814, 823 (2d Cir. 1943), *vacated sub nom., Spector Motor Service v. McLaughlin,* 323 U.S. 101, 65 S.Ct. 152, 89 L.Ed. 101 (1944); *McCray v. Abrams,* 576 F. Supp. 1244, 1246–49 (E.D.N.Y. 1983), *aff'd in part, vacated in part,* 750 F.2d 1113 (2d Cir. 1984), *vacated,* 478 U.S. 1001, 106 S.Ct. 3289, 92 L.Ed.2d 705 (1986) (the Supreme Court vacated the Second Circuit and essentially reinstated the District Court's judgment, which anticipated *Batson v. Kentucky,* 476 U.S. 79, 106 S.Ct. 1712, 90 L.Ed.2d 69 (1986)); *Barnette v. West Virginia State Board of Education,* 47 F. Supp. 251, 252–53 (S.D.W.Va. 1942), *aff'd,* 319 U.S. 624, 63 S.Ct. 1178, 87 L.Ed. 1628 (1943). *Cf. Taber v. Maine,* 67 F.3d 1029, 1043–44 (2d Cir. 1995) (Calabresi, J.). This technique is referred to as anticipatory or predictive overruling. See Eisenberg, *Nature of the Common Law,* 191 n. 43; Evan H. Caminker, *Precedent and Prediction: The Forward-Looking Aspects of Inferior Court Decisionmaking,* 73 Tex. L. Rev. 1 (1994); C. Steven Bradford, *Following Dead Precedent: The Supreme Court's Ill-Advised Rejection of Anticipatory Overruling,* 59 Fordham L. Rev. 39 (1990); David C. Bratz, *Stare Decisis in Lower Courts: Predicting the Demise of Supreme Court Precedent,* 60 Wash. L. Rev. 87 (1984); Margaret N. Kniffin, *Overruling Supreme Court Precedents: Anticipatory Action by United States Courts of Appeals,* 51 Fordham L. Rev. 53 (1982). Although the Supreme Court sometimes upbraids lower courts for anticipating impending overruling, it is worth noting that one of the strongest of these censorious statements is found in a case in which the Supreme Court upheld just such an anticipatory decision by a lower court. *See Rodriguez de Quijas v. Shearson/American Express, Inc.,* 490 U.S. 477, 484, 109 S.Ct. 1917, 1921–22, 104 L.Ed.2d 526 (1989) (overruling *Wilko v. Swan,* 346 U.S. 427, 74 S.Ct. 182, 98 L.Ed. 168 (1953) and affirming *Rodriguez de Quijas v. Shearson/Lehman Bros., Inc.,* 845 F.2d 1296 (5th Cir. 1988)).

33. *See generally* Michael Abramowicz and Maxwell Stearns, *Defining Dicta,* 57 Stan. L. Rev. 953 (2005); Julius Stone, *The Ratio of the Ratio Decidendi,* 22 Mod. L. Rev. 597 (1959); Arthur L. Goodhart, *Determining the Ratio Decidendi of a Case,* 40 Yale L.J. 161 (1930).

34. Under current English practice, the Court of Appeal is, subject to certain limited exceptions, bound by its previous decisions. *See generally Young v. Bristol Aeroplane Co.,* [1944] KB 718. By the *Practice Statement of 1966,* the House of Lords abrogated its adherence to horizontal stare decisis and left all other aspects of the doctrine unchanged. *See Practice Statement of 1966 (Judicial Precedent),* [1966] 1 WLR 1234. Notwithstanding the apparent clarity of the House's *Practice Statement,* Lord

Denning repeatedly attempted to unshackle the Court of Appeal from its own prior decisions. But just when he succeeded in persuading a majority of his position in one case, the House of Lords reversed and reiterated that the House itself is the only English appellate court not bound by its own decisions. *See Davis v. Johnson*, [1979] AC 264. Although some doubt exists as to the Court of Appeal's continuing observance of rigid horizontal stare decisis, the conventional English view is that the Court of Appeal is so bound. *See* Cross and Harris, *Precedent in English Law*, 110.

35. I borrow this term from Melvin Eisenberg (*Nature of the Common Law*, 47).

36. Eisenberg, *Nature of the Common Law*, 77 ("For some purposes . . . a useful working distinction can be drawn between principles and rules: principles are relatively general legal standards, and rules are relatively specific legal standards.") (citing Joseph Raz, *Legal Principles and the Limits of Law*, 81 Yale L.J. 823, 838 (1972)).

37. *See supra* p. 34.

38. *See* Benjamin N. Cardozo, *The Nature of the Judicial Process* (Yale University Press, 1921), 149.

39. *See, e.g., Williams v. Florida*, 399 U.S. 117, 127, 90 S.Ct. 1914, 1920, 26 L.Ed.2d 463 (1970) (stare decisis provides "the predictability required for the ordering of human affairs") (Harlan, J., concurring).

40. *See Hubbard v. United States*, 514 U.S. 695, 716, 115 S.Ct. 1754, 1765, 131 L.Ed.2d 779 (1995) ("[S]tare decisis protects the legitimate expectations of those who live under the law.").

41. *See, e.g., EEOC v. Trabucco*, 791 F.2d 1, 2 (1st Cir. 1986) (stare decisis "stems from the principles of stability and equal treatment underlying the orderly development of legal doctrine") (citation omitted); *Duffy v. Barnes*, 508 F.2d 205, 219 (3d Cir. 1974) (stare decisis means "that the courts dispense equal treatment to all litigants similarly situated") (citations omitted).

42. *See Planned Parenthood of Southeastern Pennsylvania v. Casey*, 505 U.S. 833, 854, 112 S.Ct. 2791, 2808, 120 L.Ed.2d 674 (1992) ("The obligation to follow precedent begins with necessity . . . [N]o judicial system could do society's work if it eyed each issue afresh in every case that raised it.") (citation omitted).

43. Walter F. Murphy and C. Herman Pritchett, *Courts, Judges, and Politics* (Random House, 1961), 380 (citing the four institutional values discussed *supra* in text).

44. *See Payne v. Tennessee*, 501 U.S. 808, 827, 111 S.Ct. 2597, 2609, 115 L.Ed.2d 720 (1991) (stare decisis "contributes to the actual and perceived integrity of the judicial process").

45. *Patterson*, 491 U.S. at 172, 109 S.Ct. at 2370 (citation omitted).

46. *See generally* Henry M. Hart, Jr., and Albert M. Sacks, *The Legal Process: Basic Problems in the Making and Application of Law* (Foundation Press, 1994), 568–69; Monaghan, *Stare Decisis*, 748–49. *See also* Monaghan, *Stare Decisis*, 750 ("[D]eparture from the precedent would contribute in some perceptible way to a failure of confidence in the lawfulness of fundamental features of the political order.").

47. *See, e.g., Jones v. Director of Public Prosecutions*, [1962] AC 635, 711 ("The principle [of stare decisis] does not apply only to good decisions; if it did, it would have neither value nor meaning."); *City of Detroit v. Vavro*, 177 Mich. App. 682, 686, 442 N.W.2d 730, 731 (Mich.Ct.App. 1989) ("[T]he doctrine of stare decisis requires us to follow the majority decisions of the Supreme Court, even when we disagree with

them."); Jerome Frank, *Courts on Trial: Myth and Reality in American Justice* (Princeton University Press, 1949), 275 ("The precedent system really bites viciously only when a court, regarding a precedent as undesirable, nevertheless refuses to deviate from it."); Pamela S. Karlan, *Two Concepts of Judicial Independence*, 72 S. Cal. L. Rev. 535, 548 (1999) ("Stare decisis really only matters when it constrains judges who affirmatively disagree with prior decisions."); Alexander, *Constrained by Precedent*, 4; Schauer, *Precedent*, 575–76, 592–93.

48. Christopher J. Peters, *Foolish Consistency: On Equality, Integrity, and Justice in Stare Decisis*, 105 Yale L.J. 2031, 2033 (1996).

49. *See* Michael S. Moore, "Precedent, Induction, and Ethical Generalization," in Goldstein, *Precedent in Law*, 200–210. The description of Moore's theory as a "natural model" comes from Alexander, *Constrained by Precedent*, 8.

50. *See* Peters, *Foolish Consistency*, 2112–15.

51. *See* Moore, "Precedent, Induction, and Ethical Generalization," in Goldstein, *Precedent in Law*, 210. Moore is somewhat ambivalent and ambiguous on this point.

52. Alexander, *Constrained by Precedent*, 8. *See also id.* at 50–51.

53. *See id.* at 48–49.

54. Peters, *Foolish Consistency*, 2039.

55. For discussions of the various issues and difficulties incommensurability raises for consequentialist theories, within and outside the legal context, *see* Ruth Chang, ed., *Incommensurability, Incomparability, and Practical Reason* (Harvard University Press, 1997). For specific applications of some of these problems to law, *see* Symposium, *Law and Incommensurability*, 146 U. Pa. L. Rev. 1169 (1998).

56. In fact, the consequentialist critic of stare decisis I discuss, Christopher Peters, has elsewhere suggested another nonconsequentialist justification for the legitimating effect of stare decisis on the judicial process: the ability of litigants in precedential cases "to serve as interest representatives of subsequent litigants in much the same way that we expect our elected legislators to serve as interest representatives of their constituents." Peters continues, "This form of interest representation extends the legitimacy of the judicial decision . . . from the parties immediately before the court to later parties who will be bound by the precedential effect of the court's decision" (Christopher J. Peters, *Adjudication as Representation*, 97 Colum. L. Rev. 312, 347 (1997)).

57. *See, e.g.*, Peters, *Foolish Consistency*, 2050 (defining "justice" as "treatment of a person in accordance with the net effect of all the relevant criteria, and only the relevant criteria; provided that considerations of 'equality' and 'integrity' cannot be relevant criteria").

58. Monaghan, *Stare Decisis*, 751–52.

59. *See, e.g.*, Earl M. Maltz, *Rhetoric and Reality in the Theory of Statutory Interpretation: Underenforcement, Overenforcement, and the Problem of Legislative Supremacy*, 71 B.U. L. Rev. 767, 769 (1991) (Legislative supremacy "embodies one of the most basic premises underlying the American political system"); George Winterton, *The British Grundnorm: Parliamentary Supremacy Re-examined*, 92 Law Q. Rev. 591 (1976) (describing parliamentary supremacy as the "grundnorm," or "ultimate rule of recognition," of the British legal system).

60. Here I mean vertical stare decisis. The only court in England or the United

States bound by horizontal stare decisis is the Court of Appeal, and the specific issues that constraint raises are not relevant to this discussion.

61. *See generally Van Horne's Lessee v. Dorrance*, 2 U.S. (2 Dall.) 304, 309, 1 L.Ed. 391, 28 F. Cas. 1012 (C.C.D.Pa. 1795) ("It is an important principle, which . . . ought never to be lost sight of, that the Judiciary in this country is not a subordinate, but co-ordinate, branch of the government."); *Hayburn's Case*, 2 U.S. (2 Dall.) 409, 410, 1 L.Ed. 436 (1792) ("[If] the court had proceeded, its judgments . . . might, under the same act, have been revised and controuled by the legislature, and by an officer in the executive department. Such revision and controul we deemed radically inconsistent with the independence of that judicial power which is vested in the courts; and, consequently, with that important principle which is so strictly observed by the Constitution of the United States . . . [N]o decision of any court of the United States can, under any circumstances, in our opinion, agreeable to the Constitution, be liable to a reversion, or even suspension, by the Legislature itself."); R.C. van Caenegem, *An Historical Introduction to Western Constitutional Law* (Cambridge University Press, 1995), 167; Larry D. Kramer, *Putting the Politics Back into the Political Safeguards of Federalism*, 100 Colum. L. Rev. 215, 240 (2000) ("The role of judicial review at this point was to aid in making it clear that the English doctrine of legislative supremacy had been rejected in America.").

62. Maltz, *Rhetoric and Reality*, 769.

63. *See infra* pp. 158–59, 187–88.

64. *See* Martin J. Redish and Elizabeth J. Cisar, *"If Angels Were to Govern": The Need for Pragmatic Formalism in Separation of Powers Theory*, 41 Duke L.J. 449, 460 (1991) ("One of Locke's most important contributions to modern political theory was his 'reconciliation of legislative supremacy with the ideas of the separation of powers.'") (quoting M.J.C. Vile, *Constitutionalism and the Separation of Powers* (Oxford University Press, 1967), 58).

65. *See* Earl M. Maltz, *Statutory Interpretation and Legislative Power: The Case for a Modified Intentionalist Approach*, 63 Tul. L. Rev. 1, 9 (1988) ("The best explanation for the doctrine of legislative supremacy is simply that it reflects a deeply-embedded premise of the American political system. The premise is that, within constitutional limits, the legislature (however constituted) has authority to prescribe rules of law that, until changed legislatively, bind all other governmental actors within the system."). In England, there are (at least in theory) no constitutional limits on parliamentary supremacy. Parliament's authority is legally unbounded.

66. *See generally* H.W.R. Wade, *The Basis of Legal Sovereignty*, 1955 Cambridge L.J. 172, 196 (1955) ("[S]overeignty is a political fact for which no purely legal authority can be constituted even though an Act of Parliament is passed for that very purpose."). By drawing this contrast, I am not joining the fray fomented by the Critical Legal Studies movement (and the Legal Realists before them) concerning the alleged impossibility of disaggregating law from politics. *See generally* Allan C. Hutchinson and Patrick J. Monahan, *Law, Politics, and the Critical Legal Scholars: The Unfolding Drama of American Legal Thought*, 36 Stan. L. Rev. 199, 206 (1984). I am simply tracing the different origins of different ideas.

67. The judicial recognition of legislative supremacy infuses the doctrine with its legal force. *See generally* O. Hood Phillips and Paul Jackson, *Constitutional and Admin-*

istrative Law (Sweet and Maxwell, 1987), 49–50 ("Legislative supremacy thus defined is a legal concept. The supremacy of Parliament, being recognised and acted upon by the courts, is a principle of the common law. It may indeed be called the one fundamental law of the British Constitution, for it is peculiar in that it could not be altered by ordinary statute, but only by some fundamental change of attitude on the part of the courts resulting from what would technically be a revolution."); Wade, *Basis of Legal Sovereignty*, 188, 190, 196.

68. *See, e.g.*, Maltz, *Rhetoric and Reality*, 769; Daniel A. Farber, *Statutory Interpretation and Legislative Supremacy*, 78 Geo. L.J. 281, 283 (1989).

69. Generally, where statutory language is clear, legislative history is irrelevant. *Ex Parte Collett*, 337 U.S. 55, 61, 69 S.Ct. 944, 947, 93 L.Ed. 1207 (1949) ("[T]here is no need to refer to the legislative history where the statutory language is clear.") (collecting cases). Nonetheless, even if one were to consult legislative history, I assume that it supports, with equal clarity, the plain language of the hypothetical statute at issue.

70. Despite the decision in *Collett*, cited in the previous footnote, the Supreme Court has occasionally consulted legislative history to confirm that Congress's intentions were accurately expressed by the chosen statutory language. *See, e.g., I.N.S. v. Cardoza-Fonseca*, 480 U.S. 421, 433 n. 12, 107 S.Ct. 1207, 1214 n. 12, 94 L.Ed.2d 434 (1987). Where the plain meaning of a statute's language leads to "absurd or futile results" or to an "unreasonable [result] at variance with the policy of the legislation as a whole," the Court will "follow that purpose, rather than the literal words" (*U.S. v. American Trucking Ass'ns*, 310 U.S. 534, 543, 60 S.Ct. 1059, 1064, 84 L.Ed. 1345 (1940)). This is sometimes not the judicial practice in England. For a paradigmatic example of an English court applying the words of a statute, despite the acknowledged absurdity of the result, *see Fisher v. Bell*, [1961] 1 QB 394. *But cf. McMonagle v. Westminster City Council*, [1990] 2 AC 716.

71. *See, e.g., Edwards v. Aguillard*, 482 U.S. 578, 636–39, 107 S.Ct. 2573, 2605–7, 96 L.Ed.2d 510 (1987) (Scalia, J., dissenting); Jeremy Waldron, *Law and Disagreement* (Oxford University Press, 1999), 119–46; Andrei Marmor, *Interpretation and Legal Theory* (Oxford University Press, 1992), 159–72.

72. *Compare* William N. Eskridge, Jr., *Dynamic Statutory Interpretation*, 135 U. Pa. L. Rev. 1479, 1492–94 (1987) (allowing changes in popular morality to influence judicial enforcement of clear statutory language) *with* Farber, *Statutory Interpretation and Legislative Supremacy*, 308–9 (arguing that the legitimacy and enforceability of a statute are "independent of the current state of public opinion").

73. According to those who draw this distinction, strong supremacy is "a complete specification of the judicial role," while weak supremacy is merely "a constraint on judicial action" (Farber, *Statutory Interpretation and Legislative Supremacy*, 287). To my mind, this as a distinction without a difference. The constraint on judicial action compelled by supremacy is precisely that a judge's role constrains her to enforce statutes as the legislature wrote them, provided that the statute is not unconstitutional (in the United States) or ambiguous (in England and the United States). Weak supremacy collapses into strong supremacy. This collapse is apparent in the attempt to define the distinction. Where there is strong supremacy, "courts must follow legislative directives"; where there is weak supremacy, courts "may not contravene

statutory directives" (*id.* at 284, 287). At least where statutory language is clear, as I have assumed, there is no distinction between strong and weak supremacy. *See id.* at 292 ("When statutory language and legislative intent are unambiguous, courts may not take action to the contrary.").

74. *Tennessee Valley Authority v. Hill,* 437 U.S. 153, 194, 98 S.Ct. 2279, 2301–2, 57 L.Ed.2d 117 (1978) (citation omitted).

75. The ability of American courts to strike legislation as unconstitutional is the traditional example. This power of judicial review is, of course, not currently recognized in the English system.

76. *See, e.g., British Railways Board v. Pickin,* [1974] AC 765, 782, 786–87; *Gomez v. Campbell,* 75 N.M. 86, 92, 400 P.2d 956, 960 (1965).

77. *Common School Dist. No. 85 v. Renville County,* 141 Minn. 300, 304, 170 N.W. 216, 218 (1918).

78. *See* Maltz, *Rhetoric and Reality,* 779.

79. *See* Maltz, *Rhetoric and Reality,* 771–82.

80. *See* Michael S. Moore, *A Natural Law Theory of Interpretation,* 58 S. Cal. L. Rev. 279 (1985).

81. *See supra* p. 39.

82. Moore, *Natural Law Theory of Interpretation,* 358. *See also id.* at 354 (where Moore discusses judges "constructing the morally best purpose for a statute, and construing it by reference to that purpose").

83. *See* Eskridge, *Dynamic Statutory Interpretation,* 1481–97.

84. *See* T. Alexander Aleinikoff, *Updating Statutory Interpretation,* 87 Mich. L. Rev. 20, 46–51 (1988).

85. *See* Aleinikoff, *Updating Statutory Interpretation,* 49–50; Eskridge, *Dynamic Statutory Interpretation,* 1496–97.

86. *See* Maltz, *Rhetoric and Reality,* 779–82; Farber, *Statutory Interpretation and Legislative Supremacy,* 306–9.

87. *See, e.g.,* Michael Sean Quinn, *Argument and Authority in Common Law Advocacy and Adjudication: An Irreducible Pluralism of Principles,* 74 Chi.-Kent L. Rev. 655, 657–58 (1999).

88. *See, e.g., Bloom v. American Express Co.,* 222 Minn. 249, 256, 23 N.W.2d 570, 575 (1946) (statute); *Hall v. Hall,* 109 Va. 117, 63 S.E. 420 (1909) (precedent).

89. *Cf. R. v. Secretary of State for the Home Department, ex parte Khawaja,* [1984] AC 74, 125 (stating that the age of a precedent is a "neutral factor" when assessing its ongoing validity).

90. *See* Oliver Wendell Holmes, *The Path of the Law,* 10 Harv. L. Rev. 457, 469 (1897) ("It is revolting to have no better reason for a rule than that it was laid down at the time of Henry IV. It is still more revolting if the grounds upon which it was laid down have vanished long since, and the rule simply persists from blind imitation of the past."), *quoted in Bowers v. Hardwick,* 478 U.S. 186, 199, 106 S.Ct. 2841, 2848, 92 L.Ed.2d 140 (1986) (Blackmun, J., dissenting).

91. *Magor and St. Mellons Rural District Council v. Newport Corporation,* [1952] AC 189, 191 (citations omitted).

92. *See generally* Maltz, *Rhetoric and Reality,* 792 ("The rhetorical dominance of legislative supremacy has served to detract attention from the central question—

whether it is desirable to impose strong institutional constraints on judges in cases involving statutory interpretation."). *See also* Duncan Kennedy, *Legal Formalism*, 2 J. Leg. Stud. 351, 388 para. 62, 395 para. 82 (1973).

93. Nicholas S. Zeppos, *Judicial Candor and Statutory Interpretation*, 78 Geo. L.J. 353, 357 (1989) (discussing the argument of Guido Calabresi—then professor, later dean, and now judge—in *A Common Law for the Age of Statutes* (Harvard University Press, 1982)).

Chapter 4

1. I do not assume that this process is simplistically syllogistic. *See* David Lyons, *Justification and Judicial Responsibility*, 72 Cal. L. Rev. 178, 180 (1984) ("The simplest model [of judicial reasoning] . . . may be termed a legal syllogism, which includes as its major premise a single rule of law, as its minor premise a statement of relevant facts, and as its conclusion the dispositive proposition of law. In actual practice, arguments or derivations may be much more complex, consisting of several steps, involving several rules of law.").

2. *See* Ronald Dworkin, *Law's Empire* (Harvard University Press, 1986), 31–46.

3. On the importance that the "point" of a particular practice bears for Dworkin's theory, *see id.* at 47–48, 62–65, 87–88, 92–94, 228.

4. For a discussion of the judicial function of dispute resolution according to methods of legal reasoning that require regard for authoritative sources, *see* Melvin Aron Eisenberg, *The Nature of the Common Law* (Harvard University Press, 1988), 3–7.

5. *See* Dworkin, *Law's Empire*, 88.

6. *See* Ronald Dworkin, *Taking Rights Seriously* (Harvard University Press, 1978), 37–38.

7. This, too, is open to disagreement on Dworkin's account.

8. Neil MacCormick, *Legal Reasoning and Legal Theory* (Oxford University Press, 1978), 53–54 (quotation marks deleted).

9. *Id.* at 33. *See also* Kent Greenawalt, *Law and Objectivity* (Oxford University Press, 1992), 54–55.

10. *Cf. Southern Pacific Co. v. Jensen*, 244 U.S. 205, 221, 37 S.Ct. 524, 531, 61 L.Ed. 1086 (1917) ("A common-law judge could not say, 'I think the doctrine of consideration a bit of historical nonsense and shall not enforce it in my court.'") (Holmes, J., dissenting).

11. *See generally* Dworkin, *Taking Rights Seriously*, 84–86.

12. *Id.* at 86.

13. *See supra* pp. 23–26.

14. *See, e.g.,* Dworkin, *Law's Empire*, 240–50, 350–54, 379–99.

15. *See id.* at 65–68. This is not to say that those who accept the limited domain account of legal sources assume these other factors are irrelevant to legal reasoning. The disagreement concerns whether these extratextual data are law, properly so called; whether these data are extralegal materials that may frequently have a bearing on a judge's legal ruling but that remain outside the domain of materials designated as the law of a given jurisdiction; or whether these data may be incorporated into the law of a jurisdiction in the presence of a rule of recognition to that effect.

16. *See* J. Harvie Wilkinson III, *The Role of Reason in the Rule of Law,* 56 U. Chi. L. Rev. 779, 779 (1989) ("The role of the judge involves, first and foremost, an unstinting effort to apply the law as written.").

17. *See generally id.* at 792 ("The unaccountable judge is still accountable to reason. A judge . . . must issue reasoned decisions. The judicial system as a whole is designed to promote reason as the paramount judicial virtue.").

18. *See, e.g., Bush v. Palm Beach County Canvassing Bd.,* 531 U.S. 70, 78, 121 S.Ct. 471, 474–75, 148 L.Ed.2d 366 (2000) (vacating and remanding the decision of the Florida Supreme Court because of "considerable uncertainty as to the precise grounds for the decision . . . Intelligent exercise of our appellate powers compels us to ask for the elimination of the obscurities and ambiguities from the opinions in such cases.") (quoting *Minnesota v. National Tea Co.,* 309 U.S. 551, 555, 557, 60 S.Ct. 676, 678, 679, 84 L.Ed. 920 (1940)).

19. *See* Greenawalt, *Law and Objectivity,* 49 ("Saying that a judge must decide in a certain way is to accept certain ideas about the nature of a legal system.").

20. *See, e.g.,* Thomas M. Franck, *Political Questions/Judicial Answers: Does the Rule of Law Apply to Foreign Affairs?* (Princeton University Press, 1992), 10 (By establishing judicial review of legislation, "the United States has found itself with the world's most powerful judiciary.").

21. *See* R. George Wright, "Does Positivism Matter?" in Robert P. George, ed. *The Autonomy of Law* (Oxford University Press, 1996), 66 ("Without relying on any implausibly strong claim of legal determinacy, we may still conclude that any positivist judge who finds a law profoundly immoral, but cannot fashion a plausible argument that such a law violates, say, our best understanding of the thrust of the first, fifth, ninth, or fourteenth amendments, is likely to be a judge of limited imagination.").

22. *See generally Griswold v. Connecticut,* 381 U.S. 479, 513 n. 6, 85 S.Ct. 1678, 1698 n. 6, 14 L.Ed.2d 510 (1965) ("Laws may be unjust, may be unwise, may be dangerous, may be destructive; and yet not be so unconstitutional as to justify the Judges in refusing to give them effect.") (citation omitted). *See also* Mark A. Graber, Dred Scott *and the Problem of Constitutional Evil* (Cambridge University Press, 2006), 13 ("*Dred Scott* highlights the possibility of severe conflict between constitutionality and justice.").

23. As the U.S. Supreme Court held in *Plessy v. Ferguson* (163 U.S. 537, 16 S.Ct. 1138, 41 L.Ed. 256 (1896)). For a specific, hypothetical example of such a statute, *see* David Lyons, *Ethics and the Rule of Law* (Cambridge University Press, 1984), 100–101.

24. 264 U.S. 443, 446, 44 S.Ct. 361, 362, 68 L.Ed. 781 (1924).

25. The statement under discussion here is strikingly similar in language and tone to the one examined in my discussion of legislative supremacy. *See supra* p. 44.

26. *I.N.S. v. Chadha,* 462 U.S. 919, 944, 103 S.Ct. 2764, 2780, 77 L.Ed.2d 317 (1983) (quoting *Tennessee Valley Authority v. Hill,* 437 U.S. 153, 194–95, 98 S.Ct. 2279, 2302, 57 L.Ed.2d 117 (1978)).

27. Moreover, the belief that judicial review in the United States limits judges to evaluation of government action only against the textual restraints of the written charter misconceives the historical and theoretical development of that doctrine. *See generally* Thomas C. Grey, *Do We Have an Unwritten Constitution?* 27 Stan. L. Rev. 703, 706 (1975) (defending the exercise of judicial review in light "of the courts' addi-

tional role as the expounder of basic national ideals of individual liberty and fair treatment, even when the content of these ideals is not expressed as a matter of positive law in the written Constitution"). I consider this historical and theoretical development in the next two chapters.

28. *See generally id.* at 706.

Chapter 5

1. *Dr. Bonham's Case,* (1610) 8 Co. Rep. 107a, 118a, 77 Eng. Rep. 638, 652.

2. *See, e.g.,* David Lieberman, *The Province of Legislation Determined: Legal Theory in Eighteenth-Century Britain* (Cambridge University Press, 1989), 53 (arguing that the idea that statutes contrary to common right and reason "were void in themselves and, as such, could be rejected by the common law judges . . . received its most famous airing in Coke's decision in Bonham's case"); John V. Orth, *Did Sir Edward Coke Mean What He Said?* 16 Const. Comment. 33 (1999); Edward S. Corwin, *The "Higher Law" Background of American Constitutional Law,* 42 Harv. L. Rev. 149, 371–72 (1928).

3. *See, e.g.,* S.E. Thorne, *Dr. Bonham's Case,* 54 Law Q. Rev. 543, 548–52 (1938).

4. I here postpone discussion of exactly what it might mean for a court to declare a statute void for violation of the common law. *See infra* pp. 149–50. In the specific instance of Coke's use of the phrase in *Bonham,* this question is mooted somewhat by the likelihood that even if Coke intended some notion of statutory construction, he meant that to equate with and encompass a power of judicial review in cases of extreme injustice. *See generally* Glenn Burgess, *Absolute Monarchy and the Stuart Constitution* (Yale University Press, 1996), 193.

5. I do not mean to suggest that the meaning of *Bonham* necessarily is or should be determined by Coke's intentions or beliefs. I address the question of *Bonham's* meaning from an intentionalist perspective because the scholarly debate has been framed this way for so long and because any adequate defense of the strong reading that ignored this debate would be seriously deficient.

6. Although not in the modern sense of this word. *See generally* Jeffrey Goldsworthy, *The Sovereignty of Parliament: History and Philosophy* (Oxford University Press, 1999), 38–40, 61–62, 114–17.

7. The traditional view is that the Glorious Revolution fixed Parliament's predominance within the English system of government. *See id.* at 159–65.

8. Of course, even today, the supreme English judicial tribunal called the House of Lords remains, technically, a subdivision of the legislative chamber known by the same name.

9. *See* Goldsworthy, *Sovereignty of Parliament,* 155–56; R.A. MacKay, *Coke: Parliamentary Sovereignty or the Supremacy of the Law?* 22 Mich. L. Rev. 215, 227 (1924) ("We cannot understand properly Coke's meaning without taking into consideration the general relations of the courts of the period to Parliament. Parliamentary sovereignty as understood today was far from the fact in the early Stuart period. Parliament was supreme as a court and had not yet attained superiority as a legislature."). Goldsworthy and MacKay disagree, however, about the superiority of Parliament as a legislature during this time. *See* Goldsworthy, *Sovereignty of Parliament,* 158.

10. *See* Goldsworthy, *Sovereignty of Parliament*, 123 (discussing Parliament's "desperate struggle with the King" during this period). *See also id.* at 75–77, 159–61.

11. *See* George Winterton, *The British Grundnorm: Parliamentary Supremacy Re-examined*, 92 Law Q. Rev. 591, 595 (1976) ("This alliance and mutual respect between Parliament and the common lawyers has had a profound effect on the development of English law, particularly in judicial recognition of parliamentary supremacy and parliamentary acceptance of judicial independence.") (footnotes omitted). *See also* P.S. Atiyah and R.S. Summers, *Form and Substance in Anglo-American Law: A Comparative Study of Legal Reasoning, Legal Theory, and Legal Institutions* (Oxford University Press, 1987), 227 ("Parliament and the common lawyers had been allies in the seventeenth-century struggles against the Crown; they did not see themselves as rivals.").

12. Philip Allott, *The Courts and Parliament: Who Whom?* 38 Cambridge L.J. 79, 86 (1979). Although Allott inexplicably and unsupportedly suggests that *Bonham* "should be regarded as an event rather than a source of law," he concedes its position as "a catalytic event in a fundamental process of constitutional change."

13. MacKay, *Coke,* 228–29.

14. A nascent notion of modern parliamentary supremacy existed in Coke's time. *See generally* Charles H. McIlwain, *The High Court of Parliament and Its Supremacy: An Historical Essay on the Boundaries between Legislation and Adjudication in England* (Yale University Press, 1910), 94; Corwin, *"Higher Law" Background,* 365 ("The most high and absolute power in the realm of England, consists in the Parliament . . . The Parliament abrogates old laws, makes new . . . and has the power of the whole realm, both the head and the body.") (citation omitted) (spelling updated).

15. Lon L. Fuller, *The Morality of Law* (Yale University Press, 1969), 100–101.

16. *See infra* pp. 64–69, 106–7.

17. *See generally* Theodore F.T. Plucknett, *Bonham's Case and Judicial Review,* 40 Harv. L. Rev. 30, 30 (1927) ("[Coke] was something more than a lawyer with an extraordinary knowledge of the arcana of the common law; more, too, than an antiquary of great distinction . . . for to all this he added the character of political philosopher. Urged by a presentiment of the coming conflict of Crown and Parliament, he felt the necessity of curbing the rising arrogance of both, and looked back upon his country's legal history to find the means.").

18. *Cf.* Samuel E. Thorne, ed., *A Discourse upon the Exposicion and Understandinge of Statutes* (Huntington Library/Anderson and Ritchie, 1942), 88 (arguing that in *Bonham,* Coke "must be understood to say that 'in many cases the common law will control acts of parliament'—that is, will restrict their words in order to reach sound results; and 'sometimes it will adjudge them to be completely void'—that is, will reject them completely if modification cannot serve").

19. Corwin, *"Higher Law" Background,* 372, 375.

20. For the recognition by one of Coke's contemporaries that *Bonham* stood for "a matter of public, political, and constitutional importance," *see* J.W. Gough, *Fundamental Law in English Constitutional History* (Oxford University Press, 1955), 105.

21. *See* MacKay, *Coke,* 231 ("Coke was aiming at an independent judiciary powerful enough to bring King and Parliament into line.").

22. *See infra* p. 237 n. 107.

23. The recital of the proceedings in Coke's *Reports* incorrectly notes the date as 10 November. *See Prohibitions del Roy,* (1608) 12 Co. Rep. 63, 77 Eng. Rep. 1342.

24. Catherine Drinker Bowen, *The Lion and the Throne: The Life and Times of Sir Edward Coke (1552–1634)* (Hamish Hamilton, 1957), 261.

25. *See Prohibitions del Roy,* 12 Co. Rep. at 63, 77 Eng. Rep. at 1342.

26. *Prohibitions del Roy,* 12 Co. Rep. at 64, 77 Eng. Rep. at 1343.

27. *Quoted in* Bowen, *The Lion and the Throne,* 262.

28. *Quoted in id.*

29. *Prohibitions del Roy,* 12 Co. Rep. at 64–65, 77 Eng. Rep. at 1343.

30. *Prohibitions del Roy,* 12 Co. Rep. at 65, 77 Eng. Rep. at 1343. For a discussion of contemporaneous accounts corroborating this event, *see* Bowen, *The Lion and the Throne,* 263–64.

31. *Prohibitions del Roy,* 12 Co. Rep. at 65, 77 Eng. Rep. at 1343 ("The king should not be under man, but under God and the laws.").

32. *Commendam Case, Colt & Glover v. Bishop of Coventry & Lichfield,* (1616) 80 Eng. Rep. 290.

33. *See* Bowen, *The Lion and the Throne,* 319.

34. *See id.*

35. *Quoted in id.* at 320 (emphasis deleted).

36. *Quoted in id.*

37. *Id.* at 321.

38. *Id.*

39. *Id.* at 322.

40. Hastings Lyon and Herman Block, *Edward Coke: Oracle of the Law* (Houghton Mifflin, 1929), 205.

41. Bowen, *The Lion and the Throne,* 326–27.

42. *See* 5 William S. Holdsworth, *A History of English Law* (3rd ed.) (Methuen, 1945), 478 n. 1; Bowen, *The Lion and the Throne,* 328.

43. Bowen, *The Lion and the Throne,* 328.

44. *Quoted in id.* at 334.

45. *Id.*

46. *See* Goldsworthy, *Sovereignty of Parliament,* 112–17.

47. *See, e.g.,* Anupam Chander, *Sovereignty, Referenda, and the Entrenchment of a United Kingdom Bill of Rights,* 101 Yale L.J. 457, 469 n. 73 (1991); MacKay, *Coke,* 235–47.

48. *See* Sir Matthew Hale, *The History of the Common Law of England* (Charles M. Gray, ed.) (University of Chicago Press, 1971), xii (calling Coke "the greatest lawyer in English history").

49. *See generally* 5 Holdsworth, *History of English Law,* 474 ("A very cursory acquaintance with Coke's writings will show us that he approached both law and history with the mind of a strenuous advocate. All through his life he never ceased to be an advocate of legal doctrines or political causes. Whether he is reporting a case, or arguing for the supremacy of the common law in the state, or upholding the rights and privileges of Parliament, he does it with all his strength; and the result is that he talks and writes himself into a decided view on the subject."); Harold J. Berman, *The Origins of Historical Jurisprudence: Coke, Selden, Hale,* 103 Yale L.J. 1651, 1675 (1994) ("Coke served with great distinction in each of these various capacities [as attorney general, chief justice, and member of Parliament]. As Attorney General he was completely loyal to the monarchy. As a common law judge he was com-

pletely loyal to the common law. As a member of Parliament he was an ardent supporter of parliamentary independence."). As James Stoner argues, the preceding, generally fair characterization of Coke's intellectual outlook should not be misunderstood, in Coke's case, "as the characteristic myopia of a lawyer" (James R. Stoner, Jr., *Common Law and Liberal Theory: Coke, Hobbes, and the Origins of American Constitutionalism* (University Press of Kansas, 1992), 29). *See also* Burgess, *Absolute Monarchy*, 202 ("[I]n many cases the key shifts in Coke's thinking seem to have come late, after 1625, warning us that there is no simple connection between Coke's ideas and his *career* narrowly considered" [emphasis in original]).

50. *See* Burgess, *Absolute Monarchy*, 200 (Coke "*always* believed that the operation of the royal prerogative was bounded and restricted by the common law" [emphasis in original]); Berman, *Origins of Historical Jurisprudence*, 1673–74 ("He loved the common law and fought for it against those who would curtail its scope and jurisdiction, including the king himself . . . [A]s Chief Justice from 1606 to 1616 and later as a member of Parliament, Coke fought stubbornly to limit the king's prerogative powers and to subject them to the common law and to parliamentary control.").

51. *See* Scott Gordon, *Controlling the State: Constitutionalism from Ancient Athens to Today* (Harvard University Press, 1999), 253–57; MacKay, *Coke*, 247 ("These apparent inconsistencies in Coke . . . become consistent only in their relation to his idea of the Fundamental Law."). *See also* Edward Coke, "Preface to Part Four of the *Reports*," in 1 Steve Sheppard, ed., *The Selected Writings of Sir Edward Coke* (Liberty Fund, 2003), 100 ("[T]he Magistrates to whom the execution of Laws is committed be principal observers of the same themselves . . . Whosoever will be complete Judges, . . . you must observe the laws yourselves.") (spelling updated).

52. *See* MacKay, *Coke*, 246 ("[T]hroughout his whole career there seems to be an idea of the necessity of retaining unchanged the fundamentals of the law, particularly the Common Law, but it seems clear that the method whereby he proposed to protect the law changed with the change in Coke's position from a judge to a politician.").

53. A gauge of the immediate influence of Coke's common law ideas on English legal thinking during and shortly after his life was Hobbes's use of Coke as the iconic representative of the common law mind in his later discussion of law and politics. *See* Thomas Hobbes, *A Dialogue between a Philosopher and a Student of the Common Laws of England* (Joseph Cropsey, ed.) (University of Chicago Press, 1971), 10 ("There is one master of the common law whom Hobbes takes very particularly under consideration in the *Dialogue,* and that is Sir Edward Coke . . . who is made the spokesman for the doctrine of autonomous common lawyers and thus the antagonist of what is surely Hobbes's own explicit position that sovereignty is entire in the monarch.").

54. *See infra* pp. 73–74, 79–88.

55. For an enlightening discussion of the development of Coke's thought, *see* Burgess, *Absolute Monarchy*, 200–208.

56. Like Coke, Matthew Hale understood this distinction. The latter expressed it in this way: "I Come now to . . . the Common Municipal Law of this Kingdom, which has the Superintendency of all those other particular Laws used in the beforementioned Courts, and is the common Rule for the Administration of common Jus-

tice in this great Kingdom . . . for it is not only a very just and excellent Law in it self, but it is singularly accommodated to the Frame of the English Government, and to the Disposition of the English Nation, and such as by a long Experience and Use is as it were incorporated into their very Temperament, and, in a Manner, become the Complection and Constitution of the English Commonwealth" (Hale, *History of the Common Law of England*, 30).

57. *See* Coke, "Preface to Part Four of the *Reports*," 94 (distinguishing the form of commonwealth under which the lawmakers are governed from kinds of municipal laws within a nation), 95–98 (reiterating the perils attendant to alteration of the English common law). *See also* Edward Coke, "Fourth Part of the *Institutes of the Laws of England*," in 2 Sheppard, *Selected Writings of Sir Edward Coke*, ch. 1, at 1143 ("A good caveat to Parliaments [is] to leave all causes to be measured by the golden and straight metwand of the law . . . It is not almost credible to foresee, when any Maxim, or Fundamental law of this Realm is altered (as elsewhere hath been observed) what dangerous inconveniences do follow.") (spelling updated). *Cf.* T.R.S. Allan, *Law, Liberty, and Justice: The Legal Foundations of British Constitutionalism* (Oxford University Press, 1993), 11 ("[W]hile the common law embodies many of the values traditionally associated with the rule of law, statute is necessarily more piecemeal and technical. It may supplement common law principles in specified classes of cases, or operate to overturn and defeat them (usually within fairly narrow boundaries). What it cannot do is displace the common law by providing a rival vision of the constitutional order.").

58. I address this issue in more detail later. *See infra* pp. 89–91, 173–86, 189–90. *See also supra* pp. 27–28.

59. I am not suggesting that a judge's later change of mind about the correctness of his earlier opinion is wholly irrelevant for a lawyer seeking legal authority for an argument. I am simply distinguishing between strategic choices a lawyer might make when citing cases and the status of those cases themselves.

60. Edward Coke, "First Part of the *Institutes of the Laws of England*," in 2 Sheppard, *Selected Writings of Sir Edward Coke*, sec. 138, at 701 (spelling updated).

61. *See, e.g.*, MacKay, *Coke*, 222 ("[W]e must beware of interpreting sixteenth century statements by twentieth [or twenty-first] century meanings. To understand what Coke really means we must attack the statement from a sixteenth century point of view.") Of course, Coke wrote *Bonham* in the seventeenth century. This slip in no way diminishes the gist of MacKay's message, however, with which I completely agree.

62. *Bonham*, 8 Co. Rep. at 118a n. (c), 77 Eng. Rep. at 652 n. (c) (quoting Ellesmere's *Observations on the* Reports).

63. For a further discussion of the recognition by Coke's peers that Coke intended the strong reading of *Bonham*, see Allen Dillard Boyer, *"Understanding, Authority, and Will": Sir Edward Coke and the Elizabethan Origins of Judicial Review*, 39 B.C. L. Rev. 43, 86 n. 153 (1997).

64. Thorne, *Discourse*, 86–87 (footnotes omitted).

65. Raoul Berger, *Congress v. the Supreme Court* (Harvard University Press, 1969), 351.

66. *See* Stoner, *Common Law and Liberal Theory*, 54.

67. For a contemporary edition, *see* Christopher St. German, *Doctor and Student* (T.F.T. Plucknett and J.L. Barton, eds.) (Selden Society, 1974).

68. The attentive reader will now find a reference to *Doctor and Student* in reports of *Bonham*. *See* 77 Eng. Rep. at 652–53 n. (c). This reference appears in an annotation to the decision and pertains to *City of London v. Wood*, (1702) 12 Mod. 669, 88 Eng. Rep. 1592, a case decided almost seventy years after Coke's death and in which Justice Holt cited *Bonham* approvingly. *See Wood*, 12 Mod. at 687–88, 88 Eng. Rep. at 1602.

69. *Calvin's Case*, (1608) 7 Co. Rep. 1a, 77 Eng. Rep. 377.

70. *Calvin*, 7 Co. Rep. at 3b, 77 Eng. Rep. at 381 ("This case was as elaborately, substantially, and judicially argued by the Lord Chancellor, and by my brethren the Judges, as I ever read or heard of any.").

71. *See Calvin*, 7 Co. Rep. at 2a, 77 Eng. Rep. at 379.

72. *See* Bowen, *The Lion and the Throne*, 258.

73. Berger, *Congress v. the Supreme Court*, 352.

74. *See, e.g.*, Boyer, "*Understanding, Authority, and Will*," 84 (noting that in *Bonham*, Coke "strained to the breaking point" the precedents on which he relied); Plucknett, *Bonham's Case and Judicial Review*, 40 Harv. L. Rev. at 35–45.

75. *See supra* n. 70. Some writers believe that Coke's involvement in *Calvin* was limited to the reporting of the case. *See* MacKay, *Coke*, 225 n. 19a ("Another interesting decision, in which Coke did not participate, but which he reports, illustrating the attitude of other judges at the period, is *Calvin's case*."). This is incorrect. *See Calvin*, 7 Co. Rep. at 2a, 77 Eng. Rep. at 379 (listing Coke as one of the judges who heard and offered arguments in the case).

76. Berger, *Congress v. the Supreme Court*, 352.

77. To a common lawyer like Coke, this distinction was plain enough, because, as Glenn Burgess explains, " 'common right and reason' was in the language of the sixteenth- and seventeenth-century English lawyer a synonym for 'common law' . . . [and therefore] the most likely reading of 'against common right and reason' . . . is 'against the common law'" (Burgess, *Absolute Monarchy*, 183, 185).

78. *See generally* Anthony H. Birch, *Concepts and Theories of Modern Democracy* (Routledge, 1993), 118; Lloyd L. Weinreb, *Natural Law and Justice* (Harvard University Press, 1987), 43–96 (tracing the development of natural law theory and describing its repeated and varied associations with some divine source); Kent Greenawalt, *How Persuasive Is Natural Law Theory?* 75 Notre Dame L. Rev. 1647, 1652 (2000) ("[I]n modern times, belief in natural law is strongly correlated to belief in God."); Berman, *Origins of Historical Jurisprudence*, 1661–62.

79. *See* John Finnis, *Natural Law and Natural Rights* (Oxford University Press, 1980), 388–403. *See also* Russell Hittinger, *Natural Law as "Law" Reflections on the Occasion of "Veritatis Splendor,"* 39 Am. J. Juris. 1, 32 (1994); Philip Soper, *Some Natural Confusions about Natural Law*, 90 Mich. L. Rev. 2393, 2396–2400 (1992).

80. *See, e.g.*, Robert Lowry Clinton, *God and Man in the Law: The Foundations of Anglo-American Constitutionalism* (University Press of Kansas, 1997), chs. 14–17; R. George Wright, *Legal Obligation and the Natural Law*, 23 Ga. L. Rev. 997, 1011–20 (1989).

81. *See* Burgess, *Absolute Monarchy*, 68–69; Bowen, *The Lion and the Throne*, 220–21.

82. Berman, *Origins of Historical Jurisprudence*, 1667 (footnote omitted). *Cf.* Boyer, "*Understanding, Authority, and Will*," 45 ("In Coke's day, discussions of the character

of the common law tended to conflate different theories of law—reason, custom, and nature.").

83. *Calvin,* 7 Co. Rep. at 12b–13a, 77 Eng. Rep. at 392 (citing *Doctor and Student,* cap. 2 and 4) (other citations omitted).

84. *Calvin,* 7 Co. Rep. at 4b, 77 Eng. Rep. at 382.

85. *Calvin,* 7 Co. Rep. at 13b, 14a–b, 77 Eng. Rep. at 392–94 (citing *Doctor and Student,* cap. 5 and 6) (other citations omitted).

86. *See* Berman, *Origins of Historical Jurisprudence,* 1660 ("[A] major work by Thomas Smith, *De Republica Anglorum,* first published in 1583, which is often cited as an example of distinctive English legal thought, is a straightforward account of the legal powers of the crown and the parliament and of the main features of the law applied by the common law courts. The author, who had been a Regius Professor of Roman Law at Cambridge in the reign of Henry VIII, carefully avoids philosophical questions such as the relationship of positive law to natural law and divine law.").

87. *Cf.* Corwin, *"Higher Law" Background,* 373 (differentiating *Calvin's* reliance on the law of nature from *Bonham's* focus on "the common law as applied by the ordinary courts"). For an example of a notable decision, prior to *Bonham* and *Calvin,* that relied on *Doctor and Student* as authority for voiding royal patents or acts of Parliament contrary to divine law, *see Darcy v. Allin,* (1602) Noy's Rep. 173, 180, 74 Eng. Rep. 1131, 1137 ("Now therefore it is as unlawful to prohibit a man not to live by the labour of his own trade, wherein he was brought up as an apprentice, and was lawfully used, as to prohibit him not to live by labour, which if it were by Act of Parliament, it were a void act: for an Act of Parliament against the law of God directly is void, as is expressed in the book of Doctor and Student, much more letters patents against the law of God are void."). Interestingly, Coke's report of the decision differs markedly from Noy's report. *Compare Case of Monopolies,* (1602) 11 Co. Rep. 84a, 77 Eng. Rep. 1260 *with Darcy,* Noy's Rep. 173, 74 Eng. Rep. 1131. As attorney general, Coke was cocounsel for the plaintiff in *Darcy.* Despite being decided previously, Coke's recitation of the decision appeared in his *Reports* after *Bonham* and *Calvin.* In his report, Coke omits any reference to *Doctor and Student* and carefully avoids the theistic slant of Noy's report of the case. Coke's report reads as a straightforward legal ruling that a royal grant of a monopoly over the production of playing cards was void as contrary to the common law and acts of Parliament. *See Monopolies,* 11 Co. Rep. at 86a–86b, 77 Eng. Rep. at 1262. Moreover, consistent with my argument that Coke distinguished common law from divine law, Coke's report expressly states that "the common law, *in this point,* agrees with the equity of the law of God" (*Monopolies,* 11 Co. Rep. at 86b, 77 Eng. Rep. at 1263) (emphasis supplied).

88. *See supra* pp. 59, 64–65.

89. *See supra* p. 64. St. German himself seemed to have acknowledged that common lawyers distinguished common reason from natural law. *See* St. German, *Doctor and Student,* 31–33.

90. *See* J.W. Tubbs, *The Common Law Mind: Medieval and Early Modern Conceptions* (Johns Hopkins University Press, 2000), 165–66; Boyer, *"Understanding, Authority, and Will,"* 44 ("[One of the] themes . . . central to Coke's jurisprudence [was that] artificial reason is not natural reason."); Corwin, *"Higher Law" Background,* 171–72 ("The right reason which lies at the basis of the common law, on the other hand, was

from the beginning *judicial* right reason."); MacKay, *Coke*, 229–30 ("'Common right and reason' . . . it must be remembered . . . [refers to] those learned in the law, or, to use Coke's own words, the 'artificial reason' of the law.").

91. John Underwood Lewis, *Sir Edward Coke (1552–1633): His Theory of "Artificial Reason" as a Context for Modern Basic Legal Theory*, 84 Law Q. Rev. 330, 338 (1968). For further discussion of Coke's place as a transitional figure in common law history, bridging the gap from medieval to modern legal thought, *see* Berman, *Origins of Historical Jurisprudence*, 1702 n. 130; Lewis, *Sir Edward Coke*, 330 (collecting sources).

92. Coke explicitly recognized the distinction between common law legal sources and other sources of moral or religious (but not distinctly legal) authority, and he emphasized the sole relevance of the former for legal reasoning and judicial decision making. *See, e.g.*, Coke, "Preface to Part Four of the *Reports*," 95 ("The Laws of England consist of three parts, The Common Law, Customs, & acts of parliament."); Coke, "First Part of the *Institutes of the Laws of England*," sec. 170, at 711 ("The Law of England i[s] divided, as hath been said before, into three parts, [1.] the Common Law, which is the most general and ancient Law of the Realms . . . 2. Statutes or Acts of Parliament; and 3. particular Customs . . . The Common Law appeareth in the Statute of Magna Charta and other ancient Statutes (which for the most part are affirmations of the Common Law) in the original writs, in judicial Records, and in our books of terms and years. Acts of Parliament appear in the Rolls of Parliament, and for the most part are in print. Particular customs are to be proved."); Edward Coke, "Preface to Part Six of the *Reports*," in 1 Sheppard, *Selected Writings of Sir Edward Coke*, 155–56 (citing as the exclusive "Laws of the Realm" relevant to legal determinations "Authority out of the Books of the Common Laws of this Realm, Acts of Parliament, or any legal and judicial Records"); Edward Coke, "Preface to the Fourth Part of the *Institutes of the Laws of England*," 1060 (citing as "authorities in law, [the] Rolls of Parliament, judicial Records, Warrants in law . . . because I have published nothing herein, but that which is grounded upon the authorities and reason of our books, Rolls of Parliament, and other judicial Records") (spelling updated). *Cf.* Coke, "Preface to Part Six of the *Reports*," 155 (where Coke defends one of his published case reports by emphasizing that he "dealt only with the Municipal Laws of *England*, as a subject proper to my Profession"); Edward Coke, "Second Part of the *Institutes of the Laws of England*," in 2 Sheppard, *Selected Writings of Sir Edward Coke*, ch. 29, at 848–73, especially 849, 859 (discussing various aspects of criminal procedure, due process, and civil liberties derived from Magna Carta as aspects of *legem terrae*—the "law of the land"; defining the law of the land as "the Common Law, Statute Law, or Custom of England"; and emphasizing that the *legem terrae* is the "Law of England") (spelling updated).

93. *See* Gerald J. Postema, "Philosophy of the Common Law," in Jules Coleman and Scott Shapiro, eds., *The Oxford Handbook of Jurisprudence and Philosophy of Law* (Oxford University Press, 2002), 592–95; R.C. van Caenegem, *An Historical Introduction to Western Constitutional Law* (Cambridge University Press, 1995), 27 (arguing that Coke limited himself "to strictly legal arguments and looked for precedents in medieval court rolls"; that he "did not appeal to modern natural law, which was even then taking shape on the Continent"; and that the "common law from England's medieval past had to serve in that capacity").

94. Burgess, *Absolute Monarchy*, 193.

95. *See* Mark D. Walters, *Common Law, Reason, and Sovereign Will*, 53 U. Toronto L.J. 65, 85 (2003) ("When St. German's views of constitutional theory were cited in cases or legal commentaries during the seventeenth and eighteenth centuries, it was almost always for his articulation of natural law's supremacy and immutability.").

96. Edward Coke, "Preface to Part Ten of the *Reports*," in 1 Sheppard, *Selected Writings of Sir Edward Coke*, 336–37.

97. *See, e.g.,* Bowen, *The Lion and the Throne*, 328 ("[T]he *Reports* were standard usage in all the law courts, Star Chamber included, and had been since the first volume appeared in 1600."). *See also* 5 Holdsworth, *History of English Law*, 477–78.

98. *See* Coke, "Preface to Part Ten of the *Reports*," 336 (referring to "the Arguments drawn from Books, Cases and other Authorities in Law"). For further discussion of the importance of Coke's *Reports* and *Institutes* on the standardization and development of English law, legal thinking, and legal practice, *see* Gordon, *Controlling the State*, 253–56.

99. *See supra* p. 58.

100. *See* Coke, "Preface to Part Six of the *Reports*," 155–57.

101. *See supra* n. 74.

102. Stoner, *Common Law and Liberal Theory*, 19.

103. Bowen, *The Lion and the Throne*, 259.

104. *Calvin*, 7 Co. Rep. at 4a, 77 Eng. Rep. at 381.

105. *See supra* p. 67. Berger seems to have realized his earlier mistake. *See* Raoul Berger, *Natural Law and Judicial Review: Reflections of an Earthbound Lawyer*, 61 U. Cin. L. Rev. 5, 6–8 (1992).

106. *See supra* p. 65.

107. *See, e.g.,* Charles Grove Haines, *The American Doctrine of Judicial Supremacy* (2nd ed.) (University of California Press, 1932), 36; George P. Fletcher, *Comparative Law as a Subversive Discipline*, 46 Am. J. Comp. L. 683, 683 (1998) ("Because this 17th century decision [*Bonham*] stands for invalidation of legislation on grounds of principle, it is widely regarded as the precursor to the practice of judicial review adopted in *Marbury v. Madison*."); Boyer, "*Understanding, Authority, and Will*," 45 ("The modern doctrine of judicial review traces its origins to the opinion Coke rendered in *Bonham's Case* (1610)."); Edward S. Corwin, *The Establishment of Judicial Review*, 9 Mich. L. Rev. 102, 104 (1910) ("The literary evidence with reference to the basis of judicial review is equally definite. All the law and doctrine upon that topic goes back finally to . . . *Dr. Bonham's case*.").

108. *See* Robert Lowry Clinton, Marbury v. Madison *and Judicial Review* (University Press of Kansas, 1989), 38–40.

109. 3 U.S. (3 Dall.) 365, 1 L.Ed. 638 (1797).

110. *See* Louis L. Jaffe, *The Right to Judicial Review*, 71 Harv. L. Rev. 401, 412 (1958) (discussing the origins of "the common law of judicial review"; noting that "the formative period was the seventeenth century, that great watershed of Anglo-American political doctrine"; and highlighting *Bonham*'s prominent place within this period).

111. *See, e.g., City of London v. Wood*, (1702) 12 Mod. 669, 687, 88 Eng. Rep. 1592, 1602; *Day v. Savadge*, (1615) Hob. 85, 87, 80 Eng. Rep. 235, 237.

112. *See* Haines, *American Doctrine of Judicial Supremacy*, 35; Lewis, *Sir Edward Coke*,

330–31 ("[T]he notion that previously established common law interpreted by the courts in the light of 'reason' is superior to all other [law] was continuously expressed until about 1760.") (citation omitted).

113. *See, e.g.,* Goldsworthy, *Sovereignty of Parliament,* 225.

114. (1744) 1 Atk. 22, 26 Eng. Rep. 15.

115. *Omychund,* 1 Atk. at 33, 26 Eng. Rep. at 23 (emphasis in original). Mansfield was, at the time, solicitor general, and his argument was adopted by the court.

116. *See infra* pp. 114–19

117. *See supra* pp. 27–28.

118. *Omychund,* 1 Atk. at 24, 26 Eng. Rep. at 17.

119. *Omychund,* 1 Atk. at 31, 26 Eng. Rep. at 21 (argument of Mansfield) (emphasis deleted).

120. *Omychund,* 1 Atk. at 44, 26 Eng. Rep. at 30 (emphasis deleted).

121. *Omychund,* 1 Atk. at 23, 26 Eng. Rep. at 16 (quoting the Act Concerning Artificers Strangers, 21 Hen. 8, c. 16, § 4 (1529)).

122. Berman, *Origins of Historical Jurisprudence,* 1712 n. 163.

123. For a modern example, *see Johnsrud v. Carter,* 620 F.2d 29, 31 (3d Cir. 1980) (noting that the plaintiffs' complaint claimed "violations of their rights under federal constitutional, statutory, and common law").

124. *See, e.g., State of New Jersey v. Levine,* 109 N.J.L. 503, 162 A. 909 (1932).

125. *See* Brian Z. Tamanaha, *On the Rule of Law: History, Politics, Theory* (Cambridge University Press, 2004), 56 ("[T]here was no sharp separation between public and private law; the common law rules . . . were applied equally in actions between citizens and between citizens and government officials. Accountability of government officials to ordinary law in ordinary courts was the cornerstone of this understanding."); T.R.S. Allan, *Constitutional Justice: A Liberal Theory of the Rule of Law* (Oxford University Press, 2001), 19–20, 42–43; Lord Woolf, Jeffrey Jowell, and Andrew P. Le Sueur, *De Smith, Woolf, and Jowell's Principles of Judicial Review* (Sweet and Maxwell, 1999), 54–56; Burgess, *Absolute Monarchy,* 134–35; van Caenegem, *Historical Introduction to Western Constitutional Law,* 3–4; Stoner, *Common Law and Liberal Theory,* 21; Paul Craig, *Ultra Vires and the Foundations of Judicial Review,* 57 Cambridge L.J. 63, 87 (1998) ("The absence of any formal divide between public and private law helps us to understand why it would not have appeared at all odd to a Coke . . . or a Mansfield to base judicial review on the capacity of the common law to control public power."). *Cf.* Bernard Bailyn, ed., *Pamphlets of the American Revolution, 1750–1775* (Harvard University Press, 1965), 537.

126. Lewis, *Sir Edward Coke,* 340 (footnote deleted). *See also* Craig, *Ultra Vires,* 82–83. For another example of the connection between Coke's and Mansfield's thought concerning the common law's ability to constrain parliamentary authority, *see Heathfield v. Chilton,* (1767) 4 Burr. 2015, 98 Eng. Rep. 50.

127. *See generally* Stoner, *Common Law and Liberal Theory,* 25–26; Thomas Y. Davies, *Recovering the Original Fourth Amendment,* 98 Mich. L. Rev. 547, 687, 688 (1999) (" '[U]nreasonable' had become an extremely potent pejorative in constitutional discourse because 'unreasonable'—in the form of 'against reason'—had been used in famous episodes in English constitutional history to denounce violations of fundamental legal principle . . . Coke and other legal writers . . . sometimes used 'reason'

in legal contexts as a label for the basic principles of the common law . . . To say that a statute was 'against reason' was to say that it violated basic principles of legality.").

128. *See Wiseman v. Borneman*, [1971] AC 297, 309.

Chapter 6

1. *Marbury v. Madison*, 5 U.S. (1 Cranch) 137, 2 L.Ed. 60 (1803). Although I will not address the matter here, some scholars doubt that *Marbury* itself established the power of judicial review to which Americans have grown accustomed. *See, e.g.,* Stephen M. Griffin, *American Constitutionalism: From Theory to Politics* (Princeton University Press, 1996), 94–96.

2. A.E. Dick Howard, *The Road from Runnymede: Magna Carta and Constitutionalism in America* (University Press of Virginia, 1968), 280. *See also* Edward S. Corwin, *The Establishment of Judicial Review*, 9 Mich. L. Rev. 102, 105–20 (1910).

3. Strictly speaking, it is inaccurate to refer to cases from the colonial period as "state court" opinions. Nevertheless, I use that term to mirror the familiar distinction between federal cases and cases from state (or colonial) jurisdictions.

4. Suzanna Sherry argues that Marshall's decision in *Marbury* rests on both the Constitution and "unwritten fundamental law." *See* Suzanna Sherry, *The Founders' Unwritten Constitution*, 54 U. Chi. L. Rev. 1127, 1169–70 (1987). Unfortunately, as I will later discuss in detail, Sherry does not properly distinguish among these sources of "unwritten" law (*see infra* pp. 105–7). For example, in her examination of *Marbury*, Sherry claims that Chief Justice Marshall supported his holding "that for every violation of right there exists a legal remedy" on "fundamental principles of natural law and Blackstone's *Commentaries*" (Sherry, *Founders' Unwritten Constitution*, 1169). The problem with Sherry's analysis is that the term *natural law* appears nowhere in the *Marbury* opinion. Yet Marshall refers several times, including in the portion of the opinion Sherry discusses, to the doctrines and courts "of the common law." *See Marbury*, 5 U.S. at 163, 165. Sherry's failure to differentiate common law from natural law undermines much of her analysis. Nevertheless, Sherry's effort to draw attention to the nonconstitutional legal bases for Marshall's decision in *Marbury* is commendable. Indeed, Marshall's reliance on the common law in *Marbury* lends further weight to my claims about the coexistence of common law review and constitutional review in early American law. So while I accede to the conventional belief that *Marbury* established constitutional review in the United States, it is worth remembering, as Sherry reminds us, that there is more to the story.

5. An additional felicity of the phrase from my point of view is its correspondence to the common law theories of judicial review represented in the ongoing debate about the *ultra vires* doctrine in English constitutional theory. *See generally* Christopher Forsyth, ed., *Judicial Review and the Constitution* (Hart Publishing, 2000) (anthologizing articles from prominent theorists on both sides of the debate). I discuss this *infra* at pp. 174–87.

6. *See* Michael S. Moore, "Law as a Functional Kind," in Robert P. George, *Natural Law Theory: Contemporary Essays* (Oxford University Press, 1992), 189–90. Natural lawyers conceive differently the moral realism that underpins the theory. *Compare* Michael S. Moore, *Moral Reality*, 1982 Wis. L. Rev. 1061 (1982) *and* Michael S. Moore,

Moral Reality Revisited, 90 Mich. L. Rev. 2424 (1992) *with* John Finnis, *Natural Law and Natural Rights* (Oxford University Press, 1980), 18, 24, 30–36, 59–97, 126–27, 225.

7. In this sentence, the term "law" refers to law *simpliciter*. *See* Finnis, *Natural Law and Natural Rights*, 363–64. Michael Moore refers to the intrinsic connection between the identification of the law and the moral content of the law as the "relational thesis." *See* Moore, "Law as a Functional Kind," 189–90 ("As I shall use the phrase, a 'natural law theory' contains two distinct theses: (1) there are objective moral truths; and (2) the truth of any legal proposition necessarily depends, at least in part, on the truth of some corresponding moral proposition(s). The first I shall call the moral realist thesis, and the second, the relational thesis.").

8. Individual common lawyers do, however, and these will inform and influence their understanding of the common law.

9. Defining common law and natural law as conceptually distinct does not make them mutually exclusive. Some natural law principles could conceivably be common law principles as well (and some judges viewed them this way). The importance of the conceptual distinction is that unlike natural law principles, whose authority depended on their apprehension through the exercise of practical human reason, the authority of common law principles rested exclusively on their articulation as legal sources by judges. *See infra* pp. 178–87. Moreover, this distinction recalls that between artificial reason and natural reason, which Coke emphasized and which was incorporated into the legal reasoning of certain early American judges in the decisions I analyze here. This definition and the analysis based on it conflict with the efforts of Robert Clinton to demonstrate that the Constitution rests on a common law foundation and that the common law, in turn, rests on a classical natural law foundation. Clinton's argument is ultimately tantamount to a denial of the unique status of authoritative sources for legal reasoning and of the ability of common law courts to enforce natural law principles. *See* Robert Lowry Clinton, *God and Man in the Law: The Foundations of Anglo-American Constitutionalism* (University Press of Kansas, 1997), 100–103, 189, 221. This argument seems problematic in several directions. It glosses over important dissimilarities in the thought of, for example, Coke and Blackstone. It focuses on the legal positivism of John Austin without seriously confronting the more sophisticated theories of contemporary legal positivists, such as H.L.A. Hart, Joseph Raz, or Jules Coleman—whose work as modern positivists is summarily dismissed as "self-contradictory and contrary to experience" (*id.* at 130). With his emphasis on classical natural law, as he defines it, Clinton deliberately tethers natural law theory again to an overtly theistic epistemology, without addressing the work of, for example, John Finnis. Finally, in his rejection of Austinian positivism and of the authoritative nature of legal sources, Clinton fails to note that natural lawyers, such as Finnis, do not believe that natural law theory necessitates a rejection of the place of authoritative sources for legal reasoning within the common law tradition. *See supra* p. 213 n. 12.

10. *See generally* Walter F. Murphy, James E. Fleming, Sotirios A. Barber, and Stephen Macedo, *American Constitutional Interpretation* (3rd ed.) (Foundation Press, 2003).

11. *See, e.g.,* Keith E. Whittington, *Constitutional Interpretation: Textual Meaning, Original Intent, and Judicial Review* (University Press of Kansas, 1999), 48–53.

12. Forrest McDonald, *Novus Ordo Seclorum: The Intellectual Origins of the Constitution* (University Press of Kansas, 1985), xi.

13. *See* W.J. Waluchow, *A Common Law Theory of Judicial Review: The Living Tree* (Cambridge University Press, 2007), 226–230, 261–271.

14. I add the word *written* for emphasis only. I do not argue, nor does Waluchow believe, that a constitution must be written to be a constitution. *See id.* at 47–52.

15. *See infra* pp. 188–90.

16. *See* William Michael Treanor, *The* Case of the Prisoners *and the Origins of Judicial Review,* 143 U. Pa. L. Rev. 491, 553–56 (1994).

17. *See, e.g.,* Suzanna Sherry, *Natural Law in the States,* 61 U. Cin. L. Rev. 171 (1992); Sherry, *Founders' Unwritten Constitution,* 1127.

18. *See Fullilove v. Klutznick,* 448 U.S. 448, 509–10, 100 S.Ct. 2758, 2791, 65 L.Ed.2d 902 (1980) ("[J]udicial review was the means by which action of the Legislative and Executive Branches would be required to conform to the Constitution.") (citing *Marbury*) (Powell, J., concurring). *See generally U.S. v. Nixon,* 418 U.S. 683, 94 S.Ct. 3090, 41 L.Ed.2d 1039 (1974); *Youngstown Sheet & Tube Co. v. Sawyer,* 343 U.S. 579, 72 S.Ct. 863, 96 L.Ed. 1153 (1952).

19. *Cf.* Moore, "Law as a Functional Kind," 199 ("[J]udicial review . . . [means] that every statute or case decision is subject to being overturned if contrary to the constitutional law.").

20. *See* Josiah Quincy, Jr., *Reports of Cases Argued and Adjudged in the Superior Court of Judicature of the Province of Massachusetts Bay between 1761 and 1772* (Little, Brown, 1865), 51–57.

21. *See* Robert M. Pitler, *Independent State Search and Seizure Constitutionalism: The New York State Court of Appeals' Quest for Principled Decisionmaking,* 62 Brook. L. Rev. 1, 23 (1996) ("[T]he writ of assistance was objectionable because, during the lifetime of the reigning sovereign, it served to legalize the conduct of customs officials, when they trespassed and searched at will for uncustomed and prohibited goods.") (footnotes omitted).

22. J. W. Gough, *Fundamental Law in English Constitutional History* (Oxford University Press, 1955), 192 (footnote omitted).

23. *See* William E. Nelson, *Marbury v. Madison: The Origins and Legacy of Judicial Review* (University Press of Kansas, 2000), 36. No one can seriously doubt the influence of Coke's (and Mansfield's) ideas on early American lawyers and judges. *See generally* John E. O'Connor, *William Paterson: Lawyer and Statesman, 1745–1806* (Rutgers University Press, 1979), 31 (describing Coke as "the dominant legal mind of the seventeenth century and still the most influential shaper of colonial legal ideas at the time of the Revolution"); James Q. Whitman, *Why Did the Revolutionary Lawyers Confuse Custom and Reason?* 58 U. Chi. L. Rev. 1321, 1357 (1991) (referring to Coke as "by far the seventeenth-century lawyer most influential on the American Revolutionaries"); Edward S. Corwin, *The "Higher Law" Background of American Constitutional Law,* 42 Harv. L. Rev. 149, 394–95 (1928); *Henfield's Case,* 11 F. Cas. 1099, 1106 (C.C.D.Pa. 1793) (quoting Mansfield's concept of the common law working itself pure in an important early federal case). For helpful examinations of the direct influence of Coke and *Bonham* on nascent colonial notions of a judiciary using its position and authority to subject government action to requirements of fundamen-

tal law, *see* Charles Grove Haines, *The American Doctrine of Judicial Supremacy* (2nd ed.) (University of California Press, 1932), 223–27; Thomas C. Grey, *Origins of the Unwritten Constitution: Fundamental Law in American Revolutionary Thought*, 30 Stan. L. Rev. 843, 863–69 (1978). For analysis of the factual background and political importance of *Henfield, see* David P. Currie, *The Constitution in Congress: The Third Congress, 1793–1795*, 63 U. Chi. L. Rev. 1, 14–16 (1996); Stewart Jay, *Origins of Federal Common Law*, 133 U. Pa. L. Rev. 1003, 1042–55 (1985).

24. *See* Theodore F.T. Plucknett, Bonham's Case *and Judicial Review*, 40 Harv. L. Rev. 30, 61–68 (1927); Corwin, *Establishment of Judicial Review*, 105–7, 114–15.

25. There are several other eighteenth-century state court cases in which *Bonham* and Coke are cited by the court or counsel as the basis for judicial review of legislation without scrupulously differentiating review for violations of common law, natural law, or a constitution. *See, e.g., Trevett v. Weeden*, (R.I. 1786) (unreported) (defense attorney James Varnum cited Coke in challenging a statute as unconstitutional and void because of its violation of the law of nature and common right and reason); *Rutgers v. Waddington*, (N.Y. 1784) (unreported) (*Bonham* cited by Alexander Hamilton as authority for the claim that a statute was unconstitutional and void), *discussed in* 1 Julius L. Goebel, Jr., ed., *The Law and Practice of Alexander Hamilton* (Columbia University Press, 1964), 282, 357; *Robin v. Hardaway*, 1 Jeff. 109 (Va. 1772) (George Mason, attorney for descendants of Native Americans enslaved pursuant to an act of 1682, cited *Bonham* to support the argument that the colonial statute was contrary to natural right and justice and therefore void). For a discussion of many of these cases, *see* Haines, *American Doctrine of Judicial Supremacy*, 88–121, 148–70.

26. 1 N.C. (Mart.) 48 (1787).

27. Gordon S. Wood, *The Creation of the American Republic, 1776–1787* (University of North Carolina Press, 1969), 457–61.

28. 1 Bay 93, 1 S.C. 38 (1789).

29. *Ham*, 1 Bay at 96, 98, 1 S.C. at 39, 40. The first part of the extract is a summary of counsel's argument approved by the court, and the second part is the court's ruling.

30. 1 Bay 252, 1 S.C. 101 (1792).

31. *Bowman*, 1 Bay at 254–55, 1 S.C. at 102.

32. Edward Coke, *First Institute of the Laws of England* (James and Luke Hansard, 1832), sec. 213 (spelling updated). *See also* Edward Coke, "Second Part of the *Institutes of the Laws of England*," in 2 Steve Sheppard, ed., *The Selected Writings of Sir Edward Coke* (Liberty Fund, 2003), ch. 29, at 872 ("[A]ll the Commissions of *Oier*, and *Terminer*, of goal delivery, of the peace &c. have this clause . . . to do Justice and Right, according to the rule of the law and custom of England; and that which is called common right in 2. Edw. 3. is called Common law, in 14. Edw. 3. &c.") (spelling updated). *See also supra* p. 234 n. 77.

33. 2 Bay 38 (1796).

34. *Lindsay*, 2 Bay at 58, 59–60.

35. *Lindsay*, 2 Bay at 56, 57.

36. *Lindsay*, 2 Bay at 57.

37. *See generally* James R. Stoner, Jr., *Common-Law Liberty: Rethinking American Constitutionalism* (University Press of Kansas, 2003), 16–21; George Anastaplo, *The*

Amendments to the Constitution: A Commentary (Johns Hopkins University Press, 1995), 23, 26, 75, 87–88; James R. Stoner, Jr., *Common Law and Liberal Theory: Coke, Hobbes, and the Origins of American Constitutionalism* (University Press of Kansas, 1992), 215–16; John Phillip Reid, *Constitutional History of the American Revolution: The Authority to Legislate* (University of Wisconsin Press, 1991), 6; George Anastaplo, *The Constitution of 1787: A Commentary* (Johns Hopkins University Press, 1989), 4, 134–35, 227; John Phillip Reid, *Constitutional History of the American Revolution: The Authority of Rights* (University of Wisconsin Press, 1986), 69–70; Wood, *Creation of the American Republic*, 10; Thomas M. Cooley, *A Treatise on the Constitutional Limitations Which Rest upon the Legislative Power of the States of the American Union* (Little, Brown, 1868), 37, 59–61, 175, 416–17; Leslie Friedman Goldstein, *Popular Sovereignty, the Origins of Judicial Review, and the Revival of Unwritten Law*, 48 J. Pol. 51, 59 (1986).

38. This is also why the reasoning of Judges Grimke and Waties in *Lindsay* should be read as analytically consistent with their decision in *Ham* and with the decision of Judges Grimke and Bay in *Bowman*, rather than as incompatible with "the Coke approach." *See* Goldstein, *Popular Sovereignty*, 67.

39. *See also* John V. Orth, *Due Process of Law: A Brief History* (University Press of Kansas, 2003), 99–100 n. 30 and accompanying text (discussing the view of North Carolina courts as expressed in *State v. Anonymous*, 2 N.C. 28 (1794) and *Hoke v. Henderson*, 15 N.C. 1 (1834)).

40. 1 Call. 555, 5 Va. 208 (1799).

41. *Jones*, 1 Call. at 559, 5 Va. at 209 (Carrington, J.) (emphasis supplied).

42. *See* Whittington, *Constitutional Interpretation*, 57; Wayne D. Moore, *Written and Unwritten Constitutional Law in the Founding Period: The Early New Jersey Cases*, 7 Const. Comment. 341, 353 (1990); Thomas C. Grey, *Do We Have an Unwritten Constitution?* 27 Stan. L. Rev. 703, 715 (1975).

43. Moore, *Written and Unwritten Constitutional Law*, 352. Given that the case turns on detailed requirements of the right to a jury trial, it seems more likely that this is a reference to common law rather than statute law.

44. *Id.* at 353.

45. *See* Stoner, *Common Law and Liberal Theory*, 6–7; Anastaplo, *Constitution of 1787*, 145–46.

46. *See supra* n. 36 and accompanying text.

47. *See* Stoner, *Common-Law Liberty*, 15; Thomas C. Grey, *Do We Have an Unwritten Constitution?* 715–16. *Cf.* T.R.S. Allan, *Law, Liberty, and Justice: The Legal Foundations of British Constitutionalism* (Oxford University Press, 1993), 143.

48. O'Connor, *William Paterson*, 31, 32. *See also id.* at 221 (noting that William Paterson wrote the 1799 New Jersey legislation that would "guarantee the continuing relevance of the great body of English common law that had come into existence prior to 1776").

49. Anastaplo, *Constitution of 1787*, 69. *See also* Anastaplo, *Amendments to the Constitution*, 78.

50. *See* Stoner, *Common-Law Liberty*, 12; Leonard W. Levy, *Origins of the Bill of Rights* (Yale University Press, 1999), 226–30; Gary J. Jacobsohn, *The Supreme Court and the Decline of Constitutional Aspiration* (Rowman and Littlefield, 1986), 79.

51. Herbert M. Kritzer, "Courts, Justice, and Politics in England," in Herbert Jacob

et al., *Courts, Law, and Politics in Comparative Perspective* (Yale University Press, 1996), 154. *See also* Stephen L. Carter, *Constitutional Improprieties: Reflections on* Mistretta, Morrison, *and Administrative Government,* 57 U. Chi. L. Rev. 357, 375 n. 57 (1990) ("[I]f the . . . chosen method [of judicial review] is not tied closely to the text, structure, and history of the Constitution, then far from being the 'right kind' of judicial review, it is not judicial review at all."); Stephen A. Siegel, *The Federal Government's Power to Enact Color-Conscious Laws: An Originalist Inquiry,* 92 Nw. U. L. Rev. 477, 542–43 (1998) ("[T]he Constitution authorizes judicial review only for government activity conflicting with the written text.").

52. Larry Kramer discounts the influence of Coke and *Bonham* on the development of judicial review in the United States. *See* Larry D. Kramer, *The People Themselves: Popular Constitutionalism and Judicial Review* (Oxford University Press, 2004), 18–24. This is particularly surprising, given that Kramer actually cites *Ham, Bowman,* and *Lindsay* (without noting the explicit citation to *Bonham* in *Ham* or the evident influence of Coke's language in *Bowman,* which I describe *supra* pp. 84–86). *See* Kramer, *The People Themselves,* 41, 270 n. 34. Of course, as my argument is intended to demonstrate, the explicit and implicit references to *Bonham* in these cases are not just evidence of the influence of Coke's thought on these early American jurists; they are also evidence of a broader conceptual perspective within the Anglo-American tradition of common law constitutionalism.

53. *Marbury* has been criticized and defended by various scholars. *Compare* William W. Van Alstyne, *A Critical Guide to* Marbury v. Madison, 1969 Duke L.J. 1 (1969) *with* Louise Weinberg, *Our* Marbury, 89 Va. L. Rev. 1235 (2003). I do not here take sides in this debate, with one exception. In *Marbury,* Marshall based the power of constitutional review on the features and function of the judiciary in the American system of government. *See Marbury,* 5 U.S. at 177–80. *See also* Henry P. Monaghan, Marbury *and the Administrative State,* 83 Colum. L. Rev. 1, 14 (1983) ("*Marbury's* justification of judicial review, grounded as it is in the 'ordinary and humble judicial duty' of the common law courts, seems necessarily to entail a general obligation of independent law-exposition by article III courts. This is what courts 'do'; it is their 'job.'"). While the merits of this basis for constitutional review may be debatable, my conceptual argument for the judicial obligation to develop the law is broadly sympathetic to and supported by Marshall's project. It may be, however, that conceptual arguments serve better in justifying common law review than constitutional review, given the textual constraints of the latter. *See* Antonin Scalia, *Originalism: The Lesser Evil,* 57 U. Cin. L. Rev. 849, 854 (1989) (arguing that although judicial review is "reasonably implicit" in the document, "nothing in the text of the Constitution confers upon the courts the power to inquire into, rather than passively assume, the constitutionality of federal statutes"). On the other hand, given the text's silence, Marshall had little alternative but to base constitutional review either on the governmental structure and values that underlay the Constitution or on the inherent function of the common law judiciary.

54. 3 U.S. (3 Dall.) 386, 1 L.Ed. 648 (1798).

55. *See Calder,* 3 U.S. at 386–87. The pertinent part of article 1, section 10, reads, "No State shall . . . pass any . . . ex post facto Law."

56. For criticisms of Justice Chase's view as expressed in *Calder, see* William

Winslow Crosskey, *The True Meaning of the Constitutional Prohibition of Ex-Post-Facto Laws,* 14 U. Chi. L. Rev. 539 (1947).

57. *Calder,* 3 U.S. at 388–89, 395 (some emphasis deleted).

58. *Id.* at 398–99.

59. *See id.* at 390–91, 399–400.

60. *See id.* at 389, 398–99.

61. *See generally* Bernard Bailyn, *The Ideological Origins of the American Revolution* (enlarged ed.) (Harvard University Press, 1992), 77–78; Shannon C. Stimson, *The American Revolution in the Law: Anglo-American Jurisprudence before John Marshall* (Princeton University Press, 1990), 77; Reid, *Authority of Rights,* 75.

62. *See, e.g.,* Calvin R. Massey, *The Natural Law Component of The Ninth Amendment,* 61 U. Cin. L. Rev. 49, 78 (1992); Sherry, *Founders' Unwritten Constitution,* 1172–73.

63. *See Carmell v. Texas,* 529 U.S. 513, 521–22, 120 S.Ct. 1620, 1627, 146 L.Ed.2d 577 (2000) ("In *Calder v. Bull,* Justice Chase stated that the necessary explanation [for the prohibition against *ex post facto* laws] is derived from English common law well known to the Framers . . . The common-law understanding explained by Justice Chase drew heavily upon the authoritative exposition of one of the great scholars of the common law, Richard Wooddeson.").

64. *See* Levy, *Origins of the Bill of Rights,* 254.

65. *Calder,* 3 U.S. at 388.

66. *Cf.* Levy, *Origins of the Bill of Rights,* 254–55.

67. Matthew J. Franck, *Against the Imperial Judiciary: The Supreme Court vs. the Sovereignty of the People* (University Press of Kansas, 1996), 123.

68. *Id.* at 120.

69. *Id.* at 123.

70. *Id.*

71. *Id.* at 125.

72. *Id.*

73. *Id.* at 126.

74. *Id.*

75. *See supra* n. 23.

76. *See, e.g.,* Whitman, *Why Did the Revolutionary Lawyers Confuse Custom and Reason?* 1356–68. Kramer suggests that early Americans perceived distinctions among common law, natural law, and fundamental law but failed to observe these distinctions carefully. *See* Kramer, *The People Themselves,* 9–18, 42–44.

77. 2 U.S. (2 Dall.) 419, 1 L.Ed. 440 (1793).

78. *See Chisholm,* 2 U.S. at 420.

79. *Id.* at 421.

80. *Id.* at 422.

81. *Id.* at 423.

82. *Id.* at 433–34, 435. *See generally* John V. Orth, *The Truth about Justice Iredell's Dissent in* Chisholm v. Georgia, 73 N.C. L. Rev. 255, 265 (1994).

83. *Chisholm,* 2 U.S. at 435 (emphasis supplied).

84. *Id.* at 437 (emphasis supplied).

85. *See id.* at 440, 442, 446–47.

86. *Id.* at 442.

87. Justice Souter reads *Chisholm* this way in his dissenting opinion in *Alden v. Maine*, 527 U.S. 706, 119 S.Ct. 2240, 144 L.Ed.2d 636 (1999). In that opinion, Justice Souter carefully demonstrates the historical distinction between common law and natural law conceptions of sovereign immunity during and after the colonial period, the legally authoritative status of the common law conception, and the absence of any natural law basis for the *Chisholm* decision. *See Alden,* 527 U.S. at 764–65, 772, 778, 781, 798, 119 S.Ct. at 2271, 2274–75, 2277, 2279, 2287.

88. *See* David A. Sklansky, *The Fourth Amendment and Common Law,* 100 Colum. L. Rev. 1739, 1777–78 (2000) ("[T]he common law derived much of its legitimacy from the notion that it embodied 'right reason.' Coke, as his opinion in *Bonham's Case* suggests, continued and in some ways enlarged on this rhetorical practice. Coke's seventeenth-century *Institutes,* the legal authority most revered by the American revolutionaries, celebrated the common law as a practically flawless system, 'the absolute perfection of reason.'") (footnotes omitted).

89. *See supra* n. 82.

90. *See, e.g.,* Wood, *Creation of the American Republic,* 460–61. *See also* Jack N. Rakove, *Original Meanings: Politics and Ideas in the Making of the Constitution* (Knopf, 1996), 278–79.

91. This reading of *Chisholm* helps to harmonize and integrate Iredell's thinking on these issues from *Bayard* to *Chisholm* to *Calder* and to explain why it is a mistake to assume, as some have, that Iredell's opinion in *Calder* was a disavowal of his position in *Bayard. See, e.g.,* Goldstein, *Popular Sovereignty,* 65.

92. *See* Sylvia Snowiss, *Judicial Review and the Law of the Constitution* (Yale University Press, 1990), 26–27, 66; Rakove, *Original Meanings,* 325–30, 343–44; Reid, *Authority of Rights,* 135; Wood, *Creation of the American Republic,* 461–62.

93. 8 U.S. (4 Cranch) 209, 2 L.Ed. 598 (1808).

94. *McIlvaine,* 8 U.S. at 210.

95. *Id.*

96. *Id.* at 211–15, especially at 211.

97. 10 U.S. (6 Cranch) 87, 3 L.Ed. 162 (1810).

98. *Fletcher,* 10 U.S. at 130–31.

99. *Id.* at 131–32.

100. *Id.* at 132–35.

101. *Id.* at 136–38. This is the same section of the Constitution, although a different provision, as was involved in *Chisholm.* The portion of article 1, section 10, at issue in *Fletcher* reads, "No State shall . . . pass any . . . Law impairing the Obligation of Contracts."

102. *Fletcher,* 10 U.S. at 139 (emphasis supplied).

103. *See, e.g.,* Thomas C. Grey, *The Uses of an Unwritten Constitution,* 64 Chi.-Kent L. Rev. 211, 217 (1988); Goldstein, *Popular Sovereignty,* 68.

104. *See* Grey, *Uses of an Unwritten Constitution,* 64 Chi.-Kent L. Rev. at 217 ("Justice Chase issued an opinion in *Calder v. Bull* that claimed the power of judicial review even over legislation that was not 'expressly restrained by the constitution,' and yet violated 'certain vital principles in our free Republican governments.' The unwritten constitution made up of these principles was likewise invoked as an alternate ground of decision by John Marshall in *Fletcher v. Peck,* and it was widely affirmed by ortho-

dox judges and commentators, prominently including James Kent and Joseph Story, during the early and middle years of the nineteenth century.") (footnotes omitted).

105. *See supra* pp. 57–58.

106. *Fletcher,* 10 U.S. at 136.

107. *See generally Eakin v. Raub,* 12 Sergeant & Rawle 330, 344–58 (1825) (Gibson, J., dissenting); McDonald, *Novus Ordo Seclorum,* 276; Haines, *American Doctrine of Judicial Supremacy,* 232–21; James Bradley Thayer, *The Origin and Scope of the American Doctrine of Constitutional Law,* 7 Harv. L. Rev. 129 (1893). For a discussion placing the criticisms of *Marbury* in the historical and political context of its time, *see* James M. O'Fallon, *Marbury,* 44 Stan. L. Rev. 219, 241–60 (1992).

108. *See generally* Sylvia Snowiss, *The* Marbury *of 1803 and the Modern* Marbury, 20 Const. Comment. 231, 238–45 (2003).

109. *See* Goldstein, *Popular Sovereignty,* 52.

110. The historical reasons for the shift toward constitutional review are multifaceted and largely beyond the scope of this discussion. One political pressure in the nineteenth century—the hostility of many Jacksonians to unelected judges and to the common law itself—likely compelled judges to seek refuge in the constitutional text as support for their decisions, particularly when these decisions resulted in the restriction or invalidation of legislation. *See* Gerard N. Magliocca, *Andrew Jackson and the Constitution: The Rise and Fall of Generational Regimes* (University Press of Kansas, 2007), 12, 36–37; Lewis A. Grossman, *Late Nineteenth-Century Jurisprudence Revisited: James Coolidge Carter and Mugwump Jurisprudence,* 20 Law & Hist. Rev. 577, 592 (2002). Another possible explanation, as Brian Tamanaha argues, concerns the shift from noninstrumental to instrumental conceptions of fundamental law (common law and natural law) and the attendant, increased reliance on constitutional provisions to support the exercise of judicial review. *See* Brian Z. Tamanaha, *Law as a Means to an End: Threat to the Rule of Law* (Cambridge University Press, 2006), 216–18.

111. *Marbury,* 5 U.S. at 177.

112. *See* Orth, *Due Process of Law,* 44.

113. *See, e.g.,* Letter from John Marshall to St. George Tucker (27 Nov. 1800), in 6 Charles F. Hobson and Fredrika J. Teute, eds., *The Papers of John Marshall: Correspondence, Papers, and Selected Judicial Opinions, November 1800–March 1807* (University of North Carolina Press, 1990), 24 ("My own opinion is that our ancestors brought with them the laws of England both statute & common law as existing at the settlement of each colony, so far as they were applicable to our situation. That on our revolution the preexisting law of each state remaind so far as it was not changd either expressly or necessarily by the nature of the governments which we adopted. That on adopting the existing constitution of the United States the common & statute law of each state remain as before & that the principles of the common law of the state woud apply themselves to magistrates of the general as well as to magistrates of the particular government. I do not recollect ever to have heard the opinions of a leading gentleman of the opposition which conflict with these.").

114. *E.g., Livingston v. Jefferson,* 15 F. Cas. 660 (C.C.Va. 1811) ("When our ancestors migrated to America, they brought with them the common law of their native country, so far as it was applicable to their new situation; and I do not conceive that the Revolution would, in any degree, have changed the relations of man to man, or the

law which regulated those relations. In breaking our political connection with the parent state, we did not break our connection with each other.").

115. *See* John Phillip Reid, *Rule of Law: The Jurisprudence of Liberty in the Seventeenth and Eighteenth Centuries* (Northern Illinois University Press, 2004), 78–79 ("In the American colonies the concept of rule-of-law was more historically English than contemporary British. That is, it was closer to the constitutional values of seventeenth-century England than to the newer constitutional understanding of late eighteenth-century Great Britain. We may be confident that Americans did not appreciate how deep the gulf had become. The realization that many of Britain's rulers, even some who were common lawyers, now equated law, liberty, and constitutionalism with parliamentary legislation could have staggered American constitutionalists had the fact sunk into their legal consciousness. They would never break free of the fundamentals of anti-Stuart constitutionalism in which power unrestrained was not legal."); Reid, *Authority of Rights*, 23.

116. The Supreme Court continued to void legislative action in opinions derived conceptually from *Calder* and *Fletcher* throughout most of the nineteenth century. *See, e.g., Citizens' Savings & Loan Association v. Topeka*, 87 U.S. (20 Wall.) 655, 662–63, 22 L.Ed. 455 (1874) ("[T]here are such rights in every free government beyond the control of the State. A government which recognized no such rights, which held the lives, the liberty, and the property of its citizens subject at all times to the absolute disposition and unlimited control of even the most democratic depository of power, is after all but a despotism. It is true it is a despotism of the many, of the majority, if you choose to call it so, but it is none the less a despotism . . . The theory of our governments, State and National, is opposed to the deposit of unlimited power anywhere. The executive, the legislative, and the judicial branches of these governments are all of limited and defined powers. There are limitations on such power which grow out of the essential nature of all free governments. Implied reservations of individual rights, without which the social compact could not exist, and which are respected by all governments entitled to the name.").

117. I deliberately limit the discussion in the text to Supreme Court decisions from the first twenty-five years of the nineteenth century for two reasons, each of which is open to challenge. First, the temporal limitation seems necessary to ensure that my discussion focuses on the time frame in which I am interested. Arguably, attitudes of American lawyers in the mid-nineteenth century might have changed from what they were at or relatively soon after the turn of that century. Second, I limit myself to Supreme Court arguments and decisions on the (questionable) assumption that the quality of lawyering and judging in that forum might be expected to be higher than the average of the time.

118. *See supra* n. 9.

119. John Phillip Reid, *The Concept of Liberty in the Age of the American Revolution* (University of Chicago Press, 1988), 128 n. 36.

120. *See* Reid, *Authority to Legislate*, 74; McDonald, *Novus Ordo Seclorum*, 57–59.

121. *See* Reid, *Authority of Rights*, 90–91.

122. *See id.* at 88, 91, 92.

123. *See* Reid, *Authority to Legislate*, 302.

124. *See generally* Robert E. Riggs, *Substantive Due Process in 1791*, 1990 Wis. L. Rev. 941, 984–985 (1990).

125. *See* Snowiss, *Judicial Review and the Law of the Constitution*, 68–69.

126. *Id.* at 69.

127. *Id.* at 69–70.

128. *Id.* at 126.

129. *Id.* at 126–28.

130. In addition, Snowiss bases her analysis of *Fletcher* and the crux of her argument on a claim that American judges undertaking judicial review during the late eighteenth and early nineteenth centuries were engaging in a self-consciously political, rather than legal, activity. This assertion strikes me as untenable. For specific criticisms of this part of Snowiss's position, *see* Dean Alfange, Jr., *Marbury v. Madison and Original Understandings of Judicial Review: In Defense of Traditional Wisdom*, 1993 Sup. Ct. Rev. 329, 335–40 (1993).

131. *Fletcher*, 10 U.S. at 143.

132. Snowiss, *Judicial Review and the Law of the Constitution*, 130.

133. *See* Sherry, *Natural Law in the States*, 171; Sherry, *Founders' Unwritten Constitution*, 1172–73. *See also* Robert G. McCloskey, *The American Supreme Court* (4th ed.) (University of Chicago Press, 2005), 32–33, 48. In their discussions of natural law, Sherry and McCloskey share some of the same defects of gloss that I discuss *infra* at pp. 102–7.

134. Sherry, *Natural Law in the States*, 171–72.

135. *Id.* at 214, 215.

136. *Id.* at 214.

137. *Id.* at 215.

138. *Id.* at 172, 172 n. 7.

139. *Cf.* Sherry, *Founders' Unwritten Constitution*, 1158 n. 137 ("The perceived inherent flaw in ex post facto laws might have been a violation of the natural rights of the individual, or it might have been a violation of more general fundamental law such as the principles of 'common right and reason.' In either case, the argument in the text indicates that some form of unwritten law could serve to invalidate even legislation not prohibited by the written constitution."). While I endorse Sherry's conclusion, I also believe that pinpointing the precise source of the unwritten law by which legislation is to be invalidated is an ineluctable element of the legal analysis necessary to justify the claim.

140. *See* Reid, *Authority of Rights*, 90; John Hart Ely, *Democracy and Distrust: A Theory of Judicial Review* (Harvard University Press, 1980), 48–54.

141. *See generally* Helen K. Michael, *The Role of Natural Law in Early American Constitutionalism: Did the Founders Contemplate Judicial Enforcement of "Unwritten" Individual Rights?* 69 N.C. L. Rev. 421 (1991).

142. *See* Christopher L. Eisgruber, *John Marshall's Judicial Rhetoric*, 1996 Sup. Ct. Rev. 439, 467 n. 119 (1996).

143. *See* Sherry, *Founders' Unwritten Constitution*, 54 U. Chi. L. Rev. at 1130.

144. *Id.* at 1132 (footnote omitted).

145. Coke's is grounded unequivocally on the common law. *See generally* Stoner,

Common Law and Liberal Theory, 19–20; Reid, *Concept of Liberty,* 10; Harold J. Berman, *The Origins of Historical Jurisprudence: Coke, Selden, Hale,* 103 Yale L.J. 1651, 1686 (1994) ("Implicit in these judicial decisions was the theory that the common law, viewed as a body of principles, concepts, rules, and procedures that originated in a remote past, was, in effect, the fundamental law of the English people . . . later to be called the unwritten English Constitution—to which all other law in England was subordinate.").

146. *See, e.g.,* Martin Rhonheimer, *Fundamental Rights, Moral Law, and the Legal Defense of Life in a Constitutional Democracy: A Constitutional Approach to the Encyclical* Evangelium Vitae, 43 Am. J. Juris. 135, 143 (1998) ("[W]e come to the birth of a more nuanced thought, represented by Locke and Montesquieu in line with the Anglo-Saxon tradition of the rule of law. Rights of liberty—fundamental rights directed to limiting the power of the state—are discovered, positively guaranteed, and made capable of being claimed before a judge. It is the birth of modern constitutionalism.").

147. *See supra* pp. 63–64.

148. *See supra* pp. 66–69.

149. *Cf.* Edward S. Corwin, *The Basic Doctrine of American Constitutional Law,* 12 Mich. L. Rev. 247, 254 (1914) ("[I]t is difficult to see how our judges, having set out to be defenders of 'natural rights,' were in a position to decline to defend, and therefore to define, all such rights whether mentioned in the constitution or not. The difficulty is disposed of, however, the moment we recollect that our judges envisaged their problem not as moral philosophers but as lawyers, and especially as students of the *Common Law.* 'Natural rights,' in short, were to be defined in light of Common Law precedents.") (emphasis in original).

150. R.A. MacKay, *Coke: Parliamentary Sovereignty or the Supremacy of the Law?* 22 Mich. L. Rev. 215, 246, 247 (1924) (emphasis supplied).

151. *Cf. Tillery v. Owens,* 907 F.2d 418, 431 (3d Cir. 1990) (affirming the trial court's determination that double-celling prison inmates violated the Eighth Amendment's prohibition of cruel and unusual punishment and ruling that "the district court not only had the power but the moral and legal obligation to relieve the inhumane and unconstitutional conditions to which double-celled inmates . . . are daily subjected").

152. *See infra* pp. 139–43, 144–49.

153. Steven J. Burton, *Judging in Good Faith* (Cambridge University Press, 1992), 197.

154. Haines, *American Doctrine of Judicial Supremacy,* 91 (citation omitted). There is some debate about the precise nature of the proceedings and the correct interpretation of the result in the *Josiah Philips* case. For a summary of the debate, *see* Massey, *Natural Law Component of the Ninth Amendment,* 64–67.

155. *See generally* Bailyn, *Ideological Origins of the American Revolution,* 74–75, 105–8.

156. Alexander Hamilton, John Jay, and James Madison, *The Federalist* (George W. Carey and James McClellan, eds.) (Liberty Fund, 2001), 406.

157. *Hertz Drivurself Stations, Inc. v. Siggins,* 359 Pa. 25, 33, 58 A.2d 464, 469 (1948) (citing *Marbury*) (other citations omitted). *See also Kennedy v. Mendoza-Martinez,* 372 U.S. 144, 159, 83 S.Ct. 554, 562, 9 L.Ed.2d 644 (1963) (referring to the invalidation of federal legislation as "the gravest and most delicate duty that this Court is called on to perform.") (quoting Justice Holmes's concurring opinion in *Blodgett v. Holden,* 275

U.S. 142, 148, 48 S.Ct. 105, 107, 72 L.Ed. 206 (1927)); *Ableman v. Booth*, 62 U.S. (21 How.) 506, 520, 16 L.Ed. 169 (1858).

158. *See* Frederick Pollock, *A First Book of Jurisprudence for Students of the Common Law* (6th ed.) (Macmillan, 1929), 265–66 ("Some principles of law and justice . . . described as 'common right,' were sacred against the legislature, and if Parliament were to transgress them it would be the right and duty of the judges to pay no attention to such enactments.").

159. Haines, *American Doctrine of Judicial Supremacy*, 36. *See also id.* at 227 ("The idea for which Coke had struggled so persistently in England, which had proved impossible to attain in his own country—that the common law as interpreted by the courts shall be superior to the king and Parliament—was accepted and put into operation about two centuries later with modifications necessitated by the enactment of written constitutions, in the development and adoption of the American doctrine of judicial supremacy.").

Chapter 7

1. This is not meant as a commitment to any particular method of conceptual analysis.

2. Kent Greenawalt, *Law and Objectivity* (Oxford University Press, 1992), 89. For a general discussion of some of the duties created by the acceptance of a job or other role, *see id.* at 22–25.

3. Of course, judges have many duties, including the oversight of clerical staff, managing their dockets, conducting conferences with counsel, and so on. I am interested solely in the judicial duties that arise in the resolution of legal disputes through the issuance of judicial rulings with justificatory, written opinions.

4. *See, e.g.,* Leslie Green, *Law, Legitimacy and Consent*, 62 S. Cal. L. Rev. 795, 818–21 (1989).

5. *See, e.g.,* Robert A. Burt, *Brown's Reflection*, 103 Yale L.J. 1483, 1487 (1994); Michael S. Moore, *Authority, Law, and Razian Reasons*, 62 S. Cal. L. Rev. 827, 840 (1989).

6. Kent Greenawalt, *Conflicts of Law and Morality* (Oxford University Press, 1987), 32.

7. Through the example of racially discriminatory laws, I also assume the injustice or immorality of the law at issue.

8. *See* Ronald Dworkin, *Taking Rights Seriously* (Harvard University Press, 1978), 112 (judges "are the agents through which the law works itself pure"). *See also* Ronald Dworkin, *Law's Empire* (Harvard University Press, 1986), 400–401.

9. *Cf.* Roscoe Pound, "What Is the Common Law?" in Roscoe Pound, *The Future of the Common Law* (Peter Smith, 1965), 14–15 ("One institution . . . has proved universal and significant in the polity of the English-speaking world, namely, the common-law judge."). *See also supra* p. 22.

10. *See generally English v. Emery Reimbold & Strick, Ltd.*, [2002] EWCA Civ 605, [12], [15]–[16], [2002] 1 WLR 2409, 2417–18 ("The common law countries have developed a tradition of delivering judgments that detail the evidence and explain the findings in much greater detail than is to be found in the judgments of most civil law

jurisdictions . . . Reasons are required if decisions are to be acceptable to the parties and to members of the public . . . [T]he requirement to give reasons concentrates the mind of the judge and it has even been contended that the requirement to give reasons serves a vital function in constraining the judiciary's exercise of power . . . The function that judgments play under the common law in setting precedents for the future has also been identified as one of the justifications for the requirement to give reasons . . . We would put the matter at its simplest by saying that justice will not be done if it is not apparent to the parties why one has won and the other has lost.") (citations omitted); *Grutter v. Bollinger,* 288 F.3d 732, 752–53 (6th Cir. 2002) (*en banc*) (Moore, J., concurring); Karl Llewellyn, *The Common Law Tradition: Deciding Appeals* (Little, Brown, 1960), 26; Frederick Schauer, *Giving Reasons,* 47 Stan. L. Rev. 633 (1995); Owen M. Fiss, *The Forms of Justice,* 93 Harv. L. Rev. 1, 13 (1979), reprinted in Owen Fiss, *The Law as It Could Be* (New York University Press, 2003), 11; Max Radin, *The Requirement of Written Opinions,* 18 Cal. L. Rev. 486, 489 (1930); Roscoe Pound, *The Theory of Judicial Decision,* 36 Harv. L. Rev. 940, 940–43, 952–59 (1923).

11. James Boyd White, *What's an Opinion For?* 62 U. Chi. L. Rev. 1363, 1367–68 (1995).

12. *See* Maxwell L. Stearns, *Standing Back from the Forest: Justiciability and Social Choice,* 83 Cal. L. Rev. 1309, 1376 (1995) ("[R]equiring judges to state the reasons, or to sign onto reasons stated by a colleague, for casting a vote in a particular case, whether in the majority, concurrence, or dissent, commits judges to a form of codified ordinal rankings.").

13. *Plessy v. Ferguson,* 163 U.S. 537, 552–64, 16 S.Ct. 1138, 1144–48, 41 L.Ed. 256 (1896) (Harlan, J., dissenting).

14. *Brown v. Board of Education,* 347 U.S. 483, 74 S.Ct. 686, 98 L.Ed. 873 (1954).

15. *Plessy,* 163 U.S. at 559, 16 S.Ct. at 1146 ("In my opinion, the judgment this day rendered will, in time, prove to be quite as pernicious as the decision made by this tribunal in the Dred Scott case.") (Harlan, J., dissenting).

16. *See, e.g.,* Girardeau A. Spann, *Color-Coded Standing,* 80 Cornell L. Rev. 1422, 1493 (1995) ("*Brown* . . . did not desegregate the public schools, and it certainly did not overrule *Plessy.*").

17. *See, e.g., Bryson v. United States,* 396 U.S. 64, 76, 90 S.Ct. 355, 362, 24 L.Ed.2d 264 (1969) (stating that *Plessy* belongs to a "discredited regime, though . . . it has never been officially overruled.") (Douglas, J., dissenting). *See also* Saul Brenner and Harold J. Spaeth, *Stare Indecisis: The Alteration of Precedent on the Supreme Court, 1946–1992* (Cambridge University Press, 1995), 123.

18. *See, e.g., Bolling v. Sharpe,* 347 U.S. 497, 498, 74 S.Ct. 693, 694, 98 L.Ed. 884 (1954) (citing *Brown*).

19. In less than a decade following *Brown,* the Supreme Court extirpated segregation from many areas of public life into which it had seeped. *See, e.g., Turner v. City of Memphis,* 369 U.S. 350, 82 S.Ct. 805, 7 L.Ed.2d 762 (1962) (publicly operated airport restaurant and lavatory facilities); *Bailey v. Patterson,* 369 U.S. 31, 82 S.Ct. 549, 7 L.Ed.2d 512 (1962) (interstate or intrastate common carriers and their facilities); *New Orleans City Park Improvement Ass'n v. Detiege,* 358 U.S. 54, 79 S.Ct. 99, 3 L.Ed.2d 46 (1958) (municipal parks); *Gayle v. Browder,* 352 U.S. 903, 77 S.Ct. 145, 1 L.Ed.2d 114 (1956) (buses); *Florida ex rel. Hawkins v. Board of Control,* 350 U.S. 413, 76 S.Ct. 464,

100 L.Ed. 486 (1956) (public law schools); *Holmes v. City of Atlanta,* 350 U.S. 879, 76 S.Ct. 141, 100 L.Ed. 776 (1955) (public golf courses); *Tureaud v. Board of Sup'rs of Louisiana State University,* 347 U.S. 971, 74 S.Ct. 784, 98 L.Ed. 1112 (1954) (public universities); *Muir v. Louisville Park Theatrical Ass'n,* 347 U.S. 971, 74 S.Ct. 783, 98 L.Ed. 1112 (1954) (public recreational facilities). In the wake of these decisions and others, Congress enacted the Civil Rights Act of 1964 (42 U.S.C. § 2000a *et seq.*), ten years after *Brown* was decided.

20. *See, e.g., Lonesome v. Maxwell,* 123 F. Supp. 193 (D.Md. 1954) (holding, two months after *Brown,* that segregation of Maryland's public beaches, bathhouses, and swimming pools was not precluded by *Brown,* because *Brown* prohibited segregation only in public education), *rev'd sub nom., Dawson v. Mayor and City Council of Baltimore City,* 220 F.2d 386, 387–88 (4th Cir. 1955) (citing *Brown*) (*per curiam*), *aff'd, Mayor and City Council of Baltimore City v. Dawson,* 350 U.S. 877, 76 S.Ct. 133, 100 L.Ed. 774 (1955) (*per curiam*).

21. For a discussion of the concerns of individual justices in deliberating about *Brown* and of Warren's delicate effort to draft an opinion that would maintain the tenuously unified Court he had assembled, *see* Richard Kluger, *Simple Justice: The History of* Brown v. Board of Education *and Black America's Struggle for Equality* (Vintage Books, 1977), 679–99.

22. *See Brown,* 347 U.S. at 494 n. 11, 74 S.Ct. at 692 n. 11.

23. *Brown,* 347 U.S. at 495, 74 S.Ct. at 692.

24. Lino A. Graglia, *Disaster by Decree: The Supreme Court Decisions on Race and the Schools* (Cornell University Press, 1976), 29–30.

25. *See generally* Kluger, *Simple Justice,* 711 ("Earl Warren's opinion, for all its moderation and caution, lacked the depth and persuasiveness ideal to withstand the criticism that would be directed at it even by those who strongly approved of its purpose. In the *New York Times* of May 18, 1954, columnist James Reston offered his instant analysis of *Brown;* the headline to his piece—'A Sociological Decision'—was a bellwether of the rebuke that would grow in the following months and years, even as the influence of the decision itself multiplied . . . 'Relying more on the social scientists than on legal precedents . . . The Court's opinion read more like an expert paper on sociology than a Supreme Court opinion.'"). *See also* Herbert Wechsler, *Toward Neutral Principles of Constitutional Law,* 73 Harv. L. Rev. 1, 15, 19–23 (1959) (arguing that the "main constituent of the judicial process is precisely that it must be genuinely principled, resting with respect to every step that is involved in reaching judgment on analysis and reasons quite transcending the immediate result that is achieved," and criticizing the *Brown* opinion for its lack of a principled rationale of this sort).

26. *See* Graglia, *Disaster by Decree,* 27–28; Mark G. Yudof, *School Desegregation: Legal Realism, Reasoned Elaboration, and Social Science Research in the Supreme Court,* 42 Law & Contemp. Probs. 57, 70, 87, 99, 102, 105 (1978); Ernest van den Haag, *Social Science Testimony in the Desegregation Cases: A Reply to Professor Kenneth Clark,* 6 Vill. L. Rev. 69, 77 (1960); Edmond Cahn, *Jurisprudence,* 30 N.Y.U. L. Rev. 150, 164–66 (1955).

27. *See Missouri v. Jenkins,* 515 U.S. 70, 121–22, 115 S.Ct. 2038, 2065, 132 L.Ed.2d 63 (1995) ("[T]here is no reason to think that black students cannot learn as well when surrounded by members of their own race as when they are in an integrated envi-

ronment. Indeed, it may very well be that what has been true for historically black colleges is true for black middle and high schools . . . [B]lack schools can function as the center and symbol of black communities, and provide examples of independent black leadership, success, and achievement.") (Thomas, J., concurring).

28. *See* Graglia, *Disaster by Decree*, 28–29 ("The lack of support for the Court's statement that segregation had adverse educational effects on black children led to denunciation of *Brown*, not only as applied social science rather than law, but as bad social science, and it nourished the hope, or at least the argument, that further consideration of the evidence or of new evidence would lead to permitting segregation again.").

29. *See supra* p. 207 n. 5.

30. J. Harvie Wilkinson III, *The Role of Reason in the Rule of Law*, 56 U. Chi. L. Rev. 779, 798 (1989).

31. *See generally* Cahn, *Jurisprudence*, 168–69.

32. *See, e.g., R. v. Inland Revenue Commissioners, ex parte Rossminster Ltd.*, [1980] AC 952, 1011, 1025 (adopting Lord Atkin's dissent in *Liversidge v. Anderson*, [1942] AC 206); Neal Kumar Katyal, *Judges as Advicegivers*, 50 Stan. L. Rev. 1709, 1805 n. 449 (1998) (collecting cases).

33. For statements of the judges' duty to dissent in appropriate cases, *see, e.g., Employers' Liability Cases [Howard v. Illinois Central R.R. Co.]*, 207 U.S. 463, 505, 28 S.Ct. 141, 148, 52 L.Ed.2d 297 (1908) (Moody, J., dissenting); *Briscoe v. Bank of Kentucky*, 36 U.S. (11 Pet.) 257, 329, 9 L.Ed. 709 (1837) (Story, J., dissenting).

34. *See generally* Guido Calabresi, *A Common Law for the Age of Statutes* (Harvard University Press, 1982), 167, 172–81; David L. Shapiro, *In Defense of Judicial Candor*, 100 Harv. L. Rev. 731 (1987); Robert A. Leflar, *Honest Judicial Opinions*, 74 Nw. U. L. Rev. 721 (1979).

35. *See R. v. Sussex Justices, ex parte McCarthy*, [1924] 1 KB 256, 259 ("[A] long line of cases shows that it is not merely of some importance but is of fundamental importance that justice should not only be done, but should manifestly and undoubtedly be seen to be done."); Richard A. Posner, *The Federal Courts: Challenge and Reform* (Harvard University Press, 1996), 147 ("Prolixity and lack of candor are not mere inelegances in judicial opinions . . . [T]hey reduce the opinion's usefulness as a guide to what the judges are likely to do in future cases.").

36. *See generally* Charles Evans Hughes, *The Supreme Court of the United States: Its Foundation, Methods, and Achievements* (Columbia University Press, 1928), 68.

37. *See* Dworkin, *Law's Empire*, 89–90.

38. *See supra* pp. 77–78.

39. John Gardner, *The Virtue of Justice and the Character of Law*, 53 Current Legal Probs. 1, 19, 21 (2000). *See also* Judith N. Shklar, *Legalism: Law, Morals, and Political Trials* (Harvard University Press, 1964), 117 ("The pursuit of justice does in fact express itself in specifically legal institutions of which the courts of law are the most characteristic.").

40. *See generally* T.R.S. Allan, *Constitutional Justice: A Liberal Theory of the Rule of Law* (Oxford University Press, 2001), 249; George Anastaplo, *The Constitution of 1787: A Commentary* (Johns Hopkins University Press, 1989), 3, 135; Philip Soper, *A Theory*

of Law (Harvard University Press, 1984), 55, 64; Kenneth J. Kress, *Why No Judge Should Be A Dworkinian Coherentist,* 77 Tex. L. Rev. 1375, 1410 (1999); Matthew D. Adler, *Judicial Restraint in the Administrative State: Beyond the Countermajoritarian Difficulty,* 145 U. Pa. L. Rev. 759, 784–85 (1997).

41. *See generally* Anastaplo, *Constitution of 1787,* 137–38; Melvin Aron Eisenberg, *The Nature of the Common Law,* (Harvard University Press, 1988), 80–81 ("This use of new principles to critically reexamine and refashion established rules is reflected in the concept of the law working itself pure."); Benjamin N. Cardozo, *The Nature of the Judicial Process* (Yale University Press, 1921), 22–23, 35, 42–45, 112–13, 135–36.

42. William J. Brennan, Jr., *Constitutional Adjudication and the Death Penalty: A View from the Court,* 100 Harv. L. Rev. 313, 331 (1986).

43. *See* Jerome Frank, *Courts on Trial: Myth and Reality in American Justice* (Princeton University Press, 1949), 270–71 ("When judges, refusing to depart from an unjust precedent . . . say that 'hard cases make bad law,' I think that, instead, they usually should say, 'Bad 'law' makes hard cases. If an unjust decision is the logical result of a rule, then that rule should be changed.' . . . [I]f the precedent system means the perpetuation of judge-made rules, shown to be unjust or undesirable, rules on which no one has been proved to rely, then usually the courts, when they accept that system, are not performing their function—the administration of justice. They are administering injustice.").

44. *See, e.g.,* Thomas Aquinas, *Summa Theologiae,* II-II, q. 57, a.1c (on "the judge, whose role it is to do justice"), *quoted in* John Finnis, *Natural Law and Natural Rights* (Oxford University Press, 1980), 206.

45. *Cf.* Robert G. McCloskey, *The American Supreme Court* (4th ed.) (University of Chicago Press, 2005), 17 ("[S]ince the constitutional questions that do successfully claim the attention of the Court are often those least answerable by rules of thumb, the predilections, the 'values' of the judges, must play a part in supplying answers to them."); George Anastaplo, *The Amendments to the Constitution: A Commentary* (Johns Hopkins University Press, 1995), 91 ("[T]he Constitution, from the beginning, anticipated that American courts (whether National or State) would continue acting as courts in the common-law tradition had 'always' acted. A sense of fairness, consistent with precedents, general expectations, and the political, social, economic, and religious opinions and institutions of the Country, is relied upon in how the law is to be developed and applied."). *Cf.* Cardozo, *Nature of the Judicial Process,* 112–17.

46. *See, e.g.,* Posner, *Federal Courts,* 310 ("The vastness and complexity of American law, its extension into all sorts of politically controversial areas, the lack of disciplined legislative processes, the amazing diversity of ethical and political opinion in the society, and the political character of the judicial appointing process . . . make it inevitable that many judicial decisions will be based, in part anyway, on value judgments rather than just on technical, professional judgments."); Keith E. Whittington, *"Interpose Your Friendly Hand": Political Supports for the Exercise of Judicial Review by the United States Supreme Court,* 99 Am. Pol. Sci. Rev. 583 (2005). Judge Posner distinguishes the legislative processes he describes in the American context from those in England, which seems fair enough. *See* Posner, *Federal Courts,* 310 n. 20. For the reasons I have explained and will explain, however, his more general point holds in

both systems. *See also id.* at 331 ("Candor requires admitting that the judge's personal policy preferences or values play a role in the judicial process. This admission promotes judicial self-restraint in its separation-of-powers sense.").

47. *See* Anastaplo, *Constitution of 1787*, 135; Louis L. Jaffe, *English and American Judges as Lawmakers* (Oxford University Press, 1969), 44–48.

48. Jeremy Bentham is the best-known historical example. Notable American proponents of the Benthamite view are David Dudley Field and William Sampson. They all were hostile to the common law judiciary's role and to "judge-made law" in general. They advocated the substitution of a code-based system for the common law system in England and the United States, respectively. *See generally* Jeremy Bentham, *The Theory of Legislation* (Oceana Publications, 1975), 92–95; Gerald J. Postema, *Bentham and the Common Law Tradition* (Oxford University Press, 1986), 267–301, 421–39; Lawrence M. Friedman, *A History of American Law* (2nd ed.) (Simon and Schuster, 1985), 391–92, 403–5; William Sampson, *An Anniversary Discourse Delivered before the Historical Society of New York, on Saturday, December 6, 1823, Showing the Origin, Progress, Antiquities, Curiosities, and Nature of the Common Law* (Pishey Thompson, 1826). For a more contemporary example in the same vein, *see* Gordon Tullock, *The Case against the Common Law* (Locke Institute, 1997).

49. A thoughtful examination of common law constitutionalism can be found in T.R.S. Allan, *Law, Liberty, and Justice: The Legal Foundations of British Constitutionalism* (Oxford University Press, 1993). *See also infra* pp. 162–63, 182–90.

50. Allan, *Law, Liberty, and Justice*, 4–5 ("The central role of the common law in the constitutional scheme placed unique responsibility on the shoulders of the judges of the ordinary courts . . . [T]he inherent strength of common law adjudication [is] as a basis of protection: a common law right is intrinsically related to the means of its enforcement.").

51. Ruth Bader Ginsburg, *Speaking in a Judicial Voice*, 67 N.Y.U. L. Rev. 1185, 1198 (1992). *See also* Nicholas Bamforth, "Ultra Vires and Institutional Interdependence," in Christopher Forsyth, ed., *Judicial Review and the Constitution* (Hart Publishing, 2000).

52. These points are approached in different ways throughout Llewellyn's *Common Law Tradition*. For a brief and comparatively unstilted summary of his views, *see id.* at 401–3.

53. *See* Mark A. Graber, *Dred Scott and the Problem of Constitutional Evil* (Cambridge University Press, 2006), 2, 241, 244–47, 252–53. Important as it is, I cannot here address Graber's distinction between justice-seeking constitutionalism and peace-seeking constitutionalism.

54. *See* Jeffrey Goldsworthy, *The Sovereignty of Parliament: History and Philosophy* (Oxford University Press, 1999), 13 ("Arguably, the most fundamental principle of the common law is something as abstract as 'justice.'") (discussing *Emmens v. Pottle*, (1885) 16 QB 354, 357–58).

55. *See infra* pp. 163, 180–86.

56. Common law review and constitutional review mirror one another in this regard. Where there is a written constitution, that document will typically organize the structure of the governmental system and provide substantive principles used by courts to evaluate governmental actions.

57. Allan, *Law, Liberty, and Justice,* 111.

58. *Id.* at 15 ("[T]he common law is a constantly evolving apparatus for protecting basic values. It is inherently open to changing perceptions of the requirements of justice and the demands of basic principle. It follows that the content of the common law is ultimately a matter of reason.").

59. *Griffin v. Mixon,* 38 Miss. (9 George) 424, 449–50 (1860). *See also* Posner, *Federal Courts,* 321 ("Judges who are too miserly in using their powers to check the other branches of government might as well not be a part of the system of checks and balances, though the Constitution meant them to be."). This aspect of the Constitution, like many others, incorporates preexisting common law structures and values; it does not create them. *See* Allan C. Hutchinson, *Evolution and the Common Law* (Cambridge University Press, 2005), 126. *See also infra* pp. 278–80 nn. 94–102.

60. *See generally* Judith S. Kaye, *The Human Dimension in Appellate Judging: A Brief Reflection on a Timeless Concern,* 73 Cornell L. Rev. 1004 (1988).

61. *See generally* William J. Brennan, Jr., *Reason, Passion, and "The Progress of the Law,"* 42 Record of the Ass'n of the Bar of the City of New York 948 (1987).

62. Kaye, *Human Dimension in Appellate Judging,* 1006.

63. *See generally* Robert H. Bork, *The Tempting of America: The Political Seduction of the Law* (Free Press, 1990), 176–78, 251–59, 265.

64. Brennan, *Reason, Passion, and "The Progress of the Law,"* 951–52.

65. Bork, *Tempting of America,* 259. *See also* Alpheus Thomas Mason, *The Supreme Court from Taft to Burger* (3rd ed.) (Louisiana State University Press, 1979), 293 ("[M]y fundamental commitment, if I am confirmed, will be to totally disregard my own personal belief.") (quoting William Rehnquist at his Senate Judiciary Committee hearing).

66. *See* Dworkin, *Law's Empire,* 52.

67. *See id.* at 230–31.

68. *See id.* at 379–89.

69. *Cf.* Stephen Guest, *Ronald Dworkin* (2nd ed.) (Edinburgh University Press, 1997), 56.

70. *See* Dworkin, *Law's Empire,* 66 (explaining that a proposed interpretation need not fit all aspects of the subject practice; it need only fit "enough" of the practice so that the interpreter can legitimately claim to be interpreting the practice at issue rather than something else). Dworkin's theory is sometimes criticized as underdeterminate, because he offers very little explanation of the lower limit that will satisfy the fit dimension. *See, e.g.,* Michael S. Moore, *Metaphysics, Epistemology, and Legal Theory,* 60 S. Cal. L. Rev. 453, 492 (1987). I do not propose to criticize Dworkin for or defend him from this charge.

71. Although Dworkin himself referred to "three stages" of interpretation (*see* Dworkin, *Law's Empire,* 65–66), I realize that some commentators do not believe that the interpretive dimensions of fit and justification necessarily occur in serial stages or moments of analysis. *See, e.g.,* Kress, *Why No Judge Should Be A Dworkinian Coherentist,* 1396–1402. For ease and clarity of discussion, I will nonetheless refer to the two dimensions of interpretation as distinct levels or stages.

72. *See* A.V. Dicey, *Introduction to the Study of the Law of the Constitution* (10th ed.) (Macmillan, 1959), ch. 4.

73. Kaye, *Human Dimension in Appellate Judging*, 1015. *See also* Hutchinson, *Evolution and the Common Law*, 188; Irving R. Kaufman, *The Anatomy of Decisionmaking*, 53 Fordham L. Rev. 1, 15 (1984) ("[T]he 'personal element—that individual sense of justice—is not only inextinguishable, but essential for the orderly development of the law'. . . Our gravest error may be in repressing our individual values in the hopes of achieving a pure legal result.") (quoting Irving R. Kaufman, *Chilling Judicial Independence*, 88 Yale L.J. 681, 714 (1979)) (footnote deleted).

74. I ignore two further subdivisions of the third and fourth categories. First, an interpretivist judge could use his own, rather than the community's, moral standards to inform his constitutional interpretation. Second, an individualist judge could rely on communal, rather than personal, moral principles when engaging in common law review, treating common law review as an extension of interpretivism in the extraconstitutional setting.

75. As Grant Gilmore observed, this was the dominant view of the American judicial function from just after the Civil War until just after the First (or perhaps Second) World War. *See* Grant Gilmore, *The Ages of American Law* (Yale University Press, 1977), 14-15. Gilmore described this "middle" period in American legal history as "the Age of Faith." *See id.* at 41-67.

76. Walter V. Schaefer, *Precedent and Policy*, 34 U. Chi. L. Rev. 3, 23 (1966). *See also* Jon O. Newman, *Between Legal Realism and Neutral Principles: The Legitimacy of Institutional Values*, 72 Cal. L. Rev. 200, 208-14 (1984).

77. *See* Dworkin, *Law's Empire*, 357-59. *See also* Charles M. Lamb, *Judicial Restraint Reappraised*, 31 Cath. U. L. Rev. 181, 198 (1982).

78. This point is elusive. Some commentators conclude that *Plessy* and *Brown* cannot both fit American practice, on Dworkin's scheme, because they reach contrary results. Moreover, as these scholars see it, once *Plessy* was decided, it generated more and more preinterpretive data that the later *Brown* decision could not possibly fit; *see* Robert Justin Lipkin, *Constitutional Revolutions: Pragmatism and the Role of Judicial Review in American Constitutionalism* (Duke University Press, 2000), 90. But this misconstrues Dworkin's theory. What made *Plessy* and *Brown* such difficult cases for American law is that, at the time *Plessy* and *Brown* were decided, each could reasonably be read to fit American legal and social culture, relationships, and materials. *See* Dworkin, *Law's Empire*, 30, 360. *Cf.* Richard A. Posner, *The Problems of Jurisprudence* (Harvard University Press, 1990), 307-8 ("The problem with the decision in *Plessy* was not that it had distorted the text of the equal protection clause but that it had come to seem, in the fullness of time, bad ethics and bad politics . . . As an interpretation of the equal protection clause *Plessy* could have gone either way, but so could *Brown*."). Posner mentions only the text, but his point can fairly be expanded to include the data Dworkin deems necessary to interpret the text.

79. *See* Posner, *Problems of Jurisprudence*, 304.

80. I realize that I am, perhaps, characterizing originalism here as expectation rather than semantic originalism. *See generally* Antonin Scalia, *A Matter of Interpretation: Federal Courts and the Law* (Princeton University Press, 1997), 119 (response of Ronald Dworkin). I only present this characterization to emphasize the point I am trying to make.

81. *Cf.* Richard A. Wasserstrom, *The Judicial Decision: Toward a Theory of Legal Justification* (Stanford University Press, 1961), 160–62, 168–71.

82. I should emphasize that Dworkin's theory is not the only available theoretical foundation according to which common law review might be assessed in light of the attributes of common law legal systems and the function of common law judges. For a positivistic account that supports several of the central themes for which I am arguing, *see* Frederick Schauer, "Positivism as Pariah," in Robert P. George, ed., *The Autonomy of Law: Essays on Legal Positivism* (Oxford University Press, 1996). *Cf.* Joseph Raz, "On the Authority and Interpretation of Constitutions: Some Preliminaries," in Larry Alexander, ed., *Constitutionalism: Philosophical Foundations* (Cambridge University Press, 1998), especially 183–86 (arguing that the institutional role of judges requires them not just to apply but also to develop the law when engaging in constitutional adjudication and interpretation). Raz's arguments apply *mutatis mutandis* to common law review, given the congruence between common law and constitutional adjudication.

83. *See, e.g.,* Jaffe, *English and American Judges as Lawmakers,* 21 ("A judiciary which is gagged or has the sense of being gagged in one area may well be gagged in all. The judge should have a sense of moral freedom, a sense of independence in the service of justice. We cannot look to him to resist abuse of power if he is made to feel impotent.").

84. *See generally* Charles L. Black, Jr., *The People and the Court: Judicial Review in a Democracy* (Macmillan, 1960), 34–86, especially 51–55.

85. *See* Jesse H. Choper, *Judicial Review and the National Political Process: A Functional Reconsideration of the Role of the Supreme Court* (University of Chicago Press, 1980), 233.

86. *See id.* at 230–33.

87. *See id.* at 231. *See also* Gerald Gunther, *The Subtle Vices of the "Passive Virtues": A Comment on Principle and Expediency in Judicial Review,* 64 Colum. L. Rev. 1 (1964).

88. *See generally* Fiss, *Forms of Justice,* 13 ("Judges are compelled to speak back, to respond to the grievance or the claim, and to assume individual responsibility for that response."), reprinted in Fiss, *Law as It Could Be,* 11.

89. Herbert Hovenkamp, *Social Science and Segregation before* Brown, 1985 Duke L.J. 624, 624–25 (1985) (footnotes omitted). *See also* Gerald J. Postema, "The Sins of Segregation," in Gerald J. Postema, ed., *Racism and the Law: The Legacy and Lessons of* Plessy (Kluwer Academic Publishers, 1997), 1–2, 16–17, 22–23.

90. Charles A. Lofgren, *The* Plessy *Case: A Legal-Historical Interpretation* (Oxford University Press, 1987), 200.

91. *Id.* at 201 (emphasis in original).

92. *Id.*

93. *Id.* at 202, 203 (citation omitted).

94. *See generally* Douglas S. Massey and Nancy A. Denton, *American Apartheid: Segregation and the Making of the Underclass* (Harvard University Press, 1993); Bernard R. Boxill, "Washington, Du Bois, and *Plessy v. Ferguson,*" in Postema, *Racism and the Law,* 79–110.

95. 41 U.S. (16 Pet.) 539, 10 L.Ed. 1060 (1842) (enforcing the Fugitive Slave Act and

permitting a former slave to be kidnapped in a free state and returned to a state of slavery).

96. *Dred Scott v. Sandford*, 60 U.S. (19 How.) 393, 15 L.Ed. 691 (1856) (holding that black people were not citizens who could invoke the jurisdiction of the federal courts).

97. *Hirabayashi v. U.S.*, 320 U.S. 81, 63 S.Ct. 1375, 87 L.Ed. 1774 (1943) (sustaining a conviction for the violation of a curfew order imposed on American citizens of Japanese ancestry).

98. *Korematsu v. U.S.*, 323 U.S. 214, 65 S.Ct. 193, 89 L.Ed. 194 (1944) (upholding the internment of American citizens of Japanese ancestry in "relocation centers").

99. *Cf. Prager v. Blatspiel, Stamp and Heacock, Ltd.*, [1924] 1 KB 566, 570.

100. Fiss, *Forms of Justice*, 30, reprinted in Fiss, *Law as It Could Be*, 25.

101. *See* Henry M. Hart, Jr., and Albert M. Sacks, *The Legal Process: Basic Problems in the Making and Application of Law* (Foundation Press, 1994), 343 ("[T]he courts, in their conventional operation, may . . . also make a . . . distinct contribution to the good ordering of society by holding themselves out as agencies of correction of law which is unclear or unjust.").

102. *Cf.* Dworkin, *Taking Rights Seriously*, 102–5.

103. *See generally* Lon L. Fuller, *The Forms and Limits of Adjudication*, 92 Harv. L. Rev. 353, 378 (1978) ("[A] court is not an inert mirror reflecting current mores but an active participant in the enterprise of articulating the implications of shared purposes."). *See also* Dworkin, *Law's Empire*, 175.

104. *Desist v. U.S.*, 394 U.S. 244, 259, 89 S.Ct. 1030, 1039, 22 L.Ed.2d 248 (1969) (Harlan, J., dissenting).

105. *DiSanto v. Pennsylvania*, 273 U.S. 34, 42, 47 S.Ct. 267, 270, 71 L.Ed. 524 (1927) (Brandeis, J., dissenting), *overruled in part by California v. Thompson*, 313 U.S. 109, 61 S.Ct. 930, 85 L.Ed. 1219 (1941).

106. *See Runyon v. McCrary*, 427 U.S. 160, 191, 96 S.Ct. 2586, 2604, 49 L.Ed.2d 415 (1976) ("When a rule . . . has been found to be inconsistent with the sense of justice or with the social welfare, there should be less hesitation in frank avowal and full abandonment.") (Stevens, J., concurring) (quoting Cardozo, *Nature of the Judicial Process*, 150). *See also* Justice Brandeis's statement in *Burnet*, which is quoted *supra* at p. 218 n. 10.

107. The conflict between formal justice and substantive justice also arises where strict application of an otherwise unobjectionable legal rule would frustrate the judge's sense of what justice requires in a particular circumstance. Here, again, the judge must balance the value for the law of following settled rules against the value for the law of achieving the fairest possible result. *See, e.g., Bell v. Thompson*, 545 U.S. 794, 830, 125 S.Ct. 2825, 2846, 162 L.Ed.2d 693 (2005) ("A legal system is based on rules; it also seeks justice in the individual case. Sometimes these ends conflict . . . When we tell the Court of Appeals that it cannot . . . correct the serious error it discovered here, we tell courts they are not to act to cure serious injustice in similar cases. The consequence is to divorce the rule-based result from the just result. The American judicial system has long sought to avoid that divorce.") (Breyer, J., dissenting). *See also Red Sea Insurance Co. Ltd. v. Bouygues S.A.*, [1995] 1 AC 190, 200 (quoting *Chaplin v. Boys*, [1971] AC 356, 378); *Davis v. Johnson*, [1979] AC 264, 311 (Cumming-Bruce, L.J., dissenting).

108. *See generally U.S. v. Bethlehem Steel Corporation*, 315 U.S. 289, 326, 62 S.Ct. 581, 599, 86 L.Ed. 855 (1942) ("[I]s there any principle which is more familiar or more firmly embedded in the history of Anglo-American law than the basic doctrine that the courts will not permit themselves to be used as instruments of inequity and injustice?") (Frankfurter, J., dissenting). In England, this principle is known as the common law prohibition against abuse of process. *See, e.g., A. v. Secretary of State for the Home Department (No. 2)*, [2005] UKHL 71, [19], [21]–[22], [2006] 2 AC 221 (discussing *R. v. Looseley*, [2001] UKHL 53, [2001] 1 WLR 2060; *R. v. Horseferry Road Magistrates' Court, ex parte Bennett*, [1994] 1 AC 42; *R. v. Mullen*, [2000] QB 520).

109. Postema, "Sins of Segregation," 22, 23, 24.

110. It was, however, one riddled with corruption, and it did not adequately represent the views of large segments of the Louisiana population at the time. *See generally* J. Morgan Kousser, *The Shaping of Southern Politics: Suffrage Restriction and the Establishment of the One-Party South, 1880–1910* (Yale University Press, 1974).

111. *See generally* John Hart Ely, *Democracy and Distrust: A Theory of Judicial Review* (Harvard University Press, 1980), 68–69.

112. As I discussed *supra* at pp. 55–58, 59–64, judicial independence lay at the heart of Coke's statement in *Bonham* and in his dispute with James in the *Commendam Case*. Moreover, at the turn of the eighteenth century, Parliament passed the Act of Settlement, ensuring that judicial salaries (and jobs) would not be endangered by Parliament's or the king's displeasure with any judge's decision. *See* Act of Settlement, 12 & 13 Will. 3, c. 2, § 3 (1701). *See also* 6 William S. Holdsworth, *A History of English Law* (3rd ed.) (Methuen, 1945), 234, 514.

113. Dworkin, *Law's Empire*, 356.

114. Jeremy Waldron, *Law and Disagreement* (Oxford University Press, 1999), 287–88 (footnotes omitted).

115. *Id.* at 288.

116. *See* Fiss, *Forms of Justice*, 15, reprinted in Fiss, *Law as It Could Be*, 13 ("To simply postulate the supremacy of the more majoritarian branches, the legislative or the executive, . . . is no answer, for . . . the people's preferences are not the standard, and there is no discernible connection between majoritarianism and the meaning of a constitutional [public] value.").

117. *Cf.* Fiss, *Forms of Justice*, 58, reprinted in Fiss, *Law as It Could Be*, 47 ("Judges might be seen as forever straddling two worlds, the world of the ideal and the world of the practical, the world of public value and the world of subjective preference . . . Among all the agencies of government, the judiciary is in the best position to discover the true meaning of our constitutional [public] values.").

118. Nor does Waldron deny this. *See* Jeremy Waldron, *The Core of the Case against Judicial Review*, 115 Yale L.J. 1346, 1348, 1352 (2006).

Chapter 8

1. For a specimen of these objections, specific to a version of common law review, *see* Jeffrey Goldsworthy, *The Sovereignty of Parliament: History and Philosophy* (Oxford University Press, 1999), 270–71. For a response to the objection that common law review allows judges to change or develop the law "contrary to law," *see*

N.W. Barber, *Sovereignty Re-examined: The Courts, Parliament, and Statutes,* 20 Oxford J. Legal Stud. 131, 150–53, 154 (2000).

2. Stephen R. Perry, *Second-Order Reasons, Uncertainty, and Legal Theory,* 62 S. Cal. L. Rev. 913, 967 (1989).

3. Stephen R. Perry, *Two Models of Legal Principles,* 82 Iowa L. Rev. 787, 801 (1997). *See also* Perry, *Second-Order Reasons,* 970.

4. *See* Perry, *Two Models of Legal Principles,* 800–801.

5. For a sense of what I have in mind here, *see* S.L. Hurley, *Coherence, Hypothetical Cases, and Precedent,* 10 Oxford J. Leg. Stud. 221, 247 (1990) ("It is possible that an *ex ante* mistake is so serious that the enormity of the mistake outweighs its precedential force.").

6. By this I mean to distinguish prosaic common law cases, whereby judges eliminate from the law less severe errors subject to traditional institutional constraints, from common law review, which targets only the most grievous injustices and supersedes other judicial obligations.

7. *See generally* Joseph Raz, *The Authority of Law* (Oxford University Press, 1979), 114 ("[T]he courts in common law jurisdictions . . . cannot change them [legal rules] whenever they consider that on the balance of reasons it would be better to do so. They may change them only for certain kinds of reasons. They may change them, for example, for being unjust, for iniquitous discrimination, for being out of step with the court's conception of the purpose of the body of laws to which they belong, etc.").

8. *Cf.* James Bradley Thayer, *The Origin and Scope of the American Doctrine of Constitutional Law,* 7 Harv. L. Rev. 129, 144 (1893) (the Court can refuse to enforce legislation "when those who have the right to make laws have not merely made a mistake, but have made a very clear one—so clear that it is not open to rational question"). I am not suggesting that the Thayerian view is most appropriate in the constitutional review setting.

9. *See, e.g.,* Raz, *Authority of Law,* 199–200; Joseph Raz, *Dworkin: A New Link in the Chain,* 74 Cal. L. Rev. 1103, 1110, 1115 (1986).

10. *See, e.g.,* Ronald Dworkin, *Law's Empire* (Harvard University Press, 1986), 255–56.

11. In Raz's terms, this means that common law judges must engage in "reasoning according to law" by "applying moral considerations," rather than merely "applying the law." *See* Joseph Raz, *Ethics in the Public Domain: Essays in the Morality of Law and Politics* (rev. ed.) (Oxford University Press, 1994), 332–35. The key for Raz (and exclusive positivism) is that there must be a source-based legal norm that directs or allows the judicial official to apply moral considerations, in certain circumstances, when reasoning according to law. Surely, there may be and have been legal systems that do not provide such legal norms, but the common law is not one of them. *See id.* at 338–40.

12. Joseph Raz, "Legal Principles and the Limits of Law," in Marshall Cohen, ed., *Ronald Dworkin and Contemporary Jurisprudence* (Rowman and Allanheld, 1983), 85 (written for the edited volume, this is a postscript to Joseph Raz, *Legal Principles and the Limits of Law,* 81 Yale L.J. 823 (1972)).

13. *See* Benjamin N. Cardozo, *The Nature of the Judicial Process* (Yale University

Press, 1921), 106–10; Melvin Aron Eisenberg, *The Nature of the Common Law* (Harvard University Press, 1988), 9–10, 14–26; Christopher L. Eisgruber, *Constitutional Self-Government* (Harvard University Press, 2001), 126, 131; John Rawls, *Political Liberalism* (Columbia University Press, 1993), 236. *See also* Aharon Barak, *The Judge in a Democracy* (Princeton University Press, 2006), 101–5; Harry H. Wellington, *Common Law Rules and Constitutional Double Standards: Some Notes on Adjudication,* 83 Yale L.J. 221, 244 (1973). For a discussion of Dworkin's views on the relationship between the moral views of individual judges and their community (and its bearing on judicial enforcement of unjust laws), *see* David Dyzenhaus, "The Rule of Law as the Rule of Liberal Principle," in Arthur Ripstein, ed., *Ronald Dworkin* (Cambridge University Press, 2007), 62–69.

14. *See* Eisenberg, *Nature of the Common Law,* 196–97 n. 35.

15. For some more general criticisms of Eisenberg's view that judges must evaluate law by reference to the community's, rather than their own, moral convictions, *see* Kent Greenawalt, *Law and Objectivity* (Oxford University Press, 1992), 217–18. Greenawalt notes that Eisenberg's theory concerns common law adjudication, but to the extent that Eisenberg intends his analysis to extend to constitutional adjudication, Greenawalt's criticisms extend similarly.

16. *See* Liam Murphy, "The Political Question of the Concept of Law," in Jules Coleman, ed., *Hart's Postscript: Essays on the Postscript to* The Concept of Law (Oxford University Press, 2001), 393 ("I also assume that on the best theory of adjudication judicial appeal to principles of political morality that are not incorporated into the legal order should be based on judges' own best judgment, rather than on some speculation about what the community believes; moreover, these appeals to political morality should not be hidden in a sophistical pretense of formalistic argument."). I agree with Murphy that this view generally represents "the best theory of [common law] adjudication." My reservation about Murphy's claims, however, lies in his attempt to enlist an impressively diverse group of legal theorists as proponents of this view, because I am not at all sure that they would join in his assessment of their positions. *See id.* (claiming that "Hobbes, Bentham, Austin, Holmes, legal realists such as Felix Cohen, Hart, Raz, Dworkin, and Finnis, agree" on these points). To be fair, Murphy says that he "assumes" this to be the best theory of adjudication. As my project here is designed to show, however, this must be established, not assumed. Murphy also qualifies his remarks in a footnote. *See id.* n. 83. But Murphy there says that "judges . . . should establish which is the best or the just decision given things as they are rather than as they would be in an ideal world" (citation omitted). This constraint will likely swallow judicial conscience in cases involving unjust laws. Indeed, assuming that the majority is satisfied with things "as they are" (however unjust they might happen to be), it is difficult to see much meaningful distinction between the community's conventional morality and the judge's critical morality, if the judge cannot stray too far from the status quo when appealing to moral principles not yet incorporated into the legal order.

17. Kent Greenawalt, *Policy, Rights, and Judicial Decision,* 11 Ga. L. Rev. 991, 1052–53 (1977).

18. For some criticisms of Greenawalt's "marginal cases" qualification, *see* Eisenberg, *Nature of the Common Law,* 22. Eisenberg attributes to Greenawalt the view that

a marginal case cannot be one "in which moral norms figure in the establishment of entirely new doctrines." If this is Greenawalt's view, it would be another area of disagreement for us, but I see no basis in Greenawalt's article for Eisenberg's presumption. For a view similar to Greenawalt's, *see* John Chipman Gray, *The Nature and Sources of the Law* (Ashgate/Dartmouth, 1997), 191–93.

19. 342 U.S. 165, 72 S.Ct. 205, 96 L.Ed. 183 (1952).

20. *See Rochin,* 342 U.S. at 166, 72 S.Ct. at 206.

21. *Rochin,* 342 U.S. at 166–67, 72 S.Ct. at 207 (quoting *People v. Rochin,* 101 Cal.App.2d 140, 143, 225 P.2d 1, 3 (1950)).

22. *See Rochin,* 342 U.S. at 167, 72 S.Ct. at 207 (quoting *People v. Rochin,* 101 Cal.App.2d 143, 149–50, 225 P.2d 913, 917–18 (1951)).

23. *Rochin,* 342 U.S. at 172, 173, 72 S.Ct. at 209–10 (citation omitted).

24. *See, e.g., Collins v. City of Harker Heights, Texas,* 503 U.S. 115, 126, 112 S.Ct. 1061, 1069, 117 L.Ed.2d 261 (1992) (citing *Rochin*); *McKinney v. Pate,* 20 F.3d 1550, 1556 n. 7 (11th Cir. 1994); *Hall v. Tawney,* 621 F.2d 607, 613 (4th Cir. 1980).

25. *See generally Trop v. Dulles,* 356 U.S. 86, 100–101, 78 S.Ct. 590, 598, 2 L.Ed.2d 630 (1958).

26. *Collins,* 503 U.S. at 126, 112 S.Ct. at 1069 (citation omitted).

27. *See, e.g., U.S. v. Salerno,* 481 U.S. 739, 746, 107 S.Ct. 2095, 2101, 95 L.Ed.2d 697 (1987) (quoting *Palko v. Connecticut,* 302 U.S. 319, 325–26, 58 S.Ct. 149, 151–52, 82 L.Ed. 288 (1937)).

28. *See Brown v. Mississippi,* 297 U.S. 278, 286–87, 56 S.Ct. 461, 465, 80 L.Ed. 682 (1936) ("The due process clause requires 'that state action, whether through one agency or another, shall be consistent with the fundamental principles of liberty and justice which lie at the base of all our civil and political institutions' . . . It would be difficult to conceive of methods more revolting to the sense of justice than those taken to procure the confessions of these petitioners, and the use of the confessions thus obtained as the basis for conviction and sentence was a clear denial of due process . . . 'Coercing the supposed state's criminals into confessions and using such confessions so coerced from them against them in trials has been the curse of all countries. It was the chief inequity, the crowning infamy of the Star Chamber, and the Inquisition, and other similar institutions. The constitution recognized the evils that lay behind these practices and prohibited them in this country . . . The duty of maintaining constitutional rights of a person on trial for his life rises above mere rules of procedure and wherever the court is clearly satisfied that such violations exist, it will refuse to sanction such violations and will apply the corrective.'") (Hughes, C.J.) (citations omitted); *Hovey v. Elliott,* 167 U.S. 409, 417–18, 17 S.Ct. 841, 844, 42 L.Ed. 215 (1897); *U.S. v. Toscanino,* 500 F.2d 267, 275–76 (2d Cir. 1974). In language, tone, substance, and operation, a very similar principle exists in English law as well. *See generally A. v. Secretary of State for the Home Department (No. 2),* [2005] UKHL 71, [18]–[22], [2006] 2 AC 221; *R. v. Horseferry Road Magistrates' Court, ex parte Bennett,* [1994] 1 AC 42, 61–62, 74, 76 (holding that the common law prohibition against abuse of process requires that "the judiciary [must] accept a responsibility for the maintenance of the rule of law that embraces a willingness to oversee executive action and to refuse to countenance behaviour that threatens either basic human rights or the rule of law" and that where "it offends the court's sense of justice and propri-

ety to be asked to try the accused in the circumstances of a particular case . . . the court, in order to protect its own process from being degraded and misused, must have the power to stay proceedings which have come before it and have only been made possible by acts which offend the court's conscience as being contrary to the rule of law"). *See also R. v. Looseley*, [2001] UKHL 53, [1], [2001] 1 WLR 2060; *R. v. Mullen*, [2000] QB 520, 535–36. Along with its connection to *Rochin*, the House's view in *Bennett* is echoed by Justice Kline in *Morrow*, which I discuss *infra* at pp. 153–57.

29. *See, e.g., Meyer v. Nebraska*, 262 U.S. 390, 399–400, 43 S.Ct. 625, 626–27, 67 L.Ed. 1042 (1923) ("While this Court has not attempted to define with exactness the liberty thus guaranteed [by the Fourteenth Amendment], the term [due process] has received much consideration and some of the included things have been definitely stated. Without doubt, it denotes . . . the right of the individual . . . generally to enjoy those privileges long recognized at common law as essential to the orderly pursuit of happiness by free men."); *Hurtado v. California*, 110 U.S. 516, 527–30, 532, 4 S.Ct. 111, 117–18, 119, 28 L.Ed. 232 (1884) ("As to the words from Magna Charta, . . . they were intended to secure the individual from the arbitrary exercise of the powers of government . . . [A] process of law, which is not otherwise forbidden, must be taken to be due process of law, if it can show the sanction of settled usage both in England and in this Country; but it by no means follows that nothing else can be due process of law . . . [T]o hold that such a characteristic is essential to due process of law, would be to deny every quality of the law but its age, and to render it incapable of progress or improvement . . . This would be all the more singular and surprising, in this quick and active age, when we consider that, owing to the progressive development of legal ideas and institutions in England, the words of Magna Charta stood for very different things at the time of the separation of the American colonies from what they represented originally . . . It is more consonant to the true philosophy of our historical legal institutions to say that the spirit of personal liberty and individual right . . . was preserved and developed by a progressive growth and wise adaptation to new circumstances and situations of the forms and processes found fit to give, from time to time, new expression and greater effect to modern ideas of self-government. This flexibility and capacity for growth and adaptation is the peculiar boast and excellence of the common law . . . Applied in England only as guards against executive usurpation and tyranny, here they have become bulwarks also against arbitrary legislation . . . [T]hey must be held to guarantee not particular forms of procedure, but the very substance of individual rights to life, liberty, and property.") (citations omitted).

30. *See County of Sacramento v. Lewis*, 523 U.S. 833, 846, 118 S.Ct. 1708, 1716, 140 L.Ed.2d 1043 (1998) ("[D]ue process in the substantive sense limits what the government may do in both its legislative and its executive capacities.") (citations omitted).

31. *County of Sacramento v. Lewis*, 523 U.S. at 846–47, 118 S.Ct. at 1717.

32. *See Herrera v. Collins*, 506 U.S. 390, 428, 113 S.Ct. 853, 875, 122 L.Ed.2d 203 (1993) (Scalia, J., concurring).

33. *See County of Sacramento v. Lewis*, 523 U.S. at 861 n. 2, 118 S.Ct. at 1724 n. 2 (Scalia, J., concurring).

34. *County of Sacramento v. Lewis*, 523 U.S. at 861 n. 2, 118 S.Ct. at 1724 n. 2 (Scalia, J., concurring) (citing *Salerno*, 481 U.S. at 746, 107 S.Ct. at 2101).

35. For a related discussion of the importance that a judge's sense of justice maintains for legal reasoning and judicial decision making in the common law tradition, *see* Gerald J. Postema, *"A Similibus ad Similia:* Analogical Thinking in Law," in Douglas E. Edlin, ed., *Common Law Theory* (Cambridge University Press, 2007), 126–30.

36. *See generally U.S. v. Schmidt,* 105 F.3d 82, 91 (2d Cir. 1997), *cert. denied, Schmidt v. U.S.,* 522 U.S. 846, 118 S.Ct. 130, 139 L.Ed.2d 80 (1997); *Telfair v. Gilberg,* 868 F. Supp. 1396, 1406 n. 4 (S.D. Ga. 1994), *aff'd, Telfair v. Gilberg,* 87 F.3d 1330 (11th Cir. 1996).

37. *Schmidt,* 105 F.3d at 91.

38. Richard A. Posner, *The Problematics of Moral and Legal Theory* (Harvard University Press, 1999), 142–43 (footnotes omitted). *See also id.* at 147–49; Louis L. Jaffe, *English and American Judges as Lawmakers* (Oxford University Press, 1969), 45–46; Richard A. Posner, *Legal Reasoning from the Top Down and from the Bottom Up: The Question of Unenumerated Constitutional Rights,* 59 U. Chi. L. Rev. 433, 447 (1992). Of course, the shocks the conscience test is intended to determine a constitutional violation, but the point here is that the test and common law review permit the judicial determination of legal violations based on the moral responses of individual judges rather than on a more rigidly defined legal standard. Moreover, common law review is intended to create a legal standard (akin to the test) that addresses and prevents abuses of government power, even when those abuses might not violate any specific constitutional prescription.

39. *Johnson v. Glick,* 481 F.2d 1028, 1033 (2d Cir. 1973) (citation omitted).

40. *Rochin,* 342 U.S. at 171, 72 S.Ct. at 209.

41. *Rochin,* 342 U.S. at 172, 72 S.Ct. at 209.

42. This is also true of adjudging precedents and other governmental actions void, and the discussion that follows applies to all of these authorities. I will continue to refer to statutes in the text.

43. *See supra* p. 130.

44. *See* Human Rights Act 1998, §§ 4(6)(a)–(b).

45. *See generally Norton v. Shelby County,* 118 U.S. 425, 442, 6 S.Ct. 1121, 1125, 30 L.Ed. 178 (1886); *Rodgers v. Mabelvale Extension Road Imp. Dist. No. 5 of Saline County,* 103 F.2d 844, 846–47 (8th Cir. 1939); *St. Paul Fire & Marine Ins. Co. v. Getty Oil Co.,* 782 P.2d 915, 917 (Okla. 1989).

46. *See supra* pp. 136–37.

47. *See, e.g.,* James Bradley Thayer, *"Law and Fact" in Jury Trials,* 4 Harv. L. Rev. 147, 153 (1890) ("[N]othing is law that is not a rule or standard which it is the duty of judicial tribunals to apply and enforce.").

48. *See generally* David Lyons, "Formal Justice and Judicial Precedent," in David Lyons, *Moral Aspects of Legal Theory* (Cambridge University Press, 1993), 117; Richard Posner, *The Problems of Jurisprudence* (Harvard University Press, 1990), 260–61; Dworkin, *Law's Empire,* 368; Jack Knight and Lee Epstein, *The Norm of Stare Decisis,* 40 Am. J. Pol. Sci. 1018, 1022 (1996) ("As long as justices generally comply with the norm [of stare decisis], they will be free to deviate from precedent in those cases in which their personal preferences so differ from the precedent that they feel compelled to change the existing law.").

49. *Charles v. Seigfried,* 165 Ill.2d 482, 512, 651 N.E.2d 154, 169 (1995) (McMorrow,

J., dissenting) (citations omitted). *See also Alvis v. Ribar,* 85 Ill.2d 1, 24, 421 N.E.2d 886, 896 (1981); *Brickhouse v. Hill,* 167 Ark. 513, 268 S.W. 865, 868 (1925); William O. Douglas, *Stare Decisis,* 49 Colum. L. Rev. 735, 746–55 (1949); Max Radin, *The Trail of the Calf,* 32 Cornell L.Q. 137, 150–60 (1946).

50. I postpone discussion of the specific interrelationship in England between the judicial obligation to develop the law and horizontal and vertical stare decisis. *See infra* pp. 170–73.

51. In addition to the cases I discuss in the text, *see, e.g., Wallace v. Castro,* 65 Fed. Appx. 618, 619 (9th Cir. 2003) (Pregerson, J., dissenting); *Jolly, Inc. v. Zoning Bd. of Appeals of City of Bridgeport,* 237 Conn. 184, 190–91, 676 A.2d 831, 835–36 (1996) (addressing a trial court's refusal to follow binding Connecticut Supreme Court precedent); *Stewart v. Sampson,* 285 Ky. 447, 148 S.W.2d 278, 281 (1941) ("Of course it might be the duty of an inferior court to respect and follow adjudications of the final appellate court of the same sovereignty as precedents because of higher dignity of the final appellate one, but there is no mandatory rule to that effect . . . [I]n the general practice a circuit court in this commonwealth—and we believe also in other jurisdictions—has the inherent right and power to adjudge questions coming before it according to its sound judicial discretion independently of what may have been said to the contrary by other courts of the same sovereignty, although it may be the highest court therein . . . Numerous are the instances where circuit judges are confronted with questions previously determined by this court in cases prosecuted to it, but which determinations do not meet the approval of the judge trying the particular case before him, since in the exercise of his judicial discretion he concludes that the determination made by this court is unsound and he declines to follow it.").

52. 47 F. Supp. 251, 252–53 (S.D.W.Va. 1942).

53. 310 U.S. 586, 60 S.Ct. 1010, 84 L.Ed. 1375 (1940).

54. *See Barnette,* 47 F. Supp. at 253.

55. *West Virginia Board of Education v. Barnette,* 319 U.S. 624, 63 S.Ct. 1178, 87 L.Ed. 1628 (1943).

56. 59 Cal.App.4th 924, 69 Cal.Rptr.2d 489 (1997).

57. 3 Cal.4th 273, 10 Cal.Rptr.2d 859, 834 P.2d 119 (1992).

58. *See Neary,* 3 Cal.4th at 276–77, 282, 10 Cal.Rptr.2d at 860–61, 864, 834 P.2d at 120–21, 124.

59. *Neary,* 3 Cal.4th at 286, 10 Cal.Rptr.2d at 867, 834 P.2d at 127 (Kennard, J., dissenting). According to California court rules, an appellate court ruling is depublished once the Supreme Court agrees to review the case. *See* Cal. Rules of Court, 976(d), 977. Still, the Court of Appeal's view can be gleaned from the Supreme Court's references to it. *See Neary,* 3 Cal.4th at 281, 10 Cal.Rptr.2d at 863, 834 P.2d at 124.

60. *See Neary,* 3 Cal.4th at 282, 10 Cal.Rptr.2d at 864, 834 P.2d at 124.

61. *Neary,* 3 Cal.4th at 281–82, 10 Cal.Rptr.2d at 863–64, 834 P.2d at 124 (citation omitted and emphasis deleted).

62. *Neary,* 3 Cal.4th at 282, 10 Cal.Rptr.2d at 864, 834 P.2d at 124 (citation omitted).

63. *Morrow,* 59 Cal.App.4th at 926–27, 928, 929, 930, 69 Cal.Rptr.2d at 490–91, 491–92, 493 (Kline, J., dissenting) (citing Evan H. Caminker, *Why Must Inferior Courts*

Obey Superior Court Precedents? 46 Stan. L. Rev. 817 (1994); Paul L. Colby, *Two Views on the Legitimacy of Nonacquiescence in Judicial Opinions,* 61 Tul. L. Rev. 1041 (1987)) (other citations omitted).

64. Kline made it clear in his dissent that he would not refuse to "comply with an order of the California Supreme Court to grant a particular request for stipulated reversal, a purely ministerial act" (*Morrow,* 59 Cal.App.4th at 930, 69 Cal.Rptr.2d at 493 (Kline, J., dissenting)).

65. I do not here address whether the situation presented in *Morrow* was an appropriate circumstance for judicial refusal to enforce higher court precedent.

66. *Morrow,* 59 Cal.App.4th at 930, 69 Cal.Rptr.2d at 493 (Kline, J., dissenting) (quoting Michael Stokes Paulsen, *Accusing Justice: Some Variations on the Themes of Robert M. Cover's* Justice Accused, 7 J.L. & Religion 33, 85–86 (1990)).

67. For an instance of a trial court judge refusing to apply higher court precedent, despite the certainty of a reversal on appeal, *see U.S. ex rel. Free v. Peters,* 806 F. Supp. 705, 731–32 (N.D. Ill. 1992), *aff'd in part and rev'd in part, Free v. Peters,* 12 F.3d 700, 705–7 (7th Cir. 1993).

68. Posner, *Problems of Jurisprudence,* 80.

69. *Kessler v. Associates Financial Services Co.,* 573 F.2d 577, 579 (9th Cir. 1977). *See also* Dworkin, *Law's Empire,* 229, 254 (when a judge issues a decision, "future judges confront a new tradition that includes what he [the deciding judge] has done," and "if he persuades the profession to his view," the law will change as well); Charles E. Wyzanski, Jr., *A Trial Judge's Freedom and Responsibility,* 65 Harv. L. Rev. 1281, 1302–4 (1952).

70. *Cf. Green v. Coast Line R. Co.,* 97 Ga. 15, 36–37, 24 S.E. 814, 822 (1895) ("Every direct authority known to us is against us. Nevertheless, we are right, and these authorities are all wrong, as time and further judicial study of the subject will manifest.").

71. *See* Benjamin N. Cardozo, *Law and Literature, and Other Essays and Addresses* (Harcourt, Brace, 1931), 36 ("More truly characteristic of dissent is a dignity, an elevation, of mood and thought and phrase. Deep conviction and warm feeling are saying their last say with knowledge that the cause is lost. The voice of the majority may be that of force triumphant, content with the plaudits of the hour, and recking little of the morrow. The dissenter speaks to the future, and his voice is pitched to a key that will carry through the years.").

72. *Adams Express Co. v. Beckwith,* 100 Ohio St. 348, 352, 126 N.E. 300, 301 (1919).

73. *See generally* Sambhav N. Sankar, *Disciplining the Professional Judge,* 88 Cal. L. Rev. 1233, 1234 (2000); Pamela S. Karlan, *Two Concepts of Judicial Independence,* 72 S. Cal. L. Rev. 535, 551–52 (1999).

74. The commission later dismissed the charge. *See* Sankar, *Disciplining the Professional Judge,* 1236.

75. *See id.* at 1235; Karlan, *Two Concepts of Judicial Independence,* 551–52.

76. Sankar, *Disciplining the Professional Judge,* 1235.

77. Cal.C.C.P. § 128(a)(8).

78. *See Neary,* 3 Cal.4th at 287–88, 288–89, 291–93, 10 Cal.Rptr.2d at 867, 868, 870–71, 834 P.2d at 127–28, 128–29, 130–31 (Kennard, J., dissenting); *Morrow,* 59

Cal.App.4th at 928–29, 931 n. 6, 69 Cal.Rptr.2d at 492, 493 n. 6 (Kline, J., dissenting).

79. *R. v. Secretary of State for the Home Department, ex parte Pierson,* [1998] AC 539, 589. *See also* Jaffe, *English and American Judges as Lawmakers,* 20.

80. American legislative bodies revising statutes that courts have ruled unconstitutional are the clearest demonstration of this. *See, e.g., Gully v. Kunzman,* 592 F.2d 283, 285–86 (6th Cir. 1979) (discussing the Kentucky legislature's alteration of a penal statute in response to the U.S. Supreme Court's ruling that mandatory death penalty statutes, such as the one previously in force in Kentucky, were unconstitutional).

81. *See generally Gray Panthers v. Schweiker,* 652 F.2d 146, 152 n. 15 (D.C.Cir. 1980) ("A 'due respect for the coordinate branches of government' makes courts reluctant to declare Congressionally-enacted statutes unconstitutional.") (quoting *Califano v. Yamasaki,* 442 U.S. 682, 692–93, 99 S.Ct. 2545, 2553–54, 61 L.Ed.2d 176 (1979)).

82. *Hayburn's Case,* 2 U.S. (2 Dall.) 409, 410, 1 L.Ed. 436 (1792).

83. David Dyzenhaus, *The Constitution of Law: Legality in a Time of Emergency* (Cambridge University Press, 2006), 144. *See also* David Dyzenhaus, "The Justice of the Common Law: Judges, Democracy, and the Limits of the Rule of Law," in Cheryl Saunders and Katherine Le Roy, eds., *The Rule of Law* (Federation Press, 2003), 35; David Dyzenhaus, "The Politics of Deference: Judicial Review and Democracy," in Michael Taggart, ed., *The Province of Administrative Law* (Hart Publishing, 1997), 302–7. I do not mean to give wholesale endorsement to Dyzenhaus's view of deference as respect. In particular, he considers deference as respect to be an "anti-positivist thesis" (Dyzenhaus, "Politics of Deference," 307). I do not see why deference as respect, in its more general vision of a constitutional relationship among governmental institutions, must be committed to any particular legal theory.

84. *Cf. U.S. v. Nourse,* 34 U.S. 8, 13, 9 Pet. 8, 9 L.Ed. 31 (1835) ("No questions can be brought before a judicial tribunal of greater delicacy than those which involve the constitutionality of a legislative act. If they become indispensably necessary to the case, the court must meet and decide them; but if the case may be determined on other points, a just respect for the legislature requires that the obligation of its laws should not be unnecessarily and wantonly assailed.") (Marshall, C.J.).

85. *Fletcher v. Peck,* 10 U.S. (6 Cranch) 87, 128, 3 L.Ed. 162 (1810).

86. Daniel A. Farber, *Statutory Interpretation and Legislative Supremacy,* 78 Geo. L.J. 281, 317 (1989). I am reading the term "judicial review" here to include constitutional and common law review.

87. Kermit Roosevelt suggests a way of thinking through this issue. In Roosevelt's terms, the question of balancing deference and judicial responsibility requires us to determine "whether the level of deference is appropriate" in light of five factors: (1) institutional competence, (2) defects in democracy, (3) costs of error, (4) lessons of history, and (5) rules vs. standards (or principles). *See* Kermit Roosevelt III, *The Myth of Judicial Activism: Making Sense of Supreme Court Decisions* (Yale University Press, 2006), 24–32, 44. Of course, as Roosevelt acknowledges, evaluation of these factors will sometimes direct judges toward opposing conclusions. Moreover, Roosevelt notes that certain cases appropriately require a judicial attitude of deference toward actions of other governmental entities and that other cases call for a judicial attitude that he calls "anti-deferential" or "non-deferential." I prefer Dyzenhaus's terminol-

ogy, because it avoids the impression that judicial deference operates as a binary function (deferential or not). But both Dyzenhaus and Roosevelt attempt to capture the same institutional dynamic.

88. *See* Lord Woolf of Barnes, *Droit Public—English Style,* [1995] Pub. L. 57, 68–69.

89. Kent Greenawalt, *The Nature of Rules and the Meaning of Meaning,* 72 Notre Dame L. Rev. 1449, 1476 (1997) (emphasis in original).

90. *See infra* at pp. 178–87.

91. *Anisminic Ltd. v. Foreign Compensation Commission,* [1969] 2 AC 147. *See also Andrews v. Mitchell,* [1905] AC 78.

92. Foreign Compensation Act 1950, § 4(4).

93. *Anisminic,* [1969] 2 AC at 170.

94. *Id.* at 214.

95. *See id.* at 213.

96. *Id.* at 211–12.

97. *See id.* at 169–70, 194–95, 207–8.

98. *See generally* H.W.R. Wade, *Constitutional and Administrative Aspects of the Anisminic Case,* 85 Law Q. Rev. 198 (1969).

99. *See, e.g., Calcano-Martinez v. I.N.S.,* 533 U.S. 348, 350 n. 2, 121 S.Ct. 2268, 2270, 150 L.Ed.2d 392 (2001); *Califano v. Sanders,* 430 U.S. 99, 109, 97 S.Ct. 980, 986, 51 L.Ed.2d 192 (1977); *Richardson v. Reno,* 180 F.3d 1311, 1316 n. 5 (11th Cir. 1999); *La-Guerre v. Reno,* 164 F.3d 1035, 1040 (7th Cir. 1998); *Bartlett v. Bowen,* 816 F.2d 695, 699–700 (D.C. Cir. 1987).

100. 486 U.S. 592, 108 S.Ct. 2047, 100 L.Ed.2d 632 (1988).

101. 50 U.S.C. § 403(c).

102. Quoted in *Webster,* 486 U.S. at 597, 108 S.Ct. at 2050.

103. *Webster,* 486 U.S. at 603, 108 S.Ct. at 2053.

104. *Webster,* 486 U.S. at 603, 108 S.Ct. at 2053 (citations omitted).

105. The Supreme Court has repeatedly underscored the importance of maintaining the courts' authority to review administrative action. To oust the courts' jurisdiction, Congress must express its intention with the utmost clarity. *See I.N.S. v. St. Cyr,* 533 U.S. 289, 298–99, 314, 121 S.Ct. 2271, 2278–79, 2287, 150 L.Ed.2d 347 (2001). This stipulation is reminiscent of the English courts' approach to cases of this sort. In my discussion of the *ultra vires* doctrine and the *Simms* decision in chapter 9, I will return to the issue of the clarity of legislative intentions in relation to jurisdiction and judicial maintenance of rule-of-law principles. *See infra* 185–87.

106. *See generally* Scott Gordon, *Controlling the State: Constitutionalism from Ancient Athens to Today* (Harvard University Press, 1999), 46–51, 241, 255–56, 318–21; R.C. van Caenegem, *An Historical Introduction to Western Constitutional Law* (Cambridge University Press, 1995), 17–18, 98, 117–18, 168–70.

107. *See generally Raymond v. Honey,* [1983] 1 AC 1, 13–14; *Pyx Granite Co. Ltd. v. Ministry of Housing and Local Government,* [1960] AC 260, 286; *R. (on the application of G) v. Immigration Appeal Tribunal,* [2004] EWHC 588, [9], [2004] 1 WLR 2953, 2959 ("The importance attached to the right of access to the court for judicial review has meant that express words must be used by Parliament to achieve its removal and even apparently express words will not necessarily achieve the object."); *R. v. Lord Chancel-*

lor, ex parte Witham, [1998] QB 575, 584–86; *R. v. Secretary of State for the Home Department, ex parte Leech,* [1994] QB 198, 210; *R. v. Secretary of State for the Home Department, ex parte Anderson,* [1984] QB 778, 793–94; *Commissioners of Customs and Excise v. Cure & Deeley, Ltd.,* [1962] 1 QB 340, 370; *Chester v. Bateson,* [1920] 1 KB 829, 833, 836–37.

108. These cases also serve as an additional response to the objection, which I mentioned at the beginning of this chapter, that common law review will inevitably result in the expansion of judicial authority through overuse by undisciplined judges. The refusal of English and American judges to enforce ouster clauses in cases where doing so would threaten the integrity of the courts and Anglo-American commitments to constitutionalism is an example of what I would call "defensive judicial review." Stephen Griffin describes this form of judicial authority in this way: a court "may hold acts unconstitutional only when it is necessary to defend itself from encroachments by the other branches" (Stephen M. Griffin, *American Constitutionalism: From Theory to Politics* (Princeton University Press, 1996), 92). As Griffin points out (*id.* at 94), this conception of judicial review is more restrictive than the form of judicial authority that has become entrenched in American constitutional tradition. The point here is not to argue for or against the developmental path taken by judicial review in the United States. All I want to highlight is that common law review, on this account, is actually much more limited in scope than American constitutional review.

109. For their part, positivists leveled a related charge at natural law theory. *See* Hans Kelsen, *Absolutism and Relativism in Philosophy and Politics,* 42 Am. Pol. Sci. Rev. 906, 912–13 (1948).

110. *See* H.L.A. Hart, *Positivism and the Separation of Law and Morals,* 71 Harv. L. Rev. 593, 615–21 (1958), reprinted in H.L.A. Hart, *Essays in Jurisprudence and Philosophy* (Oxford University Press, 1983), 72–78; Lon L. Fuller, *Positivism and Fidelity to Law: A Reply to Professor Hart,* 71 Harv. L. Rev. 630, 648–61 (1958).

111. Robert Alexy, "A Defence of Radbruch's Formula," in David Dyzenhaus, ed., *Recrafting the Rule of Law: The Limits of Legal Order* (Hart Publishing, 1999), 16.

112. *Id.* (quoting Radbruch).

113. *Id.* at 17.

114. Julian Rivers, "The Interpretation and Invalidity of Unjust Laws," in David Dyzenhaus, ed., *Recrafting the Rule of Law: The Limits of Legal Order* (Hart Publishing, 1999), 41.

115. *See* A.V. Dicey, *Introduction to the Study of the Law of the Constitution* (10th ed.) (Macmillan, 1959), 81.

116. *See, e.g.,* John Finnis, *Natural Law and Natural Rights* (Oxford University Press, 1980), 363–66.

117. *See* Rivers, "Interpretation and Invalidity of Unjust Laws," 61–63.

118. *Id.* at 62.

119. *Id.* at 63.

120. Ronald Dworkin, *Taking Rights Seriously* (Harvard University Press, 1978), 327. *See also* citations collected *supra* at 208–9 n. 25.

121. [1976] AC 249.

122. *See Oppenheimer,* [1976] AC at 278, 281, 283.

123. *Kuwait Airways Corp. v. Iraqi Airways Co.,* [2002] UKHL 19, [18], [2002] 2 AC 883. *See also In the Estate of Fuld (No. 3),* [1968] P 675, 698.

124. For an examination of the idea that a judge may be bound by rules she must sometimes choose not to follow, which is supportive and expressive of several themes of common law review, *see* Mortimer R. Kadish and Sanford H. Kadish, *Discretion to Disobey: A Study of Lawful Departures from Legal Rules* (Stanford University Press, 1973), 90 ("[T]he judge is indeed bound by the rules of law, and he is bound to administer justice through those rules. But sometimes the ends of justice may be disserved by following those rules. In those cases the judge's role . . . extends to him a liberty to make this judgment and to depart from the rules to achieve results consistent with the ends for which his role is set up.").

125. These are frequently grouped together under the heading "justiciability." For two helpful examinations of these issues, *see* Lea Brilmayer, *The Jurisprudence of Article III: Perspectives on the "Case or Controversy" Requirement,* 93 Harv. L. Rev. 297 (1979); R.L. Brilmayer, *Judicial Review, Justiciability, and the Limits of the Common Law Method,* 57 B.U. L. Rev. 807 (1977). *Cf. Ashwander v. Tennessee Valley Authority,* 297 U.S. 288, 346–48, 56 S.Ct. 466, 482–84, 80 L.Ed. 688 (1936) (Brandeis, J., concurring).

126. *See, e.g.,* Mark Tushnet, *Taking the Constitution Away from the Courts* (Princeton University Press, 1999), 129–76. I will not address the familiar criticism that all forms of judicial review (common law review included) are inherently countermajoritarian, undemocratic, or antidemocratic—except to say that this criticism betrays an unsound understanding of (constitutional) democracy. *See, e.g.,* Ronald Dworkin, *Freedom's Law: The Moral Reading of the American Constitution* (Harvard University Press, 1996), 17, 20, 23–25, 32–33; Raz, *Ethics in the Public Domain,* 375–76; Samuel Freeman, *Political Liberalism and the Possibility of a Just Democratic Constitution,* 69 Chi.-Kent L. Rev. 619, 659 (1994). Moreover, as the expression of a societal precommitment to preserve constitutional values and individual rights against potential threats of majoritarian overreaching, judicial review may well preserve democratic principles of equality, autonomy, and liberty more surely than "majority rules" democracy can allow. *See generally* Samuel Freeman, *Constitutional Democracy and the Legitimacy of Judicial Review,* 9 Law & Phil. 327 (1990).

Chapter 9

1. *See* Richard A. Posner, *Law and Legal Theory in the UK and USA* (Oxford University Press, 1996), 20–36.

2. The decision by the House of Lords in *A. v. Secretary of State for the Home Department* ([2004] UKHL 56, [2005] 2 AC 68) suggests that this may no longer be an accurate characterization of the English courts. In this case, the House invoked the European Convention for the Protection of Human Rights and Fundamental Freedoms (as incorporated into English law via the Human Rights Act of 1998) in its review of the potentially indefinite detention of nonnationals identified by the government as possible terrorists. The House issued a declaration that section 23 of the Anti-terrorism, Crime and Security Act of 2001 was incompatible with articles 5 and 14 of the European Convention in relation to the government's detention of these individuals.

3. *See, e.g.,* Appendix, *Comments of the Justices Concerning Their Courts,* 18 Cardozo L. Rev. 1745, 1745–47 (1997) (remarks of Lord Slynn).

4. *See, e.g., A. v. Secretary of State for the Home Department,* [2004] UKHL 56, [88], [2005] 2 AC at 130; *R. (on the application of Burke) v. General Medical Council,* [2004] EWHC 1879, [80], [116], [2005] QB 424, 453, 465; *Derbyshire County Council v. Times Newspapers Ltd.,* [1993] AC 534, 550–51; *Attorney General v. Guardian Newspapers Ltd. (No. 2),* [1990] 1 AC 109, 283–84; *Attorney General v. Guardian Newspapers Ltd.,* [1987] 1 WLR 1248, 1296–97; *R. v. Lord Chancellor, ex parte Witham,* [1998] QB 575, 585. *See also R. v. Secretary of State for the Home Department, ex parte Brind,* [1991] 1 AC 696, 717, 733–34; Lord Browne-Wilkinson, *The Infiltration of a Bill of Rights,* [1992] Pub. L. 397, 408.

5. On the nature of England's common law constitution, *see generally* T.R.S. Allan, *Law, Liberty, and Justice: The Legal Foundations of British Constitutionalism* (Oxford University Press, 1993), 4–10.

6. *Practice Statement of 1966 (Judicial Precedent),* [1966] 1 WLR 1234. Two sentences of the *Practice Statement* are especially helpful to my argument, in content and expression: "Their Lordships . . . recognize that too rigid adherence to precedent may lead to injustice in a particular case and also unduly restrict the proper development of the law. They propose therefore to modify their present practice and, while treating former decisions of this House as normally binding to depart from a previous decision when it appears right to do so."

7. [1979] AC 264.

8. The Court of Appeal is not strictly bound by its own decisions in criminal cases. *See generally R. v. Newsome,* [1970] 2 QB 711, 716; *R. v. Gould,* [1968] 2 QB 65, 68–69.

9. *See* Rupert Cross and J.W. Harris, *Precedent in English Law* (4th ed.) (Oxford University Press, 1991), 108–16.

10. *See id.* at 114.

11. *Id.* (discussing *The Vera Cruz,* (1884) 9 PD 96, 98).

12. *Id.* at 25.

13. *Id.* (citing *Re Shoesmith,* [1938] 2 KB 637, 644).

14. *See supra* p. 34.

15. *Cf.* Cross and Harris, *Precedent in English Law,* 5, 24, 25.

16. [1975] QB 416.

17. Treaty Establishing the European Economic Community, 25 March 1957, 298 UNTS 11, 4 Eur.Y.B. 412.

18. Article 106 reads, "Each member state undertakes to authorise, in the currency of the member state in which the creditor . . . resides, any payments connected with the movement of goods, services or capital, . . . to the extent that the movement of goods, services, capital and persons between member states has been liberalised pursuant to this Treaty" (*quoted in SchorschMeier G.M.B.H. v. Hennin,* [1975] QB 416, 416).

19. *See Hennin,* [1975] QB at 423–24.

20. [1961] AC 1007, 1043, 1052, 1068–69, *cited in Hennin,* [1975] QB at 424–25.

21. "The reason of the law ceasing, the law itself ceases." *See Hennin,* [1975] QB at 425.

22. [1976] AC 443.

23. *Miliangos*, [1976] AC at 459.

24. *See id.* at 467, 469–70. For Lord Simon's criticism of Lord Denning's use of the *cessante ratione* principle in *Hennin, see id.* at 471–76.

25. *Pittalis v. Grant*, [1989] QB 605, 618.

26. Cross and Harris, *Precedent in English Law*, 7. In addition to *Hennin*, the other case to which Cross and Harris refer (*see id.* at 99) is *Cassell & Co. Ltd. v. Broome*, [1972] AC 1027.

27. The materials I have discussed happen to involve the Court of Appeal, but there is no reason that the same analyses and observations do not hold for English trial courts.

28. Jeffrey Goldsworthy, *The Sovereignty of Parliament: History and Philosophy* (Oxford University Press, 1999), 176, 132, 155 (quotation marks and footnotes omitted). For a sampling of the myriad repetitions of this dogma in English legal and political writings over the years, *see id.* at 74, 102, 151, 156, 164, 177, 201–2, 226.

29. *See id.* at 28–29.

30. *Id.* at 151. *See also id.* at 155.

31. Thomas Hobbes, *Leviathan* (C.B. MacPherson, ed.) (Penguin Books, 1968), 312–13.

32. John Austin, *The Province of Jurisprudence Determined* (Wilfrid E. Rumble, ed.) (Cambridge University Press, 1995), 166.

33. Goldsworthy, *Sovereignty of Parliament*, 74 (quoting Richard Hooker, *The Works of Mr. Richard Hooker* (J. Keble, ed., 7th ed.) (Georg Olms Verlag, 1977), 445–46). *Cf. id.* at 22.

34. *See generally* Austin, *Province of Jurisprudence Determined*, 188, 205–12. *See also* Goldsworthy, *Sovereignty of Parliament*, 225. Jeremy Bentham's positivism closely fit with English legal and political theory at the time of Parliament's apparent ascendancy. *See generally* P.S. Atiyah and R.S. Summers, *Form and Substance in Anglo-American Law: A Comparative Study of Legal Reasoning, Legal Theory, and Legal Institutions* (Oxford University Press, 1987), 222–29. I mention Austin more prominently because Austin was perhaps more instrumental in disseminating Bentham's views than was Bentham himself (*see* Atiyah and Summers, *Form and Substance*, 240–45). Moreover, as Atiyah and Summers argue, even though Bentham's own thought was more nuanced than his disciple's on the subject of parliamentary sovereignty, "Austin's version of positivism . . . became the dominant tradition in England and so thoroughly influenced English lawyers and judges that it became almost literally inconceivable that the judges could ever have power to question the authority of Acts of Parliament." Atiyah and Summers continue, "English jurists were very slow to wake to the realization that the unlimited nature of Parliament's legislative powers was not a necessary truth, derived from the inherent nature of a sovereign legislature" (Atiyah and Summers, *Form and Substance*, 245).

35. *See* Goldsworthy, *Sovereignty of Parliament*, 23.

36. For Dicey's consideration of the relationship between Austinian positivism and parliamentary sovereignty, particularly as predicated on a single, legally illimitable source of legislative power, *see* A.V. Dicey, *Introduction to the Study of the Law of the Constitution* (10th ed.) (Macmillan, 1959), 61, 71–76. Dicey also notes the view in English constitutional history of this supreme legislator as being found first in the

person and office of the monarch and later in the body and institution of Parliament (or the Queen-in-Parliament). *See id.* at 69–70 n. 1.

37. *See generally* Allan, *Law, Liberty, and Justice*, 1–4, 16–19, 68–78, 130–43, 240–46, 264–90; N.W. Barber, *Sovereignty Re-examined: The Courts, Parliament, and Statutes*, 20 Oxford J. Legal Stud. 131, 134–40 (2000); Sir John Laws, *Law and Democracy*, [1995] Pub. L. 72, 82, 85–86, 90–93; Lord Woolf of Barnes, *Droit Public—English Style*, [1995] Pub. L. 57, 64–65, 68–69.

38. Allan, *Law, Liberty, and Justice*, 16.

39. The *ultra vires* model reflects the centuries-old view in English political theory that English courts cannot independently review legislative priorities or enactments, because to do so would place the courts equal to or above the Parliament, thereby positioning the judiciary as an "authority sovereign to the sovereign" (Goldsworthy, *Sovereignty of Parliament*, 183 (citation omitted)). *See also id.* at 200–202.

40. *See, e.g.*, Christopher Forsyth, *Of Fig Leaves and Fairy Tales: The Ultra Vires Doctrine, the Sovereignty of Parliament, and Judicial Review*, 55 Cambridge L.J. 122 (1996).

41. *See, e.g.*, Paul Craig, *Ultra Vires and the Foundations of Judicial Review*, 57 Cambridge L.J. 63 (1998); Laws, *Law and Democracy*, 78–80; Woolf of Barnes, *Droit Public—English Style*, 65–67; Dawn Oliver, *Is the Ultra Vires Rule the Basis of Judicial Review?* [1987] Pub. L. 543.

42. *See generally* Christopher Forsyth, ed., *Judicial Review and the Constitution* (Hart Publishing, 2000) (anthologizing many of the best essays written to date on this subject).

43. *See* Forsyth, *Of Fig Leaves and Fairy Tales*, 127–29, reprinted in Forsyth, *Judicial Review and the Constitution*, 33–35.

44. *See* T.R.S. Allan, *Constitutional Justice: A Liberal Theory of the Rule of Law* (Oxford University Press, 2001), 207.

45. *See supra* pp. 149–50.

46. Allan, *Law, Liberty, and Justice*, 17.

47. *Id.* at 68–69. *See also* Elizabeth Wicks, *The Evolution of a Constitution: Eight Key Moments in British Constitutional History* (Hart Publishing, 2006), 30.

48. *See generally* 6 William S. Holdsworth, *A History of English Law* (3rd ed.) (Methuen, 1945), 262–63.

49. T.R.S. Allan, "The Common Law as Constitution: Fundamental Rights and First Principles," in Cheryl Saunders, ed., *Courts of Final Jurisdiction: The Mason Court in Australia* (Federation Press, 1996), 161 (emphasis deleted). In this passage, Allan is discussing England specifically. *See also* Allan, *Law, Liberty, and Justice*, 130 ("It is therefore always a matter of conscience, not merely how legislation should be interpreted in the context of a particular case, but ultimately whether it should be applied at all.").

50. *Cf.* Christopher L. Eisgruber, *The Most Competent Branches: A Response to Professor Paulsen*, 83 Geo. L.J. 347, 353–64 (1994). I do not subscribe *in toto* to Eisgruber's position, but his discussion is the sort of careful, textured analysis of the balance of powers and competencies that the English (and American) system of government deserves.

51. *See* Mark D. Walters, *St. German on Reason and Parliamentary Sovereignty*, 62 Cambridge L.J. 335, 367–68 (2003).

52. *See* Barber, *Sovereignty Re-examined,* 142–54 (arguing for the abandonment in England of the simplistic unitary sovereignty model, in favor of a more sophisticated account of the relationship between the English judiciary and legislature).

53. Sir Stephen Sedley, "The Common Law and the Constitution," in Lord Nolan of Brasted and Sir Stephen Sedley, eds., *The Making and Remaking of the British Constitution* (Blackstone Press, 1997), 26–27.

54. *See generally* John Phillip Reid, *Rule of Law: The Jurisprudence of Liberty in the Seventeenth and Eighteenth Centuries* (Northern Illinois University Press, 2004), 78–79; Louis L. Jaffe, *English and American Judges as Lawmakers* (Oxford University Press, 1969), 4–5, 19.

55. *See, e.g.,* H.L.A. Hart, *The Concept of Law* (2nd ed.) (Oxford University Press, 1994), 66–71.

56. 1 William Blackstone, *Commentaries on the Laws of England* (Oxford University Press, 1765), 156.

57. *See* Wicks, *Evolution of a Constitution,* 20 ("The Parliament of 1689 was, therefore, sovereign in the sense that its laws were thereafter to be superior to the royal prerogative. But there was no suggestion at this period in history that Parliament should be unlimited in its legislative powers. The fundamental principles of the common law constitution, which had sought to bind the Crown in the earlier part of the seventeenth century, remained to bind the King-in-Parliament. The fact that they have not always been effective in doing so does not detract from their existence or their survival to the present day.").

58. *See, e.g.,* Lord Alfred Denning, *What Next in the Law* (Butterworths, 1982), 320; Lord Leslie Scarman, *English Law: The New Dimension* (Stevens and Sons, 1974), 81–83.

59. *Cf.* Christopher Forsyth, "Heat and Light: A Plea for Reconciliation," in Forsyth, *Judicial Review and the Constitution,* 394 n. 3. A possible rejoinder to this assertion is provided in the *Factortame* cases. *See R. v. Secretary of State for Transport, ex parte Factortame Ltd. (No. 2),* [1991] 1 AC 603; *Factortame Ltd. v. Secretary of State for Transport,* [1990] 2 AC 85. I do not pursue the *Factortame* point for two reasons: (1) although some English theorists view *Factortame* as the English courts' recognition of EU law as a substantive constraint on Parliament's sovereignty, others believe *Factortame* simply establishes EU law as a body of legal principle, in accordance with which Parliament is assumed to legislate but that Parliament is empowered to contravene, provided it unambiguously declares its intention; (2) I wish to focus on the implications for parliamentary sovereignty of the relationship between England's Parliament and its courts, rather than on the implications for parliamentary sovereignty of England's relationship with the European Union.

60. *Anisminic Ltd. v. Foreign Compensation Commission,* [1969] 2 AC 147. *See supra* pp. 160–61.

61. *R. v. Secretary of State for the Home Department, ex parte Simms,* [2000] 2 AC 115.

62. *Id.*

63. *Id.* at 125.

64. *Id.* at 126 (citing *Derbyshire,* [1993] AC at 550–51; *Attorney General v. Guardian Newspapers Ltd. (No. 2),* [1990] 1 AC at 283–84).

65. Another example is the common law right of access to the courts, which I mentioned in chapter 8. *See supra* p. 163 and cases cited at pp. 270–71 n. 107.

66. *Simms*, [2000] 2 AC at 126, 127.

67. *Id.* at 130–31 (citations omitted).

68. *R. v. Secretary of State for the Home Department, ex parte Pierson*, [1998] AC 539, 587–88 (citations omitted).

69. *See generally* David Dyzenhaus, Murray Hunt, and Michael Taggart, *The Principle of Legality in Administrative Law: Internationalisation as Constitutionalisation*, 1 Oxford U. Commonwealth L.J. 5, 21–23 (2001).

70. In this respect, Steyn's speech in *Simms* can be seen as a modification of his view as expressed in *Pierson*. In *Pierson*, Steyn stated that a "clear and specific" parliamentary enactment could displace the *prima facie* force of common law principles and values. By affirming in *Simms* that the common law principle of legality holds "even in the absence of an ambiguity," Steyn says that the principle of legality endures even where Parliament may have been "clear and specific."

71. *See, e.g., R. v. Secretary of State for Social Services, ex parte Stitt*, (1991) 3 Admin. L. Rep. 169.

72. *Cf. International Transport Roth GmbH v. Secretary of State for the Home Department*, [2002] EWCA Civ 158, [71], [2003] QB 728, 759; *R. (on the application of ProLife Alliance) v. British Broadcasting Corporation*, [2002] EWCA Civ 297, [36], [2002] 3 WLR 1080, 1096–97.

73. *See, e.g., R. v. Secretary of State for the Home Department, ex parte Khawaja*, [1984] AC 74, 108–12; *Conway v. Rimmer*, [1968] AC 910, 937–38, 943, 950–52, 956–58, 968, 971–72, 980, 992–93.

74. *See* Lord Steyn, *The Weakest and Least Dangerous Department of Government*, [1997] Pub. L. 84, 86 ("By the rule of law we primarily mean the principle of legality, *viz.* that every exercise of governmental power must be justified in law. But the rule of law also comprehends in a broad sense a system of principles developed by the courts to ensure that the exercise of executive power is not abused.").

75. *See supra* pp. 149–50.

76. Mark Elliott, *The Constitutional Foundations of Judicial Review* (Hart Publishing, 2001), 109–10.

77. I have deliberately chosen to refer to the modified *ultra vires* model as the most inclusive version of *vires* doctrine and as, arguably, the most accurate conception of current English law. *See generally* Forsyth, "Heat and Light," 397–98. For criticism of the modified model, *see* Allan, *Constitutional Justice*, 209–10.

78. David Dyzenhaus, *The Constitution of Law: Legality in a Time of Emergency* (Cambridge University Press, 2006), 156. *See also id.* at 115–17.

79. I am indebted to David Dyzenhaus for this hypothetical example.

80. *Simms*, [2000] 2 AC at 131.

81. *Id.* at 131.

82. *See* H.W.R. Wade, *The Basis of Legal Sovereignty*, 1955 Cambridge L.J. 172, 196 (1955) ("[T]he seat of sovereign power is not to be discovered by looking at Acts of Parliament but by looking at the courts and discovering to whom they give their obedience.").

83. *See* Barber, *Sovereignty Re-examined*, 146–48 (discussing *R. v. R.*, [1992] 1 AC 599).

84. *See* Allan, *Law, Liberty, and Justice*, 17, 62–68, 267. *See also* Allan, *Constitutional Justice*, 205.

85. *See, e.g.*, Goldsworthy, *Sovereignty of Parliament*, 252 ("It must also be admitted that in some other cases, the judges' claim to be faithful to Parliament's implicit intention has been a 'noble lie', used to conceal judicial disobedience. But such cases are relatively rare, and the fact that the lie is felt to be required indicates that the judges themselves realize that their disobedience is, legally speaking, illicit."). I fail to see the lie's "nobility." It is simply a fabrication that obscures an important common law judicial function. It would be better for judges to realize that the lie is unnecessary. *Cf.* Ian Harden and Norman Lewis, *The Noble Lie: The British Constitution and the Rule of Law* (Hutchinson, 1986) (challenging the "master ideal" of parliamentary sovereignty as inconsistent with Britain's constitutional heritage and current constitutional practice and arguing for recognition by the judiciary of its institutional obligation to maintain rule-of-law values by regulating exercises of governmental power).

86. These metaphors are not mine. For their origin, *see* Forsyth, *Of Fig Leaves and Fairy Tales*, 122, reprinted in Forsyth, *Judicial Review and the Constitution*, 29.

87. *See generally* Atiyah and Summers, *Form and Substance*, 118–56.

88. *See supra* p. 224 n. 61.

89. David Lemmings, *Professors of the Law: Barristers and English Legal Culture in the Eighteenth Century* (Oxford University Press, 2000), 247. *See also id.* at 291 ("It was this parliamentary form of 'Bodinian absolutism', even acknowledged by Blackstone in the *Commentaries*, which the American lawyers recognized as inimical to the common law tradition."); George Anastaplo, *The Amendments to the Constitution: A Commentary* (Johns Hopkins University Press, 1995), 29; George Anastaplo, *The Constitution of 1787: A Commentary* (Johns Hopkins University Press, 1989), 151.

90. *See supra* pp. 157–59.

91. Steven D. Smith, *Why Should Courts Obey The Law?* 77 Geo. L.J. 113, 133–34 (1988).

92. *See generally* Edward S. Corwin, *The Basic Doctrine of American Constitutional Law*, 12 Mich. L. Rev. 247, 247–54 (1914).

93. *See* Allan, *Law, Liberty, and Justice*, 130 ("[T]he rule of law imposes constraints on legislative sovereignty which are essential to preserve the separation of powers—a fundamental feature of constitutionalism. And I have rejected the suggestion that a court which struck down (or refused to apply) a statute which seriously violated fundamental rights would be dependent upon the terms of a written constitution.").

94. *See, e.g.*, Wicks, *Evolution of a Constitution*, 26–27; James R. Stoner, Jr., *Common-Law Liberty: Rethinking American Constitutionalism* (University Press of Kansas, 2003), 16–21; Elliott, *Constitutional Foundations of Judicial Review*, 212–16; Anastaplo, *Amendments to the Constitution*, 23, 26, 75, 87–88; Allan, *Law, Liberty, and Justice*, 135–62; James R. Stoner, Jr., *Common Law and Liberal Theory: Coke, Hobbes, and the Origins of American Constitutionalism* (University Press of Kansas, 1992), 215–16; John Phillip Reid, *Constitutional History of the American Revolution: The Authority to Legislate* (University of Wisconsin Press, 1991), 6; Anastaplo, *Constitution of 1787*, 4, 134–35, 227; John Phillip Reid, *Constitutional History of the American Revolution: The Authority of Rights* (University of Wisconsin Press, 1986), 69–70; Gordon S. Wood, *The Creation of the American Republic, 1776–1787* (University of North Carolina Press, 1969), 10; Thomas M. Cooley, *A Treatise on the Constitutional Limitations Which Rest upon the*

Legislative Power of the States of the American Union (Little, Brown, 1868), 37, 59–61, 175, 416–17; Leslie Friedman Goldstein, *Popular Sovereignty, the Origins of Judicial Review, and the Revival of Unwritten Law,* 48 J. Pol. 51, 59 (1986). *See also Burmah Oil Co. Ltd. v. Bank of England,* [1980] AC 1090, 1145; *Southern Pacific Co. v. Jensen,* 244 U.S. 205, 231, 37 S.Ct. 524, 535, 61 L.Ed. 1086 (1917) ("From them [citations of the decisions of this court] it appears beyond question, that the Constitution, the Judiciary Act of 1789, and all subsequent statutes upon the same subject, are based upon the general principles of the common law, and that, to a large extent, the legislative and judicial action of the government would be without support and without meaning if they cannot be interpreted in the light of the common law.") (Pitney, J., dissenting) (citation omitted).

95. 6 Holdsworth, *History of English Law,* 263. *See also* Gerald J. Postema, *Classical Common Law Jurisprudence (Part II),* 3 Oxford U. Commonwealth L.J. 1, 24 (2003) (discussing "Hale's striking claim that the common law is the constitution of the English people"). *See supra* pp. 232–33 n. 56.

96. Anastaplo, *Constitution of 1787,* 157–58; John Phillip Reid, *Another Origin of Judicial Review: The Constitutional Crisis of 1776 and the Need for a Dernier Judge,* 64 N.Y.U. L. Rev. 963, 971–72 (1989) ("[E]ighteenth century American constitutional theory was seventeenth century English constitutional theory . . . American constitutional principles were not *sui generis,* but were the taught principles of common law constitutionalists.").

97. *See U.S. v. Sanges,* 144 U.S. 310, 311, 12 S.Ct. 609, 36 L.Ed. 445 (1892) ("This statute, like all acts of Congress, and even the constitution itself, is to be read in the light of the common law, from which our system of jurisprudence is derived.") (citations omitted).

98. *See, e.g.,* Gary J. Jacobsohn, *The Supreme Court and the Decline of Constitutional Aspiration* (Rowman and Littlefield, 1986), 81–82.

99. *See generally* John V. Orth, *Due Process of Law: A Brief History* (University Press of Kansas, 2003), 98–102, especially at 99 ("The common law, the 'law of the land,' was anterior to all constitutions. In England, still lacking a written constitution, the common law itself supplied the rules now described as constitutional . . . In America the U.S. Constitution declared itself 'the supreme law of the land,' and constitutional amendments added the guarantee of due process. That meant, in turn, that the judges would test legislation against the norms of the common law.") (footnotes omitted).

100. *See generally* Sanford Levinson, *Constitutional Faith* (Princeton University Press, 1988), 16–17; Michael J. Perry, *Morality, Politics, and Law* (Oxford University Press, 1988), 136–45; Thomas C. Grey, *The Constitution as Scripture,* 37 Stan. L. Rev. 1, 3 (1984); Sanford Levinson, *The Constitution in American Civil Religion,* 1979 Sup. Ct. Rev. 123 (1979).

101. *See* Stoner, *Common-Law Liberty,* 15; Allan, *Law, Liberty, and Justice,* 143 ("[T]he common law is often considered inferior to bills or charters of rights as a vehicle for protecting fundamental liberties. It is mistakenly thought that *restatement* of individual rights in a constitutional document could transform their strength, when they have to be asserted in opposition to countervailing public interests.") (emphasis in original); George Winterton, *The British Grundnorm: Parliamentary Supremacy*

Re-examined, 92 Law Q. Rev. 591, 599 (1976); Thomas C. Grey, *Do We Have an Unwritten Constitution?* 27 Stan. L. Rev. 703, 715–16 (1975). *Cf.* John Hart Ely, *Democracy and Distrust: A Theory of Judicial Review* (Harvard University Press, 1980), 38.

102. *See* Anastaplo, *Amendments to the Constitution,* 22–23 ("Underlying the rule of law in the United States is the common law of England which was established on this continent in Colonial days. The common law . . . is critical to the rule of law for the English-speaking peoples, reflecting and reinforcing as it does a general constitutional system.").

103. *See* Allan, *Law, Liberty, and Justice,* 4. Many scholars may doubt this; *see generally* Stephen M. Griffin, *American Constitutionalism: From Theory to Politics* (Princeton University Press, 1996), 126 ("[T]he Constitution serves as a framework for government and politics, a role that no other law approximates."). But these scholars make the mistake, which I just mentioned, of venerating the written document at the expense of its common law foundations.

104. *Cf.* Kent Greenawalt, *The Rule of Recognition and the Constitution,* 85 Mich. L. Rev. 621, 649 (1987) ("[T]he capacity of the legislature or the makers of constitutions to *change* the nature of judicial power does not itself entail that the legal status of judicial decisions derives from implicit authorization . . . And even if the practice of giving *some* weight to prior decisions was thought to be inherent in the practice of courts or implicitly approved by legislative action, that would not mean that the full law-creating power that common law courts now have has been authorized legislatively . . . If one were trying to explain to a new judge why common-law precedents count for a good deal, one would certainly say more about these higher lawmaking authorities than that they could have eliminated or altered judicial power and have chosen not to do so.") (emphasis in original).

105. *See generally* Allan C. Hutchinson, *Evolution and the Common Law* (Cambridge University Press, 2005), 186–87. *Cf.* Jerome Frank, *Courts on Trial: Myth and Reality in American Justice* (Princeton University Press, 1949), 408–9, 412; Benjamin N. Cardozo, *The Nature of the Judicial Process* (Yale University Press, 1921), 137–38. John Adams explicitly drew the connection between the greatness of Marshall and the greatness of Coke and Mansfield. *See* Letter from John Adams to John Marshall (17 Aug. 1825), in Charles F. Hobson, ed., 10 *The Papers of John Marshall: Correspondence, Papers, and Selected Judicial Opinions, January 1824–March 1827* (University of North Carolina Press, 2000), 197 ("[I]t is the pride of my life that I have given to this nation a Chief Justice equal to Coke or Hale, Holt or Mansfield.").

106. *R. v. Wilkes,* (1770) 4 Burr. 2527, 2562–63, 98 Eng. Rep. 327, 347 (citation omitted).

107. Oliver Wendell Holmes, *The Path of the Law,* 10 Harv. L. Rev. 457, 473–74 (1897).

Chapter 10

1. *See* Harold D. Lasswell, *Politics: Who Gets What, When, How* (Meridian Books, 1958).

2. I do not here address whether the courts possess this authority to the exclusion of other branches of government.

3. *See generally* Jeremy Waldron, *The Core of the Case against Judicial Review,* 115 Yale L.J. 1346 (2006).

4. For a literary example (based on actual events) of a judge whose best option may have been resignation, *see* the character of John Hale in act 3 of Arthur Miller's "The Crucible," found in Arthur Miller, *Collected Plays* (Cresset Press, 1958), 285–311.

5. *Cf.* Benjamin N. Cardozo, *The Nature of the Judicial Process* (Yale University Press, 1921), 17 ("The method of free decision sees through the transitory particulars and reaches what is permanent behind them."); Ludwig Wittgenstein, *On Certainty* (G.E.M. Anscombe and G.H. von Wright, eds.) (Basil Blackwell, 1969), para. 97, para. 99, at 15e ("I distinguish between the movement of the waters on the river-bed and the shift of the bed itself; though there is not a sharp division of the one from the other . . . And the bank of that river consists partly of hard rock, subject to no alteration or only to an imperceptible one, partly of sand, which now in one place now in another gets washed away, or deposited."). Among other things, the comments of Cardozo and Wittgenstein relate to long-standing debates about the ontology and epistemology of law and the existential nature of judicial decisions as sources of law in themselves or as evidence of preexisting law. This book addresses aspects of these debates, but others are necessarily beyond its scope.

References

Books and Book Chapters

Alexy, Robert. "A Defence of Radbruch's Formula," in David Dyzenhaus, ed., *Recrafting the Rule of Law: The Limits of Legal Order* (Hart Publishing, 1999).

Allan, T.R.S. "The Common Law as Constitution: Fundamental Rights and First Principles," in Cheryl Saunders, ed., *Courts of Final Jurisdiction: The Mason Court in Australia* (Federation Press, 1996).

Allan, T.R.S. *Constitutional Justice: A Liberal Theory of the Rule of Law* (Oxford University Press, 2001).

Allan, T.R.S. *Law, Liberty, and Justice: The Legal Foundations of British Constitutionalism* (Oxford University Press, 1993).

Anastaplo, George. *The Amendments to the Constitution: A Commentary* (Johns Hopkins University Press, 1995).

Anastaplo, George. *The Constitution of 1787: A Commentary* (Johns Hopkins University Press, 1989).

Atiyah, P.S., and R.S. Summers. *Form and Substance in Anglo-American Law: A Comparative Study of Legal Reasoning, Legal Theory, and Legal Institutions* (Oxford University Press, 1987).

Austin, John. *The Province of Jurisprudence Determined* (Wilfrid E. Rumble, ed.) (Cambridge University Press, 1995).

Bailyn, Bernard. *The Ideological Origins of the American Revolution* (enlarged ed.) (Harvard University Press, 1992).

Bailyn, Bernard, ed. *Pamphlets of the American Revolution, 1750–1775* (Harvard University Press, 1965).

Bamforth, Nicholas. "Ultra Vires and Institutional Interdependence," in Christopher Forsyth, ed., *Judicial Review and the Constitution* (Hart Publishing, 2000).

Barak, Aharon. *The Judge in a Democracy* (Princeton University Press, 2006).

Bentham, Jeremy. *The Theory of Legislation* (Oceana Publications, 1975).

Berger, Raoul. *Congress v. the Supreme Court* (Harvard University Press, 1969).

Birch, Anthony H. *Concepts and Theories of Modern Democracy* (Routledge, 1993).

Black, Charles L., Jr. *The People and the Court: Judicial Review in a Democracy* (Macmillan, 1960).

Blackstone, William. *Commentaries on the Laws of England* (vol. 1) (Oxford University Press, 1765).

Bodenheimer, Edgar. *Jurisprudence: The Philosophy and Method of the Law* (rev. ed.) (Harvard University Press, 1974).

Bork, Robert H. *The Tempting of America: The Political Seduction of the Law* (Free Press, 1990).

Bowen, Catherine Drinker. *The Lion and the Throne: The Life and Times of Sir Edward Coke (1552–1634)* (Hamish Hamilton, 1957).

Boxill, Bernard R. "Washington, Du Bois, and *Plessy v. Ferguson*," in Gerald J. Postema, ed., *Racism and the Law: The Legacy and Lessons of Plessy* (Kluwer Academic Publishers, 1997).

Brennan, William J., Jr. "The Constitution of the United States: Contemporary Ratification," in David M. O'Brien, *Judges on Judging: Views from the Bench* (2nd ed.) (CQ Press, 2004).

Brenner, Saul, and Harold J. Spaeth. *Stare Indecisis: The Alteration of Precedent on the Supreme Court, 1946–1992* (Cambridge University Press, 1995).

Bronaugh, Richard. "Persuasive Precedent," in Laurence Goldstein, ed., *Precedent in Law* (Oxford University Press, 1987).

Burgess, Glenn. *Absolute Monarchy and the Stuart Constitution* (Yale University Press, 1996).

Burton, Steven J. *Judging in Good Faith* (Cambridge University Press, 1992).

Calabresi, Guido. *A Common Law for the Age of Statutes* (Harvard University Press, 1982).

Cardozo, Benjamin N. *Law and Literature, and Other Essays and Addresses* (Harcourt, Brace, 1931).

Cardozo, Benjamin N. *The Nature of the Judicial Process* (Yale University Press, 1921).

Chang, Ruth, ed. *Incommensurability, Incomparability, and Practical Reason* (Harvard University Press, 1997).

Choper, Jesse H. *Judicial Review and the National Political Process: A Functional Reconsideration of the Role of the Supreme Court* (University of Chicago Press, 1980).

Clinton, Robert Lowry. *God and Man in the Law: The Foundations of Anglo-American Constitutionalism* (University Press of Kansas, 1997).

Clinton, Robert Lowry. Marbury v. Madison *and Judicial Review* (University Press of Kansas, 1989).

Coke, Edward. *First Institute of the Laws of England* (James and Luke Hansard, 1832).

Coke, Edward. "First Part of the *Institutes of the Laws of England*," in 2 Steve Sheppard, *The Selected Writings of Sir Edward Coke* (Liberty Fund, 2003).

Coke, Edward. "Fourth Part of the *Institutes of the Laws of England*," in 2 Steve Sheppard, *The Selected Writings of Sir Edward Coke* (Liberty Fund, 2003).

Coke, Edward. "Preface to Part Four of the *Reports*," in 1 Steve Sheppard, ed., *The Selected Writings of Sir Edward Coke* (Liberty Fund, 2003).

Coke, Edward. "Preface to Part Six of the *Reports*," in 1 Steve Sheppard, *The Selected Writings of Sir Edward Coke* (Liberty Fund, 2003)

Coke, Edward. "Preface to Part Ten of the *Reports*," in 1 Steve Sheppard, *The Selected Writings of Sir Edward Coke* (Liberty Fund, 2003).

Coke, Edward. "Preface to the Fourth Part of the *Institutes of the Laws of England*," in 2 Steve Sheppard, *The Selected Writings of Sir Edward Coke* (Liberty Fund, 2003).

Coke, Edward. "Second Part of the *Institutes of the Laws of England*," in 2 Steve Sheppard, *The Selected Writings of Sir Edward Coke* (Liberty Fund, 2003).

Coleman, Jules. "Authority and Reason," in Robert P. George, ed., *The Autonomy of Law* (Oxford University Press, 1996).

Cooley, Thomas M. *A Treatise on the Constitutional Limitations Which Rest upon the Legislative Power of the States of the American Union* (Little, Brown, 1868).

Cover, Robert M. *Justice Accused: Antislavery and the Judicial Process* (Yale University Press, 1975).

Cross, Rupert, and J.W. Harris. *Precedent in English Law* (4th ed.) (Oxford University Press, 1991).

Denning, Lord Alfred. *What Next in the Law* (Butterworths, 1982).

Dicey, A.V. *Introduction to the Study of the Law of the Constitution* (10th ed.) (Macmillan, 1959).

Dworkin, Ronald. *Freedom's Law: The Moral Reading of the American Constitution* (Harvard University Press, 1996).

Dworkin, Ronald. *Justice in Robes* (Harvard University Press, 2006).

Dworkin, Ronald. *Law's Empire* (Harvard University Press, 1986).

Dworkin, Ronald. "A Reply by Ronald Dworkin," in Marshall Cohen, ed., *Ronald Dworkin and Contemporary Jurisprudence* (Rowman and Allanheld, 1983).

Dworkin, Ronald. *Taking Rights Seriously* (Harvard University Press, 1978).

Dyzenhaus, David. *The Constitution of Law: Legality in a Time of Emergency* (Cambridge University Press, 2006).

Dyzenhaus, David. "The Justice of the Common Law: Judges, Democracy, and the Limits of the Rule of Law," in Cheryl Saunders and Katherine Le Roy, eds., *The Rule of Law* (Federation Press, 2003).

Dyzenhaus, David. "The Politics of Deference: Judicial Review and Democracy," in Michael Taggart, ed., *The Province of Administrative Law* (Hart Publishing, 1997).

Dyzenhaus, David. "The Rule of Law as the Rule of Liberal Principle," in Arthur Ripstein, ed., *Ronald Dworkin* (Cambridge University Press, 2007).

Eisenberg, Melvin Aron. *The Nature of the Common Law* (Harvard University Press, 1988).

Eisgruber, Christopher L. *Constitutional Self-Government* (Harvard University Press, 2001).

Elliott, Mark. *The Constitutional Foundations of Judicial Review* (Hart Publishing, 2001).

Ely, John Hart. *Democracy and Distrust: A Theory of Judicial Review* (Harvard University Press, 1980).

Finnis, John. "Natural Law and Legal Reasoning," in Robert P. George, ed., *Natural Law Theory* (Oxford University Press, 1992).

Finnis, John. *Natural Law and Natural Rights* (Oxford University Press, 1980).

Fiss, Owen. *The Law as It Could Be* (New York University Press, 2003).

Forsyth, Christopher. "Heat and Light: A Plea for Reconciliation," in Christopher Forsyth, ed., *Judicial Review and the Constitution* (Hart Publishing, 2000).

Forsyth, Christopher, ed. *Judicial Review and the Constitution* (Hart Publishing, 2000).

Franck, Matthew J. *Against the Imperial Judiciary: The Supreme Court vs. the Sovereignty of the People* (University Press of Kansas, 1996).

Franck, Thomas M. *Political Questions/Judicial Answers: Does the Rule of Law Apply to Foreign Affairs?* (Princeton University Press, 1992).

Frank, Jerome. *Courts on Trial: Myth and Reality in American Justice* (Princeton University Press, 1949).

Friedman, Lawrence M. *A History of American Law* (2nd ed.) (Simon and Schuster, 1985).

Fuller, Lon L. *The Morality of Law* (Yale University Press, 1969).

Gadamer, Hans-Georg. *Truth and Method* (2nd ed.) (Continuum, 1989).

Gilmore, Grant. *The Ages of American Law* (Yale University Press, 1977).

Glenn, H. Patrick. *Legal Traditions of the World: Sustainable Diversity in Law* (2nd ed.) (Oxford University Press, 2004).

Goebel, Julius L., Jr., ed. *The Law and Practice of Alexander Hamilton* (vol. 1) (Columbia University Press, 1964).

Goldsworthy, Jeffrey. *The Sovereignty of Parliament: History and Philosophy* (Oxford University Press, 1999).

Gordon, Scott. *Controlling the State: Constitutionalism from Ancient Athens to Today* (Harvard University Press, 1999).

Gough, J.W. *Fundamental Law in English Constitutional History* (Oxford University Press, 1955).

Graber, Mark A. Dred Scott *and the Problem of Constitutional Evil* (Cambridge University Press, 2006).

Graglia, Lino A. *Disaster by Decree: The Supreme Court Decisions on Race and the Schools* (Cornell University Press, 1976).

Gray, John Chipman. *The Nature and Sources of the Law* (Ashgate/Dartmouth, 1997).

Greenawalt, Kent. *Conflicts of Law and Morality* (Oxford University Press, 1987).

Greenawalt, Kent. *Law and Objectivity* (Oxford University Press, 1992).

Griffin, Stephen M. *American Constitutionalism: From Theory to Politics* (Princeton University Press, 1996).

Guest, Stephen. *Ronald Dworkin* (2nd ed.) (Edinburgh University Press, 1997).

Haines, Charles Grove. *The American Doctrine of Judicial Supremacy* (2nd ed.) (University of California Press, 1932).

Hale, Matthew. *The History of the Common Law of England* (Charles M. Gray, ed.) (University of Chicago Press, 1971).

Hamilton, Alexander, John Jay, and James Madison. *The Federalist* (George W. Carey and James McClellan, eds.) (Liberty Fund, 2001).

Harden, Ian, and Norman Lewis. *The Noble Lie: The British Constitution and the Rule of Law* (Hutchinson, 1986).

Hart, Henry M., Jr., and Albert M. Sacks. *The Legal Process: Basic Problems in the Making and Application of Law* (Foundation Press, 1994).

Hart, H.L.A. *The Concept of Law* (2nd ed.) (Oxford University Press, 1994).

Hart, H.L.A. *Essays in Jurisprudence and Philosophy* (Oxford University Press, 1983).

Hart, H.L.A. *Essays on Bentham: Studies in Jurisprudence and Political Theory* (Oxford University Press, 1982).

Hobbes, Thomas. *A Dialogue between a Philosopher and a Student of the Common Laws of England* (Joseph Cropsey, ed.) (University of Chicago Press, 1971).

Hobbes, Thomas. *Leviathan* (C.B. MacPherson, ed.) (Penguin Books, 1968).

Hobson, Charles F., ed. *The Papers of John Marshall: Correspondence, Papers, and Selected Judicial Opinions, January 1824–March 1827* (vol. 10) (University of North Carolina Press, 2000).

Hobson, Charles F., and Fredrika J. Teute, eds. *The Papers of John Marshall: Correspondence, Papers, and Selected Judicial Opinions, November 1800–March 1807* (vol. 6) (University of North Carolina Press, 1990).

Holdsworth, William S. *A History of English Law* (3rd ed.) (vols. 5 and 6) (Methuen, 1945).

Hooker, Richard. *The Works of Mr. Richard Hooker* (J. Keble, ed., 7th ed.) (Georg Olms Verlag, 1977).

Howard, A.E. Dick. *The Road from Runnymede: Magna Carta and Constitutionalism in America* (University Press of Virginia, 1968).

Hughes, Charles Evans. *The Supreme Court of the United States: Its Foundation, Methods, and Achievements* (Columbia University Press, 1928).

Hutchinson, Allan C. *Evolution and the Common Law* (Cambridge University Press, 2005).

Jacobsohn, Gary J. *The Supreme Court and the Decline of Constitutional Aspiration* (Rowman and Littlefield, 1986).

Jaffe, Louis L. *English and American Judges as Lawmakers* (Oxford University Press, 1969).

Kadish, Mortimer R., and Sanford H. Kadish. *Discretion to Disobey: A Study of Lawful Departures from Legal Rules* (Stanford University Press, 1973).

Kearns, Thomas R., and Austin Sarat. "Legal Justice and Injustice: Toward a Situated Perspective," in Austin Sarat and Thomas R. Kearns, eds., *Justice and Injustice in Law and Legal Theory* (University of Michigan Press, 1996).

Kluger, Richard. *Simple Justice: The History of* Brown v. Board of Education *and Black America's Struggle for Equality* (Vintage Books, 1977).

Konefsky, Samuel J. *The Legacy of Holmes and Brandeis: A Study in the Influence of Ideas* (Collier Books, 1961).

Kousser, J. Morgan. *The Shaping of Southern Politics: Suffrage Restriction and the Establishment of the One-Party South, 1880–1910* (Yale University Press, 1974).

Kramer, Larry D. *The People Themselves: Popular Constitutionalism and Judicial Review* (Oxford University Press, 2004).

Kritzer, Herbert M. "Courts, Justice, and Politics in England," in Herbert Jacob et al., *Courts, Law, and Politics in Comparative Perspective* (Yale University Press, 1996).

Lasswell, Harold D. *Politics: Who Gets What, When, How* (Meridian Books, 1958).

Leiter, Brian. "Legal Realism, Hard Positivism, and the Limits of Conceptual Analysis," in Jules Coleman, ed., *Hart's Postscript: Essays on the Postscript to* The Concept of Law (Oxford University Press, 2001).

Lemmings, David. *Professors of the Law: Barristers and English Legal Culture in the Eighteenth Century* (Oxford University Press, 2000).

Levi, Edward H. *An Introduction to Legal Reasoning* (University of Chicago Press, 1949).

Levinson, Sanford. *Constitutional Faith* (Princeton University Press, 1988).

Levinson, Sanford. "Hercules, Abraham Lincoln, the United States Constitution, and the Problem of Slavery," in Arthur Ripstein, *Ronald Dworkin* (Cambridge University Press, 2007).

Levy, Leonard W. *Origins of the Bill of Rights* (Yale University Press, 1999).

Lieberman, David. *The Province of Legislation Determined: Legal Theory in Eighteenth-Century Britain* (Cambridge University Press, 1989).

Lipkin, Robert Justin. *Constitutional Revolutions: Pragmatism and the Role of Judicial Review in American Constitutionalism* (Duke University Press, 2000).

Llewellyn, Karl. *The Common Law Tradition: Deciding Appeals* (Little, Brown, 1960).

Lofgren, Charles A. *The Plessy Case: A Legal-Historical Interpretation* (Oxford University Press, 1987).

Lyon, Hastings, and Herman Block. *Edward Coke: Oracle of the Law* (Houghton Mifflin, 1929).

Lyons, David. *Ethics and the Rule of Law* (Cambridge University Press, 1984).

Lyons, David. "Formal Justice and Judicial Precedent," in David Lyons, *Moral Aspects of Legal Theory* (Cambridge University Press, 1993).

MacCormick, Neil. *Legal Reasoning and Legal Theory* (Oxford University Press, 1978).

MacCormick, Neil, and Robert S. Summers, eds. *Interpreting Precedents: A Comparative Study* (Ashgate/Dartmouth, 1997).

Magliocca, Gerard N. *Andrew Jackson and the Constitution: The Rise and Fall of Generational Regimes* (University Press of Kansas, 2007).

Marmor, Andrei. *Interpretation and Legal Theory* (Oxford University Press, 1992).

Mason, Alpheus Thomas. *The Supreme Court from Taft to Burger* (3rd ed.) (Louisiana State University Press, 1979).

Massey, Douglas S., and Nancy A. Denton. *American Apartheid: Segregation and the Making of the Underclass* (Harvard University Press, 1993).

McCloskey, Robert G. *The American Supreme Court* (4th ed.) (University of Chicago Press, 2005).

McDonald, Forrest. *Novus Ordo Seclorum: The Intellectual Origins of the Constitution* (University Press of Kansas, 1985).

McIlwain, Charles H. *The High Court of Parliament and Its Supremacy: An Historical Essay on the Boundaries between Legislation and Adjudication in England* (Yale University Press, 1910).

Miller, Arthur. *Collected Plays* (Cresset Press, 1958).

Milsom, S.F.C. *Historical Foundations of the Common Law* (2nd ed.) (Butterworths, 1981).

Moore, Michael S. "Law as a Functional Kind," in Robert P. George, ed., *Natural Law Theory: Contemporary Essays* (Oxford University Press, 1992).

Moore, Michael S. "Precedent, Induction, and Ethical Generalization," in Laurence Goldstein, ed., *Precedent in Law* (Oxford University Press, 1987).

Murphy, Liam. "The Political Question of the Concept of Law," in Jules Coleman, ed., *Hart's Postscript: Essays on the Postscript to* The Concept of Law (Oxford University Press, 2001).

Murphy, Walter F., James E. Fleming, Sotirios A. Barber, and Stephen Macedo. *American Constitutional Interpretation* (3rd ed.) (Foundation Press, 2003).

Murphy, Walter F., and C. Herman Pritchett. *Courts, Judges, and Politics* (Random House, 1961).

Nelson, William E. Marbury v. Madison: *The Origins and Legacy of Judicial Review* (University Press of Kansas, 2000).

O'Connor, John E. *William Paterson: Lawyer and Statesman, 1745–1806* (Rutgers University Press, 1979).

Oliver, Dawn. "Review of (Non-statutory) Discretions," in Christopher Forsyth, ed., *Judicial Review and the Constitution* (Hart Publishing, 2000).

Orth, John V. *Due Process of Law: A Brief History* (University Press of Kansas, 2003).

Perry, Michael J. *Morality, Politics, and Law* (Oxford University Press, 1988).

Perry, Michael J. "What Is 'the Constitution'? (and Other Fundamental Questions)," in Larry Alexander, ed., *Constitutionalism: Philosophical Foundations* (Cambridge University Press, 1998).

Phillips, O. Hood, and Paul Jackson. *Constitutional and Administrative Law* (Sweet and Maxwell, 1987).

Pollock, Frederick. *A First Book of Jurisprudence for Students of the Common Law* (6th ed.) (Macmillan, 1929).

Pollock, Frederick, and Frederic William Maitland. *The History of English Law* (2nd ed.) (vol. 1) (Cambridge University Press, 1968).

Posner, Richard A. *The Federal Courts: Challenge and Reform* (Harvard University Press, 1996).

Posner, Richard A. *Law and Legal Theory in the UK and USA* (Oxford University Press, 1996).

Posner, Richard A. *The Problematics of Moral and Legal Theory* (Harvard University Press, 1999).

Posner, Richard A. *The Problems of Jurisprudence* (Harvard University Press, 1990).

Postema, Gerald J. *Bentham and the Common Law Tradition* (Oxford University Press, 1986).

Postema, Gerald J. "Law's Autonomy and Public Practical Reason," in Robert P. George, ed., *The Autonomy of Law: Essays on Legal Positivism* (Oxford University Press, 1996).

Postema, Gerald J. "Philosophy of the Common Law," in Jules Coleman and Scott Shapiro, eds., *The Oxford Handbook of Jurisprudence and Philosophy of Law* (Oxford University Press, 2002).

Postema, Gerald J. "*A Similibus ad Similia*: Analogical Thinking in Law," in Douglas E. Edlin, ed., *Common Law Theory* (Cambridge University Press, 2007).

Postema, Gerald J. "The Sins of Segregation," in Gerald J. Postema, ed., *Racism and the Law: The Legacy and Lessons of* Plessy (Kluwer Academic Publishers, 1997).

Pound, Roscoe. *The Spirit of the Common Law* (Marshall Jones Company, 1921).

Pound, Roscoe. "What Is the Common Law?" in Roscoe Pound, ed., *The Future of the Common Law* (Peter Smith, 1965).

Quincy, Josiah, Jr. *Reports of Cases Argued and Adjudged in the Superior Court of Judicature of the Province of Massachusetts Bay between 1761 and 1772* (Little, Brown, 1865).

Rakove, Jack N. *Original Meanings: Politics and Ideas in the Making of the Constitution* (Knopf, 1996).

Rawls, John. *Political Liberalism* (Columbia University Press, 1993).

Rawls, John. *A Theory of Justice* (Harvard University Press, 1971).

Raz, Joseph. *The Authority of Law* (Oxford University Press, 1979).

Raz, Joseph. *Ethics in the Public Domain: Essays in the Morality of Law and Politics* (rev. ed.) (Oxford University Press, 1994).

Raz, Joseph. "Legal Principles and the Limits of Law," in Marshall Cohen, ed., *Ronald Dworkin and Contemporary Jurisprudence* (Rowman and Allanheld, 1983).

Raz, Joseph. "On the Authority and Interpretation of Constitutions: Some Preliminaries," in Larry Alexander, ed., *Constitutionalism: Philosophical Foundations* (Cambridge University Press, 1998).

Reid, John Phillip. *The Concept of Liberty in the Age of the American Revolution* (University of Chicago Press, 1988).

Reid, John Phillip. *Constitutional History of the American Revolution: The Authority of Rights* (University of Wisconsin Press, 1986).

Reid, John Phillip. *Constitutional History of the American Revolution: The Authority to Legislate* (University of Wisconsin Press, 1991).

Reid, John Phillip. *Rule of Law: The Jurisprudence of Liberty in the Seventeenth and Eighteenth Centuries* (Northern Illinois University Press, 2004).

Rivers, Julian. "The Interpretation and Invalidity of Unjust Laws," in David Dyzenhaus, ed., *Recrafting the Rule of Law: The Limits of Legal Order* (Hart Publishing, 1999).

Roosevelt, Kermit, III. *The Myth of Judicial Activism: Making Sense of Supreme Court Decisions* (Yale University Press, 2006).

Sampson, William. *An Anniversary Discourse Delivered before the Historical Society of New York, on Saturday, December 6, 1823, Showing the Origin, Progress, Antiquities, Curiosities, and Nature of the Common Law* (Pishey Thompson, 1826).

Scalia, Antonin. *A Matter of Interpretation: Federal Courts and the Law* (Princeton University Press, 1997).

Scarman, Lord Leslie. *English Law: The New Dimension* (Stevens and Sons, 1974).

Schauer, Frederick. "Positivism as Pariah," in Robert P. George, ed., *The Autonomy of Law: Essays on Legal Positivism* (Oxford University Press, 1996).

Sebok, Anthony J. "The Case of Chief Justice Shaw," in David Dyzenhaus, ed., *Recrafting the Rule of Law: The Limits of Legal Order* (Hart Publishing, 1999).

Sedley, Sir Stephen. "The Common Law and the Constitution," in Lord Nolan of Brasted and Sir Stephen Sedley, eds., *The Making and Remaking of the British Constitution* (Blackstone Press, 1997).

Sheppard, Steve, ed. *The Selected Writings of Sir Edward Coke* (vols. 1 and 2) (Liberty Fund, 2003).

Shklar, Judith N. *Legalism: Law, Morals, and Political Trials* (Harvard University Press, 1964).

Simpson, A.W.B. "The Common Law and Legal Theory," in A.W.B. Simpson, ed., *Oxford Essays in Jurisprudence* (2nd ser.) (Oxford University Press, 1973).

Simpson, A.W.B. "The *Ratio Decidendi* of a Case and the Doctrine of Binding Precedent," in A.G. Guest, ed., *Oxford Essays in Jurisprudence* (1st ser.) (Oxford University Press, 1961).

Snowiss, Sylvia. *Judicial Review and the Law of the Constitution* (Yale University Press, 1990).

Soper, Philip. *A Theory of Law* (Harvard University Press, 1984).

Stavropoulos, Nicos. "Hart's Semantics," in Jules Coleman, ed., *Hart's Postscript: Essays on the Postscript to* The Concept of Law (Oxford University Press, 2001).

Stavropoulos, Nicos. *Objectivity in Law* (Oxford University Press, 1996).

St. German, Christopher. *Doctor and Student* (T.F.T. Plucknett and J.L. Barton, eds.) (Selden Society, 1974).

Stimson, Shannon C. *The American Revolution in the Law: Anglo-American Jurisprudence before John Marshall* (Princeton University Press, 1990).

Stoner, James R., Jr. *Common Law and Liberal Theory: Coke, Hobbes, and the Origins of American Constitutionalism* (University Press of Kansas, 1992).

Stoner, James R., Jr. *Common-Law Liberty: Rethinking American Constitutionalism* (University Press of Kansas, 2003).

Sunstein, Cass R. *Legal Reasoning and Political Conflict* (Oxford University Press, 1996).

Tamanaha, Brian Z. *Law as a Means to an End: Threat to the Rule of Law* (Cambridge University Press, 2006).

Tamanaha, Brian Z. *On the Rule of Law: History, Politics, Theory* (Cambridge University Press, 2004).

Thorne, Samuel E., ed. *A Discourse upon the Exposicion and Understandinge of Statutes* (Huntington Library/Anderson and Ritchie, 1942).

Tribe, Laurence H., and Michael C. Dorf. *On Reading the Constitution* (Harvard University Press, 1991).

Tubbs, J.W. *The Common Law Mind: Medieval and Early Modern Conceptions* (Johns Hopkins University Press, 2000).

Tullock, Gordon. *The Case Against the Common Law* (Locke Institute, 1997).

Tushnet, Mark. *Taking the Constitution Away from the Courts* (Princeton University Press, 1999).

van Caenegem, R.C. *The Birth of the English Common Law* (2nd ed.) (Cambridge University Press, 1988).

van Caenegem, R.C. *European Law in the Past and the Future: Unity and Diversity over Two Millennia* (Cambridge University Press, 2002).

van Caenegem, R.C. *An Historical Introduction to Western Constitutional Law* (Cambridge University Press, 1995).

Vile, M.J.C. *Constitutionalism and the Separation of Powers* (Oxford University Press, 1967).

Waldron, Jeremy. *Law and Disagreement* (Oxford University Press, 1999).

Walters, Mark D. "The Common Law Constitution and Legal Cosmopolitanism," in David Dyzenhaus, ed., *The Unity of Public Law* (Hart Publishing, 2004).

Waluchow, W.J. *A Common Law Theory of Judicial Review: The Living Tree* (Cambridge University Press, 2007).

Wasserstrom, Richard A. *The Judicial Decision: Toward a Theory of Legal Justification* (Stanford University Press, 1961).

Weinreb, Lloyd L. *Natural Law and Justice* (Harvard University Press, 1987).

Wellington, Harry H. *Interpreting the Constitution* (Yale University Press, 1990).

Whittington, Keith E. *Constitutional Interpretation: Textual Meaning, Original Intent, and Judicial Review* (University Press of Kansas, 1999).

Wicks, Elizabeth. *The Evolution of a Constitution: Eight Key Moments in British Constitutional History* (Hart Publishing, 2006).

Wittgenstein, Ludwig. *On Certainty* (G.E.M. Anscombe and G.H. von Wright, eds.) (Basil Blackwell, 1969).

Wood, Gordon S. *The Creation of the American Republic, 1776–1787* (University of North Carolina Press, 1969).

Woolf, Lord, Jeffrey Jowell, and Andrew P. Le Sueur. *De Smith, Woolf, and Jowell's Principles of Judicial Review* (Sweet and Maxwell, 1999).

Wright, R. George. "Does Positivism Matter?" in Robert P. George, ed., *The Autonomy of Law* (Oxford University Press, 1996).

Articles

Abramowicz, Michael, and Maxwell Stearns. *Defining Dicta*, 57 Stan. L. Rev. 953 (2005).

Adler, Matthew D. *Judicial Restraint in the Administrative State: Beyond the Countermajoritarian Difficulty*, 145 U. Pa. L. Rev. 759 (1997).

Aleinikoff, T. Alexander. *Updating Statutory Interpretation*, 87 Mich. L. Rev. 20 (1988).

Alexander, Larry. *Constrained by Precedent*, 63 S. Cal. L. Rev. 1 (1989).

Alfange, Dean, Jr. Marbury v. Madison *and Original Understandings of Judicial Review: In Defense of Traditional Wisdom*, 1993 Sup. Ct. Rev. 329 (1993).

Allott, Philip. *The Courts and Parliament: Who Whom?* 38 Cambridge L.J. 79 (1979).

Appendix, *Comments of the Justices Concerning Their Courts*, 18 Cardozo L. Rev. 1745 (1997).

Barber, N.W. *Sovereignty Re-examined: The Courts, Parliament, and Statutes*, 20 Oxford J. Legal Stud. 131 (2000).

Berger, Raoul. *Natural Law and Judicial Review: Reflections of an Earthbound Lawyer*, 61 U. Cin. L. Rev. 5 (1992).

Berman, Harold J. *The Origins of Historical Jurisprudence: Coke, Selden, Hale*, 103 Yale L.J. 1651 (1994).

Boyer, Allen Dillard. *"Understanding, Authority, and Will": Sir Edward Coke and the Elizabethan Origins of Judicial Review*, 39 B.C. L. Rev. 43 (1997).

Bradford, C. Steven. *Following Dead Precedent: The Supreme Court's Ill-Advised Rejection of Anticipatory Overruling*, 59 Fordham L. Rev. 39 (1990).

Bratz, David C. *Stare Decisis in Lower Courts: Predicting the Demise of Supreme Court Precedent*, 60 Wash. L. Rev. 87 (1984).

Brennan, William J., Jr. *Constitutional Adjudication and the Death Penalty: A View from the Court*, 100 Harv. L. Rev. 313 (1986).

Brennan, William J., Jr. *Reason, Passion, and "The Progress of the Law,"* 42 Record of the Ass'n of the Bar of the City of New York 948 (1987).

Brest, Paul. *The Misconceived Quest for the Original Understanding*, 60 B.U. L. Rev. 204 (1980).

Brilmayer, Lea. *The Jurisprudence of Article III: Perspectives on the "Case or Controversy" Requirement*, 93 Harv. L. Rev. 297 (1979).

Brilmayer, R.L. *Judicial Review, Justiciability, and the Limits of the Common Law Method*, 57 B.U. L. Rev. 807 (1977).

Browne-Wilkinson, Lord. *The Infiltration of a Bill of Rights*, [1992] Pub. L. 397.

Burt, Robert A. Brown's *Reflection*, 103 Yale L.J. 1483 (1994).

Cahn, Edmond. *Jurisprudence*, 30 N.Y.U. L. Rev. 150 (1955).

Caminker, Evan H. *Allocating the Judicial Power in a "Unified Judiciary,"* 78 Tex. L. Rev. 1513 (2000).

Caminker, Evan H. *Precedent and Prediction: The Forward-Looking Aspects of Inferior Court Decisionmaking*, 73 Tex. L. Rev. 1 (1994).

Caminker, Evan H. *Why Must Inferior Courts Obey Superior Court Precedents?* 46 Stan. L. Rev. 817 (1994).

Carter, Stephen L. *Constitutional Improprieties: Reflections on* Mistretta, Morrison, *and* Administrative Government, 57 U. Chi. L. Rev. 357 (1990).

Chander, Anupam. *Sovereignty, Referenda, and the Entrenchment of a United Kingdom Bill of Rights*, 101 Yale L.J. 457 (1991).

Colby, Paul L. *Two Views on the Legitimacy of Nonacquiescence in Judicial Opinions*, 61 Tul. L. Rev. 1041 (1987).

Corwin, Edward S. *The Basic Doctrine of American Constitutional Law*, 12 Mich. L. Rev. 247 (1914).

Corwin, Edward S. *The Establishment of Judicial Review*, 9 Mich. L. Rev. 102 (1910).

Corwin, Edward S. *The "Higher Law" Background of American Constitutional Law*, 42 Harv. L. Rev. 149 (1928).

Craig, Paul. *Ultra Vires and the Foundations of Judicial Review*, 57 Cambridge L.J. 63 (1998).

Craig, Paul, and Nicholas Bamforth. *Constitutional Analysis, Constitutional Principle, and Judicial Review*, [2001] Pub. L. 763.

Crosskey, William Winslow. *The True Meaning of the Constitutional Prohibition of Ex-Post-Facto Laws*, 14 U. Chi. L. Rev. 539 (1947).

Currie, David P. *The Constitution in Congress: The Third Congress, 1793–1795*, 63 U. Chi. L. Rev. 1 (1996).

Davies, Thomas Y. *Recovering the Original Fourth Amendment*, 98 Mich. L. Rev. 547, 687, 688 (1999).

Dorf, Michael C. *Dicta and Article III*, 142 U. Pa. L. Rev. 1997 (1994).

Douglas, William O. *Stare Decisis*, 49 Colum. L. Rev. 735 (1949).

Dworkin, Ronald. *The Law of the Slave-Catchers*, Times Literary Supplement (5 Dec. 1975).

Dyzenhaus, David, Murray Hunt, and Michael Taggart. *The Principle of Legality in Administrative Law: Internationalisation as Constitutionalisation*, 1 Oxford U. Commonwealth L.J. 5 (2001).

Easterbrook, Frank H. *Stability and Reliability in Judicial Decisions*, 73 Cornell L. Rev. 422 (1988).

Eisenberg, Theodore, and Stewart J. Schwab. *What Shapes Perceptions of the Federal Court System?*, 56 U. Chi. L. Rev. 501 (1989).

Eisgruber, Christopher L. *John Marshall's Judicial Rhetoric*, 1996 Sup. Ct. Rev. 439 (1996).

Eisgruber, Christopher L. *Justice Story, Slavery, and the Natural Law Foundations of American Constitutionalism*, 55 U. Chi. L. Rev. 273 (1988).

Eisgruber, Christopher L. *The Most Competent Branches: A Response to Professor Paulsen,* 83 Geo. L.J. 347 (1994).

Eskridge, William N., Jr. *Dynamic Statutory Interpretation,* 135 U. Pa. L. Rev. 1479 (1987).

Farber, Daniel A. *Statutory Interpretation and Legislative Supremacy,* 78 Geo. L.J. 281 (1989).

Finkelman, Paul. *The Ten Commandments on the Courthouse Lawn and Elsewhere,* 73 Fordham L. Rev. 1477 (2005).

Fiss, Owen M. *The Forms of Justice,* 93 Harv. L. Rev. 1 (1979).

Fletcher, George P. *Comparative Law as a Subversive Discipline,* 46 Am. J. Comp. L. 683 (1998).

Forsyth, Christopher. *Of Fig Leaves and Fairy Tales: The Ultra Vires Doctrine, the Sovereignty of Parliament, and Judicial Review,* 55 Cambridge L.J. 122 (1996).

Freeman, Samuel. *Constitutional Democracy and the Legitimacy of Judicial Review,* 9 Law & Phil. 327 (1990).

Freeman, Samuel. *Political Liberalism and the Possibility of a Just Democratic Constitution,* 69 Chi.-Kent L. Rev. 619 (1994).

Fuller, Lon L. *The Forms and Limits of Adjudication,* 92 Harv. L. Rev. 353 (1978).

Fuller, Lon L. *Positivism and Fidelity to Law: A Reply to Professor Hart,* 71 Harv. L. Rev. 630 (1958).

Gardner, John. *The Virtue of Justice and the Character of Law,* 53 Current Legal Probs. 1 (2000).

Gavison, Ruth. *The Implications of Jurisprudential Theories for Judicial Election, Selection, and Accountability,* 61 S. Cal. L. Rev. 1617 (1988).

Gely, Rafael. *Of Sinking and Escalating: A (Somewhat) New Look at Stare Decisis,* 60 U. Pitt. L. Rev. 89 (1998).

Ginsburg, Ruth Bader. *Speaking in a Judicial Voice,* 67 N.Y.U. L. Rev. 1185 (1992).

Goldstein, Leslie Friedman. *Popular Sovereignty, the Origins of Judicial Review, and the Revival of Unwritten Law,* 48 J. Pol. 51 (1986).

Goodhart, Arthur L. *Determining the Ratio Decidendi of a Case,* 40 Yale L.J. 161 (1930).

Green, Leslie. *Law, Legitimacy, and Consent,* 62 S. Cal. L. Rev. 795 (1989).

Greenawalt, Kent. *How Persuasive Is Natural Law Theory?* 75 Notre Dame L. Rev. 1647 (2000).

Greenawalt, Kent. *The Nature of Rules and the Meaning of Meaning,* 72 Notre Dame L. Rev. 1449 (1997).

Greenawalt, Kent. *Policy, Rights, and Judicial Decision,* 11 Ga. L. Rev. 991 (1977).

Greenawalt, Kent. *The Rule of Recognition and the Constitution,* 85 Mich. L. Rev. 621 (1987).

Grey, Thomas C. *The Constitution as Scripture,* 37 Stan. L. Rev. 1 (1984).

Grey, Thomas C. *Do We Have an Unwritten Constitution?* 27 Stan. L. Rev. 703 (1975).

Grey, Thomas C. *Origins of the Unwritten Constitution: Fundamental Law in American Revolutionary Thought,* 30 Stan. L. Rev. 843 (1978).

Grey, Thomas C. *The Uses of an Unwritten Constitution,* 64 Chi.-Kent L. Rev. 211 (1988).

Grossman, Lewis A. *Late Nineteenth-Century Jurisprudence Revisited: James Coolidge Carter and Mugwump Jurisprudence,* 20 Law & Hist. Rev. 577 (2002).

Gunther, Gerald. *The Subtle Vices of the "Passive Virtues": A Comment on Principle and Expediency in Judicial Review*, 64 Colum. L. Rev. 1 (1964).

Hart, H.L.A. *Positivism and the Separation of Law and Morals*, 71 Harv. L. Rev. 593 (1958).

Hittinger, Russell. *Natural Law as "Law" Reflections on the Occasion of "Veritatis Splendor,"* 39 Am. J. Juris. 1 (1994).

Holmes, Oliver Wendell. *The Path of the Law*, 10 Harv. L. Rev. 457 (1897).

Hovenkamp, Herbert. *Social Science and Segregation before Brown*, 1985 Duke L.J. 624 (1985).

Hurley, S.L. *Coherence, Hypothetical Cases, and Precedent*, 10 Oxford J. Legal Stud. 221 (1990).

Hutchinson, Allan C. *Indiana Dworkin and Law's Empire*, 96 Yale L.J. 637 (1987).

Hutchinson, Allan C., and Patrick J. Monahan. *Law, Politics, and the Critical Legal Scholars: The Unfolding Drama of American Legal Thought*, 36 Stan. L. Rev. 199 (1984).

Jaffe, Louis L. *The Right to Judicial Review*, 71 Harv. L. Rev. 401 (1958).

Jay, Stewart. *Origins of Federal Common Law*, 133 U. Pa. L. Rev. 1003 (1985).

Karlan, Pamela S. *Two Concepts of Judicial Independence*, 72 S. Cal. L. Rev. 535 (1999).

Katyal, Neal Kumar. *Judges as Advicegivers*, 50 Stan. L. Rev. 1709 (1998).

Kaufman, Irving R. *The Anatomy of Decisionmaking*, 53 Fordham L. Rev. 1 (1984).

Kaufman, Irving R. *Chilling Judicial Independence*, 88 Yale L.J. 681 (1979).

Kaye, Judith S. *The Human Dimension in Appellate Judging: A Brief Reflection on a Timeless Concern*, 73 Cornell L. Rev. 1004 (1988).

Kelsen, Hans. *Absolutism and Relativism in Philosophy and Politics*, 42 Am. Pol. Sci. Rev. 906 (1948).

Kelsh, John P. *The Opinion Delivery Practices of the United States Supreme Court, 1790–1945*, 77 Wash. U. L.Q. 137 (1999).

Kennedy, Duncan. *Legal Formalism*, 2 J. Legal Stud. 351 (1973).

Kniffin, Margaret N. *Overruling Supreme Court Precedents: Anticipatory Action by United States Courts of Appeals*, 51 Fordham L. Rev. 53 (1982).

Knight, Jack, and Lee Epstein. *The Norm of Stare Decisis*, 40 Am. J. Pol. Sci. 1018 (1996).

Kramer, Larry D. *Putting the Politics Back into the Political Safeguards of Federalism*, 100 Colum. L. Rev. 215 (2000).

Kress, Kenneth J. *Why No Judge Should Be a Dworkinian Coherentist*, 77 Tex. L. Rev. 1375 (1999).

Lamb, Charles M. *Judicial Restraint Reappraised*, 31 Cath. U. L. Rev. 181 (1982).

Laws, Sir John. *Law and Democracy*, [1995] Pub. L. 72.

Leflar, Robert A. *Honest Judicial Opinions*, 74 Nw. U. L. Rev. 721 (1979).

Levine, Martin Lyon. *Forward to Symposium: The Works of Joseph Raz*, 62 S. Cal. L. Rev. 731 (1989).

Levinson, Sanford. *The Constitution in American Civil Religion*, 1979 Sup. Ct. Rev. 123 (1979).

Lewis, John Underwood. *Sir Edward Coke (1552–1633): His Theory of "Artificial Reason" as a Context for Modern Basic Legal Theory*, 84 Law Q. Rev. 330 (1968).

Lyons, David. *Justification and Judicial Responsibility*, 72 Cal. L. Rev. 178 (1984).

MacKay, R.A. *Coke: Parliamentary Sovereignty or the Supremacy of the Law?* 22 Mich. L. Rev. 215 (1924).

Maltz, Earl M. *Rhetoric and Reality in the Theory of Statutory Interpretation: Underenforcement, Overenforcement, and the Problem of Legislative Supremacy,* 71 B.U. L. Rev. 767 (1991).

Maltz, Earl M. *Statutory Interpretation and Legislative Power: The Case for a Modified Intentionalist Approach,* 63 Tul. L. Rev. 1 (1988).

Massey, Calvin R. *The Natural Law Component of the Ninth Amendment,* 61 U. Cin. L. Rev. 49 (1992).

Michael, Helen K. *The Role of Natural Law in Early American Constitutionalism: Did the Founders Contemplate Judicial Enforcement of "Unwritten" Individual Rights?* 69 N.C. L. Rev. 421 (1991).

Monaghan, Henry P. Marbury *and the Administrative State,* 83 Colum. L. Rev. 1 (1983).

Monaghan, Henry P. *Stare Decisis and Constitutional Adjudication,* 88 Colum. L. Rev. 723 (1988).

Moore, Michael S. *Authority, Law, and Razian Reasons,* 62 S. Cal. L. Rev. 827 (1989).

Moore, Michael S. *Metaphysics, Epistemology, and Legal Theory,* 60 S. Cal. L. Rev. 453 (1987).

Moore, Michael S. *Moral Reality,* 1982 Wis. L. Rev. 1061 (1982).

Moore, Michael S. *Moral Reality Revisited,* 90 Mich. L. Rev. 2424 (1992).

Moore, Michael S. *A Natural Law Theory of Interpretation,* 58 S. Cal. L. Rev. 279 (1985).

Moore, Wayne D. *Written and Unwritten Constitutional Law in the Founding Period: The Early New Jersey Cases,* 7 Const. Comment. 341 (1990).

Newman, Jon O. *Between Legal Realism and Neutral Principles: The Legitimacy of Institutional Values,* 72 Cal. L. Rev. 200 (1984).

Note, *Intent, Clear Statements, and the Common Law: Statutory Interpretation in the Supreme Court,* 95 Harv. L. Rev. 892 (1982).

O'Fallon, James M. *Marbury,* 44 Stan. L. Rev. 219 (1992).

Oliver, Dawn. *Is the Ultra Vires Rule the Basis of Judicial Review?* [1987] Pub. L. 543.

Orth, John V. *Did Sir Edward Coke Mean What He Said?* 16 Const. Comment. 33 (1999).

Orth, John V. *The Truth about Justice Iredell's Dissent in* Chisholm v. Georgia, 73 N.C. L. Rev. 255 (1994).

Paulsen, Michael Stokes. *Accusing Justice: Some Variations on the Themes of Robert M. Cover's* Justice Accused, 7 J.L. & Religion 33 (1990).

Perry, Stephen R. *Second-Order Reasons, Uncertainty, and Legal Theory,* 62 S. Cal. L. Rev. 913 (1989).

Perry, Stephen R. *Two Models of Legal Principles,* 82 Iowa L. Rev. 787 (1997).

Peters, Christopher J. *Adjudication as Representation,* 97 Colum. L. Rev. 312 (1997).

Peters, Christopher J. *Foolish Consistency: On Equality, Integrity, and Justice in Stare Decisis,* 105 Yale L.J. 2031 (1996).

Pitler, Robert M. *Independent State Search and Seizure Constitutionalism: The New York State Court of Appeals' Quest for Principled Decisionmaking,* 62 Brook. L. Rev. 1 (1996).

Plucknett, Theodore F.T. Bonham's Case *and Judicial Review,* 40 Harv. L. Rev. 30 (1927).

Posner, Richard A. *Legal Reasoning from the Top Down and from the Bottom Up: The Question of Unenumerated Constitutional Rights,* 59 U. Chi. L. Rev. 433 (1992).

Postema, Gerald J. *Classical Common Law Jurisprudence (Part II),* 3 Oxford U. Commonwealth L.J. 1 (2003).

Pound, Roscoe. *The Theory of Judicial Decision,* 36 Harv. L. Rev. 940 (1923).

Quinn, Michael Sean. *Argument and Authority in Common Law Advocacy and Adjudication: An Irreducible Pluralism of Principles,* 74 Chi.-Kent L. Rev. 655 (1999).

Radin, Max. *The Requirement of Written Opinions,* 18 Cal. L. Rev. 486 (1930).

Radin, Max. *The Trail of the Calf,* 32 Cornell L.Q. 137 (1946).

Raz, Joseph. *Dworkin: A New Link in the Chain,* 74 Cal. L. Rev. 1103 (1986).

Raz, Joseph. *Legal Principles and the Limits of Law,* 81 Yale L.J. 823 (1972).

Redish, Martin J., and Elizabeth J. Cisar. *"If Angels Were to Govern": The Need for Pragmatic Formalism in Separation of Powers Theory,* 41 Duke L.J. 449 (1991).

Reid, John Phillip. *Another Origin of Judicial Review: The Constitutional Crisis of 1776 and the Need for a Dernier Judge,* 64 N.Y.U. L. Rev. 963 (1989).

Rhonheimer, Martin. *Fundamental Rights, Moral Law, and the Legal Defense of Life in a Constitutional Democracy: A Constitutional Approach to the Encyclical Evangelium Vitae,* 43 Am. J. Juris. 135 (1998).

Riggs, Robert E. *Substantive Due Process in 1791,* 1990 Wis. L. Rev. 941 (1990).

Sankar, Sambhav N. *Disciplining the Professional Judge,* 88 Cal. L. Rev. 1233 (2000).

Scalia, Antonin. *Originalism: The Lesser Evil,* 57 U. Cin. L. Rev. 849 (1989).

Schaefer, Walter V. *Precedent and Policy,* 34 U. Chi. L. Rev. 3 (1966).

Schauer, Frederick. *Easy Cases,* 58 S. Cal. L. Rev. 399 (1985).

Schauer, Frederick. *Giving Reasons,* 47 Stan. L. Rev. 633 (1995).

Schauer, Frederick. *Is the Common Law Law?* 77 Cal. L. Rev. 455 (1989).

Schauer, Frederick. *Precedent,* 39 Stan. L. Rev. 571 (1987).

Schauer, Frederick, and Virginia Wise. *Legal Positivism as Legal Information,* 82 Cornell L. Rev. 1080 (1997).

Sebok, Anthony J. *Judging the Fugitive Slave Acts,* 100 Yale L.J. 1835 (1991).

Shapiro, David L. *In Defense of Judicial Candor,* 100 Harv. L. Rev. 731 (1987).

Sherry, Suzanna. *The Founders' Unwritten Constitution,* 54 U. Chi. L. Rev. 1127 (1987).

Sherry, Suzanna. *Natural Law in the States,* 61 U. Cin. L. Rev. 171 (1992).

Siegel, Stephen A. *The Federal Government's Power to Enact Color-Conscious Laws: An Originalist Inquiry,* 92 Nw. U. L. Rev. 477 (1998).

Sinclair, M.B.W. *The Semantics of Common Law Predicates,* 61 Ind. L.J. 373 (1986).

Sklansky, David A. *The Fourth Amendment and Common Law,* 100 Colum. L. Rev. 1739 (2000).

Smith, Steven D. *Why Should Courts Obey The Law?* 77 Geo. L.J. 113 (1988).

Snowiss, Sylvia. *The Marbury of 1803 and the Modern Marbury,* 20 Const. Comment. 231 (2003).

Soper, Philip. *Some Natural Confusions about Natural Law,* 90 Mich. L. Rev. 2393 (1992).

Spann, Girardeau A. *Color-Coded Standing,* 80 Cornell L. Rev. 1422 (1995).

Sprecher, Robert A. *The Development of the Doctrine of Stare Decisis and the Extent to Which It Should Be Applied,* 31 A.B.A. J. 501 (1945).

Stearns, Maxwell L. *Standing Back from the Forest: Justiciability and Social Choice,* 83 Cal. L. Rev. 1309 (1995).

Steyn, Lord. *The Weakest and Least Dangerous Department of Government,* [1997] Pub. L. 84.

Stone, Julius. *The Ratio of the Ratio Decidendi,* 22 Mod. L. Rev. 597 (1959).

Strauss, David A. *Common Law Constitutional Interpretation,* 63 U. Chi. L. Rev. 877 (1996).

Symposium, *Law and Incommensurability,* 146 U. Pa. L. Rev. 1169 (1998).

Thayer, James Bradley. *"Law and Fact" in Jury Trials,* 4 Harv. L. Rev. 147 (1890).

Thayer, James Bradley. *The Origin and Scope of the American Doctrine of Constitutional Law,* 7 Harv. L. Rev. 129 (1893).

Thorne, S.E. *Dr. Bonham's Case,* 54 Law Q. Rev. 543 (1938).

Treanor, William Michael. *The Case of the Prisoners and the Origins of Judicial Review,* 143 U. Pa. L. Rev. 491 (1994).

Van Alstyne, William W. *A Critical Guide to Marbury v. Madison,* 1969 Duke L.J. 1 (1969).

van den Haag, Ernest. *Social Science Testimony in the Desegregation Cases: A Reply to Professor Kenneth Clark,* 6 Vill. L. Rev. 69 (1960).

Wade, H.W.R. *The Basis of Legal Sovereignty,* 1955 Cambridge L.J. 172 (1955).

Wade, H.W.R. *Constitutional and Administrative Aspects of the Anisminic Case,* 85 Law Q. Rev. 198 (1969).

Waldron, Jeremy. *The Core of the Case against Judicial Review,* 115 Yale L.J. 1346 (2006).

Walters, Mark D. *Common Law, Reason, and Sovereign Will,* 53 U. Toronto L.J. 65 (2003).

Walters, Mark D. *St. German on Reason and Parliamentary Sovereignty,* 62 Cambridge L.J. 335 (2003).

Wechsler, Herbert. *Toward Neutral Principles of Constitutional Law,* 73 Harv. L. Rev. 1 (1959).

Weinberg, Louise. *Our Marbury,* 89 Va. L. Rev. 1235 (2003).

Wellington, Harry H. *Common Law Rules and Constitutional Double Standards: Some Notes on Adjudication,* 83 Yale L.J. 221 (1973).

White, James Boyd. *What's an Opinion For?* 62 U. Chi. L. Rev. 1363 (1995).

Whitman, James Q. *Why Did the Revolutionary Lawyers Confuse Custom and Reason?* 58 U. Chi. L. Rev. 1321 (1991).

Whittington, Keith E. *"Interpose Your Friendly Hand": Political Supports for the Exercise of Judicial Review by the United States Supreme Court,* 99 Am. Pol. Sci. Rev. 583 (2005).

Wilkinson, J. Harvie, III. *The Role of Reason in the Rule of Law,* 56 U. Chi. L. Rev. 779 (1989).

Winterton, George. *The British Grundnorm: Parliamentary Supremacy Re-examined,* 92 Law Q. Rev. 591 (1976).

Woolf of Barnes, Lord. *Droit Public—English Style,* [1995] Pub. L. 57.

Wright, R. George. *Legal Obligation and the Natural Law,* 23 Ga. L. Rev. 997 (1989).

Wyzanski, Charles E., Jr. *A Trial Judge's Freedom and Responsibility,* 65 Harv. L. Rev. 1281 (1952).

Young, Ernest. *Rediscovering Conservatism: Burkean Political Theory and Constitutional Interpretation*, 72 N.C. L. Rev. 619 (1994).

Yudof, Mark G. *School Desegregation: Legal Realism, Reasoned Elaboration, and Social Science Research in the Supreme Court*, 42 Law & Contemp. Probs. 57 (1978).

Zeppos, Nicholas S. *Judicial Candor and Statutory Interpretation*, 78 Geo. L.J. 353 (1989).

Index

Judicial decisions that appear in the text are indexed. All judicial decisions cited in this book, including those that appear only in the notes, are listed with page locations in the table of authorities.